THE FIFTH MAN

ROLAND PERRY

THE FIFTH
MAN

PAN BOOKS

First published 1994 by Sidgwick & Jackson Limited

This edition published 1995 by Pan Books
an imprint of Macmillan General Books
Cavaye Place, London SW10 9PG
and Basingstoke

Associated companies throughout the world

ISBN 0 330 34035 2

1 3 5 7 9 8 6 4 2

A CIP catalogue record for this book is available from
the British Library

Typeset by CentraCet Limited, Cambridge
Printed and bound in Great Britain by
Cox & Wyman Ltd, Reading, Berkshire

TO JACK AND ZSUZSI GROSSMAN

FOR NOURISHMENT OF THE MIND AND BODY

DURING THE RESEARCH

CONTENTS

PART SIX: EXPOSURE
1976–1990

ACKNOWLEDGEMENTS

Some of the key information in this book came from interviewees –
scientists, politicians, diplomats, businessmen and intelligence agents –
who did not wish to be acknowledged, for understandable reasons. Several
were too close to the key characters; others were bound by secrecy codes,
and the law in their countries. I spoke with and interviewed six members
of the Rothschild family, all of whom were courteous, despite the subject
matter at times being awkward to discuss. Special thanks are due to the
busy Honourable Miriam Rothschild, and Lady Tess Rothschild, who
contacted me when she learned I was writing a book concerning her
husband.

I am grateful particularly to my contacts in British Intelligence, three of
whom have been helpful since our first meetings in London in 1974 before
my initial trip to Russia and the Ukraine. As the book explains, they were
responsible for leading me to a key revelation in 1978, which finally fitted
the Fifth Man jigsaw in the 1990s.

Thanks also to my CIA contacts, who originated through former US
navy lawyer and judge, James Cardinal. His advice led me to discussions
with James Angleton in 1975 in Washington. Matters covered regarding
British Intelligence again directed me to further relevant information nearly
two decades later.

Acknowledgement must also go to the seven main KGB respondents in
1993, including Yuri Modin, Michael Bagdonov and Vladimir Stanchenko.
Despite the cover-up of the Fifth Man's identity, other respondents in
Russia also indirectly put me on the right trail. They included Lev Yelin,
Anatoli Semonov, Lev Bezymensky and ex-KGB men Vitaly Chernyavsky
and Yuri Lubimov. Representatives of ASIO (including the former
Director-General, the late Sir Charles Spry), ASIS and the French DGSE
were, as ever, accommodating if occasionally reluctant interviewees.

Documentary film-maker, Jack Grossman, who fought with both the

RAF in the Second World War, and the Haganah after it, was of assistance
with background and Israeli Intelligence. Others to give helpful hints and
leads were Malcolm Turnbull and writers Phillip Knightley, Denis Warner,
Barrie Penrose, Simon Freeman, David Gardner, John Miller, Christopher
Dobson, Ronald Payne and the late James Rusbridger.

Writers, academics, historians and journalists, along with their works, to
an unusual extent became bit players and even important figures in this
book, in part because the Fifth Man used his own writing skill and
connections to achieve his ends. Some books in the espionage genre made
the research a joy. Phillip Knightley's *Philby, KGB Masterspy* comes to
mind as does the Penrose–Freeman biography of Anthony Blunt, *Conspiracy of Silence*. John Costello's detailed *Mask of Treachery* was enlight-
ening concerning Cambridge in the 1930s, while Nigel West's prodigious
output provided clues and direction. *KGB – The Inside Story of Foreign
Operations from Lenin to Gorbachev* by Christopher Andrew and defector
Oleg Gordievsky was useful in understanding the political backdrop to
espionage events for most of the twentieth century. Chapman Pincher with
his revealing *The Spycatcher Affair*, Malcolm Turnbull with the comprehen-
sive *The Spycatcher Trial*, and Richard Hall's incisive *A Spy's Revenge*
provided background to all sides of the Peter Wright story and the
sensational trial in Sydney. Discussions with Peter Wright after the
publication of *Spycatcher*, and his two books were also necessary in tackling
the Fifth Man puzzle, as was Andrew Boyle's seminal work, *The Climate of
Treason*, which sent many writers off on hunts for the next decade.

A word of gratitude is due also to John Le Carré, whose characters and
stories re-created the atmosphere of an era – the Cold War period 1945 to
1989 – an achievement few writers in history could claim. His importance
in aiding our understanding of the mentality of the spying game was
highlighted in the 1986 *Spycatcher* trial when Judge Powell asked in court
whether Roger Hollis was the model for Bill Haydon, the traitor in *Tinker,
Tailor, Soldier, Spy*. Perhaps significantly, Malcolm Turnbull, who won the
case for the defence – publisher Heinemann and Peter Wright – was aware
of the analogy's meaning, whereas the QC for the plaintiff – the British
Government – confused Bill Haydon with Bill Hayden, Australia's foreign
minister and later Governor-General.

Appreciation for explanations of some of the more esoteric bomb and
radar technology goes to Sir Mark Oliphant, who was patient with a rusty,
former science student. His instruction was vital in comprehending the
scope of the Fifth Man's operations.

My American agent, Julian Bach, advised me well and even assisted with some important facts about John Cairncross.

Finally, I would like to thank William Armstrong, Ingrid Connell and Susan Hill at Sidgwick & Jackson, for their invaluable support, effort and contributions in producing this book.

Roland Perry, June 1994

PROLOGUE: THE HUNT FOR THE FIFTH MAN

CLUES AND CONTENDERS

'Don't ever ask about that.'

The tone of my MI6 contact chilled for the first time in several 1975 lunch meetings we had at Le Petit Club Français in St James's Place, London. (By coincidence, the restaurant was a few doors from the home of former MI5 agent, Lord Victor Rothschild, a frequenter of the Le Petit Club since it was opened during the war by the exiled French.) I had inquired about a story circulating in Fleet Street that there were Fourth and Fifth agents who made up a ring of five spies with Donald Maclean, Guy Burgess and Kim Philby. They were rumoured to have been recruited by Russian Intelligence at Cambridge University in the 1930s. The response made me curious. From that moment I became interested in the identities of numbers four and five. I began to keep files.

Rumours about penetration of British Intelligence by the Russians first came from Soviet defectors after the Second World War. They were given credence when Maclean and Burgess defected in 1951 after Maclean was exposed. Philby's defection in 1963 strengthened the case that he was number three in a larger group inside British government and Intelligence. Russian defectors in the 1960s, such as Anatoli Golitsyn, seemed to support the theory that there had been further penetration. However, real concern bubbled away for nearly thirty years in the caverns of MI6 (in charge of British intelligence operations abroad) and MI5 (which 'defended' the UK by covert operations). Then Andrew Boyle published *The Climate of Treason* in 1979. He uncovered the Fourth Man, Anthony Blunt, without actually naming him. That was left to Prime Minister Thatcher in Parliament soon after the book appeared. Boyle had speculated on the identity of the Fifth Man but had got it wrong.

He was still a mystery.

My files were expanding, but I was confused at a higher level, as were many interested writers, politicians and intelligence agents. Tantalizing information emerged during the mid-1980s when MI5 operatives such as Peter Wright and Arthur Martin went public about their concerns that British Intelligence had been compromised by spies within.

In 1985, I returned to Australia to research a book on communist writer Wilfred Burchett, who had strong KGB links. This coincided with Peter Wright's publication of *Spycatcher*. We had the same publisher and I was privy to another layer of information. Wright and other intelligence agents in the UK and Australia were convinced that there were more Russian spies than the four so far exposed. Wright was unsure about the existence of a Fifth Man, but obsessed with the belief that Roger Hollis, the former Director-General of MI5, was a spy.

By 1987, information in the West had dried up. Unless someone from the other side opened up, the true identity of number five would never be known.

A year later, after my book on Burchett, *The Exile*, and *Spycatcher* had been published, KGB masterspy, Yuri Ivanovitch Modin, retired. He had been the controller of many British agents while stationed at the Soviet Embassy in London. At that moment, the Soviet Union collapsed. Economic problems mounted. Modin and other senior ex-KGB men found their pensions eroded by inflation. To supplement meagre incomes, they were allowed to speak with Western media about their exploits in the West running spies. Limitations were set. They could not talk about any operations that MI6 did not know about, that is, those which had not been blown.

One reason the KGB has remained secretive about unnamed spies and operations is its investment in the espionage business. It has a huge multi-billion dollar budget for continued spying and still has hundreds of agents in place in Britain, the US and elsewhere. If current or past KGB agents started naming key spies it would do nothing for morale or recruitment now or in the future. Hence the prohibition against unveiling their own. The Russians will only discuss spies who are already uncovered, such as Burgess, Maclean, Blunt, Philby, Blake, Long and Cairncross.

There is also the loyalty factor. The Fifth Man was recruited in the 1930s when ideological commitment and not money was the reason for spying. The modern era is different. Communism is dead. Instead, Mammon rules. Witness the case of the CIA's 1980s equivalent to MI6's Philby, Aldrich Ames, who was paid at least $2.5 million to spy for Russia. By contrast, Modin and the KGB old guard have wished to remain true to people who gave their lives to the Communist cause.

Finally, naming the Fifth could lead to the exposure of another spy, who is living in Britain.

Consequently, despite their publicized openness, the KGB, like British Intelligence and the CIA, is paying lip-service to the idea of public scrutiny of its most important secrets.

With these limitations, Modin was on the record by 1991 in the West and in Russian magazines confirming that there had been a Ring of Five Cambridge spies: Maclean, Burgess, Philby, Blunt and the Fifth. They were the best group of agents working for the KGB during the Second World War and, importantly, after it. The Five emerged as the most valuable suppliers of espionage information in 1942. Thereafter, the Russians concentrated on them ahead of about another twenty-five notable spies operating in Britain for the KGB.

While searching for further data on Burchett, I was introduced to Russian journalists at the *Moscow New Times*, a former KGB-run magazine, which was imbued with the refreshing glow of *glasnost*. The journalists came up with a dozen KGB contacts willing to supply information about Burchett.

One was Modin. He and I discussed – via fax and contacts – making a documentary film about him and his 'running' of the ring. Information was sent to me over the next two years. I continued to fax scores of questions, some of which were answered, many of which were not. Modin would not name the Fifth Man, but did at least give me enough information to narrow the field of possibles before I arrived in Russia mid-1993 for the research proper.

Over the years, several people have been suggested and rumoured to be the Fifth Man. The leading contenders so far named by Western journalists, Russian defectors and others can be dismissed.

First there was John Cairncross, the Scottish civil servant now living in the South of France, who has not ventured back on British soil since 1952 because he fears arrest. Cairncross had a ten-month stint at Bletchley Park, the British centre for decoding enemy military secrets. He passed over much data to the Russians.

However, according to Modin and others, his file at the KGB Moscow Centre was comparatively thin. Even if all his stolen data had been acted on by the KGB, Cairncross did not pass on enough documentation of significance, except for a two month period before the biggest battle of the war between the Germans and the Russians at Kursk on the Eastern Front. This was hardly enough reason to rank him with the most important agents the Russians ever had. In fact, by 1947 he was regarded as 'dead' or useless by the KGB, until Modin reactivated him and had him steal information from the British Treasury.

In the early 1990s, during the height of the newspaper-generated speculation over whether or not Cairncross was the Fifth Man, he rang a journalist contact of his and mine, John Miller, formerly the long-time Moscow correspondent of the *Daily Telegraph*, and told him he had got rid of annoying journalists camped outside his home in the South of France by 'admitting' he was the Fifth Man.

'Do you think I'm the Fifth Man?' Cairncross asked.

'I don't know,' a bemused Miller replied. 'It's what *you* think that counts, isn't it?'

Furthermore, Cairncross was in contact in the late 1980s with my New York literary agent, Julian Bach. In several letters and telephone conversations, Cairncross denied that he was the Fifth Man, although he said he spied for Russia, independently of the Ring of Five.

(I was able to cross Cairncross off the list after my Moscow interviews with Modin. It was clear from his semantics and manner that he was using Cairncross as a red herring to cover the true identity of the Fifth Man.)

Another contender for the title was Leo Long. Like Cairncross, he was at Cambridge, but he was even less significant, acting as a sub-agent who passed on military intelligence to Blunt. A third possibility was Michael Straight, the rich American who had also attended Cambridge during the crucial years of the 1930s and had been recruited to the Soviet cause by Blunt. But he supplied no data which had any influence in stopping Hitler. The Russians wanted him for other reasons, such as his potential influence on Wall Street, although this never materialized.

A fourth candidate was British nuclear physicist, Wilfrid Basil Mann. His rare contact with Russian agents occurred in the US under supervision from the CIA and its then director, James Angleton. His lack of intelligence experience never made him a serious contender, although author Andrew Boyle had him mind as the Fifth Man when he wrote *The Climate of Treason*. Others to fall under suspicion because of their seniority were Guy Liddell, Roger Hollis and Graham Mitchell.

In considering other candidates, there were two more vital criteria that shortened the list. First, if a candidate never worked for MI5, or had no connection with it after the war, he could be eliminated. Second, all former KGB operatives agreed that the Fifth Man was an exceptional agent, who supplied the Russians with enormous amounts of vital data. This eliminated suspects who were 'sub-agents', and those who worked piecemeal for the KGB during and after the war.

In the summer of 1993 I returned to Moscow for interviews with Modin and six other key former members of the KGB, two I may name and four who wished to remain anonymous. Yuri Modin and another ex-KGB Colonel, designated 'F', knew the identity of the Fifth Man. The other five Russian intelligence service operatives knew of the Fifth's activities and the resultant espionage data. My impressions were that they did not know the exact identity of the Fifth, although they could have given me educated guesses.

Mid-1993 was a time of unrest and threat of civil war in Russia. A Russian journalist contact who had arranged some meetings offered me a handgun for protection. He always carried one in a sports bag, which was unzipped, ready for a quick response. The city was like a wild-west town: ungovernable and predatory. I was advised not to stay in a hotel. Tourists with dollars were targets for mugging and killing. In the three weeks I was there two American businessmen were murdered in separate incidents.

Ironically, some visitors were hiring ex-KGB officers for protection.

'An occasional slaying is good for business,' one interviewee remarked.

I interviewed Modin in his Moscow apartment for thirty-five hours in July and August. Although he is known to Western journalists, no one had questioned him other than superficially before.

The other interviews were conducted in several locations in Moscow, including the high-domed coffee shop at the Intourist Hotel. There were Mafia types huddled at corner tables furtively examining bird books which, I assumed, were wanted for smuggling rather than any ornithological interest. Others sipped drinks and watched young prostitutes, who in turn pretended to view wall TVs showing old American movies.

The atmosphere was seedy yet discreet enough for the interviewees to relax. The information they supplied was later checked against data collected in the West. Much but not all of this came from MI5, MI6, Mossad, the CIA, DGSE (French Intelligence), ASIS and ASIO (Australian Intelligence). I think two of the Intelligence operatives I questioned (one former MI5 agent and one former DGSE agent who knows Modin very well) know who the Fifth is. A second former MI5 agent came to a conclusion after the Sydney *Spycatcher* trial in late 1986 about who the unnamed agent was most likely to be.

The interviews in Moscow made it clear that the Fifth Man had some scientific training. He had built up an expertise in biological and nuclear weapons research. Other telling facts came out of my Russian trip. He worked for MI5 during the war. He had a connection to Churchill. The Fifth provided Stalin *almost on a daily basis* with what Churchill and Roosevelt were saying about the USSR. The spy also had particular links to the US military and intelligence during and after the war.

His work and that of the others in the ring went on for longer than originally believed by investigators. They were all involved in spying for the Russians before, during and *after* the war. Their espionage was wide-ranging and included the 1943 Anglo-American discussions on the opening of a second front in the west; information on major war projects such as the atomic bomb and biological weapons; data on Eastern European nations in exile in London (who were anti-Stalin); background to discussions on the post-war Marshall Plan to redevelop Western Europe.

Furthermore, while calling the Five a 'ring' implies they worked together, they mainly operated independently of each other. However, at times two or more would combine. Often their linking revolved around Blunt, who was the middleman most closely in contact with Soviet Controls in London from 1942 to 1963, the year Philby defected and Blunt was exposed to MI5 investigators.

Another important clue, on which those who knew the Fifth Man's identity all agreed, was that after his main spying days for the KGB finished in the UK in 1963, he went on to have a 'successful career' in both business and public life.

This again cut down the list.

Apart from fitting the many facts and clues to the Fifth Man jigsaw, intangibles such as motivation were vital. This had to go beyond the altruistic obligations of those who felt it their duty to defend Western civilization against Hitler's barbarity. The spy in question had to be inspired on a higher level than his belief, shared with the others in the Ring of Five, that Soviet Marxist ideology was superior and would eventually dominate Western capitalist democracies.

The Fifth Man's original motive was survival, for himself, family, race and country. He was compelled to supply the Soviet Union with information that would smash Hitler, for over the duration of the war its people were prepared to sacrifice and suffer more than any other to defeat him. But after the war, the Fifth Man's ideological commitment caused him to go on spying for the KGB. In so doing, he became caught in a web of betrayal and tragedy, which lasted half a century.

The Fifth Man was Nathaniel Mayer Victor Rothschild (1910 to 1990), better known as the third Lord Rothschild. He was the British head of the famous banking dynasty, which apart from prolific achievements in art, science, wine and charity, had shaped recent history by such acts as the financing of the British army at the Battle of Waterloo and the purchasing of the Suez Canal for Great Britain and Prime Minister Disraeli.

Victor Rothschild's purpose was to go a step further and change the course of history . . .

THE SCIENTIST IN QUESTION

A key factor in determining the identity of the Fifth Man was discovering how he managed to spy on all the key research facilities in Britain during the Second World War. It was clear from interviews with former KGB agents that he was a scientist, with a broad knowledge of several disciplines. The Fifth Man supplied espionage material to the Russians on work in everything from nuclear weaponry and radar to germ warfare developments at the biological centre, Porton Down. For instance, according to several KGB sources including Colonel 'F', the Russians received a succinct run-down from the Fifth Man on every major project there in 1940, the year that Victor Rothschild was on assignment at the research establishment. Of all the possible Fifth Man candidates who were involved in British Intelligence, he was the only one who had been seconded to Porton Down.

The more I delved into the Fifth Man's espionage, the more it seemed unlikely he could be just one individual. How could one person, no matter how brilliant, supply so much data, which the Russians found excellently reported and explained with diagrams and photos? It was not enough to say that research centres had to report their progress to the British Government, and that the Fifth Man, as a member of MI5, could steal documents which would be passed to Moscow and then to the many Soviet science laboratories for analysis.

The spy in question had to have regular access to British research centres. He had to have almost a hands-on comprehension of what every laboratory was doing. Again, how could this be done without arousing suspicion?

According to two MI5 sources, in 1942 Victor Rothschild became MI5's security inspector, which allowed him into every major research centre. He knew in detail about all British (and often US) weapons developments. Under the guise of the inspector who was checking facilities to see if they were vulnerable to Nazi spying, the Fifth Man himself became the espionage agent.

British scientific heads of facilities were apprehensive when the respected young lord – the Government's security man – would ring at short notice and make an appointment to check on a laboratory.

His imperious demeanour, high intelligence and diligent determination to understand every development in detail, put all who came under his scrutiny in awe and admiration of him. On occasions he actually stole equipment, examined it and sent it back by special messenger to the research centre chief concerned, with a warning that security should be tightened. Sir Mark Oliphant, one of the great scientists of the era, told me in an interview in January 1994 he experienced this late in 1942 when Rothschild secretly removed a piece of radar equipment from his Birmingham University laboratory.

Each project director lived in fear that MI5's inspector would put in a bad report and that this would lead to a sacking or a budget cut. The thought that he might be spying on them could not have been further from the minds of the scientists with whom he was in contact. (As far as is known, Rothschild never reported any one. He simply sent written warnings and reported in general that security was slack.)

Again, Colonel 'F' and Colonel 'B' said that late in 1942 or early 1943, the KGB received radar technology. They claimed that this information from the Fifth was assembled in the form of photos, diagrams and written explanations by him and Blunt. Modin confirmed that the latter used his artistic skills here to give the KGB at the Moscow Centre clear, important detail on vital technology. The clarity and visually descriptive nature of the technical data supplied by the Fifth was a trademark of his. By comparison, Rothschild demonstrated in his book, *Meditations of a Broomstick*, how he took great pride in all areas of his work for MI5 in supplying exact illustrations. For instance, he produced technical books for the British and US military, which included scale, accurate drawings on how to deal with or dismantle sabotage bombs.

Stalin's henchman, KGB chief Lavrenti Beria, had thousands of Soviet scientists working in specially constructed cities across Russia to develop copies of Western atomic weaponry. Research was supplied by a variety of spies in Britain and the US. According to ex-KGB Colonels 'F', 'B' and 'E', the Fifth Man was also the first person (in 1943) to supply the KGB with information on the creation of the plutonium route to an atomic weapon. He supplied clear, detailed diagrams and explanations three to four years before Klaus Fuchs provided the technical detail which led to the Communists detonating their first bomb in 1949. Modin confirmed that this data arrived at the Moscow Centre early in 1943, as did David Holloway, an historian at Stanford University in California.

Rothschild, acting as the security man once more, made several visits in 1943 to Professor G. P. Thompson's laboratory at London's Imperial College. He absorbed the then new alternative method of making the bomb – using plutonium as fuel rather than trying to collect the rare U-235 element of uranium.

Rothschild was again the only person suspected of being the Fifth Man, who had knowledge about this breakthrough area and fitted the other criteria concerning the double agent. The other possibles were either non-scientists within MI5 or the Foreign Office, or scientists who had no knowledge of atomic research. The one exception was Wilfrid Mann, who was at Imperial College at the appropriate time. But Mann was never in British Intelligence and had no access to MI5's secrets from 1945 to 1963, when the Fifth Man continued to be active for the KGB.

The person in question could not have suddenly started passing on data in 1940. His connection to the communist cause would have had its roots in Cambridge's scientific community at least in the 1930s. There was a contingent of support for Soviet ideals and its emphasis on science as the panacea for a world with massive economic problems brought on by depression. The Fifth Man was familiar with Soviet aims and needs through his association with communist scientists such as the Russian physicist, Peter Kapitza, who had been at Cambridge's Cavendish Laboratories from 1921 to 1934.

There was never any attempt by KGB interviewees to conceal Rothschild's links to these scientists when he was at Cambridge, or the fact that he was on a short list of ten for recruitment. They were all well aware of him, and those who had been stationed in London, such as Modin, admitted to having known him personally.

During the 1986 *Spycatcher* trial in Sydney, in which the Thatcher Government tried to ban the book by former MI5 agent, Peter Wright, he confirmed the Russians' claims by saying that Rothschild was familiar with these scientists, particularly Kapitza. Later, Rothschild was forced to admit the connection when interviewed by Scotland Yard over possible breaches of the Official Secrets Act.

According to KGB Colonels 'B' and 'F', the Russians were helped by Rothschild and other Cambridge scientists in their pursuit of technical data in the 1920s and 1930s. Kapitza was also part of the network, along with Philby and Comintern agents Theo Maly and Arnold Deutsch, who together put Rothschild on the short list for recruitment.

He was close to Kapitza and other Russians in the early 1930s. Rothschild mixed widely in scientific circles while continuing his own research into spermatozoa. He believed in a scientifically-based society, like the one envisaged in Russia, which was a radical departure from Britain. The certitude and promise of Marxist scientific principles appealed to left-wing scientists, who were hopeful of providing solutions to world problems.

THE IN-HOUSE NETWORK

An important element in the Fifth Man's activities was his proximity to others in the Ring of Five during the war in both London and Paris. This is a widely accepted fact in Britain and Russia, which was confirmed by Modin and Colonels 'B' and 'F' in my mid-1993 interviews with them in Moscow. Rothschild's links to the other agents have been extensively reported in books by British writers including: *Mask of Treachery* (John Costello); *Philby* (Phillip Knightley); *Spycatcher* (Peter Wright); *Conspiracy of Silence* (Penrose and Freeman); and *Molehunt* (Nigel West).

In 1940, Blunt and Burgess were living in Rothschild's leased three-storey maisonette as was his assistant at MI5, Tess Mayor, whom he later married, and Patricia Parry (later Baroness Llewellyn-Davies, the Wilson-appointed Labour peeress), both left-wing Cambridge graduates. Blunt was important here. Apart from his direct espionage work for the Soviets, he became a key middle-man in organizing the passing on of data from the Fifth Man and sub-agents, such as Leo Long, to their Soviet Controls.

Bentinck Street became a facility for the analysis and transfer of espionage material including microfilm and documents. According to Yuri Modin and other KGB agents, the Fifth Man and Blunt, in particular, also used their artistic talents for the Russians to draw and explain the workings of devices being developed at the various research centres for use in the war against Germany and Japan.

After Paris was liberated in 1944, the Supreme Headquarters, Allied Expeditionary Force (SHAEF), moved there. Rothschild was quick to lead the MI5 contingent, and set up a base at the family mansion at 23 Avenue Marigny by the Seine. This time the Ring of Five seemed to relax their vigil against detection. They were away from London and less concerned about being spotted together or meeting Soviet agents. Modin and Colonel 'F' confirmed that all of the Ring except for Donald Maclean, who went to the US, stayed at the Rothschild mansion. It was now easier to collect data and give it to the KGB.

Tess Mayor, assisting Rothschild, also stayed in the mansion. Her cousin-in-law, journalist and war-time MI6 agent, Malcolm Muggeridge, visited it, and for the first time became suspicious of Philby and Rothschild. One night over dinner, an argument ensued between him and the others over the issue of whether or not the Soviet Union should be given espionage information that the British had gained about the German forces. By 1944, activity at the Bletchley Park installation, where intercepted enemy messages were decoded, was at its peak. The British had broken the codes for the German Enigma machine, which was used throughout its forces. This way, the British and US military command knew the Nazis' order of battle, and every important move being made by their army, navy and air force, including those against the Soviet Union.

This information was vital to the Communists. The fierce debate started as a point of principle and drifted into a political disagreement. Muggeridge argued that the British should not share the data with the Soviets because they could not be trusted. First Rothschild, then Philby vehemently defended the Soviets' right to have the material. Again, the heady atmosphere in liberated Paris engendered by the Allied push against the Germans caused Rothschild and Philby to let down their guards. They drank more and became increasingly aggressive and loquacious. In the restraint of London and Whitehall, the two agents would have been more discreet, keeping their thoughts to themselves, secure in the knowledge that the Russians were receiving everything of importance from Bletchley via the Ring of Five.

Their argument was in essence a plea that their clandestine activity, which was accompanied by enormous strains and stresses, could be avoided if the Bletchley data were given to Moscow. The

Soviets were allies in defeating the Nazis. They should be given every assistance in their battles, because the Soviet military was taking the brunt of the Nazi war machine.

Muggeridge took the opposing view that after the Nazi-Soviet Pact of 1938, the Communists should never be trusted again. He was also influenced by the experience of having worked as a journalist in Moscow for the *Guardian*. This caused him to move away from his left-wing views of the early 1930s.

After that less than convivial, yet revealing night in the Avenue Marigny, Muggeridge never again trusted Philby or Rothschild. Writing much later, he observed that Rothschild, who was a 'curious, uneasy mixture of arrogance and diffidence', had lost his way 'somewhere between White's Club and the Ark of the Covenant, between the Old and the New Testaments, between the Kremlin and the House of Lords . . .'

Rothschild was for a short time late in 1944 the senior British officer in Paris, and during this period led interrogation of valuable German prisoners, including Otto Skorzeny, a German paratroop commander. A year earlier, Skorzeny had rescued the overthrown Italian dictator, Benito Mussolini, in a raid in Italy.

Every bit of detail obtained from the interrogations ended up in the hands of the KGB at the Moscow Centre. In our interviews, Modin admitted that Blunt had been ordered by his Controls to analyse information elicited from German prisoners. The information drawn could only have been passed on by Rothschild to Blunt, who had no role in the interrogations. The convenience of their closeness in Paris would have made this a less difficult clandestine activity.

Rothschild had close links to Burgess, Philby and Blunt from university days. During the war he was involved in a KGB operation with another member of the Ring of Five, Donald Maclean, concerning General Wladyslaw Sikorski, the premier of the exiled Polish Government and commander-in-chief of all that country's forces abroad.

Sikorski was upset by the KGB massacre of 8,000 Polish officers near the Russian city of Smolensk, and threatened to cause trouble with Stalin over it. Part of Maclean's brief at the Foreign Office was to liaise with the Poles in London. He reported Sikorski's grievances about the massacre to his other superiors in the KGB. Every threat and plan that the Pole made against the Soviet Union was reported to the KGB and then Stalin, who wanted Sikorski eliminated.

Maclean obtained the Pole's travel plans. Early in July 1943 the Polish leader was killed in a plane crash in Gibraltar, which was a suspected KGB or Nazi sabotage operation.

Sikorski's supporters in London demanded that Churchill should make an inquiry into the crash. Maclean, as the Foreign Office's link-man with the Poles, was in charge of overseeing an investigation. He made sure that Rothschild – as the UK Government's resident counter-sabotage expert – was in charge of the probe. A former Second World War MI5 operative and ex-KGB Colonel 'F' claimed that Rothschild made an inconclusive finding, which was kept secret. This had the desired effect of not embarrassing Stalin. The Poles viewed it as a cover-up.

NUMBER TEN AND NUMBER FIVE

Winston Churchill had been close to the Rothschild family from the 1890s to 1930s. He had had a political relationship and friendship with Victor's grandfather, Nathaniel Mayer, the first Lord Rothschild, a powerful backroom political operative at the end of the last century. Churchill followed Victor's career with interest. Despite their age difference (Rothschild was only twenty-eight when Britain entered the war in 1939) and some verbal jousting with Victor over his political views, they had a friendship and mutual respect which strengthened during the war years. Churchill expressed his admiration for Rothschild's courage in defusing bombs as part of his counter-sabotage operations. The wartime leader literally placed his life in the younger man's hands when Rothschild was put in charge of testing all Churchill's food before it was consumed. The two socialized often during the war years. Rothschild used his wealth and position to invite the prime minister to private parties. His entree to the wartime leader, plus access to all the key intelligence information, every major weapons development and his command of counter-sabotage operations in Britain, made Rothschild a secretly powerful figure during the war years.

KGB interviewees, including Modin and Colonels 'F' and 'B', conceded that the Fifth Man, a Cambridge graduate, MI5 agent and scientist, was also close enough to Churchill to learn his secret intentions in vital areas of the war effort.

Churchill refused to allow the valuable Bletchley Park intercepts – the deciphering of German military codes – to be sent to Stalin, mainly because the Soviet leader had not wanted an agreement on the exchange of intelligence. Stalin didn't need a formal agreement. According to Modin, and Colonels 'F' and 'B', he had all the data he needed flowing in from the Ring of Five and scores of other peripheral spies, several of whom were in a position to supply the Russians with the raw intercept data from the broken Enigma codes.

However, there were other secrets, such as the date for D-Day – the crossing of the Channel for the Allied invasion of Europe – and its location that Stalin and his military commanders wanted. The Fifth Man and others in the Ring were in a position to give the KGB and Stalin all the data they desired concerning the Allied Expeditionary Force, first in London, then after D-Day in Paris. The result was that Stalin knew as much as Churchill about vital information, often before the British High Command were informed.

THE AMERICAN CONNECTION

In 1939, Rothschild became known to the War Office when he sent Churchill a paper on the German banking system. His unorthodox yet ingenious analysis concluded that the Nazis' expansionary plans could be foretold by monitoring their financial activity. Rothschild had drawn on his family bank connections in Germany and Austria to obtain espionage data on Nazi transactions, which he used to reveal equipment purchases and predict further acquisitions.

The paper led to him being offered intelligence work in 1940 in the Commercial Espionage Unit of Section B of MI5. His first job was to determine all the threats in German business and industrial operations in Britain. In the end he recommended that many major German suppliers to industry should be dumped in favour of American companies. This naturally pleased the Americans. Consequently, Rothschild was able to form links with key US military figures.

Later his outstanding work in counter-sabotage saw him seconded to the US Army to train American forces in bomb detection in France, which led to him being decorated with the American Legion of Merit, in addition to his British George Cross. In his citation, President Truman was effusive in his praise of Rothschild.

It all helped when he wanted contacts in the US after the war for his work on nuclear fall-out, which gave him access to the main US weapons secrets, including those concerning bomb development. He built up relationships with leading American military personnel, including Admiral Lewis Strauss, who in 1946 became chairman of the American Atomic Energy Commission, which took over control of all the US's bomb projects.

According to ex-KGB Colonels 'F', 'B' and 'C', the Fifth Man spent some time in the US in the immediate post-war years, and became part of the frenetic Soviet network of spies supplying the USSR with espionage material on the US bomb missions. While not being able to supply the technical data that Klaus Fuchs and others passed to the KGB, the Fifth Man was able to give an overview of all the projects. This way, he was able to alert the Russians to possible new weapons. In our interviews, Modin confirmed that from 1945 key spies, including the Cambridge Ring, were involved in some way in acquiring bomb information.

In the post-war period, Rothschild reviewed – with other scientists such as Oliphant and physicist James Chadwick – a new, secret American bomb operation. This weapon was to incorporate radioactivity from the Cyclotron, the nuclear accelerator for producing a stream of electrically charged atoms or nuclei travelling at a very high speed. The resultant radioactivity from an explosion could destroy everything living in a big city. Details of this project were in possession of Soviet scientists in late 1946, according to Colonel 'F'.

Rothschild's reputation and position allowed him (and Philby) to form links with the CIA precursor, the OSS, during the war, facilitating KGB deception of American Intelligence until the defections of Burgess and Maclean in 1951.

Philby and Rothschild both influenced one of the US's outstanding intelligence operatives, James Angleton, from his recruitment year with OSS in London in 1944. Philby ingratiated himself to the point of becoming a mentor to the callow counter-espionage agent. Rothschild gave him contacts in Jewish underground networks in

Italy – Angleton's first posting after London – which helped the American round up German and Italian fascist agents in 1945. Angleton was beholden to both of them. He was stunned by the possible link of Philby to Burgess and Maclean, and unsure of Rothschild after Philby's defection in 1963. However, he remained in the Jewish lord's debt. Angleton ran Israeli agents when he became senior in American Counter-Intelligence and he thought Rothschild, a long-term Mossad agent, was important to him. Yet he never lost his suspicion about Rothschild's allegiances.

THE TOLL OF THE MOLE

The main mystery which has taxed British Intelligence and governments for the post-war period concerned how the Russians knew about every major intelligence operation run against them in the years 1945 to 1963. The problem emerged in public in the late 1970s and early 1980s as frustrated former agents such as Peter Wright and Arthur Martin expressed their views. Wright detailed the mystery in *Spycatcher*.

The logical conclusion that all observers made was that there had to be an agent inside MI5 – a well-buried mole – who was working for the KGB. How else, insiders Wright and Martin asked, could the Russians learn about the detail and technology of operations run against them?

After Philby defected to Russia in 1963, Wright began his investigation in earnest. He was strong on checking and cross-referencing files, and surprisingly inadequate in judging people. Like his great friend Rothschild, he was more at home in dealing with the logic of scientific principles and the new technology he was struggling to introduce to a reluctant British Intelligence. Bugging devices didn't answer back and act irrationally. They were controllable and didn't get in the way of the scientist-spy's war against the KGB.

Wright's probes into who the mole might be had all the hallmarks of detection by documentation. His theory was that if you could find a pattern in the paper trail inside MI5's files, the mole could be revealed. Along the way, he developed – on the basis of the files – suspicions about many people, who were eventually discarded as prospective moles, but who left Wright with doubts. Guy Liddell was a prime example. Liddell had been Director-General of MI5 when he retired at sixty from Intelligence in November 1952. He then joined the British Atomic Energy Authority to head its security. Wright noted that Liddell had been close to Blunt and Burgess, but thought he couldn't be the mole. He didn't fit the chronology of the mole's destructive activity from 1942 to 1963. Liddell died of a heart attack on 2 December 1958. (Victor Rothschild and his wife Tess attended the funeral. Notable for their absence were the then current head of MI5, Roger Hollis, and former head, Dick White. Rothschild and Philby were both effusive in their praise of Liddell.) He didn't involve himself with MI5 beyond normal security liaison after he left British Intelligence in 1952. Wright ruled him out as the mole, yet he was always unsure about him. He thought that Liddell might have been a Soviet agent, but not the big one.

Wright was acutely concerned with the dates for he, more than anyone, had been humiliated by the thwarting of his efforts to run spying operations against the Russians. Every single mission he had been involved in, from bugging Soviet Embassies to tracking Soviet shipping, had failed. He had been working since 1955, and was particularly concerned with the years from 1958 to 1963, which was when he had established himself as the first resident scientist at MI5. They should have been glittering years of productivity for him. But they were not.

He spent years going over the list of possible candidates for the mole until his obsessive view was distorted. The rotten rodent had partly ruined his reputation. More importantly, he or she had made sure that the KGB was on top in the techno-spy battle which became vital from the late 1950s. The mole stopped Wright from achieving his main aim in life of catching Russian agents. If he had stayed in MI5 only a short time, he may have surmounted the failure and gone on to achievements in his professional life as a scientist. Instead he stumbled on in frustration for twenty years, his passionate hatred for the apparent foe within the building festering over all that time. His bitterness was compounded by daily consultation with others equally foiled and baffled within British Intelligence.

There was no question that someone had to be informing the

Russians in advance of British operations, unless every member of counter-intelligence over two decades was a total incompetent. The intellectually-gifted and technically competent Wright drew up his penultimate list of suspects in 1963 in order of likely guilt: the then deputy-director, Graham Mitchell, who was about to retire; the director Roger Hollis; Colonel Malcolm Cumming; Hugh Winterborn; Wright himself.

Further investigation eliminated Cumming and Winterborn. Mitchell was the number one suspect. Hollis was forced to approve a probe into every aspect of the life of his own deputy. But months of investigation, which included bugging and even two-way mirror surveillance of Mitchell alone in his office, concluded only one thing: he happened to have been a senior employee of MI5 over the period of the mole's activity from 1942 to 1963.

That left Hollis and Wright. It never occurred to Wright, or he never expressed the thought, that any head of any organisation, who had seen long service, would be under suspicion for every run of adverse activity from the stealing of espionage secrets to pilfering from the biscuit tin. Hollis became the focus of doubt, suspicion, investigation and rumour for the next thirty years, which stretched two decades beyond his death in 1973. The fact that Hollis faultlessly survived an in-house MI5 interrogation in 1969 after he retired, and an independent Government (posthumous) probe in 1975, never shook Wright's tenacious belief. Hollis had to be an agent of the KGB, unless Wright himself was the mole. And this seemed too absurd to contemplate. After all, he had been the most aggressive anti-Soviet employee the service had ever had. He was, in fact, so obsessed that he was an embarrassment to the old school of British spies, who found him too boisterous for their taste. All who had ever graced his presence knew that the mole could not have been tough old Peter. Well, not exactly.

THE INSIDER–OUTSIDER

In 1958, Victor Rothschild made a direct effort to meet and cultivate Wright on the basis that they were both scientists with connections to British Intelligence. Wright had been just three years on the inside, whereas Rothschild had been on the inside through the war until 1945, and since then on the outside as an intelligence man who had a unique relationship with his wartime employer.

He had left them officially, yet unofficially still ran agents after the war in Israel, Iran, China and other nations from 1945 to at least 1969. He was the classic outsider–insider. His special place in the Establishment as a power-broker, with unsurpassed connections in every major institution in Britain, allowed him to bypass the usual restrictions on lesser-born citizens. He couldn't actually pull the files in MI5 or MI6, but he could always find someone who would do it for him, if he needed access. Rothschild was a regular visitor to British Intelligence offices. He lunched and dined constantly with its directors at his favourite clubs, Pratt's and White's, and always made it a pleasure when he picked up the tab for expense account-conscious spy chiefs.

Rothschild had been on intimate terms with most of them: Guy Liddell, Roger Hollis, Dick White, Maurice Oldfield. He became a sort of father confessor, someone who understood the machinations of intelligence and was compassionate about the chiefs' problems in defending the realm. Rothschild was always there to give sound advice, or pick up the phone to help with a contact. In dealing with directors-general, he transformed from an aloof, even sullen character to an effusively charming, extremely helpful and trusted friend. The demure, introverted lord vaporized and was replaced by the communicative fixer.

Rothschild provided relief for intelligence chiefs from the pressures of the office. He was the confidant with whom they could share the intrigues of the espionage game. In their time, every one of them in varying degrees had divulged the key intelligence secrets to him, the ones which the Russians were after.

In 1958, Rothschild's fostering of Peter Wright turned quickly to patronage on the basis that they were scientists who got on awfully well. Wright was an easy prey for the sophisticated peer. Although talented, Wright was not Oxbridge educated and therefore an outsider in a service which was run by the-old-school ties. He felt snubbed by those too ignorant to comprehend his great value in the intelligence war. Wright was also ambitious, prepared to put in many hours of overtime to achieve his goals, whether it was developing a new device, or gaining an expanded budget. His diligence and intelligence may have been unsettling to those used to the antiquated methods of defending HM, the realm and the masses.

Not so with ebullient Victor, who took him under his golden wing. For the first time in his professional life, Wright felt wanted, understood and appreciated. In this atmosphere, Wright spilled everything that was happening inside MI5. Rothschild offered help. He was in the oil group Shell, overseeing scientific development. He seconded staff to MI5. Wright told him about every piece of espionage technology under development. Rothschild offered ideas of his own and actually devised some new technology himself. He made introductions to heads of major British organizations like the AWRE (Atomic Weapons Research Establishment), which led to further expansion of MI5's R & D.

This new, powerful chum, who impressed Wright more than anyone else in his life, was in effect responsible for expanding British Intelligence budgets. This was an individual to be almost worshipped, especially in the niggardly world of Whitehall departments. It was damned hard to convince the bean-counters that Intelligence needed more funds. Why should we give you more money? the Government accountants would ask. The war is over. We're not under threat, are we?

Here was a noble obliged, apparently by his breeding, conscience and generosity, to dispense largesse and influence for the good of the services, and the nation. This way, Rothschild developed enormous goodwill within and without the services. No one was respected more, not just amongst the worker bees such as Wright and Arthur Martin, or the chiefs. Captains of industry, mandarins of Whitehall, ministers of the crown and successive prime ministers knew of his help and activity. Many wanted his services, but until 1970 – apart from the occasional Government committee – Rothschild preferred to keep the mystique of the outsider–insider and a little distance from those with whom he worked and consulted in Intelligence. His job at Shell, particularly from 1958 to 1969, allowed him all the freedom of activity and travel he desired.

It's accepted among MI5 agents that during the 1945 to 1963 period, the Russians were receiving vital information which enabled them to thwart British operations run against the Soviet Embassy and the KGB. All Russian interviewees said that the Moscow Centre received the data. Ex-KGB Colonels 'F' and 'B' and Modin admitted that the Fifth Man was at least prominent in gathering the data and informing the Russians about MI5 missions.

All through the post-war years to 1963, the Fifth Man was active in passing on vital information about MI5's plans and projects concerning the Russians and the KGB. Because of the failures, breakdown, conflict and fear this caused within British Intelligence, everyone on the inside believed that MI5 had been penetrated by someone. The inference was always that it had to be an insider. But as this book will show it wasn't Hollis or Mitchell. Even one of the leading Russian double agents working for MI6, Oleg Gordievsky, who defected to Britain in 1985, denied that the Russians had anyone of importance on the inside of MI5 in the contentious years from 1945 to 1963.

Wright, Martin and the various committees over the decades that chased around the British Intelligence maze searching for a mole, did not consider that he or she never existed. If that was correct, and all the evidence overwhelmingly suggested it was, then there was never penetration. In that case, the Fifth Man had to be an outsider who looked in often enough and listened with an expert technical ear hard enough to be more effective in compromising British Intelligence than any insider, including Philby, and for far longer.

Modin and ex-KGB Colonels 'F' and 'B' confirmed that the Fifth Man worked in tandem with the Fourth Man, Blunt, who after 1945 was the key middleman, the main receiver of espionage data from the Fifth Man and others to be passed on to the KGB Controls. That is why, under interrogation in 1964, Blunt made much of the definition of the word spying. No, he confessed, he had not *spied* for Russia, *lately*.

'Lately' implied after 1945. He, Burgess and Philby and several others interrogated, sang the same refrain. They had all done the right thing by the Allies, who included the Russians, in the Second World War by passing on information to the Moscow Centre in the drive to defeat Hitler. But they claimed they had not continued after 1945.

This was inaccurate. According to Modin and several other KGB agents, *all* of the Ring of Five went on operating *after* the war, in increasingly dangerous circumstances, as did many of the second-rank spies such as Cairncross (which Cairncross denies). Modin has become an unofficial spokesperson for Russian Intelligence in recent years. His status in KGB ranks and fame in the West is based on running the Ring of Five after 1945. He did not take up residence in Britain until 1947.

THE FUELS OF WAR

In the late 1950s, the Cold War was in deep freeze as the clandestine techno-battle expanded between the USSR and the West. The US was using Britain as a floating aircraft carrier in its preparation for an expected conflict with the Communists, which the Americans wished to confine, if that were possible, to Europe. US bomb, defence, military and communications bases linked with British bases and formed a mosaic across the length and breadth of the country.

The Moscow Centre knew about every extension to the Anglo-American network, and planned to counter it. At first it didn't know how this could be done without detection. Many Anglo-American military installations were placed in obscure locations in the country.

An ingenious suggestion to the KGB Controls from one of their British agents was that a petrol retail outlet chain should be set up. Pump stations could be built on back roads near the installations and could be used to spy on the network by, for instance, intercepting the microwave communications between bases. In preparation for war, the pump outlets could be taken over by special Soviet military forces in order to destroy the bases.

The idea seemed outstanding in principle, but any Russian-controlled company selling petrol would have to appear legitimate to fool the CIA and British Intelligence. The Russians had never set up such a capitalist enterprise before. It would have to compete with major Western retail corporations in Britain. Specialist products would have to be developed by scientists. Marketing and distribution know-how would be needed.

By coincidence or otherwise, Rothschild joined Shell in 1958 in a relatively lowly job as a part-time adviser to its research section. He immediately made his presence felt and his role was quickly expanded.

A year later, Nafta Great Britain, a Soviet retail outlet chain began operations in the UK. By the early 1960s, it was competing with the bigger Western companies. Its marketing strategy was unique in the business. Nafta set up pump stations on out-of-the-way B roads, far from the population centres and competitive outfits such as Shell and Mobil. The Russian company's managers claimed that it would compete where the big boys would not bother to go. Scores of these Nafta stations never made money in the thirty years they were open for business. They were suspiciously close to the most important defence installations in Britain.

Was Rothschild the mastermind behind Nafta? The timing for his move to Shell and the creation of the Russian company would suggest he was a prime suspect. So would his background. He had investigated commercial espionage early in his career at MI5. As its security officer during the war, he learned all there was to know about how to steal equipment and documents. Rothschild's scientific expertise also made him a candidate as Nafta's founder. His early work at Shell covered research into gas, oil, petroleum, diesel engine fuel oil and several other products, all of which were found among Nafta's offerings to the British market. But he didn't restrict his interest to science and research. Fellow executives at Shell were stunned by his inquisitiveness in all fields from production to packaging, distribution, marketing and advertising.

His great hunger for knowledge allowed him to absorb it all, and his skills did not go unnoticed at Shell. He gained quick promotion. By 1963, he was Shell's scientific research and development supremo worldwide, even though the company never quite sorted out whether their distinguished lord was a full-time employee or not. His power and position allowed him to be around when he liked, which gave him the chance to carry on his clandestine activities, such as running agents for Dick White in Israel, Iran and China. The Shell position was just right as a cover for his frequent travels to the Middle East, where the company produced its raw petroleum.

THE FOUR-DECADE SMOKESCREEN

After Burgess and Maclean defected to Russia in 1951, Rothschild spent the next four decades – the rest of his life – covering trails which linked him to them as the Fifth Man. Internal British

Intelligence investigations began in late 1951, and like every other person connected to the defectors, he was questioned. It was mild then, but when Philby defected in 1963, and Blunt 'confessed' in exchange for immunity from prosecution in 1964, the interrogations increased.

Many, including Rothschild, took Blunt's lead and opted for the immunity card. Some made the deal which prevented prosecution then made certain admissions, such as 'yes, I passed on data to people like Blunt during the war, but never to the Russians directly.'

Others said 'thanks for the immunity' to avoid first, being falsely accused, and second, guilt by association. They then proceeded to give away precisely nothing. Rothschild was in the latter category. Yet no matter what he did after that, the issue dogged him.

He protected himself legally against defamation by threatening to sue anyone who accused him of being the Fifth Man. But Rothschild never sued an accuser. Nor did he ever act like an innocent person. Someone with his clout, who *was* innocent, could have calmly waited for an accusation or innuendo, then pounced. No one, unless it was an intelligence insider with specialist knowledge, could have presented evidence which would have indicted Rothschild. Only a confession was strong enough evidence to convict major spies.

The trouble with a court action would be the skeletons it would reveal, which would have increased the suspicion that the accused was in fact a Soviet agent. This was the danger that forced him to keep up his legal threats and bluff, but to avoid the courts.

In defending himself, Rothschild instead chose the indirect but effective media route to keep the lid on accusations and deflect them from him. He wrote books and articles, and made highly publicized speeches. These improved his image away from the secret world which preoccupied him for fifty years of his life. He spoke and wrote only rarely and evasively about his links to those in the ring of five. He could hardly dismiss his close friendships with Blunt and Burgess, but he tried to distance himself from them.

He used intelligence, press and publishing contacts to create books which deflected suspicion away from him and on to others, such as the long-suffering ghost of Roger Hollis.

POMP AND CIRCUMSTANCE

The Third Lord Rothschild was camouflaged as the Fifth Man by virtue of his powerful position in the Establishment. The vast wealth of his banking dynasty embedded him in the power elite more than the other members of the Ring of Five. It was a perfect cover and served to shield him. He seemed the epitome of the ruling class of twentieth-century Britain, and therefore the least likely to be a traitor. Yet a closer scrutiny showed that he had other allegiances, which over time and on specific occasions ran contrary to British interests.

Rothschild was more loyal to his Jewish heritage than anything English. He showed this in his long commitment to his race's problems. After his political awakening at Cambridge in 1930 he supported refugees from Soviet and German pogroms. In the war, he feverishly fought the Nazis. Once Hitler was defeated, Rothschild assisted in the creation of a homeland for the Jews who had been dispossessed. When the new nation was established he again helped in guiding Israeli leaders to the people, technology and weaponry which would defend it.

He was never so committed to his country of birth and its established order. In fact, more than once when confronted with a conflict between race and country, he chose race. For instance, when the British tried to thwart the birth of Israel, which would have upset its power base in the Middle East, Rothschild intrigued against British interests. It would not have been difficult for him to make another commitment, this time to another power – the Soviet Union – and what for decades he considered was a superior cause.

As a secret communist and professed socialist he would like to have seen the collapse of the old Establishment order in Britain. There was some irony in Rothschild's secret desire to destroy the House of Lords and capitalism. These sources of power developed his own privilege and prestige, which in turn allowed him to contemplate being in the vanguard of change.

His background again gave him an international view of the world, which paralleled the aspirations of the communist movement. Its emphasis between the wars on science as the vehicle for brave, new Marxist societies appealed to him and many of his colleagues at Cambridge. It was put to him as an experimental phase in the build towards a grand, classless society. Like all experiments there would be failures, but in the end the logic of it would lead to success.

Rothschild's deep involvement in Britain's power structure protected him and may partly explain why he lived longer than anyone else in the Ring of Five. All were under enormous strain while involved in espionage. Burgess, Maclean and Philby were from the upper class but none had the wealth, privilege and prestige of the lord who bestrode politics, business, science and society. Only Blunt, as the monarch's art curator, was guarded in a similar way. But he didn't have the money to buy further protection if required.

This extra protection provided security of mind and it's not surprising that the other four were afflicted by alcoholism in varying degrees. Burgess and Maclean were killed by it. Philby nearly was too, whereas Blunt could not stand pressure without being anaesthetized by gin or Scotch. Rothschild liked his wines and spirits but remained in control.

Another factor not to be ignored in Rothschild's survival was a successful second marriage to his understanding wife, Tess. She admitted in an interview with me that her husband carried too many secrets, and that she was not privy to all of them. (Tess was Rothschild's assistant at MI5 for five years and would have known some secrets within British Intelligence.) While she would not have been aware of his activity involving the KGB, Tess held similar political views to Rothschild and thus provided stability, comfort and communication over issues about which he was passionate. Rothschild was only troubled in his final years, when the pressures brought on by his decades of covering up the past caught up with him and depressed him.

By comparison, Burgess and Blunt were homosexuals in an era when it was illegal, which brought its own pressures. Both philandered most of their lives and had many relationships. Burgess's affairs were unstable and transitory, and it is unlikely that either man could have confided anything of their KGB activity with any partner. Instead, they were forced to bottle up tensions.

According to Modin, Maclean's wife Melinda knew he was a KGB agent (something she has denied), but their marriage was unstable and Maclean was tormented by his bisexuality, especially during times of strain in his double life. Philby only found fulfilment in his fourth marriage to a Russian in Moscow late in life. His brief first marriage of convenience was to a communist agent in the 1930s, but for the greater proportion of his spying days in the West it is unlikely that his female partners knew of his true masters.

Postscript: Modin published a book of his own on the Cambridge spies in 1994, first in French, *Mes Camarades de Cambridge*, and then in English, when its title changed to *My Five Cambridge Friends*. The French edition had Modin playing his game of *not* divulging the name of The Fifth. But the English edition included some subtle changes which implied Cairncross was number Five. Confused by this, Richard Norton-Taylor of the *Guardian* newspaper rang Modin in Moscow early in November 1994. He found the Russian angry that the English edition now seemed to be saying Cairncross was the Fifth Man. He categorically stated that he had never said or written this. Daniel Korn, a researcher for the British documentary film company Touch Productions, investigated this contradiction and verified Norton-Taylor's findings. At least Molin remained consistent in his deception about number Five.

MODIN'S CONUNDRUM

A book on Russian espionage would not be complete without a conundrum. Modin supplied one during our interviews in Moscow in 1993.

'Just as the Three Musketeers were four,' he said, 'so the Cambridge five were six.'

In the tradition of the conundrum, Modin appeared to confuse the issue by also saying:

'To these five names a sixth was added: John Cairncross.'

However, the Russian would not then admit Cairncross was therefore one of the Ring of Five (which was really a Ring of Six).

Why was he playing this enigmatic game? Why not say yes, the five (six) were Philby, Burgess, Maclean, Blunt, the Fifth Man, and Cairncross?

I could find only one explanation. Cairncross, who was never in the same league as the Ring of Five (six), was added as a red herring to hide the identity of a still living number six.

A key was the use of the word names. Five names could only represent six people, if the names of two of the people were the same.

PART ONE

☭

AGENTS OF
THE CAUSE
1923 – 1938

1 · THE SALIENT SPIES

THE PUB CRAWL, APRIL 1943

Anatoli Gorsky hated the routines involved in meeting his British
agents, especially the complicated use of transport. A typical run
might include rides in a taxi, a bus and an underground train, often
taking the opposite direction to the intended rendezvous point,
before doubling back. The best agents would travel for four or five
hours to make sure they were not followed.

On this occasion Gorsky was in a hurry and had a good excuse
for cutting his run short. He had had dinner with the new KGB
resident, Konstantin Kukin, a refreshing change from his austere
predecessor, Ivan Chichayev. This made Gorsky late, and he took
the underground for a few stops before hailing a taxi. Then he
caught another underground train to Hammersmith, west London.
Despite it being a cold mid-April evening, the short, portly agent
was sweating when he emerged on to the street.

Gorsky hurried past cafés and pubs in Beadon Road which were
too close to the tube station to be used as a meeting-place. An MI5
tail could follow him unnoticed in the crowd and would spot him
entering a building. Instead he turned into Hammersmith Grove,
slowed to a stroll and using tradecraft crossed the road twice and
walked beyond the low-lit Grove Tavern.

Only a few people ventured his way from behind and they soon
disappeared into the grey, Victorian terraced houses indistinguish-
able in the Blitz-induced darkness of wartime London.[1]

Gorsky hated being late for Anthony Blunt, who was always
militarily punctual. The tall, lanky agent with the long face and
gravity-drawn mouth often complained about meeting in public
houses, but Gorsky knew he was more than partial to the Scotches

he bought, which soothed the MI5 man's perpetual worry about being seen by 'someone from Whitehall'.

Blunt, in uniform, was sitting with another military man in a corner by a coal fire. Gorsky was surprised. It was Lieutenant-Colonel Victor Rothschild, his most important agent, who rarely met directly with his control. Normally Rothschild used Blunt or another of the key five British agents, Guy Burgess, to courier his information.

Gorsky was apprehensive. He found Rothschild abrasive. The English lord, with his brooding, dark good looks had been difficult. Instead of taking directives from the Moscow Centre via the Control in the London Embassy, Rothschild often dictated through Blunt and Burgess what *he* thought Stalin, the Soviet military command and the KGB should know. At first this had caused problems, but because he was (by April 1943) the best informant the Russians had, his unique approach was accepted.[2]

Gorsky bought three malt whiskies at the bar and returned to their table. On it was a book on Picasso's art, and a rolled-up copy of *The Times*. Under the table was a black leather briefcase.

In deference to Rothschild, the Russian apologized and told them about the new Resident, which seemed to interest the aloof Englishmen less than it should. They seemed irritated with him.

Gorsky told them that the Moscow Centre wanted everyone to concentrate on the German military build-up. He acknowledged that the Centre had appreciated the data recently supplied, especially concerning the thickness of armour-plating of the new German Tiger tank. Because of it, the Russians were making shells that would pierce the tanks in the coming battle. The Centre had also been interested in the movement of Panzer divisions towards the Eastern Front.

The British MI5 agents informed him that there might be 200 at the Front by the end of the month.

The Russian asked if there was anything special in the latest data. Rothschild and Blunt told him in general about the information he would receive, which included the disposition of Luftwaffe Squadrons. They were arriving daily in a 750-mile zone stretching from Smolensk in Belorussia to the Sea of Azoz. Gorsky nodded perfunctorily as if this was of little consequence, which caused the corners of Blunt's mouth to drag. He and his fellow agents didn't like

Gorsky's apparent incapacity to show real appreciation for their efforts.

The Englishmen longed for the sort of intellectual non-Russian 'illegals', agents with the Comintern or international communist movement, who were as urbane as they were and with whom they had dealt in the halcyon days of the mid-1930s. Now the Russians were sending 'urban peasants' with no obvious aesthetic sensitivity, Blunt complained many times to Rothschild and Burgess. The pushy, demanding Gorsky was not their style.

The three men ordered a second round of drinks. Blunt and Gorsky planned another meeting. The Russian picked up *The Times*, which contained a small bag holding rolls of microfilm, then reached under the table for the briefcase, and left. Blunt and Rothschild finished their second drinks and took separate taxis home to their maisonette in Bentinck Street, near Cavendish Square. There, they expressed their grievances to Guy Burgess.[3]

TARGET: KURSK

On the morning of 6 May 1943, Soviet bombers made pre-emptive strikes on seventeen German airfields at the Eastern Front and then followed up with two further raids in the following days. In more than 1,400 flying missions, 122 Soviet aircraft were lost while obliterating 520 German planes. This held up Hitler's plans for retaking the Kursk salient, a narrow jut of Russian-held territory, so-called because it represented a bump behind German lines on the Eastern Front.[4]

The Führer increased the number of German divisions heading for Russia, in the biggest build-up of the war. His High Command regrouped its forces and the world's most powerful military machine was able to hold ground.

The Red Army's intelligence had improved in preceding months thanks to a continual stream of data flowing through to the Centre, and in that time it had liberated the city of Kharkov. However, Hitler had directed his Generals to retake it in a stunning counter-offensive, which succeeded. But the brilliant Russian General Zhukov then recaptured Voronezh. Further north, the Soviets consolidated their hold on the Kursk salient.

Hitler and his High Command had no choice but to plan the mightiest offensive in history – Operation Citadel. The Germans had to win or face losing the entire conflict with the Soviets and thus, eventually, the Second World War itself.

In response, the Centre stepped up its intelligence gathering from London. Already Moscow was unable to process all the espionage information being sent from the Soviet Embassy in London. Staff at the Centre were working till 3 a.m. every day but they did not have the technical capacity to look at every page of microfilmed information. The Centre now ordered the KGB Residents to have their Controls concentrate on obtaining data from the most important British spies, namely Rothschild, Blunt, Philby, Burgess, Maclean and, for those vital months, Cairncross and occasionally a couple of others. All other microfilm and documents piled up in vaults, never to be looked at.

The German High Command was incensed at their forces' failure to take Stalingrad during the winter and now wanted revenge. By mid-May, Operation Citadel became unavoidable as 50 German divisions lined up around the Kursk salient. By the end of June 900,000 men, with 10,000 pieces of artillery, 2,700 tanks and 2,000 aircraft – restored after the May attacks – were ready to tackle the Soviet forces.[5] The Kursk salient seemed perfect for the much-vaunted German pincer movements, where two lines of forces converged on opposing forces and crushed them.

However, the Russians were better prepared than they had been for any other battle, mainly thanks to the intelligence pumped to them by the 'Top Five' British spies. The Soviet military amassed between 1,300,000 to an unofficial 2,000,000 men, up to 20,000 guns, 3,444 tanks and 2,172 planes under the command of Generals Rokossovsky and Vatutin.

Marshal Zhukov, the victor of Moscow and Stalingrad, was in overall command. He planned Operation Kutuzov, which would let the German forces attack and exhaust themselves, before General Koniev's reserve Steppe forces counter-attacked with infantry, tank and motorized divisions.

Zhukov and his staff relied on the steady stream of intelligence coming to them via Moscow. The most vital information came from the British tapping of the German Enigma code machines at Bletchley Park in Buckinghamshire.

THE MANSION OF WAR

Bletchley Park was an ugly Victorian mansion about 50 miles north-west of London, which became the most important secret military installation in the world. By May 1943 activity there was at its peak as 8,325 people worked eight-hour shifts round the clock. They decoded and evaluated up to 12,000 intercepted enemy messages – German, Japanese and Italian – every day.[6]

The evaluations were passed daily to the War Office and the Intelligence services, MI5 and MI6. It was these summaries that Rothschild, Blunt, and Philby purloined for the Russians. The Moscow Centre was also taking an interest during these vital months in copies of the raw intercepts themselves, which Cairncross was working feverishly to deliver.

Cairncross was regarded as a second-rank spy except for the months of April and May 1943, when he removed huge amounts of data from the 'huts' or rooms in the ramshackle wooden building where German air force, army and navy Enigma messages were intercepted.[7] He familiarized himself with the huts and worked in several of them, while concentrating on decoding information from the Luftwaffe.[8]

The lean and linguistically-gifted son of an ironmonger from Lesmahagow near Glasgow, Cairncross had been at Bletchley for less than a year but was feeling the enormous strain of the double-game. While the Russians were officially being sent some data by the British Government to help them fight the Germans, it was limited because Stalin refused to agree to exchange specific intelligence material. The British, under MI6's guidance, were also cautious. They did not want to pass on data (known as Ultra intelligence) which would expose their method of eavesdropping on enemy communications and decoding signals. As early as July 1941, the Germans were known to be decoding some Soviet military traffic and if it were carrying identifiable Ultra intelligence they would realise that their code had been broken. MI6 wanted Ultra kept secret so the origin of the information was disguised by phrases such as 'a source close to the German High Command'.

As a result, only restricted general information was sent to Stalin.

An example was the 11 July 1942 Bletchley Park intercept of German army communications which was decoded as:

> 1: Increasing enemy pressure on the front of the Second Army is to be expected. The pinning down of strong enemy forces on the Army's front is desirable taking into account the operations of the Eastern Army as a whole.
>
> 2: The task of the Army Group von Weichs is, with the Second Hungarian Army, to hold the Donets Front between the mouth of the Potudan and the mouth of the Voronezh, and, together with the Second Army, to hold the bridgehead Voronezh, and the present position on the general line Olchowtka–Oserk–Bork–Kotysch station (east of Droskowo).

Two days later, MI6 had boiled the information down and disguised it so that it ended up at the British Military Mission in Moscow as:

> For information of the Russian General Staff. Our picture from various sources gives clear indication that Germans, including Hungarians, intend to hold Russians on front Livni–Voronezh–Svoboda, while armoured forces push south-eastwards between rivers Don and Donets.[9]

Stalin and his General Staff began to rely on receiving the original decoded material from the Ring of Five and Cairncross for this critical period.

Whichever way it was viewed, Cairncross's activities were illegal and dangerous, especially in wartime when alliances could change quickly. Yesterday's enemy of your enemy could be your adversary tomorrow, which would make spying for them a traitorous act.

Cairncross was tired of the constant commuting by train to and from London, which took up to four hours a day. For the past five years he had reported to Gorsky, but now he had to meet a new directing officer, Boris Krotov, who preferred meeting outside at night rather than in pubs.[10]

In mid-May, Cairncross forgot about the new arrangement and waited as usual in the Hammersmith Grove pub. When the disgruntled agent recalled that he was actually supposed to meet the Russian Control at Clapham Common, he rushed from the pub. He didn't have enough money for a taxi and was forced to take two buses, which made him 90 minutes late.

Cairncross walked to and fro close to the appointed spot and was about to leave when a man in an overcoat and hat walked parallel to him.

'Excuse me, is this where I catch the bus to Sloane Square?' the man asked, in a prearranged greeting which meant it was safe to meet. It was Krotov, the 30-year-old Russian Control.[11]

'No, I'll show you,' Cairncross said, and they walked along together. Krotov told him that Moscow was so pleased with his work in recent months, he would be given an award for it. The Scot's expression brightened for a moment before he complained about the pressure. He told Krotov that he was going to leave Bletchley Park. The Russian was disappointed, explaining that he was helping greatly in the battle against the Germans.[12]

The original intercepts Cairncross had obtained together with the evaluations passed on by other agents, had allowed the Russians to destroy the 500 Luftwaffe planes.[13] Krotov pleaded with him to stay on, at least until after the major conflict about to happen on the Eastern Front.

Cairncross replied that once the battle began his intelligence would be useless. It had either worked now or never would. He told Krotov he would still be of use as he was applying to join MI6.

The Scot informed his Control that he had contacts there, who would help him obtain a position. Krotov protested about the decision, saying that there was more than adequate intelligence coming from MI6 already. But Krotov sensed Cairncross's use-by date was up, at least at Bletchley.

The stress of espionage had taken its toll, as it eventually did for all highly active agents. Some found a few years was enough, while others with a different personality could go on for decades, with only a tendency to alcoholism or drug addiction as an outward sign of their need to escape the inner strain of constant deception.

BATTLE OF THE MILLENNIUM

The intelligence supplied by the Top Five and other agents not only gave the Russians a huge strategic advantage on the Eastern Front, it also allowed them to lay mines and dig trenches in defences which were up to twenty-five miles deep from May until late June. Despite some false information reaching the Centre about when the German assault would take place, the analysis coming from Bletchley indicated that the Germans were not ready in May or early June. In fact, the date for the attack had been set for late June or July as early as 25 April, and this gave the Soviet forces time to prepare to absorb the massive assault, which was expected to be the biggest of the war.

Operation Citadel commenced on 5 July when the German army, at its maximum strength, was hurled into action. The Luftwaffe hit first to soften up the key targets around Kursk, and then the German Ninth Army attacked southward on a thirty-five-mile front.

After forty-eight hours the Germans had only penetrated seven miles into the salient from the north. The forces coming in from the south did a little better, but after four days of fighting the northern assault had only pushed in twelve miles, while the units coming from the south had come twenty miles. But the Kursk was 150 miles long and 100 wide. The Russian defence was so fierce that some enemy units hardly moved at all.

As at Stalingrad, providence seemed to be on the side of the resisting forces. Heavy rain turned the wheat-fields around Kursk into a huge bog, something the locals had not seen for decades. This slowed the German advance literally to a crawl.

At Bletchley Park and in the War Office on 10 July there was great interest in Enigma decodes estimating the German losses and the hectic calling for reinforcements that would not come in time to bolster the German attack. On 11 July, Stalin allowed a communiqué to be released, which confirmed more or less what Churchill and his war cabinet already knew:

'Our troops have crippled or destroyed 586 enemy tanks . . . 203 enemy planes have been shot down . . . the invading army has suffered huge losses . . .'

There was amazement then celebration at these staggering figures, especially about the tanks. If true, it meant that a fifth of the entire German vehicle force had been put out of commission in just a few days. The statistics boosted the spirit of the entire Soviet military, since they had yet to deliver the counter-punch. The Russian force absorbing the German attack had more than done its job.

A *New York Times* correspondent likened the response in Moscow to the news of success to the jubilation in London when the population realised it was actually winning the Battle of Britain.

However, the Russian field commanders did not get carried away. Marshal Zhukov noted that his predictions about the Germans using too much fuel and ammunition had come true in the first few days of fighting. He was very confident on 12 July, which was such a hot day on the steppe that the swamp dried out.

Intelligence reaching him warned that the Germans would attempt to break through Russian lines simultaneously at Teploye in the north of the salient, and at Prohorovka in the south. Bletchley data informed Zhukov that German Colonel-General Hoth in the south near Belgorod was frantically trying to pull together 800 tanks, but looked likely to collect only 500 to 600. Zhukov was not particularly concerned for he was able to meet them with 850 T34 and KV tanks manned by fresh crews buoyed by their fellow countrymen's early efforts.

Hoth was personally at a further disadvantage because the Russian forces were being commanded by Lieutenant-General Rotmistrov, who had stopped him from breaking through at Stalingrad when Hoth tried to relieve surrounding forces there. The German was desperate to win, but knew he was up against a canny and forceful opponent.

The engagement between these two mighty armies, confronting each other on a narrow strip of land between the Psel River and a railway embankment, was to become the greatest tank battle in history. The German forces ran straight into anti-tank batteries and land-mines hidden in the cornfields.

So close was the fighting that the Luftwaffe and Red Air Force could not support their respective sides. The planes were left with no choice but to attack each other. In an extraordinary two-layer clash in the air and on the ground, aircraft fought and crashed in the fields below where tanks collided because of the dust clouds, smoke, burning corn, smouldering vehicles and exploding landmines. The conflict lasted nearly nine hours and shook the surrounding hills, orchards, ravines and gullies.

At the end of this historic engagement the German forces had not taken any ground. By nightfall the battle was in stalemate. In effect, this meant victory for the Russians. They had still not called up their Steppe reserves, which were waiting for the signal to come in and destroy the enemy.

The German Enigma machines at the battle sites worked overtime keeping up with directives from German commanders, who were concentrating their northern assault on Teploye, just inside the Kursk salient. The Russians were passed this intelligence via Bletchley and workers at the Moscow Centre were sending it on as soon as it came in. Learning that the Germans were robbing Peter to pay Paul by taking away forces from the Orel salient to concentrate on the Kursk, to the south, the Russian Field Generals decided to attack. Their pre-emptive counter-offensive in the Orel was so successful that the Germans were forced to pull out four divisions from the struggling Ninth Army in the Kursk.

Late in July, Hitler withdrew some troops from Russia to reinforce Axis troops in the Mediterranean. British and American forces had landed in Sicily and Italy was on the point of collapse. The Allies were relieving the pressure on the Soviet Union at just the right moment. Hitler had no choice but to call a halt to Operation Citadel.

In came the hungry Russian Steppe forces for the kill. By early August the Soviet forces had captured Orel in the north and Belgorod in the south. On 5 August 1943, the Russians could announce that they had won the battle of the Kursk salient.

Back in London, in the three-level maisonette in Bentinck Street, Rothschild was able to break out some vintage champagne in celebration, for he and his tenants Blunt and Burgess had played no small part in helping turn the tide against Nazism.

SELECTING THE BEST

On 10 December 1943, KGB agent Yuri Ivanovitch Modin, aged twenty-one, was transferred from *Smerch Pionum* (Death to Spies), the Russian counter-intelligence section aimed at foreign espionage, to the Anglo-American section of the KGB's First Directorate at Moscow Centre in the Lubyanka building on Dzerzhinsky Square.[14] Modin, tall and good-looking with an intelligent face and high forehead, had sharp eyes and a willingness to smile, despite his tough experiences in the war and, more recently, his introduction to the demi-monde of spies.

His English was just fair after a KGB-sponsored 'improvement course' but his linguistic skills were considered adequate so desperate was Russian Intelligence for translators. In 1938, Stalin's mad purges had seen many of them shot. The dictator believed this would limit communication outside Russia, and so restrict the activities of the 1919 Lenin/Trotsky-created Comintern, which was designed to spread unrest and revolution around the world. The few remaining qualified translators were serving in the forces.

The First Directorate had only twelve linguists to deal with the thousands of documents in English coming in from all over the world. Information from second-rank spies gathered by Soviet agents abroad were not being processed. There was little system apart from a random selection of documents from piles, the rest of which were left pending.

The Directorate chiefs had compromised by pulling out the information coming in from its best spies. They were all British in this Anglo-American section and were ranked from one to thirty, with the top five getting highest priority. Information from lesser spies would be considered if the Directorate was convinced by the Russian Controls in London that it was vital.

Modin began by translating technical documents, mainly political, diplomatic and economic correspondence between Britain and her allies. They also came from Australia, India, South Africa, Canada, and inside the United Kingdom.

The espionage from London was received in the form of documents and micro-film. Modin read the decoded material and classified it according to its importance. After it was passed on to Directorate chiefs for action, the documents would be returned to Modin who would file them under the agents' code-names.

During one of our long interview sessions at his Moscow apartment, Modin told me that curiosity got the better of him. As a 21-year-old agent he had become fascinated with the British spies, with their peculiar and definitive styles of espionage. He began to read the files, and so became familiar with their backgrounds, case histories and fields of work.

Modin had enormous respect for them. They had outstanding intellects, were doing great yet dangerous work for his country, and he dreamt of meeting them. He wondered what their real names were, but never expected to find out. Then in June 1944, the KGB decided to thank these top agents and a few others for their amazing work by offering them life pensions. The London Control put the proposal to them.

Each British spy wrote a letter to the Moscow Centre declining the offer. They all said they were working for the USSR for ideological and other reasons. Financial reward was not part of their commitment.

Modin had to translate the letters. Each one was signed. The young agent thus became one of a handful of people who knew the true identities of the most important espionage agents of the twentieth century.

2. SON OF A
TROTSKYITE

STALIN'S CULT OF DICTATORSHIP

When Yuri Modin was born on 8 November 1922 in the cathedral city of Suzdal in north-east Russia, it was a time of post-revolutionary turmoil. Lenin was deteriorating after having been shot by a would-be assassin four years earlier, and rivals for leadership of the Party were already positioning themselves to take power. The best known was Leon Trotsky, who stood out, especially in his public oratory and newspaper articles, as Lenin's most popular and intelligent potential successor.

Yuri's father, Ivan Vasilyevich, a Commissar in the Kadet Brigade of the Soviet army, had heard Trotsky's stirring speeches while he was stationed in Moscow. Ivan was amazed at the old Bolshevik's skill in marshalling his arguments with almost mechanical precision while still retaining their emotional call-to-arms. Ivan found him inspiring because he had all the revolutionary virtues, such as impatience and courage. He was less sure about Trotsky's audacity and sometimes rabid fanaticism but Ivan, like many in Russia, forgave him his ruthless side in those heady early years of the revolution. A 'fight fire with fire' mentality seemed the only way to stabilize and unite the country. But for Ivan, overriding all else, was the fact that Trotsky had created and controlled the army. Ivan owed his career to him and, like most of the army, would have supported him in anything, even a military coup.

Trotsky's excesses were also forgiven because many recognized that he was more dynamic and committed than Lenin himself. He wrote with more flair and urbanity than the so-called 'Father of the revolution', whose books and articles were heavy going and doctrinaire, adhering always to hardline Marxism.

Ivan regarded himself as something of an intellectual, having been educated by his commanding officer who idolized Trotsky and predicted he would lead the country once Lenin was gone. It was believed Lenin wanted Trotsky as his successor, although his written will was unclear. It praised Trotsky, but also drew attention to his weaknesses. He had been a fine foreign minister and adept at exporting revolution, yet he was inept at administration and the tactical games played within government.

After Lenin's death in 1924, Ivan became less enamoured of the revolutionary government, which promised dictatorship of the proletariat, but delivered only the dictatorship of a small clique whose power was reinforced by the iron fist of Feliks Dzerzhinsky, the head of the Cheka, the KGB forerunner. He ordered assassinations, torture, the creation of prison camps and slave labour.

Since the Civil War, which engulfed Russia from 1917 until the early 1920s, the Soviet Politburo's management of the day-to-day running of the Communist Party had fallen to a grey, uninspiring Georgian who struggled to express himself in Russian. His name was Joseph Stalin and he had surreptitiously moved from Lenin's assistant during the Civil War to coadjutor.

His work was unattractive to the intellectuals who dominated the Party and Government and the Georgian in turn was not interested in Lenin's intellectualism. Unlike the other leaders he was not dependent on Lenin's laboratory of thought, which was meant to lead to a great society. Stalin only showed more than a feigned interest in ideology and ideas if it suited his ends, such as when accusing anti-revolutionaries of transgressing against Party doctrine and aims.

He was more concerned with the techniques of control, which Lenin had set up to carry out his social experiments in everything from land reform and industrialization to economic expansion. The Cheka was already used to enforce Party policy but Stalin increased the weapons of control. He took over the mundane parts of administration that the others considered drudgery, such as the Moscow-based Central Control Commission, the purging arm of the Politburo and the Party, which he used as an instrument of his increasing power.

Initially the C.C.C. could only expel members, which it did only in extreme cases. But it taught Stalin how to manipulate all the kitchen cabals, which together determined the make-up and direction of the Party and Communism far more than any dubious, untried Marxist theory. Stalin learned how to make self-righteous accusations about 'anarchists, waverers, dissidents and doubters' and destroy their credentials, work and lives.[1] The C.C.C. became his vehicle for power, self-preservation and the creation of the perpetual fear by which he ruled. He divided and conquered in the traditional way but took it a step further to make the innocent appear to be guilty transgressors against the ever-changing and wavering Marxist–Leninist-based 'Party-line'. Then he eliminated them.

After Lenin died, leaders such as Bukharin, Zinoviev and Kemenev quarrelled with Trotsky as they all jockeyed for control of Party and Government. Stalin stayed in the background, accumulating more power through his serpent-like use of administrative levers, until he gained the position of General Secretary. All the time he was advancing the concept of 'socialism in one country', as opposed to Trotsky's idea of the Comintern and world revolution. Stalin's most telling move came in January 1925, when he managed to force Trotsky to resign as the Commissariat of War.[2]

The fledgling Soviet Union was now at a cross-roads. Trotsky had enormous support within the army. From the top to the middle and lower ranks, the forces would have been more than happy to back a coup d'état.[3]

Ivan Modin and his fellow officers across Russia discussed possible moves once Trotsky lost the job that had given him power and fame. He only had to say the word and insurrections would have occurred in garrisons across the country. But Trotsky was influenced less by the mood in the ranks and more by the people with whom he was in daily contact. They claimed that the Soviet Union had had a decade of war and now needed stability. The days of wild revolution, civil war, bloodshed and political immaturity should be replaced by steady development. The country had resisted outside challenges too – now it should show the world that it could be taken seriously as a nation.

Trotsky didn't need too much convincing. He still thought the Party was of paramount importance, no matter who led it or how they carried out government. Trotsky thought it was the only legitimate spokes-vehicle for the working class. If he were to use the army to take control, Trotsky felt he would be opposing the workers and therefore betraying them. He refused to tread the 'road of Bonapartism'.

So the most courageous and brilliant of the revolutionary leaders gave up his power without a whimper and lost his chance for a more effective role in history. He left that to a pipe-smoking, power-crazy, paranoid bureaucrat who, for the next three decades, would be responsible for the murder of more than thirty million Soviet citizens.

Stalin proceeded to under-use Trotsky's talent in menial tasks in economic administration, thus completing his political castration. Stalin even had the shrewdness to oppose Zinoviev's moves for harsh action against Trotsky and his removal from the Politburo, which was a subtle way of looking impartial as he strengthened his grip on the Party. He would finesse his talents for a few years before instituting his role as dictator. But from early 1925, the tough Georgian was *the* source of power inside Russia. Eventually his mastery of the Party allowed him to move towards expelling Trotsky.

Ivan Modin who, with a thousand other officers, had pledged his support to Trotsky in public meetings and in petitions, put down his arms and accepted the mundane new leadership, as did the rest of the nation.

PUSH TO THE PURGE

When I first spoke to Yuri Modin face to face in the rainy, sultry summer of 1993, he was seventy and in poor health. Yet the large, florid-faced former KGB Colonel still had a strong sense of humour, which surfaced often in our interview sessions. He talked sometimes guardedly, sometimes candidly about what he remembered of family life in the late 1920s and early 1930s.

He recalled his father Ivan's inspiration and hope turning to bewilderment and disappointment. Yet Ivan had steady employment where millions of others ended up in labour camps. His mobility in the army, he maintained, kept him from possible boredom and definite rebellion.

Ivan Modin's Brigade was shifted through central Russia for the next decade. In that time young Yuri found himself in ten different schools in ten regions as Soviet history was re-written by Stalin. The cunning General Secretary had Trotsky expelled from Russia and he routed all other opposition still left inside the Party and Politburo.

Yuri's disparate education made no mention of Ivan's hero, Leon Trotsky. Instead, by 1929 there had emerged a personality cult centred on Stalin. He turned fifty that year and Moscow celebrated as if it were historically important. With well-orchestrated 'spontaneity', every Party secretary in the country wrote gushing letters of praise to him. Moscow was covered with massive wrinkle-free portraits. Statues of his unprepossessing figure filled every square, public building and shop window.

Ivan Modin marched in a Moscow military ceremony early in 1930, and Stalin emerged at the top of the Lenin mausoleum in Red Square, in what looked like a general's uniform. Ivan and his fellow officers couldn't recall any mention of him during the 1917 War, or afterwards in the civil conflict, yet here was this moustachioed Georgian standing on Lenin's tomb as if it were a mere podium for his greatness.

Ivan found it confusing and even depressing, and this was compounded by the importance of not querying the weird developments engulfing the nation's Government. Doing so could mean being fired from the armed services.

Ivan recalled the news journals of the past which had concentrated on Lenin, Trotsky and others. For those like him over thirty, it was irritating. The history of the past fifteen years, *their* history, the years they had lived, fought, won and celebrated had been expunged. In their place were unconvincing re-drafts of events with Stalin at least as prominent as Lenin, while the only mentions of Trotsky managed to poison his name by blaming him for everything from the Cheka's excesses to 'revisionism'. Now he was being written out of the history books and by 1934 he was not mentioned at all. Meanwhile, the cult of Stalinism expanded.[4]

In 1936 Trotsky's exile was complete. Already forced out of Russia, Stalin now declared him a non-person while secretly marking him for assassination. Then the dictator with the chronic need for constant adulation began to use the mendacious skills he had learned and honed since the inception of the C.C.C. in 1921. He widened the methods of judgement so that the judiciary could now be used to try Party members. The notorious 'show trials' had begun.

Stalin's enemies were accused, tried, convicted and executed, sometimes in secret but often in public to maintain fear within the Party, through all organs of Government and into every layer of the population.

Yet in the Modin household the inspirational teachings about the Trotsky philosophy and ideology, taught to Ivan by his army tutor, were the vehicle by which his son Yuri now learned Marxist–Leninist principles, although the non-person was never discussed at school. It was unwise to keep any of his works on display in home libraries so his mother, Glasfina Ivanovna, hid all Trotsky's writings, including yellowed press cuttings of his articles. They helped her son comprehend the meaning of the Russian Revolution, and how it fitted with the tenets laid down by Lenin, Marx, Hegel and Trotsky himself. History was rationalized to fit doctrine, but at least it was not changed or distorted.

Modin recalled with modest pride that he excelled at Marxist theory and dialectics.[5] His superior intellect showed in everything, from his numeracy to his writing.[6] He claimed to have a superb memory, especially for fine detail, which was verified by his recall of certain events after questions were put to him in our four hour-long interview sessions. Although there were moments when he couldn't recall a location, or a document in his files, he would remember before the session was completed.

Modin's skills impressed his teachers across Russia, some of whom commented that he should become an academic. Others thought there might be openings for him if he joined the Communist Party as a theoretician.

HOMEWORK FOR LIFE

A Stalinist decree in 1931 eliminated much language training in Russia, so Yuri was not educated in foreign languages. However, the diligent Glasfina, who read widely, made sure her gangling offspring understood English.

She had a passion for literature, especially the works of Charles

Dickens, which she had first read in Middle School. Glasfina wanted her son to have at least some command of a second language so that he could learn more than the narrow and distorted view of history being forced upon the first of several Russian generations, viewed from the perspective of a twisted Marxist prism.

Yuri appreciated his mother's insistence on coaching him four times a week after school in the intricacies and vagaries of a complex language. It was difficult but he began to enjoy English through her story-telling. Like her, he admired Dickens. By the time he was thirteen, he was himself struggling through some less demanding literature, which his mother had managed to smuggle from libraries.

Glasfina was going to great lengths to give her bright son advantages. While tens of millions were being oppressed under Stalin to create his 'Socialism in one Nation', for the first time in the country's history an educated class was emerging. Tens of thousands were needed to fill the bureaucracies being formed to run the government's new departments in such areas as law, science and economics. For some it was their first chance to leap out of the squalor being made even worse for the masses by Stalin's policies.

Yuri never mastered English orally in those formative years, but he could read it. This achievement was something about which he could not boast to friends at school. Stalin was engendering such acute xenophobia that it was imprudent to show knowledge of foreign cultures. By 1936, there was much talk of spies infiltrating Russia and the secret police was beginning to enforce the Soviet dictator's vicious dictums of repression.

Glasfina also instructed Yuri in the principles of Christianity and other religions. This way the boy would not forget his roots in Suzdal. It also ensured that he had comparisons to the dogmas of the Leninist and Stalinist cults, both leaders having been effectively deified to replace outlawed religions.

Although Yuri was glad of his religious knowledge, and while he was intrigued with the mysteries of Christ, he preferred the pragmatism of Communism. Like his father, he was an atheist.

While developing into a tall, strong, curly-haired lad, young Yuri was not interested in sport, except skiing. He had many hours alone and enjoyed reading, which contributed to his habitually studious expression. Yet he had a sense of humour, which took the edge off his serious nordic-blue eyes. As he matured he developed a hearty

Russian laugh, which would be accompanied by waggling shoulders and flushed cheeks. He had a reflective rather than a rapier wit. Like all Russians he had a strong sense of irony. It was in the soul. Centuries of hardship had honed it into an art form.

Young Yuri learned quicker than most how to make friends. Because of his family's intermittent moves, he often found himself with the sometimes difficult problem of being a 'new boy'. Yet the polished manners Glasfina had taught him and the sense of strong discipline instilled by his father made him agreeable to other students and deferential to teacher authority. Yuri was never going to be a leader, but he could be a trusted friend, a confidant, someone who would offer friendship and solace.

The boy would often attract the attention of new friends by making up exotic stories about his father's former postings. He developed a practised skill at telling tales that were unverifiable and credible, and therefore usually acceptable. Young Yuri put this talent down to having read and loved the great Russian writers, especially Dostoevsky, Turgenev, Tolstoy and Chekhov.

Story-telling was also a necessary part of everyone's armoury against the constant threats in a police state. An individual had to have a believable excuse for any action. Besides, Communists argued, Lenin had made the lie a virtue in the 'struggle against capitalism'. Deception on a small or massive scale in 1930s Russia was the way of life.

It reached a peak during Stalin's purges, which became endemic in 1937. They were aimed at eliminating all traces of the old revolutionaries, Trotskyites and the Comintern. By mid-1938, he had murdered thousands of those who, twenty years earlier, had shown different political preferences to him. Stalin caused a wave of terror, first through the Party, where his ex-partners in the revolution were tortured or forced into confessions, then throughout the Comintern abroad.

All those who had risked their lives in the clandestine infiltration of nations across Western Europe were summoned back to Moscow for 'discussions', a word which became a code for execution. Most went meekly to their deaths in Moscow rather than be hunted down abroad.

In a rush to authenticate the meaning and message of the grand delusion, Stalin ordered every student to read certain documents.

Yuri, like all students in the Russian Middle School, had to study, some of it by rote, Stalin's *Short History of the Communist Party of the Soviet Union*. This boring text out-did everything that had gone before. Claiming to be the 'first accurate and doctrinally correct' work in the field, the document re-wrote the Party's history from the 'new and revealing perspective' of the show trials – the charade of Stalin's perceived enemies recanting their 'subversion' in public courts.

All previous text-books were banned and declared 'apocryphal'. The new Party bible was written by Stalin's secretaries under his direction and he composed its philosophy, a primitive digest of the Marxist theory of dialectics.

It was not criticized, for Stalin's cultism had been forced into the nation's social structure. He appeared to the people as a philosopher, constitution-maker, historian and defender of the motherland. His self-made image was that of an avuncular, strong, yet sensitive man. He never missed a photo opportunity with children, which projected him as a figure with the nation's future at heart.

THE KNOCK THAT NEVER CAME

Once these cruel initiatives against all the Old Bolsheviks who had been prominent in the Revolution were underway, Stalin turned his attention to the army, the officers of which he had distrusted since they took their commissions from Trotsky in 1917 and 1918, when Russia was in Revolution and war. In the 1920s he had not dared to move against the army. He feared insurrection long after Trotsky had departed as the War Commissariat. In the 1930s, he removed the old generals who were strong enough to oppose him and replaced them with his own appointments.

Stalin now needed to instil fear throughout the army ranks and eliminate those still brave enough to speak in praise of 'the old days' under Trotsky and the now-exiled revolutionary himself. He engineered random purges of garrisons across Russia, with the occasional military-style firing-squad executions of 'Trotskyites', a description which millions once wore as a badge of pride. It was now a smear, thanks to Stalin's relentless campaign of vilification.

Ivan feared the knock on the door in the middle of the night.

Stories of army personnel being rounded up and dragged away in darkness, never to be seen again, began circulating from garrison to garrison.

The knock never came at the Modins' barracks bungalow home. Instead, Ivan, like scores of other army officers, was visited while on duty near Moscow. In a standard ploy that was known and feared in the purge years, three KGB men turned up at the barracks and 'interviewed' officers.

'They would claim to be searching for anti-revolutionaries, Trotskyites and foreign agents,' according to former KGB Colonel 'F'. After a long discussion, if they [the KGB] were suspicious of the interviewee things would develop into a full-scale interrogation. They had a standard range of questions, which were typed up in advance. The same sheets were used for years.'

While two of the KGB men fired questions, a third took everything down in longhand. They always began by asking about background, which in Ivan's case went right back to the time when the family's ancestors in Novgorod, 150 miles south of Leningrad, were in trouble with the State authorities over trade with Sweden. They were arrested and sent to Suzdal, the religious town where Yuri was born. Even the fact that it was a haven for the Russian Orthodox Church would have taken on a sinister overtone, as if Ivan may have been wayward because of it, such was the official attitude to religion.

'Those with beliefs other than Communist doctrine,' Colonel 'F' noted, 'were regarded at least as potential political subversives.'

Once it was learnt that Ivan had been a member of the Red Army since its inception, the usual list of questions were trotted out:

Hadn't he supported Leon Trotsky?

That was easy for Ivan to answer. Everyone in the army owed their jobs to him.

Had he supported Trotsky's ideas?

Ivan knew an acceptable response to that. In 1920 one couldn't distinguish between Marxism, Leninism and Trotskyism.

The two interrogators, playing 'good cop, bad cop', challenged this. Ivan asked them to explain the differences as they were in 1920. They couldn't.

Had he supported Leon Trotsky in his bid for power in 1924 after Lenin's death?

Ivan had been forewarned of this query too. Because Trotsky was Commissariat of War, he and almost all other army officers had hoped he would become General Secretary.

The tougher secret policeman accused him of being an 'active' Trotskyite for twenty years, which Ivan denied. Leon Trotsky was the only member of the Politburo with whom he and his fellow officers were familiar. None of the others, certainly not Stalin, had anything to do with the army.

This brought further anger from the main inquisitor, who demanded to know if Ivan had read about recent articles in the papers about the Great Leader's [Stalin's] key advice to Army generals during the Civil War.

Ivan said he had. All the while, the third man scribbled down his every word. The tough interrogator again accused him of being active in support of Trotsky since his exile from Russia nearly a decade ago.

Ivan denied it again. The 'softer' questioner asked if he had ever put his name to 'illegal' petitions in support of 'the Jewish traitor, Leon Trotsky'.

The army Commissar said he couldn't recall doing that.

The other policeman claimed they had documents with his name on it in support of Trotsky.

Ivan wanted to know when this was. The two men said the documents ranged from 1924 to 1937. Ivan replied that they were mistaken. The less aggressive inquisitor then pulled out sheets of paper with sworn statements from alleged fellow officers in other Brigades who had named him, amongst scores of other army personnel who were 'recognized, active supporters of the anti-Soviet traitor, Leon Trotsky'. It was another bluff, which by 1938 most interrogators knew about.

Ivan thought he may have known only one of the accusers – a man whom he had heard had disappeared from the Yaroslavl garrison.

The questioning remained intense and at times fierce until the 'good cop' asked if they could speak with other members of his family. Ivan had no way of avoiding this. It was a standard threat and he had to acquiese. He warned his family that there could easily be a visit by the secret police.

Modin told me he could still remember the fear in his heart

throughout many months of 1938. However, he was prepared for any interrogation. His parents had not mentioned Trotsky in recent years. He knew his father had been a strong supporter, but that was more than a decade ago. He was also aware that Ivan was not a traitor and certainly did not support Trotsky or any overthrow of Stalin. This gave him enough courage to face whatever questions were put to him.[7]

To his relief the interrogation never came. Ivan was finally told that he would be informed of his fate 'in the near future'.

There was a fearful gloom in the Modin household for the next week while Ivan contemplated his fate. No one could sleep well. They were all worried again about the knock on the door. But instead, after ten days, Ivan was summoned to his commanding officer's quarters and told that he was to be cashiered. It came as a shock, for the Commissar had been a member of the Army for two decades. The military had been his life and now he was receiving a dishonourable discharge for 'rebellious views . . . and active support of an exiled traitor, who was intent on destroying the motherland and the Union of Soviet Socialist Republics . . .'[8]

The family was ordered to return by train to Suzdal in late 1938. After they had taken up lodgings with friends for a few weeks, a surprising thing happened. Ivan received his army pay-cheque in the mail. It was the same amount as usual.

After seveal months of pay-cheques, he wondered if he had been the subject of a not-unheard-of bureaucratic bungle. He and his wife worried about the consequences of accepting the money. Then at a convivial army reunion in Leningrad, he learned that other officers who had been accused of being Trotskyites were also still on full pay – in effect, on reserve call-up. Stalin was expecting war and wanted all experienced personnel ready for a return to active duty at any time, even if they were real or imagined Trotskyites.

When the Modin family settled down again, his father advised Yuri to join the Young Communists, *Komsomols*, which would give him many advantages. Not the least of these, his parents pointed out with chagrin, would be full knowledge of what was 'politically correct'. Young Yuri would learn which 'isms' and 'ites' would bring him progress in life rather than persecution.

3. SON OF A BANKER

THE FOUR BURDENS

On October 12, 1923, Charles Rothschild committed suicide by lacerating his throat with a razor at Tring Park, Buckinghamshire. This act of a man driven insane over six years by the then incurable disease of sleeping sickness, was to change the life of his twelve-year-old son Victor dramatically.[1]

Victor was shocked but not deeply moved for he had not been close to either of his parents, regarding them as 'policemen' rather than loving kin. They had regimented his life and to a lesser extent those of his three sisters Miriam, Elizabeth and Kathleen, from a distance, always with a succession of nannies and governesses as filters and go-betweens in their upbringing. Charles' severe illness also prevented him having a close relationship with anyone.[2,3]

His death, however, was 'an absolute disaster' for the family, particularly for Victor, according to his sister Miriam, two years his senior.[4] He was too young for the responsibilities that would come with being heir to a famous banking dynasty. The new head of the family, Uncle Walter, was too much of a misfit and rogue to take on the exacting role completely.

The name 'Rothschild' – meaning 'red shield', an insignia which adorned the home of the family's founder, Mayer Amschel – had been synonymous with wealth and power for nearly two centuries, ever since it emerged from the ghetto of eighteenth-century Frankfurt. In that time, the family had moved from dependence on the support of princelings to a position where they backed governments and financed major European wars in the interests of their country. The English Rothschilds led by Nathan, Victor's great-great-grandfather, had financed the greatest of all British victories – against

Napoleon at Waterloo. Victor's great-grandfather, Lionel, had bought the Suez Canal for Disraeli. Nothing had been too complex or ambitious on the world stage for the family.

Yet no matter how bright, no one so young could cope with the enormous responsibility of his heritage as the next head of the family's British branch. The spotlight would be on young Victor at least a decade early. Even some Rothschild adults who had gone before had buckled under the pressure of the family name.

Until Charles' premature death, life at Tring Park had been peaceful and the children had been brought up appreciating the world's flora and fauna. Charles was a dedicated naturalist and reluctant banker, and eccentric bachelor-uncle Walter, who lived at the family mansion, was a shy, nervous zoologist. This lovable miscreant had virtually been banished from the Bank to Tring after near bankruptcy in 1908. The company of this wayward genius had its advantages for young Victor. He developed an interest in zoology and could identify butterfly species before he could read their names.

Perhaps as a compensation or counter to the over-sensitivity of his uncle, who had a debilitating speech defect, and the reclusive depressions of Charles, Victor could be a naughty prankster who would not let his sisters dominate him.

His father's demise hardened him, as he learned at a young age how to handle the triple burdens of race, name and intellect. He was a Jew and had already had his shins kicked by a bully at the Stanmore Park prep school for this. Victor, born 31 October 1910, had been unaware of anything particularly Jewish about him or his family until that bruising notification, which had been accompanied by the salutation 'you dirty Jew', a phrase at that time beginning to float across from a specific part of the Continent with increasing regularity.[5]

He considered his parents to be atheists or agnostics. The only hint of any religious leanings on their part came from the children having to say a non-denominational prayer at the foot of their mother's bed before saying good night or good morning. This offering to a vague deity was an all-encompassing plea to bless everyone. (Victor didn't recall a single response from an omniscient God, but he kept an open mind.) Yet his racial inheritance came to isolate him from the mainstream, while awakening his curiosity.

Intellect was also a cross to bear. Young Victor was endowed with much of it, always a misdemeanour in the minds of the less well endowed. School bullies attacked him for his brain capacity, while others sneered as teachers responded to this child with a first-rate, hungry mind.

What kept him from being ostracized at Stanmore and then Harrow was his exceptional sporting skills, especially at cricket, tennis and golf. (His ball sense came from his mother, who had been Hungarian Ladies lawn tennis champion. She introduced overarm to the women's game.) Cricket appealed to him most. He looked on it as 'the nearest thing to chess that sport could bring'. He liked the physical challenge of facing speed as a batsman, or the intricacies of delivering slow-medium variations such as in the leg- or off-cutter. According to his sister Miriam, herself a skilled cricketer who saw Victor play often, he was also an excellent slips fieldsman.

Later, she saw his now legendary performance against the fierce speed of Harold Larwood, who was practising his 'leg theory' bowling, which later was employed against the Australians and became known as 'bodyline'. Larwood hurled the cricket ball at speeds approaching 100 miles an hour and directed his deliveries at the batsman's ribcage – around the righthander's heart – or head. Larwood was so fast and accurate that with almost every delivery the batsman faced three options: getting hit, fending the ball off with the bat and risking a catch to the fieldsmen crowded on the leg side, or getting out of the way.

Victor, on that famous occasion, played his natural batting game of graceful aggression. He refused to take evasive action and took many blows on the body from Larwood, who had no compunction about hitting the future Lord Rothschild. He made 36 for Northamptonshire that day in a memorable stay of 75 minutes against the brilliant, terror bowling. Victor came away bruised from the encounter, Miriam recalled, and added proudly that he seemed to enjoy the challenge and never flinched.[6]

The young Victor saw the benefit of analysing any match as it unfurled and devising keen strategies against opponents. He was an incessant changer of fields on the odd occasion he bowled himself or captained a side, always looking for a tactical advantage when others may have been in despair against a rampaging opposing bat. Cricket, even more than compulsory house rugby, brought out an aggressive athleticism in the boy, which lay undetected in the class-room, where he appeared more taciturn than tactical.

Another saving grace was the boy's wit. He was not the type that larked about and was cheeky to teachers in order to show bravado and draw attention to himself. Rather, Victor was adept at sharp, sardonic humour, which sometimes cut deep into the sensibilities of the shin-kickers and the odd tormentor. But he still enjoyed the thrust and parry between teacher and boys in the class-room. When one master dangled a boy out of the window by the hair, Victor watched in as much hopeful anticipation as the other on-lookers. When another drunken teacher tried to remove a student's appendix with a pen-knife, young Rothschild was in awe rather than fear of this outrageous act of amateur surgery. Belly-laughs were loud from him too when fellow students felt the sting of chalk or blackboard duster on the ear or nose.[7]

Another burden or badge for him, depending on the moment, was the family name. It conjured up an exceptional sense of history, power and wealth in the minds of his contemporaries, even if they too came from the highest ruling and moneyed class in the land. This brought a certain schizophrenia to Victor's make-up as he battled with his breeding and circumstances. At times, when he wished to appear superior, he would be 'an aloof, overbearing little snob'.[8]

At other times, in his formative pre-teenage and teenage years, he would be generous and egalitarian in his attitude, especially when he realized it was performance on the sporting field that brought the greatest prestige. Hitting fifty runs always brought genuine, heartfelt applause, whereas being delivered to school in a Rolls-Royce never would.

The name Rothschild always brought an uncomfortable certainty to his future. It was always assumed that no matter what he did or excelled in, he would end up in the Bank. His school-chums told him so, and teachers occasionally mentioned it, as did family members.

Secretly, this irked and troubled Victor. What if he wanted to be a naturalist as his father had been in his non-banking relaxation hours? Charles, a benign, unassuming gentleman until the depression of his disease possessed him, was an expert on fleas. In the late nineteenth and early twentieth century it was fashionable to examine such small creatures. They were carriers of disease which then preoccupied health authorities because of the epidemics they caused. Charles had even written an important tome called *Synopsis of British Siphonaptera* (fleas).

Young Victor had rarely spoken of his ambivalent feelings about being a regular face in the City of London. Thinking his father might show understanding because of his flea hobby, he had mentioned it *en passant*. His father had replied patronizingly that there was nothing wrong with being a scientist, part-time. Flustered, the boy, then just nine, asked about being a cricketer. Even this largely amateur sport was a career for some, and the fine young batsman showed later that he was of first-class standard, and even had Test potential if he really persevered. There was, after all, Victor explained to his sport-ignorant father, Dr W. G. Grace as an example of the right background and excellence on the field in combination. Charles' response was to laugh at him, not derisively but dismissively.

While it was never said in as many words, only the Bank had real credibility in the eyes of the world as the place for a true, modern-day Rothschild. In some ways Charles' untimely departure was a blessing, for Victor felt less constrained by family tradition. If his father had been alive the bank career route would have been inevitable. Charles' self-destruction helped *make* his only son and primary heir. Victor felt freer to consider other possibilities for his life.

His father's suicide also meant that the young man was faced with a new obligation – money. He inherited 2.5 million pounds, which was put in trust for him until he turned twenty-one. When he later fully realized the enormity of the responsibility and privilege it accompanied, his wealth cornered and troubled him. His imma-ture mind could not accept that some people should have a lot of money without having earned it, which became an uneasy philos-ophy for him later in life as he became more aware of the inequalities of society and his own wealth.

The problem left him restless but not sleepless. The pounds had their uses, and meant he could afford luxuries which he less guiltily revelled in. Again, twinned with his father's passing, Victor's inheritance allowed him an independence of thought and prospect.

It was a heady mix for a hitherto predestined member of the city's bowler hat and umbrella brigade.

Harrow took him down the usual, well-documented top English public school path of extracurricular Latin, beatings, striving for educational and professional elitism, more than latent-homosexuality, eccentricity and over-dosing on mundanities such as compulsory sport. Victor was vaguely aware of something dramatic happening in his first term at Harrow when 'eleven boys were fired' from his house, apparently for homosexual acts. During this time he was beaten up by school bullies for giving cheek, or 'lip' as it was known. Aware of this, another boy threatened to report him to the head of his house unless he agreed to a homosexual relationship with him. Rothschild was 'sufficiently unnerved by this blackmail' to report the boy to his house-master. The blackmailer was punished and for some unexplained reason, perhaps because of Rothschild's integrity or even his declared heterosexuality, he thereafter became one of the house-master's 'favourites'.[9]

Through all this Victor showed his scientific bent, although he eschewed entomology in a defiant reaction to his father's obsessions. He loved biology, but showed an unfamily-like inclination towards the Classics, which were compulsory until he was sixteen, for which he remained eternally grateful.[10]

The young Rothschild was also herded into his own separate state of Jewishness, not by the school, which strove for a bland, non-denominational purvey of religion, but by a number of parents who wanted definite Judaic instruction for their sons. On each Saturday the Jewish boys were corralled into a classroom known as the Tin Tabernacle, where a distinguished Shakespearian scholar, Sir Isaac Gollancz, attempted to teach them the principles of Judaism. Victor was not happy with this isolation, which his family had not requested. But out of duty and sensitivity to his race, he joined the other boys.

RISE OF THE BEER-HALL BARBARIAN

Meanwhile in Germany a much more sinister racial apartheid was fermenting in the mind of a former First World War corporal, who was to make up for his intellectual short-comings by a capacity to incite particular hatreds in others and to unite them in their disturbed feelings and ignorance.

His name was Adolf Hitler and he emerged in the 1920s during the period of Germany's unstable Weimar Republic when post-war economic conditions were poor and the nation was humiliated by having to pay war reparations to the Allies. His thoughts manifested and festered in a weirdly derivative two-volume book called *Mein Kampf*, which was based on a twisted view of both Darwinism and a potted, if not potty, racial history. Hitler's writings managed to demonstrate his brutality and insanity to such an extent that the book might have been considered risible, had it not proved so dangerous.

Mein Kampf was Hitler's blueprint for the Third Reich, which would be set up to 'last for a thousand years'. He maintained that a strong State could only build power by not allowing races to mix and by eliminating what he judged to be inferior people, primarily Jews. He blamed them for 'internationalism', which was the appreciation of things foreign – a poison that caused people to underestimate their own cultural values. Jews also tended towards 'egalitarianism, democracy and majority rule', which were 'hostile to all creativity and leadership, the origin of all progress'.

Hitler also took offence at 'pacifism', and distorted Darwin's theories into a social observation that this destroyed a people's healthy, natural instincts for self-preservation. In other words, the Jewish mentality tended to thwart one nation's inclination to destroy another.

In order to develop a powerful state one had to dominate and/or eliminate these nasty, pacifist, democratic internationalists. Hitler felt that Bolshevik Russia – in the mid-1920s exemplified by the Trotskyite concept of international socialism using the Comintern as an infiltrating vehicle – exhibited all these undesirable tendencies. Hitler linked Russia with a 'Jewish world conspiracy'.

In the mid-1920s, the beer-hall agitator suggested that Germany should look east to Russia to 'extend its living space', an unsubtle euphemism for 'attack and occupy'. In one swoop, Hitler suggested, Germany could thus wipe out the base of international Jewry and Marxism.

He wrote much of *Mein Kampf* while in prison before his release at Christmas 1924. He used the ideas in his book for all his frenzied speeches, which excited the great mass of disaffected voters across Germany. He appealed to the population by promising better government than the democratic parties, which had been discredited by continual failure in the 1920s. Hitler also said he would create a strong anti-communist front across Europe and restore the confidence of the nation. He was careful not to spell out policies and spoke to emotions rather than reason.

The Nazis were clever at producing drama and pageantry, which ignited a response among a population disinterested in the normal drab political offerings. The images evoked at rallies were jingoistic, ruthless and youthful, allowing a defeated country to fantasize about regaining its power. Hitler's subconscious preoccupation with themes of struggle, death and hatred of what he saw as inferior races, such as the Jews, came through and coalesced a negative force in the Germany of the 1920s and 1930s.

It took ten years – from the formation of the Nazi movement on 24 February 1920 out of the tiny German Workers' Party, to the Parliament (Reichstag) elections on 24 September 1930 – for Hitler to have a national impact. The Nazis won 107 seats and 6.5 million votes, outscoring its main rival, the Communists, who took 77 seats and 4 million votes.

By 1930, Hitler's rise was feeding the complexes of Jews around the world as his ranting reminded them of their long history of inhuman persecution. The Rothschild family, which extended across Europe, was particularly aware of the developments in Germany for its members represented everything Hitler hated about Jews – sophistication, cultured internationalism and well-organized capitalism.

Yet one member of the famous family, the spoiled and sport-loving Victor, seemed blissfully unaware of the threat as in 1930 he prepared to enter Cambridge University on a scholarship.

4. CAMBRIDGE CAULDRON

A BLUNT AWAKENING

Rothschild found Trinity College's cloistered, privileged life a welcome change from Harrow, and although he could not escape his three burdens, he found some respite from them. His dark good looks, which through his undergraduate years would appear to grow more mysterious, arrogant and surly, made him attractive to both sexes, as did his penchant for fast cars (he had a Bugati) and sport.[1]

He played county cricket for Northamptonshire and Cambridge, first-grade tennis and enjoyed whittling down his golf handicap to single figures. Rothschild also liked entertaining, and turned from the chore of classical piano, learnt at an early age, to the delights of jazz. He was a party hit at the keyboard wherever he went.

With all this extracurricular distraction, it was not surprising that he did not do as well as expected in the first year of his course, Part I of the Natural Sciences Tripos (examination). The result didn't please his Hungarian-born mother, Rozsika, who was descended from a Habsburg court Jew and was active in Zionist politics. She had a strong influence over him and took advantage of this academic lapse to persuade him, against his will, to leave Cambridge and help out at the Rothschild Bank in the City of London. The Depression had hit the banks, which were in disarray worldwide.[2]

Reluctantly in 1931, the just turned 21-year-old swapped open-neck shirt and tweed jacket for the banker's pinstripe-suited uniform. After the relaxed atmosphere of Cambridge, he hated the stuffy, anti-intellectual ambience of New Court, in the City. Rothschild found it 'moribund, boring, rather painful.' He wrote in his autobiography, *Meditations of a Broomstick*: 'I did not like banking which consists essentially of facilitating the movement of money from Point A, where it is, to Point B where it is needed.'

This lack of appreciation led to many arguments with his strong-willed mother as he showed his resentment to the world of capital and in particular the business's gold refinery, where he spent some time. His mother reminded him that it was banking that had given him his wealth and status, and that it wasn't for a Rothschild to turn his nose up at the family profession and tradition.

Victor responded by saying that tradition should not be allowed to cage him. In the end, his mother heard from others at the bank that her son was uncooperative and therefore 'a liability'. As such it was better that he be 'expunged'. The dogged young sophisticate 'retired' after the shortest run ever – less than six months – at the profession by one of the family.

He went back to Cambridge, and persuaded his professor to let him attend Part II of the Natural Sciences Tripos lectures and practical classes, while also commencing research into animal sperm for a doctorate. At that time a student could research for a PhD without a degree but soon after he began, the university Statutes were changed and he had to get a degree.

Rothschild wanted to continue his research as soon as possible, which meant taking the shortest, easiest route to undergraduate qualification. He took a Pass degree in Physiology, French – which he could speak well enough after a succession of native governesses – and English. However, the latter didn't prove to be the problem-free course he had anticipated.

'We had not been encouraged to read as children,' he wrote in *Meditations*. '*Alice in Wonderland*, for example, was forbidden, presumably because my mother had read Freud.'

He gave credit to his tutors who helped him on his way to a Triple First in his 'contemptible Ordinary Degree.'

Anthony Blunt, three years his senior at twenty-four, was one of his occasional French tutors. The homosexual aesthete considered his pupil 'darkly romantic looking'. Rothschild found his blue-eyed, languidly affected mentor was a seductive figure because of his artistic knowledge and rebellious, anti-Establishment mind. Blunt took time in the one-on-one tutorials to tantalize his charge with innuendo about the secretive world he inhabited, including his membership of the Apostles.

Rothschild's appetite was whetted when Blunt refused to answer questions about the clandestine society.[3] However, he did inform him of its origins. The intellectual brotherhood had been founded in 1820 by twelve Evangelical undergraduates ('apostles'). Blunt had been elected in May 1928, late in his second year, and he mischievously informed Rothschild that before 1914, a new member was chosen for his 'good looks', which economist John Maynard Keynes referred to less bashfully as 'the higher sodomy'.[4]

More lately, Blunt also told the inquisitive novice, they were selected for their IQ, scholastic achievements, and 'social motivations'. The latter turned out to be their political persuasion. Blunt added cheekily that a handsome appearance could still be advantageous to those wanting to enter.

Rothschild admitted to Blunt early in 1932 that he felt 'socialist inclinations'. Blunt then introduced him to two contemporary Apostles at King's College, Dennis Proctor, a first-class economics undergraduate and Alister Watson. The latter impressed Victor more because of his desire for a scientific career, which Rothschild was also contemplating. Like Blunt, Watson had studied mathematics. Rothschild liked Watson and thought his logical, precise articulation of Marxist principles, which he managed to harness to science and maths in theory, seemed plausible. The appeal, which was at times emotional as much as rational, influenced many scientists of the era, who were caught up in a wide and growing attraction to Marxism amongst the intellectual class. Academics in general were aware of Hitler and fascism by the early 1930s and viewed communism as the antidote to the poisonous elements of its social doctrine. A broad selection of intellectuals joined the trend towards attempting change – even revolution – in the economically struggling Britain, which was still in a depression.

THE KAPITZA CLUB

Watson introduced Victor to several Russian scientists at Cambridge, including physicists Peter Kapitza and Lev D. Landau, and mathematician George Gamow, at the University's Cavendish Laboratories. The charismatic Kapitza, who would go on to be a Nobel Laureate, was the most influential of the three. He had been sponsored by the British Royal Society to come to the Cavendish in 1921 to work with Lord Rutherford. Immediately on arrival he formed the 'Kapitza Club' – a gathering of scientists which met to discuss their latest discoveries.[5] Colleagues joked that he had formed the club to keep in touch with advances in physics so that he wouldn't have to do the reading himself. They were half right. Everything he learned and the written papers presented on the various topics were sent back to Moscow.

The Russian had been encouraged by Lenin and Trotsky, who believed science would broaden economic growth in Russia. All Russian scientists abroad had to be members of the KGB-linked Soviet Scientific Mission. It did legitimate purchasing of laboratory equipment and gathered scientific literature which could further the cause.[6]

The Mission's members were under instructions to talent-spot and engage in espionage. Kapitza travelled back to Russia each year to report on his activity. He, the other Russians and the Westerners they recruited, targeted X-ray crystallography, nuclear physics, electronics, and radioactivity. The field was widened in the 1930s to include every area that could be adapted for offensive and defensive weaponry.

The undergraduate Rothschild was inspired by the belief that the Soviet Union would develop the world's first political system based on scientific principles, which the nation's theoreticians were desperately trying to fit with Marxist tenets.[7] They were boasting that science would solve the world's problems. To Rothschild and many others, the excitement of the Soviet experiment had much more appeal than the seemingly archaic and outmoded attitudes in Britain which fostered the old order of privilege and class. It was the scientific aspect of Soviet ideology more than anything that lured Rothschild to the Communist cause.

MEETING DIABLO

Rothschild spent several French tutorials discussing what he was learning from the Russians concerning scientific developments. Blunt attempted to impress him further by trying to connect impressionist and post-impressionist art with French culture, the French Revolution and Marxist precepts.[8] Rothschild found this fascinating, mainly because it revealed the hidden networks which revolutionary thought at the university was building.

But while he admired Blunt's passionate analysis, he thought these artistic longbows drawn on Marxism were obscure compared to the pragmatic links the ideology seemed to have with science.

Yet he was intrigued. He felt he was getting close to the heart of a secret Communist movement. At first, Rothschild was uneasy about what this meant for his family's banking network. He thought about the effect on his wealthier relations in Europe when all that property became controlled by the State. If he sided with the workers, he wondered what his mother would say. These thoughts remained unexpressed, except to those in the family, such as Miriam, who understood, although she always regarded herself as a socialist, as distinct from a communist. Nevertheless he was mesmerized by the prospect of revolution and its historically romantic connections with France and, more recently, Russia.

The clever, shrewd Blunt, with his feminine instinct for fathoming character, anticipated what could be prodding Rothschild to rebellion. He asked how he felt about the family Bank. This brought an irked response from Rothschild, who railed against the mindlessness of money movements and the international banking system itself. He spoke bitterly about his experiences at New Court.

Blunt sympathized but without reinforcing the negative thoughts. He even suggested that the banking system would have its uses when revolution occurred. This appeased Rothschild's worry about his background and his heritage's place in an upturned future Europe.[9]

Blunt then introduced his new chum to Guy Burgess. This could have been a bad move had not Rothschild already been aware of the homosexual culture and rampant communism at the university, which in terms of networks and exploitation were related. Burgess was the excessive embodiment of both. His boyish good-looks accentuated his waspish wit, free-thinking, and licentious behaviour. He was a seducer of any like-minded male on or off campus, and took his erotic indulgences a dangerous step further by buying favours and picking up everyone from barrow boys to bus conductors. He invented the vulgarly snobbish term 'rough trade', and for him it was a matter of the rougher the better.

From sailors to sales clerks, bar attendants to bohemians, Burgess gained a reputation for being a brutal fucker extraordinaire. His devil-may-care attitude endeared him to others who were more squeamish about their then illegal sexuality. Where Blunt fretted about his mother, vicar father and heterosexual friends learning of his preferences, Burgess regaled his intimates with his grubby adventures, exaggerating and showing off at every opportunity. He knew his outrageous approach was refreshing to his contemporaries of both sexes. It was all part of his cultivated image as a libertine which, with the saving grace of his intellect, brought not just homosexuality but also communism from their subterranean lurkings into the open.

Like Alister Watson and the more subtle Kapitza, Burgess was a communist proselytizer. He had gone to great lengths to learn by heart long communist tracts such as Marx's *Das Kapital* and Engels's *Communist Party Manifesto*. David Haden-Guest, the son of a Labour MP and a fellow Trinity undergraduate, guided him through Marx's laborious writings about dialectical materialism, which encouraged him to devour even more austere works by Lenin.[10]

Burgess would back up thought with action. He took part in strikes on behalf of Cambridge dustmen and employees at Trinity College. This endeared him even more to the closet communists in his set and inspired him to spout Marxist lines as if they were as mellifluous as Shakespeare, always without doubts about their prophetic meaning.

Stalin's Russia was a haven, he claimed, and Rothschild was reminded again – this time with more emphasis on the basic theory – that the communist dictator was applying Marx *scientifically* to society, in a way that would allow his ideology to triumph over capitalism in the next few decades.

If a rumour circulated about imperfections in the Soviet Union, it was either dismissed as bourgeois misunderstanding or explained away as a necessary sideways push to make way for the greater good in the modern Marxist society's development. When Rothschild challenged Burgess and others about the lack of democracy in Russia, the crushing of political opposition, persecution of minorities, or the stories of gulags, the questions were brushed off by comparing Russia's development to experiments in a science laboratory. Of course there would be mistakes, but when the breakthroughs were made they would leave capitalism, with its multitude of inequities, for dead.

In the early 1930s, with the crash of stock markets and businesses and the sudden rise of unemployment, the communists seemed to have all the answers, especially when facts about the failures of, for instance, the five-year economic production plans in the closed Soviet Union were not forthcoming. The world depression simply fuelled the certitude of communists outside Russia about the rightness of their position. Capitalism did seem extremely ill, although nobody was as yet prepared to administer last rites.

The one point that reached even deeper into Rothschild's psyche than the exaggerated prospects for Soviet science concerned survival. Hitler's Nazi doctrine saw 'the inferior Slavs of the Russia' and its 'Jewish co-conspirators' as the number one enemy. Increasingly in the minds of Jews everywhere was the thought that any enemy of the Nazi Party was a friend of theirs.

Russia seemed set on a collision course with Germany, which therefore made Stalin a figure to be supported, despite the vicious Jewish pogroms in the Soviet Union. At least the communists did not seem to have a hidden programme for eliminating the whole Jewish race. By mid-1932 the Nazi Party had more than doubled its vote in national elections to 13,745,000 votes, holding 230 seats in the Reichstag. It was now the largest party in Germany. Despite political setbacks, it seemed likely that Hitler would soon be Chancellor, bringing communist and Jewish fears closer to fruition.

Blunt, Kapitza, Watson and Burgess noticed their young target's natural concern when it came to talk about Stalin standing up to Hitler, and they worked on it gently in order to get him on-side. They saw him, with his money, brains and connections, as the kind of person who would be most useful in the infiltration of high places in preparation for revolution in Britain.

Late in 1932, Rothschild became a secret member of the British Communist Party. It was a bold move for the scion of a conservative banking family, none of whom he informed. However, his mother noticed the change in her son. He seemed much happier than he had been at Harrow, the Bank or in his first year at Cambridge. During his first year she would ask him each term if he had made any new friends – apart from Harrovians who went up at the same time.

'I had to say I had not,' Rothschild wrote, 'something of which I was very ashamed.'

However, his widening interests in his second year saw him blossom in character and personality. He was enjoying every aspect of his student life. He had slipped into the Bloomsbury set, through his friendships with Blunt, Maynard Keynes and left-wing writers like Rosamond Lehmann, her brother John, Lytton Strachey and Julian Bell. The males were all in or connected to the Apostles. When his mother asked about friends in 1932 he was able to answer differently.

'I was able to announce, and from time to time produce, Garrett Moore (who became Lord Drogheda), Dick Sheepshanks (killed in the Spanish Civil War), Sammy Hood, Gerald Cuthbert (killed in the Second World War), Anthony Blunt and a clever, dissolute young man called Guy Burgess, with whom my mother got on very well. Perhaps he was a Soviet agent even then.'[11]

Not all the family hit it off with Burgess. Victor's older sister Miriam, perhaps the most intellectually gifted of the family after her brother, would argue with him while Burgess tried to shout her down. They used to argue because he was incapable of debating, Miriam recalled. She took a conventional socialist line, while he wanted bloody revolution and was a self-confessed Marxist. On one occasion she reduced him to a flood of tears. After that, Miriam didn't have the heart to bait him again.[12]

Miriam never debated with Blunt, but nevertheless thought him an excellent conversationalist. He impressed all the family with his knowledge of the Rothschild art collection in England and France.[13]

THE HOARDER'S COMPANION

Rothschild also sought a more practical understanding of socialism through his friendship with the brilliant economist John Maynard Keynes, a former Apostle who lectured at Cambridge and had a room at King's. Keynes did not espouse communism, but saw the value of government intervention, especially in an economic crisis when there was mass unemployment.

In these conditions, Keynes had long said that governments should step in and control all forms of investment so as to better regulate the economy. His greatest contribution to the debate on which way governments should behave in crisis was the idea that public expenditure – particularly directed to such things as building and construction projects – should be increased at the onset of a recession. He argued that this would increase employment and thus, through the payment of wages, raise spending power and stimulate business investment. This was innovative lateral thinking, which turned most economic theory on its head. Later his views influenced the 'New Deal' under President Roosevelt in the US and 'Full Employment' policies in Great Britain.

Rothschild thought his views more pragmatic than Marxist doctrine. The tyro also admired the 48-year-old (in 1931) Keynes' wider interests, which went beyond economics to literature and book-collecting.

Rothschild had the hoarding gene – a centuries-old trait in his family – activated by his English tutor George Hylands, an authority on Shakespearian theatre. The undergraduate started acquiring English eighteenth-century first editions, particularly those of Jonathan Swift whose 'scintillating prose, irony, and sense of ridicule' appealed to Rothschild.

'Book-collecting also contributed to my friendship with Maynard Keynes,' Rothschild noted in *Meditations*, 'whose many gifts included treating the young as if they were contemporaries. He was an avid book-collector. On Monday mornings the second-hand book catalogues of Gregory used to arrive at Cambridge from Bath. If there was a volume which specially interested him, usually a seventeenth-century work, he would get out his car and tear off to Bath.'

Rothschild used to visit Keynes, unannounced, in his room at King's and in his youthful ignorance was puzzled that he never found him 'working'.

'He was always in an armchair with his feet up reading an edition of Locke, Hume or some other English philosopher or economist. When did he do his day's work? I never found out. The rumour was that he finished it in bed early in the morning.'

Rothschild chatted with the indulgent Keynes about a range of topics and was interested in the great man's views on the gold standard, the importance of which he had learnt during his aborted stay at the Bank's gold refinery. Keynes told him that Britain would not get off the gold standard, a currency system whereby the Bank of England was required to exchange gold for currency, and vice versa, at a fixed rate, thus stabilizing the exchange rates for currencies. The gold standard was the basic international monetary fund system before 1914 and between 1925 and 1931. Ten days after Keynes' pronouncement, Britain went off the standard.

Rothschild wanted to know why such an eminent observer as Keynes had got it wrong.

'Victor, I made a mistake,' Keynes replied in a refreshingly honest manner. 'You know, I am the economy's dentist. When it seems in good shape nobody wants to talk to me or even to see me for a check. It is only when the symptoms of a cavity appear that they call for me. The sad thing is I could have prevented the cavity developing.'

The elder man's candour impressed the undergraduate, who had not expected such humility in one so accomplished. It was a revelation which would stay with him and by which Rothschild would judge others and himself in the future.

THE FAVOUR

Blunt made much play towards the end of 1932 about his efforts to have Rothschild and Burgess elected to the Apostles. He complained that King's College men had dominated in the past, and he was doing what he could to wrest the initiative for the 'more enlightened at Trinity'.

Both potential recruits wanted to know what was discussed. Blunt refused to tell them, saying that a strength of the secret society was its discretion, which rang true with the questioners. They didn't even know who the other members were, although they had some idea. Burgess claimed that he knew what went on, but when challenged was found wanting.

Blunt built up the mystery until both men were quite excited about the prospect of being elected. He had become the Apostles' key figure since he joined it four and a half years earlier by engineering himself and his Marxist friends into positions of control. They included Richard Llewellyn-Davies, who went on to be an architect, the poet Hugh Sykes Davies, Alister Watson, Julian Bell, who was killed in the Spanish Civil War, and Andrew Cohen, who became a distinguished diplomat.

This cosy little cabal of Marxist/communist rebels even had their photo taken together to mark their takeover of the Society and its agenda. In so doing they broke the Apostles' rules of secrecy.

On 12 November 1932 Burgess and Victor were both voted in, and Rothschild threw a champagne party to celebrate without letting any of the guests know the reason. One partygoer recalled that 'Victor was most chuffed about something but was sworn to secrecy. I assumed he had inherited something spectacular, a chateau in a remote principality perhaps . . .'[14]

The Apostles' main function was to have a member deliver a paper and discuss it. Burgess swung into paper writing with enthusiasm. His prose-style was rambling but good and he liked the sound of his own words. Naturally he chose Marxist expositions, which aired his doctrinal knowledge. He often punctuated his papers by extemporizing and breaking away from the stated topic. In two years he delivered six lectures, three of them while inebriated, but always with the verve and enthusiasm of the obsessively committed. Every paper was dogmatically, esoterically communist.[15]

Rothschild was at a loss for a subject to submit to the Apostles' agenda-setters. He consulted Blunt, who said it would probably be wise to stay with the hot theme of 'socialism', just to start with. Victor, a strong speaker and articulate writer chose 'Communism and the future of Banking'. His paper was witty, politically correct and pragmatic. The discussion it generated was only moderate and the Apostles showed their almost complete ignorance of business and the outside world. Rothschild submitted eight ideas in his years with the Apostles and only three, all on 'suitable' left-wing topics, were chosen as papers.[16] 'They preferred to fall-back in debate on the theoretical and the doctrinaire,' he told a close family member.[17]

They would be lectured often by past members such as Keynes, who enthralled Rothschild because of his worldly experience, which rose above the usual level of undergraduate diatribe. After hearing his paper on 'Government Intervention', which was appreciated by most of the members, a frustrated Rothschild later wrote to his friend and mentor:

'We [the Apostles] talk endlessly in the Society about Communism which is rather dull. Guy [Burgess] and Alister [Watson] and

Richard [Llewellyn-]Davies speak with shining eyes and sweaty foreheads about this all-pervading topic, vehemently but somewhat illogically, it seems to me. (I believe I have found a fallacy in the whole racket; no doubt you could tell me a hundred.) Hugh Sykes Davies prates endlessly about Sadism and Swinburne, which I believe is due to the new Italian book; while Gray, Walter and I content ourselves with obscure jokes about electric currents. The fact is an atmosphere of decadence is appearing and we need your presence . . .'[18]

However, a paper Rothschild delivered entitled, 'Communism and the Hope of Science', was appreciated. It dwelt more on the practical aims of the field now being experimented in and showed how developments could make for a better society. It was clear that Rothschild had to be given a rational, credible outcome for him to in any way appreciate communist theory. *Then* he might become a committed revolutionary.

Blunt knew his introductions to people and organizations had obligated Rothschild, although he did not ask a favour in return until April 1933, when the young art expert stumbled across a painting in a dealer's shop in Cambridge. Blunt was almost obsessive about the French painter Nicolas Poussin, and easily detected one of his works.

This particular painting was in need of restoration, but Blunt was beside himself when he noticed the familiar signature of his favourite painter. Pretending to be only vaguely interested, he asked the dealer its price then rushed to a phone to ring Rothschild. Blunt told Cambridge contemporary Alister Macdonald and others about the conversation, which he dined out on for years. It was, he said, one of the 'most thrilling moments of my life'.

'Victor, I've come across a very interesting investment,' Blunt said.

'What, Anthony?'

'It's a painting by Poussin, "Elizier and Rebecca at the Well".'

'How much is it?'

'Three hundred pounds.'

'That sounds very cheap.'

'Oh, it most surely is. The owner doesn't know what it is. I wondered if you might consider investing?'

'How much?'

'A hundred, perhaps.'

'You're sure it's a Poussin?'

'Victor, please!'

There was a pause before Victor remarked in his 'booming' voice: 'Well Anthony, you're not really talking about an investment. What you mean is that you want me to buy it for you.'

Rothschild, in a gesture typical of his generosity to his close friends, gave him the £300 outright. (Sixty years later the painting was valued at a million pounds.)

KIM OF TRINITY

This act of largesse bonded Rothschild and Blunt even more and the latter went further out of his way to keep his friend on-side with introductions. Blunt thought it would be useful, in particular, to introduce him to a like-minded character who was dedicated to action for the cause. This was to the taciturn, stammering Kim Philby, the son of rebel Arabist, Harry St John, who helped create Saudi Arabia. Rothschild found Kim an interesting, if not intriguing figure. He was treasurer of the Socialist Society at Cambridge and his views were far less strident than those of Burgess, Watson and Co., and more in keeping with Rothschild's moderation.

At the time, June 1933, Philby had just taken his finals in Economics at Cambridge having gained good second-class honours, and a Trinity College prize of £14, with which he had bought the collected works of Karl Marx. With additional money from his father and another source, he had also acquired a second-hand motor-bike, with which he intended to tour Europe.[19]

This impressed Rothschild, who had never done anything so adventurous. He asked Philby where he might go. Philby claimed he wanted to improve his chances of getting into the Foreign Service. An Austrian visit would help him brush up on his German. Rothschild was fascinated and he discussed the recent collapse of democratic government in Austria.

Engelbert Dollfuss was governing by decree, trying to hold extremists at bay. Hitler had taken power in Germany and had done much to restore national unity and morale. He now wanted

Anschluss, union with Austria. There were reports of Nazi forces on both sides of the border agitating for the merger.

Philby responded that he would be avoiding trouble and would monitor events to make sure he wasn't trapped there. Rothschild asked him to keep in touch over his observations and Philby promised to contact him as soon as he returned to England.[20]

A week later, on a visit to the Tring estate, Blunt asked Rothschild about his thoughts on Philby. He said he found him 'amusing', though shy and wondered if there was something more going on behind his retiring manner, especially as he was biking over to a European trouble spot like Vienna.

A MARRIAGE OF CONVENTION

A few months later, Rothschild informed his mother he intended to marry the lively and intelligent Barbara Hutchinson, who had been in his small, regular circle of friends at Cambridge. Barbara was the daughter of St John Hutchinson, a leading barrister.

Rozsika had mixed feelings. She felt that Victor was 'too immature, too adolescent' to marry in his early twenties.[21] However, she was also relieved. Although she liked Burgess, Blunt and the other homosexuals in his circle, she hoped that her son was not of the same persuasion. Rozsika was also surprised at the suddenness of the affair and thought that her son was probably a virgin before becoming involved with Barbara, who had 'plenty of sex appeal' for the untried Victor, according to a close Rothschild relative.[22]

However, Rozsika was pleased that Barbara wanted to become Jewish and she was converted with full Orthodox rites into the faith.

The marriage did little to change the undergraduate's lifestyle. Governesses and nannies would be employed for young Sarah, who was born the following year in 1934. Rothschild continued his studies, sport, book-collecting, membership of the Apostles and partying. The privileges of money, tradition and position ensured he could carry on the way he liked. However, he had taken up another interest, which would become an obsession over and above everything else in his existence.

He had become a Hitler-watcher.

5. THE CONVERSION

HOOK OF DESTINY

Rothschild met Philby again a few weeks after he returned to London in May 1934 and was introduced to Philby's new bride of semi-convenience, Litzi Friedmann, a Jewish communist working underground for the Comintern in Austria. The tiny, dark, sensual Litzi had married Philby to escape Nazi persecution.

They spoke about the vicious Nazi attacks, the collapse of the Austrian Socialist Movement, the murder of its leaders, and the Nazis' revival of beheading for political offences. It all had a stinging resonance for Rothschild, who was hearing similar stories from family members in the Bank in Austria. Litzi talked about communism now being the only way to stop Hitler and added that Jews everywhere should join the movement to fight fascism. Rothschild said he was willing to help.

A week later, Burgess met him and told him that 'Kim has asked me to raise money for the fight against fascism in Vienna'. Rothschild gave him 'several hundred' pounds for the cause.[1]

A few days later Rothschild travelled down to London and met Philby alone at a coffee shop in West End Lane, West Hampstead, not far from where Philby was staying with Litzi in his mother's home. Rothschild was riveted by Philby's account of his adventures in Vienna, where he took risks to help the underground freedom movement. He joined the defenders of fired-on council estates, assisted trapped workers to escape from sewers, and carried out dangerous missions as a courier, using journalism as a cover.[2]

Philby said he was going to do more in 'the fight'. He intended to go anywhere he was directed to push back the Nazis. It was more than fighting talk, theorizing in the stuffy Apostles meetings or bravado at communist rallies. Here was action man, in the form of a half-smiling, pipe-smoking and stutteringly reticent son of a famous explorer.

Philby was someone Rothschild thought he himself might never be, restricted as he was by his background, wealth, and inherited responsibilities. Yet Philby's independent life and willingness to take up challenges were things to which the young Victor aspired.

Towards the end of the meeting Philby asked if Rothschild would be willing to do more than contribute funds for the cause.[3]

In a moment that would make any heart beat faster, the scion of one of the world's richest families replied positively. In rebellion against everything he had been bred to do, but in support of his race, his personal independence and his sense of self-worth, he had taken a step towards a line, beyond which was an alluring, clandestine void.

Rothschild asked what he should do.

'Nothing,' Philby responded sphinx-like, 'and you had better get used to it.'[4]

At that moment, Philby felt he had all but hooked one of the ten people he had listed to follow him into operations as a secret agent for the Soviet Union.

The KGB at Moscow Centre were already well aware of Rothschild. Peter Kapitza had recommended him when he returned to Moscow for the last time in mid-1934. Stalin, in the process of crushing the Comintern and getting rid of the last of the old guard Bolsheviks, ordered Kapitza along with other scientists and agents back to Russia. They were told to nominate replacements at Cambridge. Rothschild was high on Kapitza's list, despite him not being directly linked with the key research areas targeted. He could be relied on to secure any information the Soviet scientists required.[5]

Kapitza, meanwhile, was asked to set up a new research organisation – the Institute for Physical Problems, which was to replicate Rutherford's work on atom-splitting at the Cavendish.

THE CONTROL

Rothschild received a mysterious invitation with a single ticket to a London concert in August 1934. A hand-written note, which listed the recitals of piano, harp and violin, had the word 'harp' circled, with a line leading to the words 'suggests we should meet'. This was connected to another word – Otto – which was the name of a violinist playing a Rachmaninoff concerto. Rothschild applied his mighty mind to the puzzle with doodles and arrows of his own, but couldn't work it out until he received a note from Kim Philby, which was signed Harold Adrian Russell Philby – HARP. Rothschild had only ever known him as 'Kim'. The note said simply: 'Dear Victor, Had any good invitations lately?'

Rothschild was thankful for the clue. Ten days later he sped down to London in his sports car, did some personal business concerning his income and investments, then drove to the concert in Hammersmith which featured musicians and artists from Hungary.

The seat next to him was empty until seconds before the lights dimmed. A tall, handsome man in his early forties, with thinning, swept-back hair and a dark moustache took the seat. The stranger's sky-blue eyes locked with Rothschild's for a second before it was dark. At the interval, the man smiled and spoke about the concert, mentioning that his brother was performing in the second half of the programme.

They had a drink together during the break, as two strangers might. The older man introduced himself as 'Otto'. During their short chat, Otto, alias Teodor Maly, spoke knowledgeably about the composers and performers. He even knew the home towns of several of the musicians, which made it clear that he was Hungarian. Rothschild didn't mention he was doing scientific research for a Prize Fellowship at Trinity. Nor did he even say his surname. They were just two music lovers passing time.[6]

At one point, Rothschild mentioned his visit to such an event as being a 'nice break from Cambridge'. Otto remarked that he was coming there for business in a week and suggested they meet for lunch at a pub in Huntingdon, about fifteen miles away.

ACQUAINTANCESHIP

They set a time and met. Normally Rothschild would have avoided such a contact. However, this stranger was so urbane and cultured that he might have got in touch again for that reason alone. But he knew Otto had to be Philby's contact.

They sat outside in warm August sunshine, and this time Otto, as relaxed and suave as before, came round to the real reason for their rendezvous. Every so often, Rothschild caught a glimpse of the steel behind those warm eyes. He learnt that when the First World War broke out, Otto, a newly ordained priest, became a regimental chaplain with the Austro-Hungarian army. During a battle with the Russian Tsar's army on the Carpathian front, he was captured. He witnessed the suffering caused by disease and starvation in the prisoner-of-war camps. It changed his life. No longer could he be the passive priest dispensing succour to the dying and dispossessed. He had to play a more active role.

In three or four subsequent meetings stretching into September 1934, Maly let Rothschild know more of his background.

'The POW camps did it,' he told him. 'I didn't see how a God, a caring supernatural power, could let that careless brutality happen on such a scale. I abandoned the church, but not to run away. If a God couldn't fight such inhumanity then I wanted to be with men who could.'

This was his reason for joining the Cheka and the Red Army during the Civil War against the White Russians. He was one of scores of foreign Communists working for secret police chief, Dzerzhinski, who justified his own brutality by saying it was necessary in order to destroy the decaying Tsarist empire.

Titbits about his past were slipped into the conversation with his usual charm over the course of the meetings as Otto quietly 'sold' himself and the cause.[7] At the same time, he was assessing the potential recruit without asking any direct question. How deep was Rothschild? Could he be trusted? How committed could he be? Would he crack when the pressure was applied to betray his class and even his country? Was he mentally and physically courageous like Philby? Was he devious and strong enough to act out a double life, which had seen many commit suicide in despair at the insidious schizophrenic nature of the espionage business.

If the personality was not powerful enough it would first fragment, then disintegrate. The spy would reach for alcohol or drugs. This would widen the split in the mind caused by being two characters, if not more, as the agent took on different identities for assignments under cover. At first, playing someone else was exciting for the recruit. But when the crunch came, was he or she actually a fair actor? Under a little pressure at a passport counter in a foreign country, and perhaps in a second language, could a new player carry off the deception without faltering?

Otto had yet to see an agent unaffected by the strain as the years slipped by and the near-misses, mistakes and other stress-causing factors accumulated. Most, in fact, either collapsed or retired to prune roses, which was all they were good for after a career in the double game. Their belief in the cause had to be strong, or else there had to be another compelling reason for commitment. Like survival.

There were other questions on Otto's mind. Intestinal fortitude and nerve were important. But was this aloof young man patient? Could he wait years until 'activated'? Or was his impressive intellect too hungry, which meant he would lose interest, or let something incriminating slip?

It was also useful to be adaptable. Clearly Rothschild's eclectic mind, which was interested in a wide range of pursuits from science to the arts, was flexible. Yet would he be pragmatic enough to use a camera, pick a lock or even one day place a bugging microphone?

Then there was the awkward question of his spouse. Otto had been forewarned that she had a conservative background. It always caused problems if the wife or husband was not politically in accord or at least compliant. How would Barbara react if she suspected her husband was an agent? It was always better if the partner was a supporter of the cause.[8]

A politically correct marriage had other advantages. The spy in question could safely confide on the pillow or anywhere with his wife, who would usually enjoy the secretiveness. This would relieve the spy of the danger of 'bottling up' the stresses of deception.

Perhaps equally important was the strengthening bond that

knowing meant to a spy and his partner. Espionage, if shared, could cement a relationship. If it wasn't, the spy's disintegration could be faster and greater. Keeping his secret life from a perceptive woman led to increased tensions.

THE BAIT

While making his assessment, the ever gracious Otto delivered his polished lines of enticement. Philby, Blunt and Burgess had warned him that Rothschild had to be reeled in on the Jewish, anti-Hitler line. Too much clap-trap about the 'rightness' of the communist view might cause his eyes to glaze over with uncertainty and boredom. He had heard and comprehended all the theory but was unconvinced. He knew too much about Stalin's Jewish pogroms in Russia.

Rothschild judged Stalin and Hitler to be about equal in their appalling treatment of Jews. A dictator was a dictator, and a dead, starving or tortured human was the same on either side of the Eastern border.

Otto found he had to be more careful in his sales pitch with Rothschild than any other of the key targets that he, his protégé Arnold Deutsch, and Philby had been after. Victor would not be seduced like Burgess and Philby by ideology and the panacea of a perfect communist world with a post-Stalinist figure astride East and West. Nor could this target be lured like Blunt by appealing to his artistic vanity and his detestation of the foibles and conservatism of his own, elite class.

Rothschild, like Watson, was influenced into believing that Russia's laboratories of social and scientific experimentation would lead to a better, albeit Godless world with test-tube man in charge. Otto had been briefed by Blunt and Kapitza that this could be used as a second line of argument. Rothschild, Otto had been informed, was a believer in the certainties of scientific development even if it went down spurious or counterfeit trails.

Young Victor's chosen line of research was some proof of this. He was investigating how fast sperm swam, and why only one sperm managed to fertilize an egg. 'It occurred to me,' he wrote in

Meditations, 'that light might be shed on this problem by treating an egg in a suspension of sperm as if it were a sphere being bombarded by gas molecules.'

In one sense this may not have been deemed a 'sexy' topic, but it was neither spurious nor counterfeit. In the secret laboratories of Nazi Germany and Communist Russia, scientists were already scanning Rothschild's published literature (in Russia this would continue for a quarter of a century) for data that would help in cloning a German super race, or a Soviet superman.

Rothschild's work would contribute to the build-up of data Hitler's scientists would use to weed out the non-survivors and the weak in his cock-eyed grand design. It would also assist Stalin's white-coated brigade in their inhuman experiments with drugs, social behaviour, genetics, and psychiatry.

Otto was well briefed about Victor's research and even feigned knowledgeable interest in the subject. Rothschild's smugness about being at the forefront of his field was fortified by flattery. Otto, with his worldliness and articulate elegance, managed conversational insertions about communism providing the best facilities for improving modern man's lot.

The work Rothschild was doing was germane to a 'brave new world', and he knew it, although he was not then aware of the hideous attempted and actual uses to which it would be put.

The main anti-Hitler argument had to be delivered with equal care also, for despite his youthful naïvety, the young Victor on some levels was already shrewd and perceptive. For that reason, Blunt had advized that the other key Comintern control, Arnold Deutsch, should not be used first in attracting Victor. Deutsch was a Jew. If he dwelt too much on the persecutions, he might make the target suspicious that his recruitment was too contrived. Philby had convinced the Controls that Rothschild was potentially their most important catch. He had to be wooed with great subtlety and finesse.

Rothschild was well aware of the stark choices emerging because of Hitler's rise to power. The German 'Third Reich' was to last, according to its architect, for a thousand years, which for civilization would mean a barbaric period in history, a darker age than had ever gone before. There was a sense of noblesse oblige in Rothschild's response. His privileged, hereditary position would mean he could influence events if he so chose. Tackling Hitler, via communist opposition, seemed the only effective route.

Many British politicians had no stomach for another conflict like the Great War. They had let the military run down to the point that even a middle European power could challenge Britain. Leaders were already talking about appeasement with Hitler, which was tantamount to political capitulation and eventual concessions to German expansionism. This led to a sense of impotence and frustration amongst those who sensed the dangers posed by Hitler.

Rothschild's status in society and his political leanings meant that he was, in a sense, 'ripe' for persuasion to take up a cause against Nazism and fascism. He was an elite rebel with a cause, but in search of a way to exercise it. The Comintern's secret path was the only one available to him, unless he turned to more active politics, like his friend Churchill. But Rothschild was not about to contemplate that. He preferred, like his powerful antecedents especially his grandfather, Nathaniel Mayer ('Natty'), the first Lord Rothschild, to keep his politics as private as possible. Like Natty, he would employ his ability to get things done and influence major events from behind the scenes.

Natty was a powerful back-room manipulator of late Victorian politics, who supported Disraeli and intrigued against Gladstone. In addition, the splendour of Tring Park was the setting for negotiations ranging from the extension of Cecil Rhodes' diamond empire to the reconstruction of London University. Churchill became a regular visitor as Natty supervised the destruction of Liberalism in the hope of strengthening the Conservative Party, which was his most notable political accomplishment.

Aware of all this, Otto first painted a raw picture of the expected mighty battle between fascism and the left. He then dabbed in points about the skirmishes already begun in Austria, which would ring true from what Philby and the Viennese Rothschilds were saying. The Control next added a few big brushstrokes about the might of Germany and the danger this posed to civilization, without mentioning the Soviet Union just yet.

'Hitler is marking time,' he told the target, 'so he can build his military force. Then he will move. Nothing is surer. We have to be ready.'[9]

Otto also worked on demonstrating that only Russia would have the will and might to tackle fascism. He did this by reminding Rothschild that he, Otto, had experienced at first hand the Allied efforts, which included the might of half the world, to crush the fledgling communist revolution in Russia in the early 1920s. The control then spoke of the financial, military and trade deals on-going between Germany and Britain.

This touched a nerve, for young Victor had seen this during his time at the Bank. Making money overrode moral principles in some international dealing and he became more disgusted with this as his political sensitivities became more acute.

Otto obliquely referred to glowing editorials about Hitler in some leading conservative papers, implying that the ruling classes were pandering to the German dictator. That gave Rothschild pause before he agreed dejectedly that he too had sensed this. Even at his mother's dinner parties there had been ignorant talk about the importance of forging links with Germany and pacifying the strutting demagogue with bribes and concessions.[10]

There were also Hitlerites amongst the City's merchant-bankers and businessmen. They were combining with right-wing Tories in favour of rapprochement and conciliation with the Nazis, no matter what they did. Otto warned that the far right elements amongst the Tories were gaining the ascendancy within the party. More moderate members such as Winston Churchill were 'unlikely to gain power'.[11]

Otto suggested that it was conceivable Germany and Britain would combine in an attempt to overthrow the Soviet Union. This struck a further chord with Rothschild. There had been much discussion about it at Cambridge.

Later, Otto switched to the obvious line that Hitler and fascism had to be obliterated. Only a nation the size of the Soviet Union, if it was strong and prepared by Intelligence reports, could do that. Agents in Britain could play their part by climbing into positions of power and decision-making. They could then guard against conspiracies between Britain and Germany, by informing the Soviet Union if there were any. Otto even suggested there could one day be a link between Britain and a strong Soviet Union, especially if the right people were in positions of influence in Whitehall.

Details from Otto were few. The objective had been to arouse Rothschild's interest in secret work to defeat Hitler and that meant supporting the Soviet Union. It was an accumulated appeal to his survival instinct as a Jew, his protective urges towards the family, his ego, and his rebellion against the Establishment, which he believed would be overturned and replaced by a better, science-driven society.

Otto made his proposals sound as if the new recruit would be able to take part in history-making events. He could even shape them, as Rothschilds had done for two hundred years.

THE ROLE

The Comintern considered the question of Rothschild's immediate role. A person of his name and stature could hardly slip away like Philby with a false ID and pose as a freelance journalist in fascist-controlled countries. Although the dirty word 'espionage' was never used, the next Lord Rothschild was not the type to act as a straight agent. It was ludicrous to suggest he could be used to infiltrate extreme right-wing groups.

Otto suggested, however, that he might consider helping to finance the setting up of a front to assist other operatives in order to create the right credentials for infiltration. Otto explained that it would be useful for those supporting the cause to become members of, for instance, the Anglo-German Fellowship. It attracted the circles in which the Prince of Wales, the future King Edward VIII, moved. He, himself, was pro-Hitler, as were several of the upper-class members who filled the Fellowship's banquets.

Rothschild was inquisitive about who would be asked to penetrate that circle.

'Guy Burgess is enthusiastic,' Otto replied. 'So is Kim.'[12]

It was the first time Rothschild had been given direct evidence that members of his circle had joined the cause. The thought of the quieter, shrewder Kim changing his image was plausible. But Victor scoffed at the idea Burgess could present himself as a fascist.

Otto was adamant. Guy, he claimed, was qualified for the job. All he needed was a preparatory link to neo-fascism. The concept was straightforward. Rothschild was asked to contribute towards funding a newsletter specializing in economics, finance and business with strong links to Germany. Burgess was ignorant of such matters so a professional journalist sympathizer, German communist Rudolph Katz, was ready to be brought in to do most of the donkey work in London by writing and editing the newsletter. Burgess acted as the titular editor and, under Katz's direction, researched and wrote some contributing articles.

It would be an entrée to the fascist networks linked with the Anglo-German Fellowship. Burgess could roam free in these circles. Again, Otto didn't have to spell out some of the methods randy, debauched Guy would use to extract information and develop contacts. Rothschild's thoughts changed from bemusement to amusement. Grubby Guy's frenzied dalliances had their uses, it seemed. He could be discriminating after all.

Rothschild was able to go further and use his family contacts to introduce Burgess to influential members of the Conservative Party. According to Modin, these included George Ball, an MI5 agent and founder of the Conservative Research Unit – the Party's information service. (This led to Burgess becoming parliamentary assistant to a young, extreme-right Conservative, Jack Macnamara. He was a homosexual and a member of the Anglo-German Fellowship.)[13]

In further discussions with Otto, Rothschild brought up his own image. How could he be seen financing a right-wing business letter? It wouldn't be good for the family name, or the Bank. Otto explained that no one would need to know he was behind it. In any case, some of the funds would be provided from elsewhere. Rothschild volunteered that they could always claim his mother Rozsika was financing Burgess's ventures. Technically this was accurate because she looked after most of Victor's finances. Burgess was on a retainer from her of £100 a month for advising her on stock investments.[14,15]

Rothschild warmed to the idea and even volunteered that Burgess and Philby could act as couriers for the family banking operations, if a front was needed. Victor's family was familiar with private intelligence networks – they had their 'spies' at court, in governments, the military and business – people retained to inform the family's decision-makers of a business deal here, a political intrigue there.

More than a hundred years ago Nathan Mayer Rothschild, the founder of the British dynasty, had run a swifter spy service than those of the British or French Government. His agents followed

the armies everywhere and were so efficient that Nathan knew
Napoleon had been defeated at Waterloo before either government.[16] The Rothschild network had remained intact since 1815.
What's more, it had already been activated to help Jews in trouble
in Germany.

Victor's cousin James had influenced him into supporting the
setting up of Israel in order to give the tens of thousands of
dispossessed a 'home'.[17] James, a Liberal MP, was giving financial
backing to creating many Jewish cooperatives in Palestine. However,
expansion of the settlements was being held up by a 'pro-Arab'
lobby in Whitehall. Britain didn't seem likely to honour the declaration of Foreign Secretary Balfour who in 1917 had promised to
recognize Zionism and had called for a Jewish homeland.

At the last of their initial meetings in 1934, Otto and Victor
discussed Rothschild's plans for the future. He didn't really see
himself ever reaching for a position of influence within Government,
mainly because he was loving his research and being at Cambridge.

'I can see myself going on to the age of forty or fifty,' he told Otto
and many contemporaries.

The Control was not happy with this response at first. He
suggested it would be most helpful if he could set his mind on a key
position now. Otto flattered him by saying he could achieve great
things for Britain.

Rothschild wanted to know why it was so important to join
Whitehall. The Control gave the stock reply he had been using with
some sincerity in discussions with other recruits.

'War is inevitable,' he maintained. 'That is when positioning
really counts.'

This gave Rothschild more to consider, but he did not respond.
Otto had already concluded that this young man would be the most
difficult to direct. Normally this would cause a Control to not
proceed with the recruitment. Yet he understood why Philby had
been keen to add Rothschild to the network of agents. Apart from
his intelligence, he was single-minded, independent, and apparently
in awe of no one.

Otto salvaged something by suggesting it would be useful to
know of the secret work of scientists at the major institutions, such
as Cambridge. The Comintern agent said he was aware that secret
research had been going on in the area of 'gas' warfare since the First

World War. Knowing how far it had gone would be helpful. Rothschild agreed that he would assist where he could, as he had in gaining information for Kapitza over the last two years.

Otto wrote to Moscow about Rothschild, explaining the unconventional nature of his activation as a functionary, and his usefulness in financially supporting other agents and supplying useful scientific data.[18]

According to several KGB sources, Otto, Deutsch and the Moscow Centre were then ambivalent about 'fully recruiting' Rothschild to a point where he would be regarded as more than a subagent, that is, someone on the fringe who could help with finance and information from time to time, or as a supplier of intelligence data to full agents such as Burgess, Blunt and Philby.[19]

They had other misgivings because the target had no obvious ambition to join British Intelligence or the government. They were impressed by his intellect but worried about his wife Barbara not being 'suitable' for the cause. There were further concerns about his attitude to Palestine and the campaign to create a Zionist state which confused the Moscow Centre. The Soviet Union had no firm policy on the issue and it was unable to voice an opinion when Otto asked for one to give Rothschild. The Centre also found problematic the fact that Rothschild had independent means. It was harder to manipulate or 'keep' agents who were not financially dependent in some way, even if it just meant the odd cash payment for expenses.

Otto sent numerous communications to the Centre about several agents in the last few months of 1934. Despite Moscow's uncertainty about Rothschild, this period marked the beginning of his secret life. Otto advised him, as he did Burgess, Philby, Maclean and Blunt, to sever all relationships with the far left. Rothschild gave up his links to the Communist Party.

PART TWO

☭

THE SWITCHES
OF WAR
1939–1945

6. BLACKMAIL FOR LIFE

THE SIEGE

Despite the Nazi–Soviet non-aggression pact of August 1939, Stalin was preparing for war and the defence of Russia as fast as strained Soviet resources would allow. The able-bodied population was being quietly mobilized and readied. Late in the year, Yuri Modin, just seventeen, decided to try for the School of Naval Engineering in Leningrad. He passed the tough entrance exam which tested his education in mathematics and writing skills. He then had a year's training as an engineer specializing in building fortifications for heavy weaponry on the coast. Just as he graduated in early 1941, war broke out and he was sent for further training in expectation of an invasion by the German army.

It came on 22 June 1941 under the code-name Operation Barbarossa when three million German soldiers marched into the Soviet Union on a 4,000 mile front. Modin's battalion of Engineers began constructing forts on several sea fronts as the Germans stormed towards Leningrad.

Hitler had one thing in mind: razing the city to the ground. He was obsessed with the fact that this beautiful port, with its gracious buildings, museums and canals, had been the bosom of the revolution, the place where the communists' dreams came true.

Hitler told his generals that obliterating it would be a massive psychological blow and a great boost for his forces and plans. German Intelligence had informed the Nazi leaders how best to attack the vulnerable sea port and choke off its food supplies.

The prediction in the German High Command was that Leningrad would not be difficult to take, and that the real battle to defeat Stalin would occur at Stalingrad. However, the Nazis did not take into account the courage of Leningrad's inhabitants. This was not Paris, where the French capitulated in favour of preserving themselves and their magnificent city. The tougher Russians were prepared to challenge Hitler's dream of destruction.

Almost everyone was called up for defence work. The only groups exempt were the ill, the elderly, pregnant women, those caring for small children, and workers in vital industries.

Fierce resistance slowed the invader's advance by three months and it was September not July before the enemy reached Leningrad's outskirts. The closer the Germans came, the tougher was the opposition. Fifteen miles out, the advancing army was blocked at Oranienbaum by the Soviet Eighth Army.

So determined were the Russians, that Hitler changed his tactics to ensure he didn't deplete his forces. Aided by the Finns to the north, he decided to strangle the city by surrounding it and cutting food and other supplies coming in while hammering it with artillery bombardment. The Führer thus hoped to starve out the Leningradians. On 8 September the Germans took Schlusselburg, east of the city on the shores of Lake Ladoga.

Inside the besieged Leningrad, where three million were trapped, the 300,000-strong People's Militia were helped by 200,000 armed servicemen, including the Leningrad Engineers. Soldiers stood alongside workers building 22,000 gun emplacements, digging anti-tank ditches, putting up concrete blocks, and placing barbed wire entanglements.

While every street corner became a machine-gun post, the nation geared itself for a possible defeat, although it was inspired by the determination, courage and discipline of Leningrad's inhabitants. There would be no question of anything but maximum resistance. The Germans would have to take the city, not building by building, but paving stone by paving stone.

There was one major weakness in the city's defences. Leningrad imported most of its food and wood, and all of its coal, iron, steel and cotton. It was poorly prepared for a siege and there were only limited local supplies of vegetables, dairy products, peat and firewood. By 11 September food and fuel were already running down and electricity had to be rationed. Hitler's intelligence agents in the city had informed him correctly. The city could not hold out long, especially without food.

It was being shelled and bombed from the air as soldiers' and workers' rations were reduced to only 1 lb 2 oz of bread a day. The hunt for food continued every hour they were not on duty. Dogs and cats fetched high prices on the black-market and the city became empty of animal life. Every bird was grabbed. Even rats became a luxury. There were rumours of dead soldiers and militia being carved up and eaten.

Modin heard of people boiling pieces of leather such as straps and belts to extract the minutest nourishment. People were even attempting to eat glue by mixing it with any digestible substance. The floors of bakeries, breweries and meat factories were ripped up to salvage slithers of anything even remotely edible.

All the fighters weakened. Their morale was not helped by the news in early November that the Germans had taken Tikhvin, 140 miles east of Leningrad, in their attempt to control all the eastern shore of Lake Ladoga. The lake was the key to breaking the resistance. If the invaders controlled the 125 miles by 78 miles stretch of water, they would cut off the supplies coming across to Leningrad by boat.

By mid-November, the lake began to freeze over, reducing supplies to a dribble. Air drops of essentials supplemented this a little, but there were just too few planes available to make a significant difference. On 20 November soldiers' rations dipped to 9 oz of bread daily, which was being made from rye flour but included left-overs from paper production, fuel for ship's furnaces and chaff. People began devouring this with the aid of refined industrial oil.

As the ice thickened on Ladoga, Andrei Zhdanov, the chairman of the city Soviet, ordered a reconnaissance party out at night to see if there was a way over it. The party reported back that the ice was too thin to support vehicles. They would have to wait another month.

'We are finished,' Zhdanov told them, 'if we can't get supplies in.'

He called in the Commander of the Navy and they sent a team to attempt to cross the shortest neck of the lake, which was iced but only 18 miles wide. The sailors made it.

Zhdanov then directed that a road should be constructed over the ice from Osinovets near the south-west corner of Lake Ladoga to the eastern side. The road continued across land to the nearest Russian-controlled railway stations.

Troops worked at night, building a crude road where the ice was thickest. As it was being made, horse-drawn sledges, then motor vehicles followed the construction team. Horses and trucks fell through the ice and many perished, but the survivors salvaged the horses' bodies and ate them. Once they were over the ice and on land clear of German troops and patrols, the construction team worked faster.

At a station in Karpino, the exhausted workers were rewarded with bigger rations for their superhuman effort. Then they helped load the incoming sledges and vehicles for the return journey, which would take them back over the ice in the dark.

On 23 November they managed to return from the railway stations with 33 tonnes of rations. The next day there were less than 20 tonnes, but it was a beginning. The opening of the supply track lifted the city's spirits as the soldiers returned, their magnificent job done.

AT THE FRONT

Modin and his fellow kadets were called up to the Leningrad front over the months of November and December 1941 and January 1942. Two days after arriving in groups, the Engineers assembled at KGB Headquarters on the Neva River not far from Nevskii Prospekt, for a briefing on how to patrol the city in the search for spies and snipers.

Modin's first assignment was to hunt down enemy agents – Russians and Germans – who were shooting at Russians from vantage points, such as roof tops. Modin had to follow up on reports of suspicious individuals or groups throughout the encircled city. This entailed detective work. Suspects had to be followed, checked and investigated. If they did anything out of the ordinary or were seen stealing with weapons to vantage points, an urgent report would be made.

Modin saw himself as a scout. The engineers were younger and stronger than the KGB men. They could run up staircases to the tops of buildings to do the checking. At times it wasn't that hard to detect the snipers. There was house-to-house fighting but locals didn't often fire from the tops of their own buildings. It would invite return fire and no one wanted their homes destroyed. The attacks were worst when workers were going to and from work.[1]

Modin spent many a dangerous day and night scouring buildings and roof tops. It wasn't as physically demanding as the work being done on the ice road, but it was nerve-racking and drained precious energy. Many times he would creep up a building via a fire-escape and wait in the shadows on the roof, close to a suspected sniper's nest. Occasionally, he would spot a rifle or sub-machine-gun being angled down towards a street. At one point Modin and his fellow Engineers were searching for three men firing rockets on the *Smolnei*, which used to be the Tsarist Women's Union building but during the war housed the leaders of Leningrad.

An alert brought into action the KGB's crack counter-sabotage unit, which sent agents to arrest or kill the snipers. They knew the German agents were on a near-suicide mission and would do everything to avoid capture, which would lead to KGB interrogation, torture and then execution, usually by hanging. Bullets would not be wasted on enemy agents; ammunition was too precious.

Modin was impressed with the work of the secret police. They were meticulous, efficient and brutal. He got to know several secret police officers, who regarded him as one of the best of the young investigators. Modin learned all he could about their operations and was interested in the fate of those he had detained. Had they given useful information? Could it be used to seek out other agents? What techniques were employed in interrogating them?

As winter deepened, the Engineers prepared themselves for a tough struggle, but Modin never became pessimistic. By contrast, his father Ivan, who was also at the front, was not hopeful. At forty-seven, he was in the middle of his second war. He had been wounded in battle in 1918 and he confided to his son that now he did not expect to survive.

Modin noted that Ivan hid his fears well. One of his main duties was to lecture troops at the front and raise their morale. Whenever Ivan met up with Yuri, he brought something to eat. Yuri thought his mother, who was safely in Suzdal, somehow got it to him via courier.

In mid-December, Modin found himself assigned to the ice road.

The Russians had recaptured Tikhvin and the supply route could be shortened. A week later supplies of up to a 1,000 tonnes of provisions a day started coming over the ice. The Germans picked out the movement and bombed and strafed the convoys day and night. The Russians sent more militia to help as blizzards made it hard for drivers. Trucks fell through the ice, yet the supply was now unstoppable. The troops worked literally like slaves, helping to build bridges over ice holes and weak patches.

During a tea break in an interview session, Modin recalled those days of hunger at the end of 1941.

'We dared not even dream of something like this,' he said, ruefully gesturing to a biscuit, 'but suddenly on 25 December the reward for the mammoth effort of survival paid off as the bread ration was increased, giving soldiers and workers an extra 4 oz. We received 7 oz.'

Modin recalled a lift in spirits amongst the troops and the entire city population. Despite the increase being equivalent to only one slice of unappetizing bread, it was as welcome as a banquet. Strangers congratulated each other and there was excited hope for further increases. The Leningradians convinced themselves that further relief would soon come. Then they ran into the extreme cold of January and February which, coupled with the meagre rations, made them the worst months of the entire siege. Nearly 200,000 people died of cold, hunger and disease. It was common to see someone just collapse in the street, Modin remembered. Entire families were found dead, huddled together in homes where water and sewerage pipes had frozen and snapped.

In this most bitter period, electricity and public transport stopped. Modin continued to work on the ice road, which became the escape route for many who were too young, frail or old to survive in the city.

March was still freezing cold, but rations were lifted again as the ice-road became more efficient and the population thinned because of the dead or evacuated.

Like all kadets, Modin found that his healthy 6 ft 1 in, 185 pound body lost weight in the months he was inside the city until he dipped below 130 pounds. Emaciation was normal in Leningrad. His condition stabilized at just below 132 pounds in March –

dangerously low for a man of his height, but not life-threatening. He wrote to his mother, telling of his experiences and his survival.

In mid-April, the last truck crossed the frozen lake and trams began to run in the city, bringing tears of joy to on-lookers, who never thought they would see them in service again. A limited amount of electricity was available after a local peat supply had been re-opened and fuel was brought in.

The warmer weather thawed the lake and water pipes that had not burst began to flow. Modin and his Engineers were now detailed to join the population in a massive clean up. They uncovered festering piles of rubbish and bodies, which had been lying undiscovered in back alleys for months.

There was a temporary dip in rations while boats waited to replace the trucks that had braved the ice but spring allowed vegetable production in the city, improving the people's diet.

By May, Modin's Naval Engineers were at last allowed to leave the siege, and were replaced by fresh troops crossing Lake Ladoga. Leningrad was soon turned into a fortress city as civilians were evacuated and new defences were built.

The Naval Engineers retreated to Yaroslavl, east of Moscow, for rest and medical treatment. But food rationing was still enforced and Modin remained weak for months until his weight improved.

THE DUTY

During this recuperation period, the war was at its peak and every kadet engineer was still very conscious of food rationing. Each man was given the same amount of bread each day. Butter, oil and sugar were luxuries, and each was measured as if it was gold. Though every member of the military dreamt of gorging on bread, butter and sausage washed down with vodka, stealing was rare.

In this time of crisis, people dependent on each other for their lives in battle rarely abused comradeship by pilfering. But when it occurred, punishment was severe. Depending on the offence, Stalin decreed in June 1942, it could even be punished by death.

A month later, Modin was ordered by his superior officer to manage and guard the kitchen, a job he had done several times before because he was trusted to distribute food equitably. The manager he was relieving, Boris Dementiev, told Modin that a locked cupboard in the kitchen might contain stolen food. He had tried and failed to open it.

The kitchen staff were embarrassed by the suggestion, but they confirmed that the cook had the key at his home. Modin checked and re-checked his food inventory and went several times through every item stored in the kitchen. Some butter *was* missing.

He agonized over what to do. It was unlikely that the outgoing manager would be crass enough to steal something and then draw Modin's attention to it. The cook was the main suspect in view of the locked cupboard.[2] It seemed that he had relied on Dementiev's laziness in not checking his inventory to see if anything was missing. Modin was a more diligent character, who would carry out his duty to the letter.

Modin knew the penalty for theft would be tough. He suddenly had enormous power over the career and future of a fellow kadet. Modin thought about confronting the cook, but calculated he would deny any wrongdoing. If word got out about the theft, then Modin's failure to notify the authorities would reflect on him. He could even be seen as an accomplice, especially as food theft was drummed into the kadets as a major crime. Modin finally decided that he had no choice but to report the missing butter to his superior officer.

The officer found a locksmith who was able to break into the cupboard. A kilo of butter was found wrapped in paper. The KGB was informed and they came to the barracks to hold an inquiry.

'We were all very, very afraid of the KGB,' Modin claimed.

He was summoned to an office, ordered to sit at a table, and given a pencil and writing pad. A KGB officer put queries to him.[3]

Had Modin known the thief very long?

No, only since being stationed at Yaroslavl.

Had he had any dispute with the cook?

No.

Modin would not have placed the butter there himself?

No, he didn't have a key to that cupboard.

Did he know the butter had been stored in the cupboard?

No, not until it was opened.

The KGB man was sombre and efficient. He asked many detailed questions. At times it seemed as if Modin himself were under suspicion. Then the questioning became more personal.

'You are a member of the Komsomol?' the senior officer asked.

The apprehensive young Engineer nodded.

'You speak English?'

He nodded again.

'You realize the severity of the accusation against your fellow kadet?'

Modin nodded uncertainly.

'Why did you inform on him?'

The earnest young Engineer mumbled something about his duty, and tried to explain that he had reported his suspicion about the locked cupboard, not the thief himself.

There was another reflective pause.

'Kadet Yuri Ivanovitch Modin, if you are in any way uncertain about this information you have given me in this interrogation, you may withdraw it.'

Modin frowned. Where was this heading? Why was he bringing up such an option? What did he mean by interrogation?

'You don't wish to withdraw?' the KGB man asked.

Modin spoke again about duty.

'Remember, be precise in your responses, which ensures precision in thought. Then the information stands?'

Modin said it did.[4]

The KGB man left, warning Modin not to say anything to anyone about the matter at hand.

When Modin next encountered the cook in the kitchen he found it difficult to communicate with him. A few days later, the cook did not turn up for work. The kadets were asked to assemble in the barracks courtyard and they were informed by the KGB officer about the theft of the butter. Finally, in a voice which Modin found cold and almost robotic, the KGB man said: 'The cook will be shot tomorrow at dawn.'

The accused was not able to appeal. The execution was carried out the next morning as announced and it stunned the Engineers. Modin felt some guilt for the incident which stayed with him for the rest of the war and a long time afterwards.

THE CORNERING

The war was at a critical point as the Germans advanced across the Ukraine towards Stalingrad. The Naval Engineers were ordered to regroup for a return to Stalingrad via the Volga River. At the town of Kostroma they began training in how to handle battery armaments. Modin took time to join the Communist Party while waiting for the call-up to the front. No one who went to Stalingrad expected to return. In 1942, being sent to fight there was the near-equivalent of a death sentence.

Modin wrote to his family and friends, knowing that it might be the last communication he would have with them.

Two days later, he was summoned to the local office of the KGB. He was apprehensive, but the officer there chatted to him about his work in Leningrad.

'There are excellent reports of your investigative efforts there.'

Modin was not sure if the officer meant him personally or the Engineers in general. He responded that he had been honoured to do that work.

'Hunting German spies is important.'

Modin sensed a change in mood. He replied that he thought the work was *noble*.

That pleased the secret-police officer.

'Would you like to join our organization?' the officer asked.

Modin was surprised.

'You would be trained and your language skills improved,' the officer added.

Modin wanted to know if that was for longer than the duration of the war.

'No,' the KGB man replied, 'once your patriotic duty is complete, you will be free to leave and follow any profession you choose.'

Just like other members of the military? Modin wanted to know.

'Exactly.'

Modin was reeling from the offer. He wanted to join but needed time to reflect on it.

'You would be based at Moscow headquarters,' the KGB man told him.

Modin asked about the nature of his job.

'You will work for *Smerch*. It's the section responsible for fighting German spies.'

Modin asked when the work would commence.

'Immediately.'

Modin accepted the offer. The recruiter for Russia's secret police force shook hands with him.

'This means you will miss the Stalingrad front,' he said with a grin.[5]

7. THE POSITIONING

MOSCOW CALLS

Victor Rothschild, like several Comintern supporters, waited through the early months of 1937, but did not hear from Otto or Deutsch. The death of his uncle Walter meant that the newly-titled 26-year-old had taken his seat in the Lords and was busier than ever. Having been elected to a Fellowship at Trinity in 1935, he was now lecturing in Zoology and advancing his study into sperm movement and fertilization.

In June 1937, Rothschild learnt that Otto had returned to Moscow at Stalin's orders. The Soviet Dictator had been purging the Comintern in an attempt to eliminate all remnants of Trotskyism. At their last meeting eight months earlier Otto had hinted that he might be in danger. He knew that Stalin's assassins had been hunting down some of the leading Comintern people in several countries, and he expected trouble.

Blunt, who saw more of Otto and Deutsch, the two key agents in England, and acted as a conduit for any information Rothschild might wish to pass on, thought Otto's life might be at risk.

The information chilled the other three key British agents then working for Moscow: Philby, Burgess and Donald Maclean, the main Cambridge spy at the Foreign Office. It worried Rothschild too. Although he had less direct contact with the Comintern Controls, he had met Otto and Deutsch on at least six occasions for discussions, and several more times socially.[1] The two Comintern agents had from time to time turned up at private functions involving the five and other British agents.

Rothschild was still on the fringe of Comintern activity, but his sponsorship of the Katz-edited financial magazine had allowed

Burgess to join the Anglo-German Fellowship. Burgess had successfully buried his far-left connections to emerge as a fascist-
sympathizer, using his homosexuality to insinuate himself further
into important far-right circles.

Rothschild kept in contact with Kapitza in Moscow and wrote
reports on scientific developments to accompany data published in
obscure journals and papers, largely restricted to the international
scientific community. These covered a range of subjects, including
biological toxins and nuclear physics, which would eventually lead
to research into germ warfare and atomic weaponry. Some of the
data he passed on was classified. It was all of enormous help to
Russian scientists.[2]

If anything, his prose style was even more deft than the brilliant
yet verbose Burgess, and the precise Philby. Furthermore, Rothschild was breaking down far more esoteric information than the
others. His reports would often be accompanied by explanatory
drawings, which demonstrated his extraordinary capacity for comprehending anything scientific.

Whether it was the very early rudiments of the gas centrifuge
method of collecting 'fissionable' uranium or the experimentation
of scientist Mark Oliphant in 'Hydrogen power' at the Cavendish
Laboratory at Cambridge, Rothschild could twist his mind around
the theory and picture it, in much the same way as Einstein visually
perceived his theory of relativity.

He built up friendships with the relevant science departments at
Cambridge and other strategically-placed agents such as Alister
Watson, who met in discussion groups and in relaxation hours to
inform each other about developments in their respective specialties.
Rothschild would dwell on areas outside his discipline until he could
understand the principles well enough to hold his own with the
experts.

'Knowing other [scientific] developments allowed us to cross-
fertilize,' he later told his MI5 scientist friend Peter Wright. 'It
stimulated the imagination. For instance, after a discussion with
nuclear physicists, who were forever in discourse about bombarding
this and that with gas molecules, I applied it to my own work.'[3]

Apart from regular talks with his scientific peers, Rothschild daily
had his face buried in papers and journals. He made a point of
reading *everything*. He stood above many dons in his comprehension

of several disciplines. While some aired their great knowledge of various fields of research, Rothschild aired his understanding.

He could also be a fine communicator to the lay person when he wished. It came through in his writing. Much later in *The Times*, for example, he showed a formidable grasp of nuclear physics in a clear and explanatory article, 'I think the future will (not) look after the future', which examined whether nuclear power could be used for good or evil.[4] The theme of that piece and others, demonstrating the problem of how or whether to harness the nuclear genie, had given him cause for deep thought.

Rothschild's ascension to the House of Lords saw him opened up to not quite the real world, but a world outside the feverish labs of Cambridge. It introduced him to peers of another sort, for whom he secretly did not much care. However, he broadened his contacts beyond the Woolsack as he was introduced to the workings of government and committees.

Even if he had been a dilettante, his name alone would have given him an unsurpassable array of contacts amongst Britain's power elite. His experiences at Cambridge in science, politics and intrigue broadened and deepened his connections. Rothschild was on first name terms with such eminent politicians as Winston Churchill, who knew Victor's family well. He had been close to Victor's grandfather Natty, especially during the latter's back-room manipulation of British politics in the late nineteenth and early twentieth centuries. Churchill naturally followed Victor's development, being a regular visitor to Tring Park, where 'country house politics' were perfected. Churchill's famous signature scrawl adorned the guest book there and at Waddesdon Manor from the 1890s to the 1930s. He was also sympathetic to the efforts of Victor's uncle Walter, who fought hard for a Jewish homeland. They had a common enemy in Adolf Hitler, and, as the Nazi menace grew in Germany, Churchill gave support to persecuted Jews.

However, Victor and Winston, two independent thinkers, clashed soon after Rothschild's first appearance in Parliament. It happened at a dinner party in Cambridge late in 1937, following Churchill's address to the Conservative Union. He was frustrated by his years in the political wilderness with no direct influence on government. He sat next to Rothschild and they engaged in small talk about their respective smoking habits. Then Churchill growled in reference to his younger companion's decision to start politically neutral in the Lords: 'So you're on the cross benches?'

'For the time being, yes.'

'Sitting on your dividends, I suppose.'

'With great respect,' Rothschild replied, taking umbrage, 'I seem to recall reading about a young Churchill abandoning Toryism for Radicalism.'

'Not the same thing.'

For the rest of the night they hardly said a word to each other.[5] Rothschild was incensed at the reference to his wealth, but when he settled down saw it as an opportunity to excuse his sitting on the Labour benches. A day after the spat with Churchill he arranged to be interviewed by a reporter from the popular working-class daily *Reynolds News* about his indignant reasons for supporting the Socialists.

The reporter, however, matched Churchill's insensitivity by asking questions that indicated he thought the Rothschild family grew money trees at Tring and drank from gold goblets at breakfast.

Partly in justification for his political move, Victor remarked: 'I do not believe that people should be allowed to have a lot of money unless they have earned it. Being the son of a rich man is not good enough.'

What he didn't say was that the publicity and his new seating arrangements allowed him to become more easily acquainted with the power-brokers in the Labour Party and the far left, who were more sympathetic to the plight of Jews on the run from the Nazis.

At the time, Rothschild and his family across Europe were doing all they could to resist the Nazis' attacks on Jews in Germany and Austria. Increasing numbers were being isolated, dispossessed, jailed, brutalized and murdered. The refugees needed support in their plight and a solution to it. The Rothschilds were the most prominent family involved in the campaign to create a Jewish homeland in Palestine. Meanwhile, Hitler was plotting his depraved 'final solution', which he hoped would see all Jews end up in gas chambers.

Rothschild had a burgeoning connection to networks such as the Haganah which was formed in 1929 and was the secret intelligence forerunner to the Mossad (formed in 1948). The Haganah set up its own information service, named Shai, which aimed at creating an independent state of Israel. To achieve this it concentrated on infiltrating the British administration in Palestine, in order to inform Jewish leaders about British attitudes. It also spied on Arab opponents in countries such as Syria, TransJordan and Egypt, which surrounded Palestine.

The Haganah's espionage and surveillance extended to Europe, where it monitored all groups hostile to Zionism. The Rothschild family, led in Britain by the second baron, Walter, and Rozsika, lobbied the British government hard over a homeland for the Jews and was secretly intertwined with Jewish Intelligence. The family and its network provided money, political influence and organization to the Jewish movement.

Victor was always aware of the Zionists' aspirations. He was drawn more to the Haganah (led by Chaim Weizmann, with whom he developed a strong friendship) when the family's underground network of agents and security people linked with its operations to establish escape channels in the mid-1930s for Jewish refugees fleeing Nazi oppression. Victor and Miriam organized the British family network and lobbied the government to gain support for visas. In 1937, when the British moved slowly, they lobbied other countries such as Australia, Canada and New Zealand. Money was needed to facilitate the exodus from Germany. Couriers had to be organized and paid for. Officials across Germany had to be bribed and methods had to be found to move out refugees and their possessions.

Even helpful governments in Australia and Canada were not able to process documents fast enough, and the Rothschilds had to approach unlikely consulates from Central and Latin America. These would sometimes agree to supply visas for exorbitant payments but the documents often had no validity. The refugees would arrive in Britain and find that these countries would not recognize them, leaving them stranded and stateless. This served to stress the need for the 'promised land'.

The Rothschilds would then have to lobby the British Government to prevent the refugees being deported back to Germany. Miriam adopted fifty-nine refugees from Germany and so saved them from Nazi persecution.

The instant brood had to be fed, housed, educated and medically supervised. She recalled the chaos when taking fifteen at a time to an oculist.[6]

PRESSURE IN VIENNA

By 1938 Philby had become the most important Russian agent in Britain. Not only had he, like Burgess, penetrated the Anglo-German Fellowship, he had also become a celebrated Spanish War correspondent for *The Times*, insinuating himself into right-wing political circles via his pro-Franco reporting. He had even been decorated by General Franco, the Spanish dictator.

Rothschild meanwhile worked on as a sub-agent, while busying himself at Cambridge and in Parliament. At the University he was still mixing with the fashionable Bloomsbury set of writers and artists, but these days were numbered. He remained very sportive, and also found time for his ever-growing passion for collecting eighteenth-century books and manuscripts.

Rothschild was extending himself in his main love, scientific research, and had become one of the hardest-working dons at the University. He was fascinated by the use of cinematography to observe bull semen under the microscope.

'I'm the only person in the world,' he told any visitor to his laboratories, 'who is able to show you a movie of a bull's spermatozoon joining a female egg.'

There wasn't much time left in his private life for wife Barbara, and his two children, Sarah, now three, and Jacob, aged two, who was born in 1936. He kept his university research and his growing involvement in the secret world of Intelligence to himself. This bottling up of part of his life manifested itself in impatience and he became increasingly difficult to live with at home. Both he and Barbara were headstrong and this led to incessant clashes.[7] By his own admission he had never been an easy person to get on with. Rothschild described this characteristic as a 'quick anti-reaction'. In other words he didn't suffer fools, and could be aloof and arrogant.[8] Where Philby, Blunt, Burgess and Maclean drank or had homosexual partners as an outlet, Rothschild took on more projects and relied on the few people he could trust, or those who shared his secrets.

Malcolm Muggeridge knew him from the 1930s and described him in this period and later as a 'man who had lost his way'. 'Embedded deep down in him there was something touching and vulnerable and perceptive; at times lovable even,' Muggeridge wrote in an *Observer* article, 'but so overlaid with the bogus certainties of science, and the equally bogus respect, accorded and expected, on account of his wealth and famous name that it was only rarely apparent.'[9]

Another writer described him in a way which would have applied as much in 1938 as 1988:

'When asked about Victor Rothschild his friends variously describe him as a genius, an oaf, an academic success, a man of the world, a frustrated failure, a remnant of the old Bloomsbury set, a fierce perfectionist, a character out of one of Scott Fitzgerald's poorer novels, and an administrator of immense skill. They all agree [he is] one of the most complicated personalities in contemporary life.'[10]

His surface manner could, in part, be explained by the pressures on all Rothschilds for the decade from 1938 to the creation of the Jewish homeland in 1948. As the richest, most successful Jewish clan in the world, they had chosen to confront Nazism.

In March 1938, Austrian Chancellor Schuschnigg announced a referendum on the proposed political union with Germany. This annoyed Hitler, who feared that his fellow Austrians would reject him. Before the free vote he moved up to the Austro-German frontier.

On 12 March Hitler led his army into the neighbouring country and ordered the arrest of prominent citizens. At the top of the list was Baron Louis Rothschild, Austria's leading banker, whom Victor admired more than any other member of his family.

Three hours after Hitler had bullied through his *Anschluss*, two Nazi officers drove up to the Baron's residence and rang the door bell. The butler appeared. The Nazis demanded to see the Baron. The butler disappeared up a winding staircase while the Nazis waited.

'I very much regret,' the butler said on his return, 'that Baron de Rothschild is at dinner and cannot be disturbed.' He stepped away from the door and approached a desk with a book open on it. 'Do you wish to make an appointment?'[11] The Nazis strode off angrily and drove away.

The next day the Baron received a telephone call from Victor, who urged him to leave Austria, but he wasted half a day putting his affairs, and those of his bank employees, in order. The Baron was arrested the next day and thrown in prison. He was interrogated and forced to do hard labour.

Victor and others in the family initiated demands for Louis' release, but the Nazis would not budge. Victor then activated his own contacts by organizing for Burgess to fly to Vienna, ostensibly on business for the Anglo-German Fellowship. His real mission was to find out what the Baron's problem was. Burgess reported back that the Nazis were trying to acquire all the Rothschild property they could, especially an iron and coal complex at Wittkowitz in Czechoslovakia. They needed such sources of raw material to feed the insatiable demands of their munitions factories.[12]

Family connections in Vienna smuggled Louis a message suggesting he should try to convince the Czech and Austrian governments that Wittkowitz would be safer in the hands of a 'foreign-based company, preferably in the UK'.

Louis, still in his prison cell, began a secret restructure of the company and attempted to have its controlling interests transferred to the London-based Alliance Insurance Company. The paper-work was approved in Prague, then in Vienna, and escaped the notice of the Nazis. Only when the deal was sealed did they discover that the major shareholder in Alliance was London's N. M. Rothschild & Sons.

Hitler was furious. The Nazis threatened Louis with more time in prison. The Baron told them that the iron and steel works were not his to hand over any more. They would have to negotiate with London. The Nazis then offered him freedom and payment in return for the works. He shrugged them off again. Hitler was told he would have to negotiate with the English owners. The Führer wanted to avoid any form of direct confrontation with Britain for the moment, so he agreed to the price demanded. The Baron's freedom and two million pounds.

Once the papers were signed, Hitler ordered his release. The Baron was woken from a nap after an early evening meal and told he was free to go. Louis, showing his famous *sang-froid*, told his guards it was too late to turn up on the doorstep of his friends.

'I'll leave in the morning,' he said, and went back to sleep.

Victor and the Rothschild family thus 'won' their first confrontation with Hitler. Louis's great courage gave Victor heart. The clear message was that the Führer had to be stood up to everywhere. Yet talk in Whitehall and parliament was disturbing. The Conservatives wanted a rapprochement with the rampaging Nazis. They considered the German army was already far too strong for Britain or anybody else to fight.

Churchill's warnings against appeasement were being ignored.

EXCUSE TO ESCALATE

Another Jew to challenge the Nazis was a Pole, Herschel Reibel Grynsban. His approach was understandable yet misdirected.

Grynsban had just received a letter from his parents describing their suffering after having been expelled from Germany. Incensed by Nazi thuggery and murder in Germany and Austria, Grynsban slipped into the German Embassy in Paris on 7 November 1938, saying he had important papers for the Ambassador's secretary.

Grynsban was sent upstairs to the appropriate floor. He walked into an office annexe and shot the Embassy's Third Secretary, Herr vom Rath, the nephew of Herr Koester, a former German Ambassador in Paris. Vom Rath was seriously wounded and later died. It provided an excuse for the Nazis to step up their brutality.

Within forty-eight hours Jewish activities of all kind were attacked and cultural life for them was brought to a standstill. All their papers and magazines were shut down. Synagogues in Germany were closed. A day later, businesses were attacked by rampaging swastika-marked gangs, mainly led by young Nazis and members of the Hitler Youth. Synagogues were burnt and shops looted. Jews were bashed, mugged and murdered.

Goebbels worked his propaganda machine and claimed the violence was spontaneous. In response, Rothschild wrote a carefully-composed letter to *The Times*, which demonstrated his deep and agonizing preoccupation:

Sir,

May I remind your readers of two points concerning yesterday's pogroms in Germany:

(1) Some people may think, from reading the newspapers, that pogroms are something new in the treatment of the Jews in Germany. That is untrue. The difference between the treatment of the Jews during the last three or four days is quantitative. Qualitatively, these things have been going on continuously.

(2) The reports from Germany that the pogroms are 'spontaneous demonstrations by the German people' are a terrible defamation of the character of the German people as a whole. The German people are very much like the British. They detest the persecution of innocent people.

I have received letters from Germany, from Germans who are not Jews and not even 'liberals'; from people who sympathize with the Nazi regime. But they have told me that they abhor the persecution of the Jews just as much as they and we abhor the beating up of the Cardinal Innitzer or the 'protective detention' of a brave and good man, Pastor Niemoller. It has been announced in the newspapers that any criticisms made in foreign countries of the treatment of the Jews will only increase their torments in Germany. I have no fear of doing this, because their torments cannot be increased except by such refinements of torture as would create general horror in Germany itself. Almost the only thing left for them is death; for some this would be a blessed relief.

May I add that, like Mr Laski and Mr Montefiore [two prominent British Jews], I deeply deplore and condemn the assassination of the Third Secretary to the German Embassy in Paris. The Polish boy who did this was not in a condition to appreciate what he was doing. He was mad. Your readers will doubtless know why.[13]

Rothschild had come out in the open for the first time in his personal struggle against the Nazis. In private and through his growing underground links, his war with them was already well underway.

THE COMINTERN'S CRUSHING

At about the same time in 1938, a very distressed Anthony Blunt arrived unannounced at Rothschild's Cambridge quarters to give

him sad and shocking news. Otto had been executed by a firing
squad in Moscow. It was a huge blow, for everyone appreciated the
'human face of communism' presented by Otto and Deutsch, whose
fate was still unknown.

Blunt could not say if there would be any replacement for them.
In the meantime they would send their information via an agent
from the Soviet Embassy. It would be the first time the British
agents had dealt with any other than an 'illegal' agent. He or she
would also be a Russian, which was unusual. All the British agents
were very concerned about the change. British counter-intelligence
was much more likely to be able to trace them when they made
contact with a 'legal', since they monitored the Embassy and all its
residents.

The five and the other agents, such as John Cairncross who was
at the Foreign Office with Donald Maclean, wondered if this marked
the end of their network. Had Stalin killed it off in his insane efforts
to destroy his arch-enemy, Trotsky, and remnants of the Old
Bolshevik guard?

Later in the year the agents learned that Anatoli Gorsky would
be their Control. He was a Russian Jew in his early thirties who had
been in the Embassy for more than a year. He did not endear himself
to Blunt because of his business-like manner.

'A bit hard for my taste,' he told Philby, who gave the new man
the benefit of the doubt because of his rough, ironic wit.

'He is Russian, don't forget,' Philby said, and later joked that
'Anthony was upset because he was portly, bespectacled and far less
attractive than his predecessors.'[14]

All the key agents were sending their information and requests in
writing to the Centre via Gorsky. Burgess wrote in December 1938
and explained that he was working for Major Laurence D. Grand,
the head of D section of MI6, which was British Intelligence's
'dirty tricks' department, a position for which Rothschild had
recommended him. It operated under cover of the Department of
Statistical Research at the War Office.[15]

'My first assignment from Grand was to work on the Jewish
question and Palestine,' Burgess said in a letter to the Moscow
Centre. His task was to 'activate Lord Rothschild in a political tactic
to split the Jewish movement' in order to 'create an opposition
towards Zionism and Dr Weitzmann [sic. Dr Chaim Weizmann, the

head of Zionism in Britain]'. Such a tactic was meant to allow the British Government to strike deals with the Arabs more easily.

Burgess claimed to have asked for Rothschild's help in establishing a Jewish community – separate from the main Zionist plans for Palestine – between Lebanon and Egypt. Grand and his political strategists thought this would divide the Zionist lobby while acting as a buffer against any more ambitious Italian moves north towards Egypt, then a British Protectorate, after they had annexed Abyssinia. Grand had no idea Rothschild was pro-Zionist and unlikely to try to split them.[16]

Commenting on the report, Gorsky asked Burgess if it were wise to involve another agent like this, and an argument ensued. Gorsky reminded the Englishman that it was not his right, as a Soviet agent, to question him or Moscow Centre.[17]

Burgess complained to Philby about this and all of them longed for the less combative and more urbane Otto. The British agents, reporting to each other after meetings with Gorsky, concluded that he was rude, demanding and unappreciative of their efforts.

However, for the remainder of 1938 they were subsumed by a far more meaningful issue, the Nazi–Soviet Pact signed on 23 August, which gave them all pause, especially as it coincided with the end of their connection to Otto. In theory the Pact would prevent either party attacking each other so long as they stayed away from their recognized territories. It gave Hitler a huge advantage since it neutralized Russia, put an end to an Anglo–French–Russian coalition to block German designs on Eastern Europe, and isolated Poland.

The agents thought of abandoning their commitment until Gorsky made contact. He reassured them of their importance and told them that Stalin was simply buying time, as was Hitler. Fascism, he reiterated, would always be the *true* enemy.

Blunt and Rothschild were cautious, while Maclean, Philby and Burgess gave Stalin the benefit of the doubt and took, in Philby's words, 'the long view'. Blunt agreed to continue on as an agent, without giving his approval to Soviet foreign policy. Rothschild was certain that Hitler would turn on Stalin. He calculated that with weak government in Britain, Russia was the big hope to combat the Nazis. He, too, would help Stalin.

However, the Russians were left wondering how much Rothschild would cooperate. Despite Burgess's occasional disobedience of

Moscow's instructions, it was Rothschild who remained the least dictated to of the subagents, those on the fringe willing to help the Soviets as major conflict in Europe loomed.[18]

Even though he was not yet thirty he had a commanding presence. The Soviets did not wish to lose him because of his increasing power and influence. The Centre was well aware of Rothschild's proximity to Churchill, now jockeying behind the scenes for leadership as they learnt from Rothschild himself. The Soviet Controls decided at first that they would use his close friends to influence him. Blunt in particular could usually persuade him.

Gorsky set about 'activating' all his agents. The Nazi-Soviet Pact marked the beginning of the key agents' and second division of sub-agents' attempts to get important jobs, preferably within the Intelligence community. To many, war seemed inevitable but in Britain until it was declared there was a reluctance to put funds into developing Intelligence departments.

A few days after the Pact, the Führer, now free to bully whom he wished, marched on Poland, which the West was ill-prepared to defend.

8. THE PLACEMENTS

THE OLD-SCHOOL TIES

Moscow wanted spies in all sections of British Intelligence, the Foreign Office, and the military, but they couldn't make real penetration until Britain declared war on Germany in September 1939. Then both MI5 and MI6 expanded by recruiting the best minds from Oxbridge.

The incestuous network helped themselves. Burgess, at MI6 and still on a retainer from Rothschild, recommended Philby for a job in Section D of MI6. Rothschild, who had helped nudge Burgess into his position before the war, had been in turn recommended to MI5 by Burgess, and Guy Liddell, then deputy director of MI5's B division, who had in turn been introduced by Burgess to the young lord.

However, according to ex-KGB Colonel 'F' and Modin, Rothschild was the key to most of the Cambridge ring's penetration of British Intelligence.

'He had the contacts,' Modin noted. 'He was able to introduce Burgess, Blunt and others to important figures in Intelligence such as Stewart Menzies, Dick White and Robert Vansittart, the Permanent Under-secretary of State in the Foreign Office, who controlled MI6.'[1]

Churchill and Rothschild had long since patched up their minor differences, and the still-frustrated politician had put in a good word for his brilliant young friend after he had submitted a paper on the German banking system to the War Office. The paper showed how, using spies in the international banking system, the Nazis' plans could be predicted. The science all-rounder left his research at Cambridge for a position in the Commercial Espionage Unit of MI5's Section B.[2] According to Susan Watson, Rothschild also found her husband Alister a job in the Admiralty Research Laboratory. Rothschild hoped that Watson would supply the KGB with defence secrets. As the leading Marxist amongst the Apostles, he was expected to deliver espionage material, but he never had the inclination or nerve to do it. (This so angered Rothschild, Blunt and Philby that when from 1951 to 1967 they deceived MI5 investigators about British spies working for the KGB, all three pointed the finger at Watson.)

Finally, Blunt was recommended by his close friend Victor for a position in D division of MI5.

In the wings were many more Russian agents, such as John Cairncross who moved from the Foreign Office to become private secretary to Lord Hankey, a war cabinet minister under Chamberlain. The Centre was supposed to be giving directions to these minor agents to join specific espionage operations, but they were waiting to see which sections of the British spy apparatus would be most useful to them.

First, those already in place, like Philby and Burgess, had to learn where spots should be filled. Then Gorsky or the other Controls, such as Ivan Chichayev and Sergei Krotov, could make suggestions or get their agents to do it for them.

These three Controls all began to receive a myriad of data, both microfilmed and in document form, which was flown back to the Centre for analysis. In the first year the system was chaotic. The Centre asked the Controls to concentrate on the better spies supplying the best and most important espionage material for the Soviet war preparation.[3]

As the months slipped by, the top agents began to emerge as Philby, Maclean, Burgess, Blunt and Rothschild consolidated their positions in MI5, MI6 and the Foreign Office. The Controls started using them more but there was still a data overload in Moscow.[4]

Rothschild went about his work diligently and soon showed his forceful analytical powers. He had access to vast amounts of commercial intelligence data, which he filtered to Gorsky. His first job was to determine all the German business and industrial operations in the UK, and to discover which constituted a threat.

In early 1940, he summarized his activity for MI5. His spying had uncovered many organizations which were controlled by Germans or by those with strong links to the Nazis. These 'undertakings' could spy on the British war effort. Rothschild wanted 'drastic action' to stop 'a system of espionage which is so extensive and so subtle and so difficult to combat' that he thought it could prove 'an important strategic factor in the conduct of the war'.[5]

He concentrated on the machine tool industry and discovered it was heavily dependent on German suppliers. Rothschild suggested the German suppliers should be dumped in favour of American companies.

The US Embassy in London was very pleased. So was Rothschild's boss, Guy Liddell, who sent the young man to the US Embassy to start negotiations. It was Rothschild's first major link with the US, and he made a big impression. Gorsky took note and informed Moscow of the important connection.

THE HOUSE ON BENTINCK STREET

Rothschild had bought a short lease on a five-year-old three-storey maisonette at 5 Bentinck Street, London, above the ground floor offices of the *Practitioner*, a medical magazine, not far from Harley, Wigmore and Oxford Streets. However, with Barbara pregnant with their third child he decided to retreat to their Cambridge home, a large, low, sprawling white-brick house with a complex of cottages and garages. It had several acres of land, a garden, a tennis court and croquet lawn. Later Victor added a spectacular enclosed swimming pool complete with sauna. The pool had a dome, which could be slid open or closed according to the weather.

This was a move back to his 'spiritual' home, but it turned out to be only a base. His work for four intelligence agencies – MI5, the KGB, the Haganah and the family network – saw him constantly moving between Cambridge and London, around the country and occasionally abroad.

Despite the birth of their second child Jacob in April 1936, it was obvious to most friends that all was not as it should be in the Rothschild household. Barbara felt more and more isolated, for Victor refused to share his secrets with her and he was far from the perfect husband and father. His moods, his egocentric nature, and his capacity for spending many solitary hours reading, thinking or experimenting caused more estrangement from his family.

He was not a man who mixed with his children and enjoyed them. He treated them like little adults and kept them at arm's length. He regarded his work, research, and creative time as far more important than the warmth of family life. Bringing up children was for nannies, governesses, and wives if they so desired.

Rothschild was not alone in Britain's upper and middle classes in this attitude. But he was unusually distant and lofty towards his family. Of course, there was a war on, and this gave him an excuse, if indeed he needed one, to remove himself further from the home environment.

With the family ensconced in Cambridge, Blunt and Burgess moved into Bentinck Street. This allowed the network to more efficiently co-ordinate its spying. Another level in the maisonette was occupied by two attractive young women who were oblivious to the espionage activity carried out on the other floor. One was Teresa ('Tess') Mayor, a great-niece of writer Beatrice Webb and the daughter of Robin Mayor, a Cambridge philosopher and educationalist. The other was Patricia Rawdon-Smith née Parry (who later married Richard Llewellyn-Davies, an Apostle and close friend of Blunt. She became a Life Peeress in 1967 when Harold Wilson made her a baroness.) They had just been bombed out of their flat in Gower Street, London. Both were friends of Rothschild and Blunt.

Rothschild was attracted to the stunningly beautiful, dark-haired Tess, who had sensual eyes and a wide mouth, which gave her a 'slight look of decadence'.[6] She and Patricia had earned reputations as left-wing sympathizers during their time at Cambridge (1935 to 1938). Tess had recently been prevented from joining the Communist Party by American Michael Straight, whom Blunt had tried to recruit as a Soviet agent. Straight exercised his veto, as chairman of the Socialist Society, against Tess's enrolment.[7]

Like Rothschild, Straight had been enchanted by the young firebrand Tess's smouldering good looks and fell in love with her. Straight was 'stricken' with her 'unearthly beauty'. Tess had 'the gaunt nobility of Yeats's beloved Maud Gonne', and some of her 'cold fire'. He tried to make love to her at Whewell's Court in Cambridge. He set the scene by reading Yeats's love poetry, with Mozart's concertos playing in the background, but Tess didn't respond in the way he hoped. 'There was a knot within her I could not untie,' Straight noted.[8]

Rothschild had more success in releasing Tess's passions. She liked the way he 'got things done' and found him handsome but enigmatic, mainly because of his 'many secrets'.[9] She appreciated his understanding of her outspoken political views, and the trio of spies at Bentinck Street felt comfortable with her in the maisonette. If she had known about their connections to the KGB, it may have bothered her, but they did not take her into their confidence. Tess was fond of Blunt and Burgess, but fell for the handsome young lord, who was finding more and more excuses to stay in London.

When the lease ran out, the four permanent occupants and Victor all pooled their resources to take it over. The meticulous Blunt handled the details of managing the household accounts and the five shared a common kitchen and sitting room, which was used for much entertaining. Blunt had à boyfriend installed, whereas, true to long-term form, Burgess had homosexual parties with friends and boys.

Malcolm Muggeridge, then at MI6, described the Bentinck flat as a 'millionaire's nest' in which he felt 'morally afflicted'. On his one visit, there was a heavy air-raid going on and he found himself amongst 'a whole revolutionary *Who's Who*'. He felt uncomfortable and corrupted while sheltering in 'so distinguished a company – Cabinet Minister-to-be, honoured Guru of the extreme Left-to-be, Connoisseur Extraordinary-to-be, and other notabilities all grouped round Burgess, Etonian mudlark and sick toast of a sick society.'

Muggeridge noted rubber bones from the doctor's office were available to bite on, if the excitement of the very close company became too much. The writer found the ambience was of 'decay and dissolution . . . it was the end of a class, of a way of life'.[10]

Yet that life and the partying went on and attracted many visitors, who were often too drunk to leave. Maclean, Philby and Guy Liddell were frequent guests. When the alcohol ran out, whatever male grouping happened to be there would roll on to the Reform Club, the Gargoyle or the risqué *Le Boeuf sur le Toit*, where Rothschild would need little encouragement to play some jazz. After these drunken forays, Tess often found herself assisting an inebriated Blunt or Burgess from the front door of the maisonette to bed.

MOVING UP

In June 1940, Rothschild's mother, Rozsika, died. After her husband's death in 1923, she had gradually taken over the administration of the Tring estate, and the finances of every family member. Her progressive political thinking, and her drive for a Jewish homeland had deeply influenced Victor.[11] With Rozsika gone, he felt answerable to no one. He could make any decision he liked concerning the family, his private and public life, and his all-consuming involvement in the secret world.

The death marked his drift away from his family and the beginnings of a closer connection to Tess. It also was the moment when he stepped up his spying activities for the Russians.

Also in 1940, Blunt, operating on Gorsky's behalf, suggested Rothschild could use his scientific connections to find out about a secret war project at Porton Down, in Wiltshire. Coincidentally, Rothschild felt that his work in commercial intelligence was essentially completed with his 'sell off' of German companies to the Americans. He was looking for new challenges.[12]

Gorsky claimed that Stalin himself was interested in knowing what was happening in the development of special weaponry in British research establishments. He had never used this incentive before, so Blunt, at least, did not take it lightly. He persuaded Rothschild to think over the idea.

Rothschild was enticed by the thought of returning to research, especially in such clandestine and important areas. He had read much in the science journals since the early 1930s about developments that were now being researched at Cambridge and Porton Down.

Germany looked almost invincible, and Rothschild was more than eager to aid the Soviets in their knowledge of *any* potential weaponry. Even before they were at war, he perceived them as the only force in Europe that could stop Hitler, the liquidation of his race and democratic Britain. Despite the resilience the British exhibited in the blitz and the inspiration of Churchill, they seemed no match for the German military, the mightiest ever assembled.

Rothschild had Blunt warn Gorsky that his installation at the secret facility could take some time. This way, Rothschild stalled to see if the Nazi–Soviet Pact would hold up or fall apart as Gorsky had predicted it would.

Early in 1940, information from all British intelligence sources was clear. It was only a matter of time before Hitler reneged on the Pact and attacked Russia. Rothschild urged Churchill and other Government members to warn Stalin. However, the Soviet dictator ignored all the appeals from Churchill and would not communicate with him in case Hitler learned of it. Stalin was frightened to antagonize the Nazis.

Convinced that the Pact would be over before the end of 1940, Rothschild used his connections at Cambridge to secure himself a research position at Porton Down. Here he learnt much about poisons and acquired a cyanide capsule, which he carried in his wallet for the duration of the war. He would rather swallow it than be captured. His main priority at the Porton Down laboratories was a top secret project, of which he already had some knowledge simply on the basis of the biochemists assigned to it. The project involved experimentation in making germ bombs.

The aim was mass production within three years. They were being developed as 'weapons of last resort'. At best, they could be used as a threat to deter aggression if Hitler looked like taking Britain. At worst, they could be used to destroy an enemy. However, the teams of scientists were well aware that they were venturing into a dangerous unknown with such weapons. If misused the results could be disastrous.

Porton Down had been a top secret establishment researching chemical and biological weapons for a decade before the war. Its main focus from 1940 was on the making of botulinus toxin. It had already been discovered that anthrax spores, which caused cholera, could be spread either in the form of a dry powder, or in a 'slurry'. No satisfactory method of immunization against anthrax spores had been developed.

Research was continuing into both this kind of germ bomb and its antidote. Much data was coming in from the US research facilities at Camp Detrick, Maryland. There was also a field-testing station at Horn Island, Mississippi.[13] The work at Porton Down was one of the most closely guarded secrets of the war. It wasn't until much later, in an address on 'The Future' at Imperial College on becoming an Honorary Fellow and Special Visitor, that Rothschild indirectly referred in public to the developments there:

> There is, potentially, an unpleasant side to genetic engineering and again, I fear, we drift into the military or geopolitical sphere. It seems certain that, again in your lifetime, genes controlling toxins such as those of cholera and botulinus will be able to be put into the bacterium *E. Coli*, a normal inhabitant of most human intestines.
>
> Deliberately or inadvertently, this could cause appalling trouble. A teaspoon full of Botulinus toxin is enough to kill everyone in London. For comparison, a teaspoon full of cyanide, usually thought of as a very deadly poison, would only kill a busload of people.
>
> Although some people think the dangers associated with genetic engineering are exaggerated, I am sure this subject will not merely be left to the good sense of us scientists . . .[14]

Within four months of Rothschild's arrival at Porton Down, the Moscow Centre had enough data to help their own research in germ warfare. They were up-to-date with efforts in both the US and Britain. Suddenly Rothschild's stock was high in the eyes of the Controls and the Centre. His commercial espionage intelligence had been useful but the latest data placed him amongst the most important agents they had.

After this, Moscow needed Rothschild to move closer to the centre of British Intelligence.[15] The ordinary Russian soldiers and civilians had been taken by surprise by the invasion of the Soviet Union on 22 June 1941 when the German Army of three million men crossed the 4,000 mile front. Even before the declaration of war by the Germans on the Soviet Union, the Luftwaffe had struck airfields and Red Army troop concentrations.

Several hundred planes and tanks, and other equipment were destroyed before they could be deployed. Communications were disrupted throughout the Soviet armed forces. Hitler's Operation Barbarossa had been a smashing success, stunning the Soviet Union with its secretiveness and sudden ferocity.

Stalin thought Hitler had been bluffing and didn't put troops on the border so he could avoid the Germans using the long-tried excuse that they had been provoked. Had the Soviet leader heeded correct intelligence about the intentions of Hitler and his High

Command, he would have been better prepared and could have repelled the attack, saving millions of lives.

Churchill, by now Prime Minister of Britain, had been doing his best to warn Stalin of the specifics of the impending danger with hundreds of messages informing the Russian leader of German military plans directed against him. But the Soviet dictator, in his usual paranoid state, had again feared the British were trying to disrupt his uneasy Pact with the Nazis. Once more he ignored Churchill's offers of intelligence data.

Even after the shock of Hitler's attack, Stalin refused communication with Churchill. Instead he decided to build his espionage sources within the British intelligence agencies.

The Centre sent urgent messages to the London Embassy. Gorsky was soon working with Blunt, Philby and Burgess, who were used to persuade others to penetrate the heart of MI5 and MI6. Stalin didn't want any more surprises like Barbarossa. Rothschild realized that his war activity would be based in London and wanted more privacy than Bentinck Street allowed, so he bought a flat at 23 St James's Place, very close to MI5. However, he remained a frequent visitor to Bentinck Street and often stayed overnight.

MOVING IN

Churchill's ascension to the leadership in May 1940 led to a big shake-up of British intelligence and Guy Liddell was given control of counter-espionage. He found a suitable job in MI5's St James's building in September 1941 for Rothschild, now twenty-nine, which combined his intelligence-gathering, technical and political skills.

He headed up a section dealing with counter-sabotage, which meant detecting and catching saboteurs who had, for instance, been sent to Britain by the Nazis to disrupt shipping and transport. He also organized the dismantling of sabotage bombs coming into the country. It was an important enough role, for it included looking after the personal well-being of his friend Churchill, who was a key assassination target for the Nazis. But Rothschild's work was neither overly high-powered nor time-consuming. He had plenty of time for his main activity in the Second World War – spying.

Most importantly Rothschild now had access to all the vital military and other Intelligence data, whether raw or processed, circulating from Bletchley park, MI5, MI6, and the armed services. Furthermore, he regularly discussed aspects of intelligence and military operations with Churchill, with whom he socialized at private lunches and dinners.[16] Rothschild thus knew all the key Intelligence reaching the War Cabinet and at times would predict how Churchill and the Cabinet might act on it. From mid-1941, no spy was better placed to inform Moscow Centre of everything the British had on the Nazi war machine, and on British intentions.

However, Rothschild could not just hope to sit out the war in the new position created for him by Liddell. He had to prove his value in a new field from a standing start. He also had to demonstrate great physical courage. The sabotage bombs made by the Germans were new and ingenious. They were always camouflaged to appear as innocuous objects such as lumps of coal, a thermos flask, a mackintosh, a walking stick, or even a coat hanger.

Coal, for instance, would be packed around the disguised bomb. If lumps were removed carelessly, the bomb's fuse would be activated and an explosion would result. In the case of a mackintosh, parts of the lining would be filled with explosive. When the coat's belt was pulled and tied, it would activate a fuse, which caused the bomb to go off.

The bombs often had a fuse connected to a delay mechanism, which was activated by a clock or by acid eating through metal. The Nazis made their bombs complicated. Sometimes the fuse itself was booby-trapped so that it exploded when it was being examined after removal.

Because many of the German devices had never been seen before, Rothschild and his team had few experts to turn to for help. It was a case of the dismantlers backing their knowledge of science against the Nazi scientists' deadly cleverness.

The team needed a variety of data, but British Intelligence could not help. Rothschild told Gorsky he wanted everything the Russians had on the German Secret Service's development of bombs and fuses.[17] The Centre sent information on twenty German sabotage fuses and their delay mechanisms. If the delays included clocks, they came from Switzerland.

That wasn't enough for Rothschild. He would not feel prepared to understand a bomb's mechanism unless he first saw a comprehensible drawing of it that could be explained to a layperson. He loved sketching such things himself, but he needed a professional to make the artwork perfect. Anything less might mean the difference between life and death.

'Many of those who might have come across sabotage bombs were not technically trained and experienced difficulty in visualizing the fuse mechanisms – and how to dismantle them,' Rothschild commented in his book, *Random Variables*, published in 1984.

He wanted a draughtsman 'who could make perspective drawings to scale, with parts of the casing and innards removed or opened up, to show how the fuse worked.' The drawings also had to show how to undo the fuse without activating any booby trap 'that might be incorporated to prevent, by exploding it or the whole bomb, an understanding of in fact how the fuse did work.'

Rothschild found that a police inspector in the sabotage team had a son who was a draughtsman. He was peeling potatoes in the Air Ministry. Rothschild met him and showed him a sabotage bomb fuse.

'If you explain to me how it works,' the young man said, 'I think I can draw it.'

Rothschild tried him out and the result was beyond his 'most optimistic expectations.' He now had an understanding of every possible mechanism and pictures of them. A little piece of fortune added to his confidence one day when Rothschild was buying a watch at the jeweller, Cartier, in Bond Street. Meeting a friend there, they were chatting about his dangerous work when Rothschild happened to mention that he had trouble finding first-class screwdrivers for undoing the tiny screws in the delay mechanisms. The Swiss watchmakers had made them well. One slip in a defusing operation could mean an explosion.

The conversation had been overheard and soon afterwards, Rothschild received a surprise gift from Cartier – a fine set of steel screwdrivers, some delicate enough for the smallest screws the Swiss professionals had designed for the German weapons.[18]

Apart from the data, the drawings and the right defusing tools, the MI5 team of counter-sabotage agents had also to uncover the creative methods the Germans were using to get the bombs into Britain. The Nazis even went to the trouble, with the help of

Spanish fascists, of sinking a boat outside Spain's Algeciras Harbour as part of a sabotage operation.

The vessel held supplies of food and equipment for German divers, who slept on land. At night they swam the quarter of a mile to the British colony of Gibraltar in order to place their bombs in Allied shipping. The divers would sneak aboard the ships bound for England and slip the bombs inside vegetable crates or other articles.

Dismantling bombs, Rothschild was told early in the job, was a question of trial and error. Too much trial could lead to error. One mistake and the dismantler would have limbs blown off, or be killed. When told of the job, Churchill said it was ideal for the combination of Rothschild's brilliant scientific brain and his dexterous jazz-playing fingers. Rothschild replied ruefully that he was 'counting on both. If they fail me, I shall have nothing to count on, or with.'[19]

Rothschild still enjoyed relaxing with the piano in private or in nightclubs. It was fast becoming his only escape from the pressures of family life, and spying. He wasn't about to have it literally blown away. His main fear became German ingenuity in creating some new device or a bomb that had been so deviously disguised as to defeat his detection.

After much sweat and practice he gained confidence in dismantling bombs himself. It put his faith in scientific knowledge and his practical, rational view of life into sharp perspective. Rothschild was more than glad to report to family and friends that each time he defused another bomb his 'faith' was revitalized. Those receiving the good news wondered if Rothschild had a death-wish or was subconsciously putting himself as close to death as his Jewish brethren being hunted by the Nazis.

In July and August 1942 intercepts at Bletchley Park confirmed what the Rothschild underground network had already heard rumoured: Jews were being exterminated in their thousands at concentration and death camps. SS communications spoke of more than 8,000 deaths at Auschwitz in Poland by mid-1942. There was also an outbreak of typhus, which added to the devastation at the camp. The SS complained that the disease prevented a thousand prisoners being taken to help build the Danube railway.

The news shocked the Rothschilds.

'Victor was stunned,' a member of his family recalled. 'He went into a depression for several days and wouldn't speak to anyone.

After that he threw himself into the sabotage work. Auschwitz affected him deeply. It was crushing. A nightmare for all of us.'

As for the death-wish: 'He wouldn't consider this during the war,' the relative added. 'Victor only admitted to nerves, especially at the beginning of the war. After Auschwitz, he became obsessed with what he was doing and concentrated on that. I don't believe he dwelt on anything "deep and meaningful" about the dangers. [Decades] later, though, I think he reflected a lot about those days, but he rarely expressed an opinion, or a feeling [about his work in the war].'[20]

The daily terror became a way of life for him and his small band of assistants. On one occasion, after travelling to Liverpool to give a lecture to the police on sabotage, an officer asked him to examine a big can of liquid eggs which they suspected had a fuse inside it. It had come in from China, but was believed to have been tampered with in Gibraltar. A naval officer three weeks earlier had been seriously wounded when taking apart a fuse from a similar can.

Rothschild drove back to London and took the can containing the fuse into the MI5 office, told everyone to stay clear and got down to work. He put the can on the floor, and knelt down behind a padded armchair, 'so that if it was booby-trapped, only my hands and the lower parts of my arms would be damaged.'

He was able to take the fuse to pieces without mishap.

News of his skills spread through the services and soon his office was being inundated with calls for help, especially from Northampton, where goods coming via Gibraltar were unloaded. One of the most harrowing jobs was the dismantling of a booby-trapped device in a crate of onions.

Rothschild dictated the exercise into a microphone. 'I thought it desirable for there to be a record in case of accidents,' he explained.

'It is a crate in three dimensions,' he began. 'The right-hand compartment has onions in it . . . I can see, right at the bottom, one characteristic block of German TNT. Next to it is some material which looks rather like plastic explosive and in that there is a hole in one bit which is about the size a detonator would need . . .'

Rothschild stopped dictating and removed the onions. He then noted two blocks of TNT in the middle compartment and went on:

'I am looking for the delay mechanism or initiating device . . . I

am having difficulty in the middle compartment because the onions
have grown and are difficult to pull out . . .'

Rothschild's voice remained calm, but his tempo quickened as he
spotted 'a sort of putty-like thing' next to the TNT. He could not
see a fuse. He paused then said:

'I am now going very gently to take out the cast brick of high
explosive . . .'

He had to be extra cautious when extracting the TNT, and the
'plastic block' with which it was in contact. He was learning as he
went and was testing his scientific knowledge in the most exacting
way – with his life. Rothschild's dictation gave an insight into his
fast-computing brain, which constantly sought precision. The
'putty-like thing' became a 'plastic-block' then 'plastic-explosive'.
His next move was to examine it.

'I am now going to start trying to take this plastic explosive to
pieces. I see a primer inside one of them. I am going to try to take
one out.'

There was a longer pause this time. Rothschild was only too well
aware that this was the most crucial moment.

'I have taken the primer out,' he noted with a just discernible
trace of relief. 'I can now see the detonator buried in the middle of
the plastic. It is a twenty-one-day Mark II German time clock. I
have unscrewed the electric detonator from the Mark II delay so
that one is safe. I am now going to look at the other piece of plastic.
I can just see the other Mark II delay inside the other piece of
plastic.'

There was a prolonged silence.

'I have taken the primer off. The other detonator is off.'

Finally Rothschild added with a hint of triumph: 'All over, all safe
now.'[21]

As a result of this action he was awarded the George Cross, the
highest medal for civilian bravery. His position at MI5 made him
ineligible for a military decoration.

Later he joked about becoming 'off-handed' about his work,
although he still found it all rather a 'disarming experience'. Black
humour for the anti-saboteurs became a way of 'defusing the
tension' Rothschild told colleagues.[22]

The work was secret because the team was part of MI5, and
Rothschild's name appears little in the history books covering the

Second World War, except as a passing reference. In fact, if he had not retained and later circulated the transcript about defusing the onion crate bombs, it might never have become public. Normally, secret service members were never singled out for recognition. Yet both the British and American authorities recognized the courage needed for his work and its great value in preserving life, limb and leadership. It all helped build Rothschild's image as a heroic patriot, which would prove useful to him later.

Towards the end of the war he was seconded by the US army to lecture Americans in counter-sabotage. Rothschild then led Allied teams around France, disarming mines and booby-traps left by the retreating Germans, using crude yet effective metal detectors.

Rothschild later received the American Legion of Merit. He was also awarded the US Bronze Star for his work. In the citation, President Truman referred to him as 'one of the world's greatest experts in counter-sabotage'. 'He gave unstintingly of his time and energy', the President noted, 'in personally training American officers as counter-sabotage specialists. He wrote and edited many technical manuals used as text-books by the US Army, especially by bomb disposal engineers and counter-intelligence personnel.'

These texts again showed Rothschild's exceptional didactic skills using diagrammatic explanations. They demonstrated his three-dimensional comprehension of every scientific device he came across, from tiny contraptions that could remove a limb to bigger devices that could destroy a large city.

9 . AT THE PIVOT

AT THE PIVOT

Rothschild's relationship with Tess Mayor strengthened in 1941 when she began working for him at MI5 as his secretary/personal assistant. This was an important move. His clandestine operations demanded an assistant he could trust and confide in; someone who would not gossip about his schedule, movements, views and work. Tess was also sympathetic to his political positions.

She was an unabashed left-wing supporter. Like her new boss, as well as Blunt and Burgess, Tess felt that the Allies could do more to help the Soviet Union in terms of Intelligence provided about the German military and its intentions – as did Churchill at the beginning of the war.

While Rothschild kept her ignorant of the data he was having passed on to Soviet agents, he could at least confide in her about his sympathies, which were decidedly pro-Russian, the country that was taking the brunt of the German military's attacks in Europe.

Churchill had never trusted Stalin and this mistrust was accentuated by the Nazi–Soviet Pact. But still the British Prime Minister sought to warn the Soviet leader that Hitler was planning to attack Russia. Once the Pact was broken, Churchill used his agents and diplomats to try to gain a greater exchange of Intelligence with the Soviets concerning the Nazis. The British Prime Minister was puzzled to learn that the Russians were reluctant to cooperate, and this coloured his attitude to further links with them.

There was good reason for Stalin's reluctance. He was getting as much data as Churchill thanks to Rothschild, Philby, Blunt, Burgess and Maclean. There was no need to bother about formalizing the arrangement. Indeed, had Stalin done this, MI5 and MI6 would soon have realized that they were being sent data they already had from Bletchley and elsewhere and this would have led to the uncovering of the famous Five.

Presumably Tess would have toned down her left-wing utterings when she arrived at MI5. It would have been an interesting position for someone who was politically opposed to the Conservative forces running the country. Now she was working for the powerful institution that defended them. The struggle against fascism had united the whole political spectrum in Britain.

Nevertheless, Tess enjoyed her work and the very close friend-ships she had developed with Rothschild, Blunt and Burgess during those days at Bentinck Street. She liked being close to the centre of MI5's espionage and counter-sabotage action, and Lord Rothschild. He had been promoted to the rank of Colonel for his courageous work and was accepted as the nation's leading authority on bomb-dismantling.

MI5 was approached by Churchill's aides, who had become worried about the mounting death threats against him. Liddell put the organized Colonel with the efficient, loyal assistant in charge. Rothschild found it his toughest job in counter-intelligence.

'Apart from the obvious pleasure he derived from personal danger,' Rothschild noted, 'Winston was continually receiving cigars from all over the world.' After his experience at Porton Down, Rothschild thought it too easy 'to coat the proximal end of one of them with cyanide or better (in one sense) botulinus toxin.' He also worried that a 'small, high explosive charge could be activated by the heat of lighting the distal end'.[1]

Rothschild had Churchill's aides send him all the Prime Minister's cigars for examination. There were so many of them that a statistical technique for testing a certain percentage was calculated. The cigars were X-rayed, then doubtful ones were ground up in saline and injected into mice. If the mice were affected or died, Churchill didn't get his beloved Havanas or whatever brand they were. Rothschild explained the proceedings for his safety.

'I feel certain to miss the mice vote at the next general election,' Churchill joked. But he was less amused by delays. Impatient aides were often at Rothschild's office with 'irate' messages from the leader demanding that his addictive pleasure not be denied him. Tess sometimes handled them and asked whether they wanted their superior in good health or not. That ended the aides' arguments, but not Churchill's. He would send even more angry notes.

Cigars were not the only problem. As the war progressed and people in Britain and around the world realized that Churchill was a great, fighting war-time leader, he was sent many unsolicited gifts. He enjoyed the adulation and would accept presents happily, but aides became concerned.

Once Churchill was striding from 10 Downing Street to the House of Commons when a French General in full uniform hurried across Parliament Square towards him, carrying a brown-paper parcel. Police accompanying the Prime Minister rushed to restrain the General but Churchill allowed him to come close. The Frenchman stood sharply to attention, saluted and handed him the parcel.

'It is 'am, sir,' the General said with a smile, 'a Virginia 'am.'

Churchill accepted it.

'I will have it for breakfast tomorrow morning,' he responded, beaming. 'Thank you very much, General.'

The Frenchman stepped away, saluted again and disappeared. Churchill ordered an aide to make sure he had the ham and that the General be sent a note of thanks. The aide panicked and rang Rothschild.

'How can the ham be tested?' the aide demanded to know.

'Where is it?'

'With Winston. He said he will deposit it at the kitchen himself.'

'When he does, get it and bring it to me.'[2]

The aide did as commanded and the thinnest of slices was surgically removed from the pink and succulent leg.

An urgent meeting was called and the possibly offending slice became the subject of earnest discussion between MI5 and the Medical Research Council. Time was short. The ham had to be in front of Churchill for breakfast. None of the assembled geniuses could come up with a suitable, quick test.

'Let's feed it to a cat,' Rothschild suggested. Everyone agreed this was an excellent idea. The Medical Research Council cat was found and duly fed the tasty morsel. It devoured the ham in two minutes while eight interested humans stood over it, waiting. Nothing happened. Someone was left to monitor the cat all night. It lived. The ham was sped to the Prime Minister's cooks and he had it for breakfast as ordered.

Later, when Churchill visited General de Gaulle, the French resistance leader in exile in Britain, he was presented with twelve bottles of 1798 Armagnac by a French admirer.

'I felt it was essential for the donor to produce a thirteenth bottle (for testing),' Rothschild wrote, 'which my colleagues and I sampled with pleasure. After that, the Prime Minister was allowed to have the other twelve.'

10. SILENCE OF
THE LUBYANKA

BERIA'S BOMB

Modin was trained in espionage tradecraft and put on a crash course
to improve his English in 1943, before moving into an office on the
fourth floor of KGB headquarters in the Lubyanka on Dzherzhinsky
Square, a few blocks from the Kremlin. The six-storey Gothic
building, owned by an insurance company before the Revolution,
was built in a rectangle around the Lubyanka prison, where
innumerable prisoners were tortured and murdered.

Modin's day at the KGB's First Directorate – responsible for all
clandestine Soviet activities abroad – began at 8 a.m. when he joined
the thousands of other KGB personnel trudging up the stairway
with its well-worn red carpet to a dingy green corridor and a
crowded office. His day consisted mainly of reading the steady
stream of information flowing in from British agents. He would then
translate the important data, which would be passed to his Chief for
action. After that, it would be his duty to file the information.

Modin's training had briefed him on what was vital and what
could wait or be ignored, but as the war progressed it became
increasingly his decision on what to pass higher. In effect, he and a
handful of other agent/translators were the arbiters of useful intelligence. If they ignored a microfilm it would never be moved up for
action.[1]

His training had emphasized the importance of intelligence on
the Western rush to make an atomic bomb to stop Hitler. An
assistant to Secret Police Chief Beria had lectured Modin and other
inductees on Beria's setting up of at least twelve secret Russian sites
for atomic bomb production in a nuclear archipelago running
north–south and mostly 500 miles or more east of Moscow. There

were also sites for research and development into chemical and biological warfare, and radar.[2]

According to Andrei Sakharov, the secret centres were developed as 'a symbiosis between an ultra-modern scientific research institute and a large labour camp'. Sakharov spent sixteen years working at Arzamas-16, some 250 miles south of Moscow, which was the most important town in the archipelago.[3]

Beria had chosen remote places so that they could not be sabotaged, but all had a nearby railway and prison camp to supply labour. Secrecy was paramount. Scientists would meet at warehouses in Moscow and be taken by KGB escorts to trains which would then transport them to the sites.[4]

These centres were shown on a map in a locked conference room close to Modin's office. Each site was marked with its particular role, so that relevant data from the West would be sent to scientists and engineers there.

The data filtering through from Britain and the US in 1941 showed that the Allied scientists were concentrating on trying to produce the core of an atom bomb from uranium 235, a rare isotype of uranium that had to be separated from the more common U-238. Early Western reports suggested that Cambridge scientists were leading the way in collecting U-235.

The Russians copied their methods, but had little success. Beria responded by creating further clandestine nuclear cities in the hope of supplying the bomb-makers with weapons-grade uranium. The secret police chief was furious when told that his scientists were having trouble in separating the two uranium isotopes and trapping the vital U-235. He threatened leading nuclear physicists with execution.[5] They claimed that snaring the U-235, which was only 0.7 per cent of natural uranium (that is, one part U-235 to 140 parts U-238) was impossible on a large scale.

Modin was instructed to comb incoming spy data for any new material on bomb-manufacture. It was ranked the second highest priority, only just behind Intelligence on the immediate locations and intentions of the German army.

THE CENTRE'S COMPLEX

Life for Modin improved at the Centre. No longer was he under threat of dying at the front with his former Kadet Engineers, and he was able to endure the long hours spent examining the information coming from London. He and the other eleven translators on the Anglo-American desk at the Centre worked on all the documents coming through. It meant Modin would often finish at 3 a.m. and collapse back at his Moscow flat a mile away. The exhaustion was mental now rather than physical, as it had been on the Lagoda ice-road, but it took its toll.

Yet Modin looked on the bright side, for he enjoyed the opportunity to use his intellect to the full. At just twenty-one, his work was giving him the equivalent of a crash multi-university course in languages, literature, science, geography and modern warfare.

If he wasn't walking around Moscow in his lunch and dinner breaks he would often go to the KGB library. After being chided by his Chief for not having been educated widely enough, Modin regarded these break times as vital to his education. The Chief would encourage him with suggestions on which books would improve his knowledge.

The extensive library was on a higher floor and he would slip upstairs after a meal in the basement canteen. At night, in the empty, dimly-lit stairwell, the muffled screams of the tortured – victims of Beria's depravity – in the interior prison could be heard. Modin blocked them from his mind, but could not escape the reminders in the early hours when he was leaving Dzherzhinsky Square. There would be cleaning crews coming and going from their duty of washing blood from the Lubyanka's stone walls, swabbing gore off the oak floors and carting away the bodies of those who had not survived the brutality and deprivation. It was a further sharp lesson in who held the power in the Soviet Union. It resided with Stalin in the nearby Kremlin and those real or imagined individuals who opposed him were given a one-way ride to the torture chambers of the Lubyanka.

As time slipped by, Modin began to find flaws in the system at the Centre. Extra staff were needed, but he noted more fundamental problems. With a few exceptions, he felt that his superiors lacked initiative. An urgent request might come through from a Control at, say, the London Embassy, and it might take days for a response, which would often be ambiguous. Sometimes the Chiefs would not act because Beria had not decreed in a certain area, and they were too frightened to make a move. It had got to the point where some of the key agents, especially in Britain would make moves, such as switching from one department to another, without consulting a Control.

Modin was frustrated by the order to destroy coded telegrams from the British agents, which was issued after Stalin became fearful of spies within the Lubyanka. Beria sent a note to the Chiefs, who ordered the destruction. Modin wanted to protest, but felt he might incur the wrath of his superiors. Instead, he and others in the translator group shredded some telegrams and filed others. That way a few would be left in the archives over time, which would assist the Centre to track some of the agents' communications.

But it did not allow effective long-term analysis, which was another weakness. Modin also felt that his superiors were slack in their working methods and not nearly as diligent as he and his fellow translators, who did most of the thinking.

'There was a blind consideration for the here and now,' Modin remarked, 'without a thought for analysing problems or operations over a longer period. There were, of course, the pressures of fighting a war. But no one took the initiative to supply broader, better intelligence. It was more a case of what Beria (or Stalin) wanted, he got.'[6]

Modin was spurred on by Beria's feverish directive about obtaining as much data as possible on the atomic bomb. The science involved was difficult for the layman, because the project was so new and needed specialist knowledge. Modin became familiar with the attempts – started in the West and copied in Russia – to make a weapon using the U-235 route.

All the top British agents had passed data on the project to the Centre. But Blunt seemed to have passed on the most telling information from an agent closely connected to him. It contained detail, which began appearing in mid-1943, on an alternative method of making the ultimate weapon.[7]

11. THE ATOMIC ALTERNATIVE

THE REAL FINAL SOLUTION

From mid-1942, the Rothschild network in Europe had begun to hear word from refugees of Hitler's 'Final Solution' to exterminate the Jewish race. It was more a confirmation of what had already been evident from the SS and Nazi Party's habitual indiscriminate killing of large numbers of Jews, Poles and Slavs. It began with 'euthanasia' programmes in Germany and occupied Poland and was extended as Hitler invaded Russia. He gave the SS 'special tasks', which amounted to ordering the Wehrmacht – German Army – to slaughter certain of its prisoners of war.

With this background of sanctioned mass murder, SS officers began to take the initiative as a minute from one of them illustrated in a discussion about moving 300,000 Jews to a camp in Poland:

> This winter there is a danger that not all the Jews will be able to be fed. Serious consideration must be given as to whether the most humane solution might not be to finish those Jews who are incapable of work with some quick-acting preparation. This would be more pleasant than letting them starve.
>
> Furthermore it was proposed to sterilize all those Jewesses who are still fertile so that the Jewish Problem will be finally solved with the present generation.

The mentality was reflected in the language. Such developments had the effect of preparing everyone in power in Germany for the full expression of the Führer's demonic lunacy. By early 1943, the phrase 'Final Solution' was common in the Jewish underground network. The terminology was chilling and horrific, not the least for Rothschild who remarked to his friend, Chaim Weizmann:

'We must find a *real* Final Solution. Something that will finish *them*.'

When Weizmann asked if this were possible, Rothschild said he was 'working on it with everything I have.'[1]

THE RACE FOR THE BOMB

As well as keeping abreast of research at Porton Down, Rothschild monitored the other secret weapon development – the race to make an atomic bomb – and offered his assistance in October 1941, when a secret directorate was set up in London to accelerate the research programme. Until then, work at Cambridge and other universities had been pushed forward under Churchill, but no faster than the projects to develop radar. Atomic research had been given a boost by two French physicists who smuggled some 'heavy water', necessary in bomb production, from Norway.

The new directorate, under the control of Sir William Akers of ICI, was called Tube Alloys. Rothschild used his influence to help obtain government grants for laboratory research and joined a committee to oversee the venture. He was the most knowledgeable of all British and American intelligence operatives on the race to make a bomb.[2]

The major terror was that the Nazis would get there first. Rothschild would have been in charge of finding and dismantling the device, should it be smuggled into Britain for detonation rather than dropped on London from a plane. At that early stage, no one had much idea what an atomic device would look like, or how heavy it would be. (Later, the weight and numbers that could be produced by the Allies would become an important secret the Russians wanted.)

Before the end of 1941, two leading US scientists from Columbia University came out to 'exchange ideas'. The Japanese had attacked Pearl Harbor, thus catapulting America into the hostilities. The US and Britain decided to pool resources in a desperate effort to make a deliverable atomic bomb before the Nazis could develop one.

Churchill, who had been briefed by Rothschild and others on progress, and President Roosevelt ratified the arrangement when they met at the President's country retreat.[3] They discussed the efforts the Nazis were making to procure supplies of heavy water, which Churchill said was 'a sinister term, eerie, unnatural, which began to creep into our secret papers.'

'What if the enemy should get the atomic bomb before we did!' Churchill pondered. 'However sceptical one might feel about the assertions of scientists, much disputed among themselves and expressed in jargon incomprehensible to laymen, we could not run the mortal risk of being outstripped in this awful sphere.'[4]

Rothschild saw every secret paper and he made sure that he was able to understand them. In fact, according to colleagues, he often suggested changes in experimentation, even though this was not his field of expertise.

Gorsky became anxious for every detail on Tube Alloys. He and other Controls were running atomic spies, Dr Allan Nunn May, Dr Klaus Fuchs, Bruno Pontecorvo and other nuclear physicists. But they were only delivering data from their individual spheres of research.

Rothschild had the overview and was able to summarize exactly what the combined Anglo-American project was achieving, and where it was headed.

When the KGB were forced, for processing purposes, to rank their top British spies from one to ten, with emphasis on the top five, Rothschild emerged in 1941 as the Fifth Man – or fifth most important agent. However, his closeness to Churchill and his access to Bletchley's decoding of Nazi operations saw him ranked equally by early 1942 with the other four as foreign suppliers of key intelligence.

Before the war was out, Rothschild's capacity to access and articulate the most important scientific development of the war would make him number one.

As MI5's resident scientist and expert on sabotage weapons, he could have arranged for summaries of research to be sent to him. But Rothschild wanted to go much further. He wished to know *everything* that was happening, especially in England.

He knew, for instance, of the advanced work of Rudolf Peierls, a Jewish nuclear physicist, who had emigrated to Britain in 1933. Peierls had shown that a nuclear chain reaction was possible, allowing the building of a reactor which would produce bomb fuel. He worked with fellow German refugee, Otto Frisch, in Birmingham, where they were first to calculate that less than a kilogram of separated U-235 isotope could make a bomb. Until then (1940), scientists had been thinking it would take tonnes.

Peierls was at first horrified by the thought of developing a bomb that could destroy a city, but as the war progressed his fear of Germany grew greater. He and Frisch had experienced the brutality of the Nazis and Hitler at firsthand.

'If we could see this so could the Germans,' Peierls remarked recently, 'and the thought of Hitler getting a bomb like that was frightening.'[5]

The Professor of Physics at Birmingham University was the brilliant Australian scientist, Sir Mark Oliphant, who appointed Peierls and Frisch as applied theoretical physicists. (In the Spring of 1941, Oliphant authorized their employ of Dr Klaus Fuchs, who was then passing secrets to his Russian Controls.)

'Ironically, these two highly-trained and skilled scientists (Peierls and Frisch) were not allowed to work in Radar because of their German backgrounds,' Oliphant recalled. 'But they *were* allowed to work in nuclear physics.'[6]

He got them to put their alarms about a bomb on paper and they wrote the famous 'Memorandum', which Oliphant drew to the attention of the British Government. It concerned the properties of a radioactive 'super-bomb'. They were the first scientists to set out the technical feasibility of building an atomic weapon. Their project would rely on the separation of U-235. MI5 received a copy of the Memorandum.

Rothschild made sure this early suggestion was passed to Krotov, a Control at the British Embassy.[7] Beria's team of scientists in the secret cities got to work copying the method, but failed. As Hitler pressed forward into Russia in late 1942 and early 1943, Beria, with urging from Peter Kapitza, changed the emphasis of his directives to his agents in Britain and the US. They had to find an alternative method of atomic bomb production. Controls demanded that their scientist spies concentrate on any new, feasible approaches.

A break-through seemed likely in Britain first, because scientists there had started work two years before the US began its Manhattan

Project. But despite the slow start, Enrico Fermi made a big leap forward with his 1942 Chicago Experiment. This relied on Peierls' chain reaction concept but demonstrated that the bomb could be made using plutonium. This was done by building a reactor using natural uranium fuel – that is, 99.3 per cent U-238 and 0.7 per cent U-235 – encased in graphite. During the chain reaction some of the uranium was transformed into plutonium, and it could then be separated chemically and used as bomb fuel.

Peierls, Frisch and Co. were not impressed with this experiment, and Rothschild couldn't rely on information about plutonium – or any other secret work – coming through from them to the Government and MI5, as with the famous Memorandum. And since not all scientists were as motivated to stir the Government to action as these two outstanding Jewish physicists, Rothschild instead had to go out and glean facts from his other contacts in England and the US like an assistant researcher in order to comprehend the fundamentals.[8] This meant visiting every defence research establishment and asking questions about all aspects of a project. The problem was, how could he do this and remain above suspicion?

THE SECURITY INSPECTOR

Rothschild found an ingenious legitimate way of learning everything he needed in all areas of secret research involving not only nuclear and biological weapons but also radar. He wrote a memo to Guy Liddell reminding him of the laxity he had found in commercial organizations in his earlier intelligence work. There was now an urgent need to tighten security in all defence and research establishments. Liddell put him in charge of security, giving Rothschild the right to examine any building he wished. It also meant, if he was doing his job properly, that he should understand every development in order to make sure it was secure.

Late in 1942 he visited Birmingham University and examined every aspect of the Peierls/Frisch laboratory. Then he went next door to check on Oliphant who was refining the magnetron, which would turn radar into a war-winning weapon for Britain.

'It was our one and only meeting,' Oliphant told me in an interview in January 1994. 'Rothschild wanted to know everything about it [the operation of the magnetron]. He went over the whole lab and absorbed information like blotting paper. He wasn't an expert but he didn't pretend to know things. He asked a lot of questions, and took notes in a long discussion which ranged across our areas of scientific expertise. Rothschild was cheerful enough in that meeting. He was a very bright individual and I liked him very much.'[9]

The MI5 security inspector did more than learn about the secret work. He slipped a three-inch diameter magnetron into his pocket when Oliphant wasn't looking. That night Rothschild drove to his Cambridge home and copied the design of the device, with its three terminal electrodes, which generated short radio-waves.[10]

Early the next morning Rothschild drove to London, gave the magnetron and drawing with explanatory notes to Blunt at Bentinck Street for passing on to the Russians, who microfilmed everything by the afternoon. They gave it back to Blunt, who returned the device to Rothschild at his MI5 office in St James's.[11]

Rothschild wrote a note to Oliphant, attached it to the magnetron, packaged it and sent it back to Birmingham by special messenger. Oliphant was shocked to receive it. The note said:

Perhaps you should tighten up your security.
   Enjoyed our meeting,
      Yours etc
         Rothschild

Oliphant had no reason to suspect Rothschild was doing other than his appointed security job. In fact, the scientist was most grateful, even beholden to him.

'He could have caused us trouble by reporting our slackness,' Oliphant commented. 'But he didn't. I immediately tightened up our procedures and made sure no equipment was left lying around. Rothschild never commented about us, but in a report he was scathing about security in general.'

Early in 1943, Rothschild visited Professor G. P. Thompson's laboratory at London's Imperial College, again for 'security' reasons. There he had the plutonium route to the bomb explained to him. Thompson's team had the right principle for generating plutonium but had failed by using heavy water instead of graphite as a moderator in the reactor.

Rothschild was able to inform Blunt, again with his trademark diagrams of explanation, how it worked and Blunt wasted no time in passing it all on to a Control.[12]

According to former KGB Colonel 'F': 'This was the kind of data our scientists were looking for. It took us some time to develop a nuclear weapon using plutonium, but that initial clue was the start. We admit it [the first Russian bomb, exploded in 1949] was just a copy of the American design, which led to 'Fat Man'. [The bomb, 'Fat Man', exploded on Nagasaki soon after 'Little Boy' – fuelled by U-235 – was exploded over Hiroshima on 6 August 1945.] It also educated us in the rudiments of [plutonium] breeder reactors for industry.'[13]

By March 1943, Rothschild had achieved his aim of having a complete overview of the struggle to be first to make a 'super-bomb'. Through his diligence as MI5's security inspector, he had developed a knowledge of every major scientific development in the Allied war effort. No one in Britain or America, not even Churchill's scientific adviser Baron Cherwell, knew as much as Rothschild. He made sure Russia's scientists had the basics of every secret project from biological warfare to radar and the various types of potential nuclear bomb.

12. MISSION: DESTROY
AND COVER-UP

THE SIKORSKI INCIDENT

In April 1943 German troops uncovered the Katyn Woods site not far from the Soviet city of Smolensk where the KGB had massacred 8,000 Polish officers. Most had been shot in the back of the neck. It was known that these officers had been interned by the Russians in the winter of 1939, after Soviet forces had occupied eastern Poland.

The Nazis made quick propaganda out of the grisly discovery and it caused outrage amongst the exiled Poles, notably General Wladyslaw Sikorski, the premier of the exiled Polish Government and commander-in-chief of all that country's forces abroad.

The first man to bring him the news was Donald Maclean from the Foreign Office, who was in charge of 'administrative liaison' with Allied troops in Britain – at this time mostly Poles and French.

On 15 April Sikorski and Count Racynski, the Polish Ambassador in London, went to see Churchill at 10 Downing Street.

'Alas', Churchill told them, 'the German revelations are probably true. The Bolsheviks can be very cruel.'[1]

KGB agent Maclean had reported to Gorsky that the Poles were suspicious of Stalin, who had similar feelings towards Sikorski. Now he informed his Control that the Poles were going to call for an investigation into the Katyn murders by the International Red Cross. Sikorski did this publicly the day after his meeting with Churchill and against the British Prime Minister's advice. Moscow was well prepared and it retaliated by breaking off relations with Sikorski's Government. It called the Poles 'Fascist Collaborators' and blamed the massacre on the Germans.

Maclean's assignment caused him great strain, especially as he was trotting between the aggrieved Sikorski, who wanted the blood of the KGB, and Gorsky, the uncompromising, unsympathetic Control, with whom the Five and other British agents had grown uncomfortable.[2]

Maclean reported that Sikorski planned to put 'great pressure' on Stalin and to embarrass him as much as possible with the Allies. There would never be a future *rapprochement* between the Soviet Union and Poland while Sikorski was the leader-in-exile.

Stalin was furious with the reports. It was the latest of many confrontations between Sikorski and the Soviets beginning with the First World War when the Pole supported the policy of the restoration of Poland by the Central Powers, and later when he commanded an army in the Polish-Soviet War of 1919–20.

In 1922, when he became prime minister, he again upset Lenin, Trotsky, Stalin and the other Bolsheviks by obtaining recognition of the Russo-Polish line of demarcation. After a coup in 1926 Sikorski was exiled to Paris for a decade, where he continued to rail against Stalin. In 1936 he returned home but after just three years he was pushed out of Poland by Soviet pressure.

When the Germans occupied the country, Sikorski created a formidable army in exile and in 1940 set up in London. In the same year, with the Nazis occupying his country, he signed a treaty in Moscow restoring diplomatic relations with the Soviet Union. This annulled the Nazi–Soviet partition of Poland but in practice was nothing more than cosmetic diplomacy and propaganda against the Nazis.

Churchill wasn't going to take the opportunity to attack Stalin over the massacre in the Katyn Woods because of the delicate relationship with Russia, but Sikorski had his confidence and support. He and his troops were independent, anti-German and anti-Soviet. The British Prime Minister also regarded the Poles as excellent military men and fighters. At Sikorski's request in 1940, he made every effort to save tens of thousands of Polish troops fighting in France.[3]

Yet Churchill took the big view. He went to great lengths to smooth relations between Stalin and Sikorski. The Polish leader wanted to send a blistering communiqué to Stalin, which Churchill saw as a 'declaration of mortal war'. Conciliation was 'the only line of safety for the Poles and indeed for us'. There was 'no use prowling morbidly round the three-year-old graves of Smolenski'.[4]

On the night of 27 April, Churchill redrafted the Polish Communiqué, in Sikorski's name. 'We have persuaded them [the Poles] to shift the argument from the dead to the living and from the past to the future,' he telegraphed President Roosevelt. Churchill then wrote an inspired letter to Stalin.

He started by rebuking the Soviet leader for the haste with which he had broken off relations with the Poles. This had not given Churchill enough time to report to Stalin on the progress of his earlier talks with Sikorski.

'I had hoped,' Churchill wrote, 'that, in the spirit of our Treaty last year, we should always consult each other about such important matters, more especially as they affect the combined strength of the United Nations.'

Churchill told Stalin he had urged the Poles not to make 'charges of an insulting character' against the Soviet Government. 'I am glad to tell you,' he added, 'that they have accepted our view and that they want to work loyally with you.'[5]

Thanks to Maclean, Stalin knew this was untrue. While the exchanges between the leaders were going on, the British agent was feeding Stalin the facts about the Polish reaction to Katyn. The Soviet leader and Beria asked Maclean for a report on the reaction in Britain if Sikorski were to be eliminated.[6]

Maclean's response was translated in London. When it reached the Centre it was not processed in the normal manner but sent direct to Stalin. Maclean's message said essentially that although Churchill was close to Sikorski and admired him, his demise might be seen in Whitehall as 'solving a problem'.[7] As long as the Poles were mollified by concessions there would be minimum hostility towards the Soviet Union.

Stalin was well aware of what these concessions were and Churchill had reiterated them in his letter. The Poles wanted the dependants of the Polish Army in Persia, and the fighting Poles still in the Soviet Union, to be allowed to join those Poles whom Stalin had already allowed to go to Persia.

'We think the request is reasonable,' Churchill commented. He asked Stalin to consider it 'in the spirit of magnanimity'. For its part, Britain would ensure 'proper discipline' in the Polish press in Britain.[8]

Stalin paid particular attention to Churchill's remark that matters 'to our joint detriment' must be stopped, and 'will be stopped'.

Towards the end of April, Gorsky asked Maclean to inform him of Sikorski's travel itinerary. The agent learnt that the Pole planned to meet other exiles in Gibraltar in July.[9]

On 4 July 1944, Sikorski was in a Liberator plane taking off from Gibraltar, along with his daughter and two British MPs, Victor Cazalet and Brigadier John Whiteley. It reached about 1,000 feet, then crashed, killing everyone on board.

THE INVESTIGATOR

Churchill wept when he was given the news of Sikorski's death by Frank Roberts at the Foreign Office.[10] His emotional response was probably due to his closeness to Sikorski, and the fact that he himself had narrowly missed death a month earlier when flying out of Gibraltar for Plymouth. Bad weather had persuaded Churchill to stay on board a solid Liberator rather than transfer to a more comfortable but less weather-worthy Clipper flying boat.

That same day, a Clipper flying from Lisbon to Plymouth, on a similar flight path to the Liberator, had been shot down, killing all its passengers, including the actor Leslie Howard. MI6 was sure that the attack had been intended for Churchill.[11]

The burden of relaying bad news fell once more to the aloof and unemotional liaison, Maclean. He was forced to inform the remaining Polish leadership in London of Sikorski's death. Shocked and confused, they questioned whether the Nazis or the KGB were behind the attack.

The man from the Foreign Office tried to tell them that there was no reason to suspect assassination. The angry Poles would not believe him. They wanted to know if there was going to be an investigation. When Maclean said he didn't know, they demanded one. Maclean promised to pass on their request to his superiors, which he did, but to those at the Soviet Embassy as well as the Foreign Office.[12] Gorsky told him that if there was an investigation, he had to make sure it was undertaken by Rothschild.[13]

The uproar after the crash caused wild speculation, for several parties had a motive for the possible assassination, including the Nazis, the Soviets, and other Polish exiles competing for power with Sikorski. Even the British fell under suspicion because Sikorski had been a threat to their relationship with Stalin, and Churchill in particular did not want anything to stand in the way of the combined effort to defeat Hitler. At the time it seemed that he was prepared to safeguard good relations with Stalin at almost any cost.

A Polish delegation to 10 Downing Street asked for an official inquiry. In order to appease Polish demands and to quash the false speculation, Churchill ordered the Foreign Office to make an investigation, which meant Intelligence services' involvement. Maclean monitored the affair and made sure he was consulted because of his liaison work with the Poles.[14]

He suggested that the inquiry would probably need a counter-sabotage expert, just in case a bomb had been on board the Liberator. The experts were in MI5, under Guy Liddell. He referred the investigation to Colonel Rothschild, who thought the matter important enough to head up himself.

As usual, Rothschild was thorough. He flew out to the crash-site himself, took eye-witness testimony, asked for a coroner's report, and had bits of the plane flown to London for examination. His secret investigation concluded that there may have been an explosion on board the Liberator, which indicated sabotage.

The break-up of the aircraft was consistent with that caused by a small bomb, probably with a time-mechanism. No fragments of the device were found, so he could not discover the make or the type of weapon. There was not, therefore, any way of knowing who was responsible.[15]

His inconclusive report was kept secret, which had the desired effect for both the British and Soviet Governments of not causing any further embarrassment to Stalin and the KGB. However, the exiled Polish community remained suspicious. Its leaders felt that the British would have disclosed the outcome of the Rothschild investigation if the Nazis had been linked to the assassination. Gibraltar, after all, had been the target for much Nazi sabotage.

This left the Poles with one conclusion. There had been a cover-up.

13. ENTER THE
MEXICAN WARRIOR

CENTRE OF PROGRESS

By mid-1944, Yuri Modin's hopes for himself and his country surviving and triumphing were lifted. There was a renewed confidence in Moscow and across Russia as the Soviet Army rolled back the invaders, first in Russia then through Belorussia and the Ukraine. There would always be paranoia at the Centre under Beria. His use of murder, rape and torture kept agents in a state of permanent fear. But that aside, the atmosphere began to change inside the overworked Directorates as military success began to reflect well on all areas of Government.

Promotions inside the Lubyanka began to increase, as did food rations. Modin and his fellow agents of the First Directorate, however, could not rest as an avalanche of espionage data poured into the Centre. Beria did not lessen his demand to feed Soviet nuclear scientists with data as the emphasis swung towards firstly making a plutonium bomb, and secondly the longer-term aim of creating a new, totally Russian-developed weapon.[1]

Modin still rarely left the Dzherzinski Square before 3 a.m. and had learnt how to survive on a few hours sleep a day. Yet there was an extra inspiration at work which helped keep him enthusiastic. He had met and fallen in love with a beautiful, dark-haired translator, Anne, who, like him, had been recruited because of her basic knowledge of English.

While there could be no courting in working hours, Modin and Anne began seeing each other in the evening break and on their days off, which they made sure coincided. Their affair was encouraged. An inside relationship which led to marriage would enhance opportunities for advancement, especially for foreign postings.

Having the correct partner was an unwritten law for appoint-ments to Western Embassies. The temptation to defect would be strong once agents were exposed to life in the West. Single agents could be vulnerable to seductions of several sorts from sex to money. A committed Communist couple would be far less likely to abandon the cause, no matter what the inducements.

Anne found Modin attractive 'both physically and mentally'. She admired his ideological knowledge, intellectual depth and thorough-ness. But she found his serious side was balanced by his capacity to laugh, even at himself, and claimed that his sense of humour, love of life and compassion were warm traits.

Modin found his new love stunning and an even more meticulous translator than him. They spent many hours pondering an English word or phrase. Their common work in such an intense and challenging atmosphere drew them together, according to Modin.

They often found themselves secretly discussing the key British agents and the great job they were doing for the Soviet Union and the cause. They and the Soviet Intelligence hierarchy were also concerned that the agents might be uncovered early in 1944 when Churchill demanded that every single communist be flushed from all British Intelligence departments. The Prime Minister had done this 'after having to sentence two quite high-grade people to long terms of penal servitude for their betrayal of important military secrets to the Soviet Union.'[2]

The first of these betrayers was Douglas Frank Springhall, the national organizer of the British Communist Party, who had obtained details of the jet engine from an Air Ministry clerk for passing to the Russians. Springhall had been given a seven-year sentence in July 1943 after a secret trial. The Prime Minister also took exception to the activities of Ormond Leyton Uren, a captain in the Special Operations Executive (SOE), who had given Spring-hall a description of SOE HQ. He too received a seven-year sentence.

Churchill's attitude to communism had not wavered despite his cooperation with Stalin in fighting the Nazis. He was looking beyond Hitler's eventual defeat and was already considering the problems which would arise in confronting communism and Stalin's mono-lithic power, especially in Europe.

The apprehension felt at the Centre was more than matched by the agents in the field, for the activities of the Five and others had been far more pervasive and vital than that of Springhall and Uren. Modin and Anne thought that their Chiefs and Beria might ease up demands on the Controls and foreign spies. But it wasn't to be.

'If anything,' Modin recalled, 'the pressure for better and more Intelligence increased. Winston Churchill's attacks [on communists] caused [British] Intelligence to consider setting up a section dealing strictly with anti-communist operations.'[3]

The new Section – Nine – was created to do exactly that. The Centre told Philby he had to do 'everything in his power' to become its boss. Using his great guile in internal politics, Philby manipulated his way into the position.

'My own suitability for the post was explained [by his superior at MI6] in flattering detail,' Philby told his biographer, Phillip Knightley. 'Strangely enough, the recital of my virtues omitted my most serious qualification – the fact that I knew something about communism.'

Section Nine was supposed to handle *counter*-espionage, working to protect Britain from communist penetration. But it was soon attempting to penetrate communist countries in order to mount espionage operations.

Philby, as its boss, was thus in a position to protect all Russian agents, including himself. What's more, he was able to let the Centre know about all British spying operations mounted against the Soviet Union.

Instead, therefore, of clamping down on communist agents in Britain, Churchill's remorseless anti-communism ironically gave them greater protection and encouraged a burgeoning of their activities. For the moment, Burgess, Maclean, Blunt and the ubiquitous Rothschild could breathe easier. If they were in potential trouble, Philby would know about it, inform them and head off the dangers.

Section Nine also gave Philby an excuse for closer liaison with its American counterpart – the Office of Strategic Services (OSS), the CIA forerunner. He would be able to monitor its more dedicated anti-communist personnel. In fact, the most important anti-Soviet operator the CIA ever had began his apprenticeship under Philby early in 1944. His name was James Jesus Angleton.

One month after he arrived, in February 1944, at OSS's London offices in Ryder Street, the young American's thin dossier was already being perused by the Moscow Centre.

ANGLETON'S ACCESS

Angleton, 6 feet 1 inch tall, handsome, very slender and stooped, had just turned twenty-six when he joined the small London OSS team. In appearance and manner, he was an Anglicized American, despite his upbringing in Idaho and Ohio, and his Mexican mother. He had been initiated into the rites of the British private school system, with its moral focus and emphasis on elitism in all its forms, from a striving for excellence in study to class distinction and snobbery.

Angleton's American father, Hugh, joined NCR in Milan and James was sent to England. He spent his most formative years, from fourteen to seventeen, being educated first at Chartridge Hall House in Buckinghamshire, then at Malvern House in Worcestershire, where he stayed for three years. He was popular enough with the teachers to be made a prefect, the traditional appointment for all-round achievers in the system, and did his compulsory stint in the school's Officers' Training Corps but disliked it. He avoided the extra training needed to become a school Under-Officer and was appointed a corporal, which was the automatic school military grading after three years.

'Jim didn't have much time for the regimentation,' a Malvern House school friend recalled. 'He enjoyed the Scouts more, where you could show individual initiative. One against the elements . . . He was quiet, likeable, respectful . . .'[4]

His experience was broadened by his love of Europe. He spent summer vacations hiking and camping in France and attending Boy Scout jamborees in Hungary, Holland and Scotland. In the summer of 1938, he joined his family in Italy. In 1941, he graduated with a modest Bachelor of Arts from Yale, where he spent more time on artistic pursuits such as the editing of a literary magazine called *Furioso*, and going to jazz clubs than on his studies. In the autumn of 1941 he entered Harvard Law School, but this discipline did not hold Angleton's attention.

A room-mate, William Wick, remembered Angleton's life as an insomniac there:

'He could talk knowledgeably on any subject, and the ladies adored him . . . Rooming with Angleton was a fascinating experience. He knew no schedule, ate when hungry at whatever hour of the day or night, attended classes when he felt so inclined . . . Come nightfall, Jim kept me up to the wee hours, discussing girls, the war, international politics, famous poets . . . philosophy, *Time* magazine's unique writing style, bowling (which Jim had newly mastered), raising orchids and law . . . I would often arise [in the morning] to find Jim still reading or furiously writing, ashtrays stuffed with cigarette butts, and the room littered with library books.'[5]

War intervened and Angleton was drafted into the Army on 19 March 1943. His old English Professor at Yale, Norman Pearson, got him a job at OSS Counter-intelligence in London, which Pearson then headed.

From the beginning of his professional life, Angleton affected an English style, from his dark pure-wool suits to his polite manner and softened, elongated vowels. This and his experience at school eased his acceptance by his superiors amongst the British in the cramped OSS offices shared with MI6. One man in particular with whom he had a good relationship was Philby.

In the heady atmosphere of the Allied effort, which promised to defeat Hitler (with a lot of help from the Soviet Union), the intelligent, dedicated espionage tyro learned much from Philby, the young master.

He was introduced to the techniques of 'turning' enemy agents rather than executing them, so that they would send home false information. Angleton learned the value of using a constant flow of enemy intelligence data ('Ultra' technology allowed the British to crack the German Enigma machines, which were of vital importance throughout the enemy military). He also became familiar with the use of harmful propaganda against the enemy, and in measuring how successful it had been.

Most importantly, he began to understand the art of penetrating the enemy's Intelligence services, which was aimed not only at gathering secrets but, in the process, also destroyed the enemy's morale by sowing doubt, suspicion and paranoia.

Superficially, he and Philby seemed compatible because of their mutual respect for logic, and their understanding of people's strong and weak points. They were both patient and had a capacity for hard work beyond the call of duty, labouring into the early hours. They both enjoyed the company of sensual women and spent many nights attempting to drink each other under the table. They became close friends. At least that was what the younger Angleton thought.

Some of the same qualities drew Angleton to Rothschild, although they were not close. However, they had a rapport of a kind. According to Intelligence sources, they met early in 1944 when Rothschild made many visits to Ryder Street liaising with both MI6 and the OSS, where he was known and highly thought of for his Intelligence and sabotage work.

Twenty years later, after Philby had defected to Russia, Angleton was forced to reconsider the larger picture of all their acquaintances, including Rothschild as he was in London in 1944. Angleton remembered that he was a fine piano player, especially jazz. He also recalled his preoccupation with the plight of Jewish refugees, which he spoke about often, and that Rothschild had a different political attitude to a Jewish State being set up than the British Foreign Office.[6]

A former CIA agent also recalled that Angleton 'always had his ears – his antennae – open for different thoughts and attitudes. Don't forget Jim was an Hispanic. He had a Mexican mother, whose parents were poor refugees. This gave him another dimension, an intuitiveness, a side to his intellect that was emotional. Rothschild too was different, unconventional in his approach . . . I think he was responsible, at least in some part, for Jim's [later] strong support for Israel.'

Angleton was posted to Rome in October 1944. Within six months he was promoted to First Lieutenant of X-2, the counter-intelligence branch of OSS in charge of all operations in Italy, making him at twenty-seven the youngest OSS chief. Rothschild gave him contacts in the underground Jewish networks, which helped America to mop up fascists in Italy.[7]

The links would be useful later in his CIA career and in influencing his support for Israel.

14. 1944: THE TURNING

FALL IN PARIS

Rothschild threw a dinner party in a private room at the Savoy Hotel on 7 February 1944 for a dozen friends, including Churchill, his wife and daughter, Brendan Bracken, Minister of Information, and a close confidant of the Prime Minister's, and John Colville, Churchill's Private Secretary. It was no ordinary show. In keeping with the family style, Rothschild prepared the best.

'Dinner was excellent,' Colville noted in his diary, 'and the wine, from the Tring cellars, included Pol Roger 1921, the Rothschild Château Yquem and a remarkable old brandy.'[1]

An 'extremely good conjuror' performed at the end of the dinner. There was a rabbit, cards and a dove.[2]

'I've never seen anything better than that,' Churchill declared, sucking on a non-lethal Havana cigar, *never.*'

The British Prime Minister had the capacity to relax on such occasions and he consumed more than his usual quantity of liquor. Nevertheless, on his mind that night was the Allied invasion of Europe. Churchill was in the process of drafting a directive to the Supreme Commander of the Allied Expeditionary Force, US General Dwight Eisenhower. This set out his task and command, the logistics and the date, May, for crossing the Channel – 'D-Day'.

The timing for the invasion was in dispute since Eisenhower and Lt-General Montgomery both thought it should be in early June.[3]

Churchill did not want Stalin to know either of the prospective dates. It was in the Soviet dictator's interest to keep quiet about them because a successful Allied attack across the Channel would help the Soviet Union in the war against Hitler's forces. But Bletchley had evidence that the Germans had broken some of the

Soviet military code systems. Data that the British Government transmitted to Moscow was being sent to Soviet Commanders and then intercepted by the Germans.

However, as usual Stalin knew as much as Churchill did, and often before he did.[4] The Moscow Centre had notified its Controls that Stalin wanted the key British agents to move with the Supreme Commander's staff, wherever it went. The Allied Force's HQ on the Continent would be Paris.

Early on 6 June 1944, the Allies hit the beaches of Normandy with a huge invasion force to engage the Germans. Eleven days later 550,000 Allied troops were ashore and prepared for the drive across France in a series of battles which would decide the outcome of the war. Paris was liberated and cleared of Germans by late August. A few weeks later, SHAEF – the Supreme Headquarters, Allied Expeditionary Force – set up in Paris and there was a rush by British and American Intelligence personnel (already inside SHAEF in London) to create their own bases.

WAR AND PLAY AT AVENUE MARIGNY

The agents, with their customary agility at using the Intelligence services' old-boy network, managed to get attached to SHAEF. Burgess had joined the Foreign Office, which the KGB had wanted so that Maclean's 'loss' to Washington would not be missed so much. Blunt had been part of a D-Day deception plan to make the Germans think that the landing would be at Pas de Calais. But it was Rothschild who led the charge. He could not wait to get to Paris for several reasons, not the least being the restoration of the family mansion at 23 Avenue de Marigny by the Seine. There was some evidence of the German army's hurried evacuation. Apart from the inevitable sniper-smashed windows and boarded-up doorways all over the city, there was a burnt-out vehicle in the Place de La Concorde and the remains of a tank in the Tuileries Gardens, which seemed to have been left as a monument to the past four years.

Rothschild found the liberated city was an exciting place to be as bars, cafés and clubs opened up to celebrate the pushing back of the Nazis. He wasted no time in frequenting the Ritz in the Place

Vendôme and the Travellers Club on the Champs Elysees, where he lingered till the early hours, occasionally playing jazz on the piano.

He was surprised to find 23 Avenue de Marigny more or less intact. Unlike most other large houses taken over by the Germans, it had not been looted. Hermann Goering, the second most powerful individual in Germany, had put the commander of the Luftwaffe in France in the mansion. Apart from storing some artefacts and paintings in the basement, he had left it unspoiled.

Rothschild moved part of his counter-sabotage unit in, but when he started defusing explosives in some of the rooms, which contained antique furniture, he was persuaded to transfer these activities to the Rue Petrach offices of 105 Special Counter-Intelligence attached to SHAEF.

However, there was no objection to moving in his fellow agents Blunt and Burgess, and Philby intermittently. Rothschild wanted the first two close at hand, as they had been at Bentinck Street in London, so that he could furnish them with any data, verbal or written, that would be useful to the Soviet Controls – including Boris Krotov (Gorsky went to Washington in July after D-Day to look after Maclean who had been placed there by the Foreign Office).

Rothschild not only provided the base for the Ring of Five in Paris, he also took virtual control of the small, dedicated KGB network. He caused the Russian Controls to shift temporarily from London to Paris to receive espionage data, which he had no trouble collecting, especially as he was one of the senior British officers (and for a time the senior officer) in the city. Events were happening too fast with the Allied forces' thrust into the Continent for the Controls to dictate what data would be useful to the Moscow Centre. Even Stalin's insatiable appetite for knowing what the Allied High Command was thinking was being anticipated as far as possible by Rothschild.

He dictated which intelligence should be purloined and from where. The KGB Controls were controllers in name only in this period and it caused some tensions, although they were never openly expressed. The KGB was so magnificently served by him that the Controls and Residents in London and Paris were receiving consistent praise for the first time in the war. The Centre and Stalin were increasingly pleased with the data they were receiving.

When Tess Mayor arrived at the mansion, still as assistant to Rothschild, whose duties had widened, she was pleased to see her former Bentinck house-mates. 'How nice to have the buggers in the house!' she remarked to Malcolm Muggeridge, who was married to her cousin, Kitty and arrived in Paris early in October.[5]

Muggeridge, at that time a conscientious MI6 officer, was not amused by other experiences in Paris involving the network, which at that point he began to suspect of being Soviet agents. Three incidents created doubt. Over dinner one night with Rothschild and Philby at the mansion an argument developed about the rights and wrongs of withholding important Bletchley intercepts from the Soviet Union.

Rothschild started the discussion. He had access to the great amount of intelligence now flowing into SHAEF daily from Bletchley Park. The intercepts told of the German military's struggle to cut its losses as it retreated everywhere across Europe. It was vital for the Soviet Union, he argued, to learn where the remaining Nazi strengths were so it could organize its response and be more effective in destroying the enemy.

Rothschild was 'vehement' about the fact the British should not be withholding this intelligence from the Russians. This was an act on his part, for he had been passing on the data himself, but he wanted to make his indignant point to Muggeridge. Enough alcohol had flowed during the angry discussion for Rothschild to let down his guard, especially as his guest was in his element in a political debate.[6]

Muggeridge made several counter-points which fuelled the fierce responses. '[Withholding the intercepts from the Russians] was legitimate,' he claimed, 'especially in view of the way the Russians had passed on to the Germans everything they knew about us and our intentions during the period of the Nazi–Soviet Pact. Another similar occasion for treachery might arise, and we were right to guard against it . . .'[7]

Rothschild replied that the immediate past was irrelevant. The Russians had taken the brunt of the war against Hitler, and they should be given every assistance.

'Every German tank destroyed or Luftwaffe plane shot down is one less against us,' was another argument of his.

Muggeridge felt that the exchange was drifting towards a left–right political stance. He had been a left-wing sympathizer, but had been put off Marxism by the excesses of Stalin, which he had witnessed as a newspaper correspondent in Moscow in the 1930s. Now he was more conservative. His two colleagues, he felt, were much more pro-Stalin. Rothschild was disdainful of Muggeridge's political change of heart and suggested that this had coloured his view of reality. The Soviet Union had sacrificed most in the war, Rothschild reminded him, and it was now fighting on the same side as the British and the Americans.

The cross-fire intensified, Philby joined in and got so irritated that he began to stammer, a sure sign that his normal self-control was slipping. Muggeridge recalled: 'He spluttered and shouted that we were duty-bound to do everything within our power, whatever it might be, to support the Red Army, including risking – if there was a risk – the security of Bletchley material.'

Muggeridge suddenly felt 'like a skeleton at the feast'. There was no way of persuading these two that they were morally and politically incorrect. Muggeridge mistakenly suspected that this was the beginning of Philby's treachery.

His doubts hardened in the next few weeks after two further incidents. He was surprised at how disinterested Philby was in Soviet sabotage and subversion in France, especially at a time when he was supposed to be consumed with setting up his Section Nine networks. And, in a bizarre incident one drunken night, they found themselves strolling by the Seine. Instead of returning to the mansion, Philby wanted to go to the Soviet Embassy in Rue de Grenelle.

'"How are we going to get in there?" Kim kept saying,' Muggeridge remembered. '[He] went on to expatiate upon the special difficulties of penetrating a Soviet Embassy as compared with others ... [there was] no chance of planting a servant when all the staff, down to the lowliest kitchen maids and porters and chauffeurs, are imported from the USSR and sometimes in reality hold quite senior posts in the intelligence *apparat*.'

Muggeridge was astounded that Philby carried on like this 'in an almost demented way; not exactly shaking his fists, but gesticulating and shouting . . .'

Muggeridge later surmised that his friend was making a play to employ him in his new Section Nine.

'His Soviet friends possibly persuaded him to try it on me, reasoning that a recruit whose name was down in the Kremlin's black books would strengthen rather than weaken Kim's position in the eyes of his [British] superiors . . .'[8]

THE INTERROGATOR

Rothschild's excellent relations with the Americans continued soon after his arrival in Paris when he was seconded to them for a short time. The manuals Rothschild had written were now used by all the Allies and he was asked to instruct American counter-sabotage people, in lectures and field work. He and Tess demonstrated how bombs could be detected and defused. But before he could begin he had to go through the secondment formality of an IQ test, which he found easy.

A week later, he was summoned by US General B. Conrad, in charge of US operations in Paris.

'I have a serious question to put to you,' he told Rothschild, 'which I hope you will answer with complete frankness.'

'Of course, General.'

'You did our IQ test a week ago; can I have an absolute assurance from you that you had not seen the papers before, nor discussed their contents with anyone?'

'I can give you that assurance, General.'

'Colonel Rothschild, you have an IQ of 184. There is only one person the US army has examined with as high an IQ, and that is Dr Schacht [Hitler's finance minister], at present interned.'

Without another word, Rothschild saluted and left.[9]

The incident added further to his reputation as an exceptional all-round operator during the war, which pleased the Soviet Controls. They were keen to have an insider with a foot in both US and British Intelligence at SHAEF as the Allies closed in on the stumbling German army.

On finishing his secondment Rothschild was, for a few weeks in November, the senior British officer in Paris.[10] He took advantage of this elevation to take part in the interrogation of important German prisoners, including Otto Skorzeny, a German paratroop commander who in September 1943 had rescued the overthrown Italian dictator, Benito Mussolini, in a raid on Campo Imperatore in Italy's Abruzze Mountains.

It was an effective psychological ploy to have a Rothschild doing the questioning, for he was from the family which Hitler had personally set up as the epitome of everything Jewish that the Germans should despise and destroy. In many documents, such as the Führer's decrees about art confiscation or bank acquisitions in occupied cities, the Rothschilds were used as an example.[11]

The fact that they were Europe's richest, most powerful Jewish family had already triggered Hitler's hate. But the incident with Baron Louis in Austria, when he disdainfully ignored the threats of the goose-stepping Nazis and then made the secret deal with his British relatives to avoid Hitler getting his grasp on the family assets, made Rothschilds everywhere an object of revenge. They bore the brunt of anti-Jewish abuse and denigration in Nazi-influenced and -dominated newspapers from 1938. Every officer knew how Hitler, Goering and Himmler felt about the family.

Now, in an unnerving twist for captured Nazi officers, the most enigmatic, controlled and cool member of the family was in command of their fates. The strains of the war had modified Rothschild's boyish good looks and the double life he had been leading had etched itself into his solemn features. His jowls were heavier, and while he was still handsome there was a maturity in his appearance beyond his years.

In half a decade, Rothschild had made the transition from a fringe sub-agent, whose life was preoccupied with researching spermatozoa activity, playing tennis, women and fast sports cars, to a fully-fledged spy. By the time of his thirty-fourth birthday in Paris he had the intellectual strength and experience to cope with his 'too many secrets'.[12]

His character was complex, layered and variable, but he was buffered against the stresses of espionage, betrayal and an unsatisfactory personal life, by his heritage, money and drive. His desire to be influential in Hitler's destruction had overridden or submerged other considerations, which would have ruined more vulnerable, less inspired individuals.

Now the real visage of the enemy was in front of him, and he thrived on the opportunity to witness the Nazi submission. Yet he did not rant, strut, fume or threaten in the interrogations. Instead, calling on his English patrician background, he subtly and coldly probed his targets, wearing them down with long, telling stares, silently daring them to lie. Obfuscation was met with repetitive questions or incessant reiteration. Nothing was hurried. Pertinent queries were put and responses were weighed, measured and pondered as if he were back in his Cambridge research laboratory.[13]

Skorzeny, the German war hero SS officer, was 'nervous and forthcoming' about his skilful and bold coup in the rescuing of Mussolini by air from his mountain prison. At first, he clammed up when the interrogation turned to Mussolini presiding over a German-sponsored Italian Republic in the North. Yet when asked about his own exploits involving the German rear-guard actions in other parts of Europe, he opened up here and there, allowing the Allies to piece together, with the help of other POWs and Intelligence, a picture of the German High Command's likely plans.[14]

Apart from his demeanour, Rothschild had another enormous advantage: the Bletchley intercepts. They were never mentioned, but instead, 'our informants in the German High Command' were referred to as if there were highly-placed spies who knew a great deal. Allied interrogators kept Ultra secret throughout the war, and prisoners were intimidated and stunned by the amount of detail in the hands of the enemy. It often shocked them into tripping and divulging information, which otherwise would be withheld. It was all passed to Blunt and then the Controls in Paris and London for transmission to the Moscow Centre.

On 30 April 1945, Hitler committed suicide in his Berlin bunker – twelve years and three months after he had become Chancellor of the German Reich. The same evening, a Russian soldier planted the Red Victory Banner on top of the Reichstag. General Chuikov, the heroic defender of Stalingrad, received the surrendor of the city.

A week later, on 7 May, the German military forces surrendered unconditionally and the Third Reich was ended. With it went the Nazi tyranny that had terrorized Europe for six years. A jubilant

Rothschild joined the three powers arrangement in Germany and continued screening refugees in the chaotic rush across the German border. Eastern Europeans and others from several countries threatened with control by the Soviets attempted to get into Germany by posing as Germans.

Rothschild, acting as a British representative, journeyed to places such as Pilsen near the Czechoslovakian border, joining officers from the CIA and the KGB as they screened hundreds of honest refugees, imposters and Nazis wishing to avoid being sent to a Soviet gulag, or worse.

A majority vote of at least two to one was needed to decide whether an individual went East or West. There was never overt collusion, but usually the British and American representatives agreed about a refugee's status and there was more often than not a three-way agreement. In Pilsen, there was no connivance between Rothschild and his KGB counterpart, who had no idea of the British agent's secret affiliation.

A MATTER OF LIFE OR DEATH

Asja Mercer was a young Latvian medical student when the Soviets took over her country in 1940. She helped organize the resistance and was soon raiding weapons factories, arming guerrillas, blowing up bridges and throwing grenades into Red Army barracks. Later the Germans took Latvia, but they were enemies too, and she became involved in playing one off against the other. At the end of the war she fled across central Europe, trying to escape the clutches of the KGB, who were unrelenting in their liquidation of 'terrorists' who had resisted them.

Mercer made it to the Czechoslovakian border, posing as a German refugee. She managed to steal across the border to Pilsen, where she slept in an abandoned Gestapo building. She was discovered there by American forces. Asja was told she could go temporarily to a hotel they had taken over. She had to report daily to American HQ.

The first day she visited the HQ, a former police station near the badly-bombed Skoda works, she was frank with her interrogators.

'If the Russians take me prisoner,' she said, 'I'll be sent to Riga for trial. I'll be either shot on the spot, or transported to Siberia. Any Latvian on the run faces this fate.'[15]

The Americans complimented her on her command of German and told her not to be concerned. At the hotel she sat sipping Pilsen beer in the lounge with others while listening to Churchill on the radio. His words were comforting, for some. She felt he had 'peered into the future and seen the dark things [in the partition of Europe] that were to happen.'

'On the Continent of Europe,' Churchill said, 'we have yet to make sure that the honourable purposes for which we entered the war are not brushed aside or overlooked in the methods following our successes, and that the words "freedom", "democracy" and "liberation" are not distorted from their meaning as we have understood them.'

The next remark chilled Asja.

'There would be little use in punishing the Hitlerites for their crimes if law and justice did not rule and the totalitarian or police governments were to take the place of the German invaders . . . It is the victors who must search their hearts in their glowing hours and be worthy of their nobility, of the immense forces that they wield.'

The fears stirred by these words became reality a few hours later when Asja was told she would have to leave the hotel. She was forced to stay in a filthy, crowded doss-house. In the middle of the night 'zealous' Czech underground members woke her and the scores of other refugees and demanded to see their clearance papers.

They were rough and rude in exerting the small authority the Americans had granted them. Asja explained that she was a German awaiting clearance.

'My heart was filled with despair,' Asja recalled. 'I was haunted by the thought that the Russians might still snatch me away. The future took on the black and hopeless appearance it had done so often in the past.' Her 'despondency deepened' at the thought of 'the last supreme ordeal', facing the occupying tribunal which would decide if she was a harmless German, a Nazi war criminal, or someone to be handed over to Soviet authorities.

Asja turned up every day at the American HQ, not knowing when the tribunal would examine her case. On the seventh day of reporting in, she had been waiting in a corridor for some time when a military policeman approached her.

'Come with me,' he said and led her into a room. She stepped in and the door was closed behind her. Asja faced three men sitting behind a trestle table. The KGB man was scowling. The CIA officer was smiling and friendly. Rothschild sat sphinx-like behind a pall of smoke from his Balkan Sobranie.[16]

'Sit down, *fräulein*,' the American said. He offered her a cigarette. She refused. The American leant back on his chair, tilting it. He tried to put her at ease, asking her name, occupation and length of service.

'I am a nursing sister of the Wehrmacht,' she explained.

'You look like a Baltic national to me,' the Russian growled. 'Why don't you want to go home?'

'Surely,' Rothschild said, 'if she's a German, she is already at home.'

The American had read the notes from her first interrogation in which she had expressed her fear of the Russians. They told a different story but he didn't question her current position and was well-disposed towards her. Rothschild was less friendly. His questions were blunt and phrased in 'legal language'. 'If he had a heart, it was certainly not on display,' Asja noted.

The Russian attacked, saying she had been seen consorting with Baltic nationals at Dobrzani. Why had she run when Soviet forces were near the hospital?

'I was frightened,' Asja replied. 'I wanted to get to Hanover, where my mother is.'

The Russian was adamant she was from a Baltic state. He banged the table and shouted: 'I will be responsible for sending her back there.'

Asja felt weak with the strain.

The American said he believed her. 'My vote is that she is a German national.'

'And my vote is for her repatriation to the Baltic states where she belongs,' the Russian countered.

The two men looked at Rothschild. He held the casting vote, and Asja's life, in his hands. Would he vote with the Russian, the way his companions amongst the top five British agents probably would have? They would no doubt have taken the 'long view' in deciding the woman's fate. Rothschild's ideological commitment and subservience to the cause could at times be just as steadfast, in his low-key way, as the other members of the ring but his mind was more flexible. His main aim of defeating Hitler had been achieved and this sad, beautiful woman had been trapped in a conflict not of her making. He looked on this minor episode as unimportant to the East–West struggle. Rothschild drew on his cigarette and stared at Asja, who had fixed her frightened gaze at a damp patch on a wall.

'I say she is German,' he said in the same dispassionate manner. 'That makes two votes to one.'

The Russian was furious but under the rules governing the occupation powers he had no choice but to sign the clearance papers. Asja heard the scratching of pens on paper.

'*Fräulein*,' Rothschild remarked, 'we have decided you will go to Hanover as soon as transport is available.'

Asja felt faint. She couldn't stand up. The three men stared.

'You may go, *fräulein*,' Rothschild confirmed. 'You are free to go now.'

With a supreme effort, Asja stood up, smiled and left the room.[17]

DATELINE SUDETENLAND

Rothschild did as much touring and observing as time would allow during his weeks near the Czech border. He was particularly interested in the Sudetenland, that part of Czechoslovakia annexed by Germany in 1938, with Stalin's agreement, as part of the Munich Pact. In March 1939, Hitler went further and annexed all of Czechoslovakia.

The town of Zatec near the German border was the centre of a huge industrial area where the Nazis used slave labour to build armaments from Messerschmitts to artillery for their war effort. Rothschild learned of factories where planes, half-finished but in good condition, had been abandoned once the Nazis were defeated and the slave labour was liberated.[18] There were buildings full of machinery and partly-assembled weaponry – all the nuts and bolts of the weapons of war. The observant visitor wondered how these arms would be put to use and by whom in the coming carve-up of Europe, which was shortly to see the closing of Stalin's Iron Curtain.

Czechoslovakia, as Churchill had feared and predicted, would soon be under the Soviet yoke.

Rothschild determined then to report what he had learned to his connections, but not in the KGB or MI5. His thoughts were directed at the Jewish spy network.[19]

PART THREE

MY ALLY,
MY ENEMY
1945–1951

15. THE REASSESSMENT

PANIC IN THE KREMLIN

A blinding flash was followed by scorching heat as the first atomic bomb was exploded at Trinity Site, New Mexico, on 16 July 1945. The explosion was accompanied by a cyclone of hot wind that flattened every building within 30 miles. A pillar of black smoke was speared by a scarlet thread that glowed until the smoke too went red. The desert was charred around the collapsed buildings, and the low, thunderous boom sent shock waves around the world and into the heart of the Kremlin.

All the cynicism and doubt that had surrounded attempts to create a nuclear weapon evaporated along with the prefabricated structures at Trinity in the Manhattan Project's test. In their place was depression in Moscow, particularly at the Centre where there was also a sense of failure. The bomb detonated had been made using plutonium, which Soviet scientists had known about since Rothschild's data had reached them in 1943. Yet a breakthrough was still years away, Beria and Stalin were informed. Additional funds were allocated to extending the existing secret nuclear research sites as well as building even more.

Meanwhile the Allied war with Japan was still in progress in the Pacific. US military commanders had the choice of attacking the Japanese mainland and suffering enormous casualties or bombing the enemy into submission. There was a growing peace movement in Japan but no sign of a military surrender. A decision was made by the US to use an atomic weapon.

On 6 August 1945, news flashed around the world of the detonation of 'Little Boy' over Hiroshima. It killed more than 150,000 people and flattened the city, leaving a hideous radioactive

zone for 30 square miles. That bomb effectively finished the Pacific
war between the US and its allies and the Japanese.

Moscow's depression turned to fear. The US had been prepared
to use the weapon as soon as possible. Furthermore, it had been
made using U-235, unlike the Trinity bomb, demonstrating that the
Anglo-American combined Manhattan Project had succeeded with
two types of super-weapon, where the Soviet scientists had failed at
everything.

Fear became panic three days later on 9 August when another
plutonium bomb, 'Fat Man', was gratuitously blasted over Nagasaki.
Apart from again showing off US weapons superiority, it demonstrated how ruthless Washington could be in dealing with its
enemies. Japan would probably have surrendered after Hiroshima.
It capitulated on 15 August.

From that moment, the hawks under Stalin had their power
boosted. After emergency meetings with Stalin and his closest
advisers, Beria was directed to find the best German scientists and
force them into work for the Soviet Union. Those already captured
were given new directives. For instance, a day after Nagasaki,
Manfred von Ardenne was summoned to a high-level meeting in
Moscow. He headed an entire German physics laboratory which
had been settled in Sukhumi, a Georgian city on the Black Sea. Von
Ardenne was told that he and his team had to create a copy of the
Hiroshima bomb.

'I was given about ten seconds to consider what to do,' Ardenne
recalled. 'I thought that if we [his team of scientists] made the
bomb ourselves, we would never see our homeland again.' However,
he and scores of other physicists had little choice. With the current
mood in the Kremlin, it was that or death. All of them preferred to
live and work.[1]

Meanwhile, established Soviet scientists, such as Kapitza, gave
th∶ KGB specific requests for information about the bombs which
the US had exploded: how were they exploded; how was implosion
used; how were the explosive and nuclear material used; how were
the yield and neutron diffusion calculated; what was the critical
mass (which determined how big the reactor had to be to produce
the nuclear fuel)?[2]

The KGB had moles working at Los Alamos, Oak Ridge, Tennes-
see, and Chicago, according to former KGB Colonel 'F'.

'We had important people – [J. Robert] Oppenheimer, [Enrico] Fermi, [Niels] Bohr and others – who were willing to give us information to help us.'

How did they assist the KGB?

'By comments and documents – and answers to our specific requests.'

You are saying they were agents?

'No. But they knew Fuchs was. He was given extraordinary access to the vital data – as were others of our people.'

Why did Oppenheimer and Co. do this? Because of guilt, conscience . . .?

'They believed in the balance of power. It would have been dangerous for peace if the Americans had the power to destroy us.'[3]

The Beria push irritated Kapitza. He hated the idea of copying the US/British method. He wrote to Stalin in 1945 and complained about Beria being the conductor who waved the baton, 'but [who didn't] understand the score. In this respect Beria is weak.'[4] Kapitza asked to be taken off the atomic bomb project, but compromised when Stalin allowed him to create his own project on a specifically Soviet developed bomb.

REVIEW AT THE CENTRE

With Germany defeated, the Centre's number one espionage target became Intelligence on the bomb. Modin and other agents were ordered to review the roles of the Five and the other top twenty-five agents, and edge their work, if possible, towards every aspect of the weapon's production from scientific research to budget allocation.

Maclean was already usefully placed in Washington. Gorsky ordered him to better position himself to obtain data from the British Mission to the Manhattan Project. Burgess, also attached to the Foreign Office, was needed for espionage involving the Big Powers conferences, but he was told of the new priority and directed to report on the mood of his department. Were FO officials disposed towards war or peace? Would they advise using the bomb against new 'enemies' such as the Russians?

Philby at MI6 was given similar orders, though he was mainly con-cerned with the operations of Section Nine – counter-intelligence against the Soviets — an aspect of British Intelligence which had increased in significance with the end of the war. The Russians, the great ally of the West from 1942 to early 1945 were, by the end of that year, enemy number one. All political activity, espionage and weapons development were to be directed with that in mind as the world superpowers quickly adjusted to the new, different realities of the Cold War.

Modin was fascinated by the case of Anthony Blunt at MI5. He had told his Controls that he was planning to leave the service to join the staff at Buckingham Palace as the King's art curator. Blunt had endeared himself to King George VI at the end of the war when he successfully carried out an assignment for him, in which he was sent to Germany to acquire art and retrieve documents — mainly letters in the hands of the Royal Family's many German relations. One particular objective had been the 'long and intimate' correspondence between Queen Victoria and her eldest daughter, the mother of Kaiser Wilhelm II. There were fears that old but intimate secrets might be made public by American journalists. Even more pertinent were communications between Hitler and the Duke of Windsor, the former King Edward VIII, which could have embarrassed the Royals and the Government.[5]

The Centre at first tried to dissuade Blunt from moving out of MI5 and into the Royal Court. But he argued that he could still be of service because 'the monarch's private secretary had access to all the secrets of government and knew nearly everything that went on' in the British circles of power.

This gave the Centre pause, and they considered Blunt's argument. The Chiefs asked for an assessment of Blunt's spying capabilities. The Controls suggested he had not lost his nerve and that he could still be of value. He was, however, 'fatigued' by his tremendous war-time effort in passing on so much Intelligence. The risks had not destroyed him, but they had worn him down. On top of that he was not a committed ideologue in the mould of Philby, Maclean, Burgess or even Rothschild.[6]

The Centre was not convinced he would be of value at the Palace, but let him go after he assured them that he would continue in the KGB's service.

Rothschild was another issue. There could be no cajoling, bullying or financial seduction of this super-agent. He was as committed as ever, but above the normal directives because of his independence and power. Approaches by Controls were usually done via Blunt, although there were opportunities for 'discussions' on issues at official functions at the Soviet Embassy in London and elsewhere.[7] The Centre always believed that Rothschild would assist them, but it seems likely that, in the interests of his race, he was now expecting favours in return for his exceptional work. Rothschild asked the Soviet Union to ease restrictions on Jewish refugees trying to leave the Communist bloc.

This was granted, but Rothschild warned that there would be further requests because the Jewish homeland question would soon be a major issue.[8] The Centre expected in return that he would still be useful in targeting information on atomic developments.[9]

The Centre was now almost totally concentrating on the American-controlled Manhattan Project. According to Leonard R. Kvasnikov, the KGB officer who collated all the atomic information flowing into the Centre, spies involved in the Project at Los Alamos provided big leads on the way the Soviet scientists should go. There was an agent code-named HURON, who was 'close to' the Project's director, Robert Oppenheimer (who had assisted the Soviet Union since 1942). There was also a physicist, PERSEUS, who began delivering information from early 1943 to Anatoly Yatskov, a KGB officer in Washington who travelled to New York by train to make contact. KGB files in Moscow show that there were also agents coded as BULL, CAT, SHOT and TIFF.[10]

As the Cold War began these and another ten agents were in place in the Manhattan Project network, pumping data on the bomb developments to the Centre. They included Klaus Fuchs, Bruno Pontecorvo, Allan Nunn May, Harry Gold, David Greenglass, Julius and Ethel Rosenberg. The Russians could not provide the huge money resources needed to turn a chain reaction into an explosive so they had to steal the research using thousands of scientists at home and several efficient spy networks abroad.

THE WILDERNESS OF MIRRORS

With so many agents in the field connected to the same massive operation, there were bound to be mistakes which would lead to some being caught. On top of that, the Cold War marked the beginning of defections from Russia by those who had experienced a better life in the West. The defectors needed to have something to sell.

This put the Soviet bomb espionage networks in jeopardy. Those Russians abandoning their posts enhanced the concept of 'the wilderness of mirrors' in which defectors became wittingly or unwittingly involved in molehunts based on the new data they gave. If a KGB defector suggested there were spies inside Western services nearly everyone became a suspect, because the game was to be undetectable which meant that possible moles ranged from the most to the least obvious.

The first major Russian to leave his post in the West post-war with promises of major secrets was a 25-year-old cipher clerk in the Ottawa Embassy named Igor Gouzenko. In September 1945, he claimed that Moscow had an important spy at the heart of British Intelligence. But Gouzenko couldn't make up his mind whether he worked for MI5, or Section Five of MI6.

Gouzenko was speaking about a spy who had operated until 1945, which at first could have meant any one of twenty people. Over time it narrowed down to a handful, including Blunt, Roger Hollis (then in charge of monitoring the British Communist Party), Guy Liddell and Rothschild – all at MI5 – and Philby at MI6.

A few weeks later, KGB operative Konstantin Volkov in Istanbul told a British Embassy official that he wanted to defect. His deal was £27,500 and sanctuary in Britain in exchange for data about five British double agents in Intelligence and two in the Foreign Office. The key spy again was initially thought to be in MI6, but over the years Volkov's claims were reassessed and could have meant a section head of MI5, which then pointed to Hollis once more. But Liddell and Rothschild's roles could also be interpreted to mean head of section until 1945. (Philby alerted the Centre and Volkov was taken back to Moscow and executed.)

The upshot of such defections and accusations was to make both British Intelligence and the FBI (the CIA was not yet in operation) far more alert to moles inside espionage agencies and spies within vital operations such as the Manhattan Project. The agents and their Controls were suddenly under far more stress than they had ever experienced in wartime as the hunts began.

16. CHANGE OF FOCUS

MORE FOR MOSSAD

The end of the war signalled a confirmation of the commitment of the Ring of Five to their espionage work for the Soviet Union. But now a clandestine approach was paramount. They were working for the new enemy of the West. If exposed now as KGB agents, they would be viewed as full-blown traitors.

Rothschild decided to formalize his relationship with his close assistant, Tess. In 1946, he divorced Barbara and married Tess, thus beginning a far more settled and successful private life for the versatile spy. He officially gave up service for MI5 after helping to reorganize its structure. In public, he lifted his profile in keeping with his background by continuing to do research at Cambridge and by taking up directorships, such as with the British airline BOAC. He accepted war honours and awards in Britain and the US, and continued his work in the House of Lords.

In private, unlike others who left the service, he was addicted to the secret world and could not give it up. Because of his independence, position and the reputation he had gained during the war, he was able to keep in touch with the secret services' most powerful men.

He could afford to dabble when and how he liked. But as always with Rothschild, there were strong motives behind his affiliations. He was closely connected to the Jewish drive for a homeland for the millions of refugees made homeless by the upheaval of the war and used his position in the Lords to make powerful, cogent public statements, which would get wide press attention.

His unseen contacts with Intelligence were useful in helping the Jewish Haganah – the precursor to Mossad – learn what the British

were thinking and doing, for the Foreign Office jealously guarded its
influence in the Middle East.

The Arab nations were against any form of a Jewish state in their
region. The FO was determined to maintain its standing with the
Arabs and it was difficult for Zionists to get support for the radical
idea of a new country in the midst of hostile nations.

The political campaign for it had to be subtle, thoughtful and
persistent. There was much education to be done in a parliament
and political system that had not exactly been feverish in its support
of the Jews during the war. There had been some sympathy,
especially in the Labour movement, but there had also been
ignorance, even hostility before the war amongst Conservative
elements, including newspapers, who backed Hitler. Despite the
horrors of the death camps there was a deal of work needed to turn
the pre-war apathy into post-war support.

As the months of the first post-war year were eaten up with his
various public and clandestine activities, everything Rothschild did
seemed increasingly to be inspired by the Jewish refugee/homeland
problem. It was a continuation of his work in the 1930s, but now
with the possibility of a humane solution, he was redoubling his
efforts in public and in secret.

Rothschild had cleverly cultivated a 'neutral' position concerning
the politics of the issue and had friends in the press comment that he
was 'the most pro-Arab Jew in the UK'. He went further in a Lords
speech and stated 'I have never been a supporter of Zionism, or
what is called political Zionism; nor have I been connected officially
or unofficially with any Zionist organisation.'[1] But in a debate on 'The
Situation in Palestine' on 31 July 1946, he came out into the open.

The debate coincided with great unrest in Palestine, a few days
after the King David Hotel was blown up by Jewish terrorists –
members of the notorious Irgun and Stern Gang. British soldiers
were killed in the incident.[2]

Rothschild made his speech in response to an official Anglo-
American Commission recommendation, which wanted Palestine
partitioned into four areas with the right of entry, into a 'Jewish
Province in Palestine, of 100,000 Jews to be selected primarily from
Germany, Austria and Italy.'

Rothschild started by again denying that he was a Zionist or
connected with its intelligence operations, and then proceeded to

make a near-emotional (for him), but always rational case for Jews being allowed to have their part of the partition.

He pointed out that, in the worldwide tradition of the past few hundred years, pogroms were still going on, the latest as recently as July 1946 in Kielce, Poland. Rothschild reminded their lordships that 'almost all the young Jews in Palestine had fathers, mothers and relations who were among the six million Jews tortured or gassed to death by Hitler'.

He gave a graphic account of an aunt, 'whom one loved dearly – she was seventy-five years old and quite blind – [who was] . . . clubbed to death by the SS on the railway station outside an extermination camp . . .'

Rothschild then spoke of a Foreign Office-influenced, 1939 British White Paper, which was against a Jewish settlement. It was viewed by many Jews as 'a betrayal of previous promises' going back to the Balfour Declaration in November 1917, in which the British Secretary of State for Foreign Affairs wrote the following reply to Lord Walter Rothschild, Victor's uncle:

Dear Lord Rothschild,

I have much pleasure in conveying to you, on behalf of His Majesty's Government, the following declaration of sympathy with Jewish Zionist aspirations which have been submitted to, and approved by, the Cabinet:

'His Majesty's Government view with favour the establishment in Palestine of a national home for the Jewish people, and will use their best endeavours to facilitate the achievement of this object, it being clearly understood that nothing shall be done which may prejudice the civil and religious rights of the existing non-Jewish communities in Palestine, or the rights and political status enjoyed by Jews in any other country.'

I should be grateful if you would bring this declaration to the knowledge of the Zionist Federation.

Yours sincerely,

Arthur Balfour

Victor invoked Churchill's reaction to parts of the White Paper:

'That is a plain breach of a solemn obligation, a breach of faith . . . What will those who have been stirring up the Arab agitators think? Will they not be tempted to say, "They are on the run again. This is another Munich."'

Rothschild attacked some Arab nations for their anti-British and pro-Hitler stances and then commented on the Anglo-American recommendation:

'A prerequisite of this recommendation being implemented was that no further acts of terrorism should take place . . . that illegal armies in Palestine should all disarm before these displaced people were allowed into Palestine. The Jews, constrained to Palestine, felt, quite wrongly no doubt, that this added condition was directed against them, rather than against the Arabs, who had all the surrounding countries such as TransJordan and Syria, in which to prepare for resistance.'

Rothschild defended the Jewish Army and at the same time showed the English connection to it by noting that many of its members 'did many acts of valour for England during the war', and that it was trained 'by a national hero of ours,' General Wingate.

Rothschild added an historical perspective: 'Palestine . . . is the only country where the Jews, after 2,000 years, have been able to get back to their business of tilling the soil and living on the land . . .' Then he invoked some passion by speaking of Gestapo torture, which explained why the Jews had become desperate for a safe refuge from persecution.

He ended his speech with a back-handed compliment: 'I remember that only a few years ago my grandfather was the first Jew your Lordships allowed to sit in this House, and I therefore felt it my duty to try and explain something of the trials and torments of my co-religionists in Palestine.'[3]

The speech attracted worldwide attention and signalled that Rothschild's war had not ended. He would put the same fervour into setting up Israel as he did in defeating Hitler. This meant he would court the Americans with whom he had built such superb relations during the war. Money and support would come from the powerful Jewish lobby in the US, but Rothschild had not forgotten his contacts in the Kremlin. If they *and* the Americans backed a Jewish homeland it would more than cancel out British intransigence.

The KGB were hoping that Rothschild could still help them as they geared up their efforts to steal Western bomb intelligence. He was secretly anti-American when it came to their drive to be the biggest military power and, like Oppenheimer, he was keen to do what he could to create a 'balance of terror', where each of the superpowers had the bomb as a deterrent to each other's aggression. He also still held a strong ideological belief that Socialism should be the dominant system on earth.

One way the Russians could be sure of his help would be if they acceded to his demands about a Jewish homeland. In 1946, he kept lobbying for more refugees to be released from behind the Iron Curtain, and news kept coming in that more than a trickle of Jews were moving across the borders.

MISSION LESS POSSIBLE

In 1946, the heavily guarded Los Alamos compound at a secret spot in the desert of New Mexico became a place of confusion as the Manhattan Project fell into limbo for more than a year as scientists tried but failed to bring it under civilian control. This period hampered the KGB's access to secrets as scientists came and went, without leadership and direction. The situation was salvaged when the Atomic Energy Act formed the AEC, which resuscitated the Project, followed by the McMahon Act on 1 August, which put civilian control over the military.

These changes didn't worry the Russians but they were concerned that the new Act would affect all Anglo-American scientific exchanges. Section 10 of the Bill made the distinction between 'basic scientific data', which could be shared with other nations, and 'technical processes', which could not. Only US citizens could have access to 'restricted data' – information concerned with the use of atomic weapons and the production of fissionable material.

This severely cut the amount of data the British Mission at Los Alamos could access and saw a steady drift of scientists, including Fuchs in 1946, back to research, or academia in Britain. Fuchs had emerged over a five-year period as the key atomic scientist spying for the KGB. He had worked overtime at Los Alamos, helping in as many areas apart from his own speciality as time would allow, and his departure was a major blow to the Russians. The KGB would either have to increase its espionage in the US, or find other ways of obtaining data from the new AEC.

Controls had urgent discussions with their top agents in the US and Britain. In the US, more was required from the agents coded PERSEUS, BULL, SHOT and TIFF, as well as conduits such as Gold, Greenglass and the Rosenbergs. Amongst the now excluded foreigners, only one, Rothschild, had the flexibility and connections to adjust to the new dilemma. He had used the brilliant ploy of making himself security inspector during the war, now he had to find an excuse to visit Washington and the AEC.[4]

This time, through his friendship with the head of the British Mission, physicist James Chadwick, he had himself appointed as a special liaison with American scientists concerning the development of a dubious new atomic weapon based on releasing radioactive material.[5]

An American scientist had thought of using the radioactivity from the cyclotron – the nuclear accelerator for producing a stream of electrically charged atoms or nuclei travelling at a very high speed – in a bomb. This could destroy the human population of a large city.[6]

Some of the British scientists, such as Oliphant, were against it, but US General Leslie R. Groves, head of the Manhattan Project, wanted it to be considered in depth. He ordered Chadwick, Oliphant, Rothschild and others not to say anything in Britain about the possible new bomb in case the discovery became public.[7]

Rothschild was a friend of the Chairman of the AEC, Admiral Lewis Strauss, and made several trips to the US. He combined his liaison work with US scientists, which broadened from the consideration of the hideous new radioactive bomb to fallout in general, with his other roles such as his position on the Anglo-American Commission on Palestine.

Rothschild was given access in his scientific role to major atomic weapons secrets, but he couldn't stay in Washington to monitor AEC–Manhattan Project progress. He hoped to persuade the Americans to ignore or avoid the McMahon Act and to return to the 'spirit of cooperation' engendered between the two nations during the war after the agreements between Churchill and Roosevelt. However, there was a new mood in Washington under President Harry Truman, who was against sharing, not the least because he was suspicious of the new Labour government under Clement Attlee. He was aware of some of the current cabinet members' efforts to improve relations with the British Communist Party before the war. Truman's appointees at places such as the AEC were of a like mind.

Nevertheless, Rothschild lobbied Strauss concerning the proposed shut-off of US atomic secrets under the McMahon Act. On one visit, Strauss arranged a dinner for him with several other senior military and scientific personnel. Rothschild again raised the subject of exchange of atomic secrets. The Americans became 'edgy'.[8]

Strauss had been quiet on the subject when he suddenly responded in front of the gathering at the end of the dinner:

'Why should we let you have secret information when you've got Mr John Strachey, a communist, as War Minister?'

Strachey had been a frequent visitor to Bentinck Street during the war and was more than an acquaintance of Burgess and Rothschild.

'So that's what's bothering you,' a stunned Rothschild eventually replied.

'Yes, and you can tell the Prime Minister.'

'I can assure you and everyone else,' Rothschild said, trying to salvage some ground, 'that the information I have will not go to him [Strachey].'[9]

The Americans accepted the assurance, but were not impressed. Rothschild informed Attlee, who addressed his cabinet on the matter, warning them off any association with the Communist Party.

By 1947, not even Rothschild was allowed access to AEC data, although the KGB still had an 'in' via Donald Maclean, who had been appointed as Secretary to the British Delegation on the Combined Policy Committee. The Committee determined the nuclear policy of the US, Britain and Canada in tandem, but as the McMahon Act had thwarted meaningful cooperation on the important secrets, it was a lame duck.

At this point there was a marked lull in top nuclear intelligence coming through to the Centre. Beria was desperate. It didn't seem that the Soviets could deliver the much-desired bomb for Stalin. Beria had instructions and letters sent to scientists such as the Dane, Niels Bohr, who had been helpful before, asking for the latest research data. Bohr sent a message back saying that the Americans had denied him access. [10]

Beria gave instructions to London and Washington that more had to be done. With guidance from Rothschild and others Maclean could gather 'basic scientific data' from the AEC, such as the type and amount of raw materials used, the weight of bombs, and patents, which were filed in order to legally protect any device or process developed at Los Alamos.[11]

Maclean had been issued by the AEC with a 'permanent pass to the Commissioners' Headquarters'. He made at least twelve visits, five of them at night according to AEC records, between June 1947 and his departure for an appointment in Cairo a year later.

A later AEC damage assessment found he had access to estimates of uranium ore supply and requirement forecasts for the period 1948–52, although these later turned out to be inaccurate.[12]

Pressure on the KGB increased after America's successful tests at Bikini Atoll in the Pacific. They revived Russian fears about their own capacities and Beria began to fret that the Soviet Union would never detonate anything like the American productions. However, in 1947 the indefatigable Fuchs, who was at Britain's atomic research station at Harwell, was able to furnish Beria with refined details of the plutonium route to the bomb, which had first been supplied in principle by Rothschild in 1943.

Fuchs had not originally worked in the plutonium field, but after the explosion of the 'Fat Man' bomb over Nagasaki and his transfer from Birmingham to Los Alamos, he garnered – with Oppenheimer's acquiescence – as much data on the alternative weapon technology as possible. Everyone in the Manhattan Project remembered Fuchs's extraordinary diligence and selflessness in helping out in areas outside his expertise.

By late 1947, Igor Kurchatov, who directed scientific work on the bomb, was so sure that the Russian scientists finally had the technical skills to build the weapon that he took the nuclear charge of the first proposed Soviet atomic bomb – a nickel-plated plutonium ball about ten centimetres in diameter – to Stalin in his study at the Kremlin.

'And how do we know that this is plutonium, not a sparkling piece of iron?' Stalin asked. 'And why this glitter? Why this window dressing?'

'The charge has been nickel-plated so that it would be safe to touch,' Kurchatov replied. 'Plutonium is very toxic, but nickel-plated it's safe.'

Stalin handled it. He noticed its heat.

'Is it always warm?' he asked.

'It always is,' Kurchatov replied. 'The continuous nuclear reaction of alpha-disintegration is underway inside. It warms up. But we shall excite a powerful fission reaction in it. This will be an explosion of great power.'[13]

Stalin was not completely convinced but he later authorized the testing of the first bomb. It was to take until September 1949.

17. MR MODIN GOES
TO LONDON

AVOIDING THE WATCHERS

In late June 1947, Modin flew to London via Paris with Anne, his wife of one year, and their young baby Olga. On the first night of their stop in the French capital, the family stayed at the Soviet Embassy on Rue de Grenelle, where V. M. Molotov was also staying. The Soviet Foreign Minister was in Paris for a special conference of all European countries to discuss a joint European programme of mutual self-help to be prepared by an Anglo–French–Russian committee.

Modin, then twenty-four, immediately went to work translating reports from Guy Burgess, who was with the British Foreign Office team. This political espionage allowed Molotov to go to his meetings with a complete background picture of what the British were saying in public and thinking in private about the issues.

Molotov upset the conference by rejecting the Anglo-French initiative, which provided for the recovery of Germany rather than forcing the defeated enemy to pay war reparations.

On the first night in Paris, baby Olga cried all night, keeping Molotov awake. He complained the next morning and the Modin family was removed from the Embassy.

'We were put in one of Paris's best hotels on the Rue de Rivoli,' Modin recalled with a chuckle. 'We learned that Westerners were not quite as deprived as we were told in Moscow.'[1]

Early in July, the family moved on to London to begin an open-ended assignment. It could last a few months or years, depending on the young spy's performance in the field. It was not Modin's first visit. In 1945, he had stayed for ten days with the World Democratic

Youth Organization, a Communist front which was used to recruit young agents.

That had given him a look at the war-torn capital, which was still luxurious compared with home. He was even more impressed with the recovery, improved living standards and life in general in 1947. Despite an early attack of homesickness, both he and Anne found some pleasurable advantages in London living.

'We could take a taxi somewhere, go to art galleries and dine in nice restaurants,' Modin said. 'These things were just unheard of in Moscow.'

The Modins improved their English by going to the cinema.

'We went every day we could,' Modin remembered with a laugh. 'I became an expert and critic on the films of Greta Garbo, Vivien Leigh and Laurence Olivier.'

They also went to the theatre, watched village cricket and the tennis at Wimbledon and even attended the annual Oxford–Cambridge boat race.

When asked whom he supported, Modin looked cagey.

'Arh, now that would be telling!' he replied, his ruddy face swelling and his shoulders waggling as he laughed heartily.

He and Anne were trained to cultivate the British Establishment. This could take years, but the KGB objective was simple. All agents had to focus on ingratiating themselves with people in positions of power and influence from parliament, the bureaucracy, the press, society, business, science and academia.[2]

Communists, socialists and those with left or Soviet-leaning sympathies were prime targets, but the KGB did not limit themselves. Even staff at Buckingham Palace were approached, especially with the influential Anthony Blunt employed and available to help facilitate an appreciation of all things Soviet.

The Soviet Embassy organized social functions around cultural exchanges, parties to celebrate the 1917 October Revolution, British–Soviet joint 'enterprises', in fact any excuse for meeting the nation's power elite.

The Western press in London, which included locals, Americans and other European correspondents, was cultivated. The KGB made a few early post-war 'hits' with journalists from leading broadsheets, who were willing to take secret payments for the cause.

The recruited journalists were different from newspeople acting as agents of influence, who were expected to insert pro-Soviet propaganda in their stories. Instead, this group were directed to report on off-the-record briefings, especially in the area of military and defence. Modin, whose cover was a 'press attaché', felt the potential in this area had not been exploited.

His main mission, however, was to develop into a leading agent-runner – a Control. He was about to put into practice the considerable knowledge he had of the top British agents working for the Russians. Modin had studied their files until he knew them as well as if they were members of his own family.

'I was especially thrilled to work on Burgess's reports in Paris,' he said, 'although I did not meet him at that point. It was exciting to see how this [spying and supplying data for immediate use] operated at first hand, and to be part of it. I knew his style so well. His reports were thoughtful, layered and clear – easy to translate. He was by then a great pro, despite his reputation as a disreputable, drunken, homosexual philanderer. People like Molotov didn't care much about that as long as the foreign minister was being so brilliantly informed in advance when dealing with Western leaders.'

Before Modin could be activated as a Control he had to settle in at the London Embassy and learn the tradecraft of how to operate in a major Western city. He spent weeks familiarizing himself with the underground, bus routes and streets with as much diligence as a taxi driver. His career depended on it. If he was caught and expelled early on, his first mission could be his last.

His first boss and mentor was the KGB Resident, Konstantin Kukin, the man in charge of all KGB operations in Britain. In many ways, he was secretly more important and powerful than the Soviet Ambassador. But the exercise of power depended on the character of the KGB man. Kukin, on assignment since 1943, was considered by many to be a 'narrow-minded bureaucrat', who kept his distance from the Ambassador and showed him due deference.[3]

Modin was taught the fundamentals of avoiding the 'watchers', the MI5 agents assigned to follow him each day to the office and home at night. It seemed strange at first, to always find them waiting for him at the same bus-stop near his flat in Notting Hill Gate and following him to the Soviet Embassy in nearby Kensington Palace Gardens. It worried Anne, who was also followed, even when she went shopping with the baby. She complained to the Soviet Ambassador.

'Don't be concerned,' he responded. 'Think of them as your bodyguards. You are unlikely to come to any harm in London with them there to protect you!'

The Modins got to know the faces of the MI5 men, who always dressed the same in their dark suits. Modin began to have breakfast in a small cafe near the Embassy. This must have pleased his watchers who began to turn up there too.[4]

Soon Modin found himself in conflict with Kukin, who was more concerned with administration than his real job of running and extracting data from the top British agents. Modin was one of three agents at the Embassy processing data coming in from them. It was no longer just microfilm, but also real stolen documents. He had to classify and photograph them before the Controls returned them to the British spies, who put them back in their original safes and drawers.

Modin also clashed with Ivan Milovzorov, the directing officer for the top Five agents and others since Gorsky had been moved to Washington to look after Maclean. His heavy-handed, brusque ways had caused him to fall out with all of them. Modin was appalled. He appreciated how great the top agents had been and he felt embarrassed and depressed by the authoritarian and neglectful way they were being treated.

'With Kukin as boss and Milovzorov the top Control,' Modin reflected, 'we were not gathering all the espionage material we could have. They were underachieving bureaucrats, with no sensitivity to their agents' needs, desires and potential.'

After a few months, Modin's luck changed, when a more amenable, urbane KGB Resident, Nikolai Rodin (alias Korovin), took over from Kukin. Rodin was not the diplomatic bureaucrat his predecessor had been and he would, on occasions, show his arrogance by taking the Ambassador's car spot at the Embassy, daring a challenge.

Yet Rodin appreciated the British agents, having spent time at the Centre during the war. He realized their value and that they had not been utilized nearly enough since 1945. He set out to change the attitudes and work rate of his Controls. More translators and processors of espionage material were brought into the Embassy.

Rodin liked to delegate and saw the young Modin as potentially a fine Control. 'He knew that I knew more about the top agents than anyone,' Modin mused. 'But he did not know if I could direct them. I had to be tested.'

MEETING THE LEGENDS

Soon after arriving in early 1948, Rodin decided it was time for Modin to meet and run a British agent in the field.

John Cairncross was the choice. He was considered 'dead', of little or no importance to the KGB, although he had served them well in the war years. The whole KGB culture in 1948 was geared to gathering data on the atomic bomb, any information at all which would inch the Soviet Union towards its first detonation and then mass production of the weapon. This meant learning about everything from the supply of uranium raw material to the various technologies needed en route to an explosion. Cairncross was in the finance department at the Treasury and there didn't seem to be anything he could steal that was relevant. If Modin botched this assignment or even got himself caught with Cairncross, there would be little lost, except to Modin himself as a failed Control.

Modin was nervous about the first rendezvous at the Grove Tavern in Hammersmith. Even the less important Cairncross was a legend in Modin's mind for the work he had done, especially over the Battle of the Kursk.

'I was in awe of him,' Modin recalled over a glass of malt whisky from a bottle I had given him as a gift. 'I also didn't like the environment [in the pub]. People stared. If you weren't a local, who were you? Their glances showed some suspicion. And I couldn't eat anything. I wanted to concentrate all my energies on the meeting.

'Rodin was different, as were other agents. They could relax, eat and drink. I was more cautious. I just couldn't concentrate in a pub. I preferred the anonymity of the street. I liked being on the move in the open – a park, a road. Especially in the shadows of the night.'

When he met Cairncross he showed his nerves but the serious Scot put him at ease and chatted amiably to him. Modin immediately felt beholden to him. He wanted to use this supposedly retired agent but how should he reactivate him?

After the introduction, the two planned to meet again a fortnight later. Cairncross preferred a day-time rendezvous so they arranged to see each other in the street near a church, not far from the pub in Hammersmith Grove.

Modin's mind was concentrated by the watchers, who were furious that he had given them the slip the previous day. The next morning, three of them turned up outside his apartment looking menacing. They followed him more closely than ever and didn't let him out of their sight until he walked into the Soviet Embassy.

But they were the least of his worries. Modin spent the two weeks wondering how he could get Cairncross operating again.

On the day of the next meeting, he followed his tradecraft to perfection, again slipping away two hours earlier at 6 a.m. in order to avoid the watchers, who would probably not have an agent on the job so early in the morning. In order to play safe, in case one dawn tail had been assigned to him, Modin travelled systematically for five hours until he took a bus to Hammersmith. He was nervous, but certain no one had managed to tail him for long, if at all.

They met as planned. Modin quizzed Cairncross about his office at the Treasury. He questioned him for half an hour as they walked the street, stopped in a park, sat for a while on a bench and moved on. Cairncross became fidgety, then testy.

'I really can't procure anything like the data I could before,' Cairncross kept saying. All the time, Modin was assessing whether the spy still had the stomach for the work. Was he shell-shocked from too many risks taken during the war, or was there a deeper, untapped reservoir of desire to perform in their nerve-racking, clandestine business?

'Could you get me the internal directory?' Modin asked.

Cairncross was bemused by the request but agreed. At the next meeting the two spies went through the directory. Again Modin queried him. What is this woman's function? Do you know her? Who is this man? What is the scope of his work?

Finally the Russian asked about the other man in Cairncross's office.

'Oh, he works in budget assessment for Britain's nuclear weapons programme.'

The two agents stared at one another. Without expressing it, they knew what had to be done.

'Has he a safe?' Modin asked.

'Yes, but it's locked.'

Cairncross stole a key, had it copied and prepared to steal from the safe. His reactivation put an extra spring in the Scot's step, for he was more excited by working for the cause than anything else in life. There had been a three-year lapse since his last mission and five since his exhaustive effort at Bletchley Park over the Battle of the Kursk. He was refreshed, ready and eager.

Then came disappointment. Before he could open the safe, Cairncross was transferred to the personnel and planning section of the department which planned the finance of the defence industry. However, this proved fruitful for the KGB since the section's brief included NATO, which was due to be formally established in 1949. Modin felt he had triumphed:

'Every day, Cairncross had his hands on files concerning the manpower of future NATO forces, the part each nation would play, the equipment they would use from fatigues to tanks, and the positioning of garrisons in Europe and elsewhere.'[4]

The frowning, hard-working Scot eventually stole the proposal for NATO's entire structure.

'I had struck, if not gold, then silver,' Modin said.

However, Cairncross was not easy to run, despite the two building up a strong bond of trust and friendship.

'He was easily distracted from the job and forgetful,' Modin recalled. 'He also lacked attention to detail. He had some strange quirks.'

The KGB decided Cairncross should have a car. Modin gave him some money but his charge kept turning up on foot.

'When are you going to get a vehicle?' Modin asked him.

'I bought a Vauxhall,' Cairncross replied and added balefully, 'I haven't got a driving licence.'

'Are you going to get one?'

'I've failed the test three times.'

The Scot finally gained his licence, but Modin discovered why it had taken so many attempts when they decided to go on a trip outside London for a talk. They met in Chelsea's Sloane Square and were driving around it when Cairncross stalled the Vauxhall. He tried everything but could not get it started.

Modin became anxious. He noticed a policeman standing in a doorway with his eye on the vehicle.

'He walked from his post to us,' Modin said. 'He motioned for John to get out and then sat in the driver's seat. He played with the choke and a few other things and then got it started. He got out and returned to his doorway. He did not say a word in the entire incident. But I was petrified he would speak to me, ask questions and hear my accent. I am sure he would have been suspicious.'

Despite near calamities such as this, Cairncross again proved a useful agent. While he would never achieve the heights of the Kursk data, he once more served the KGB with distinction.

Modin was commended by Rodin for his first up achievement. If he kept up such a standard he would be introduced to some members of the top Five and other important spies. Modin was delighted. He had expected to leave the KGB at the end of the war, but had stayed on. He felt, at that moment, that he had a career for life.[5]

IN EXTROVERT COMPANY

Before long, Rodin felt Modin was ready to be one of the Controls running Burgess and Blunt, two of the top Five, who were also on the slide after years of great, enduring and at times brilliant service. He met Burgess in a park in the London suburb of Ruislip at 6 p.m. on a winter's night. With each new agent, Modin would work out a routine should they be questioned by police.

'That's no problem, old boy,' Burgess said. 'You're a very good looking chap. Just pretend we are lovers on a date.'

Modin stared at Burgess, who at thirty-seven was already showing the signs of his debauchery and alcoholism. Burgess laughed.

'I'm serious,' he said. 'With my track record across London, it's the best excuse.'

Modin liked Burgess a great deal and quickly regarded him as a good friend.

'He was stimulating, engaging and fun despite his escapades and unpredictable character,' Modin remembered.

Burgess considered himself a 'fully-fledged Soviet agent' who was working for world revolution. His new Russian Control was impressed by his knowledge of Soviet ideology – a subject in which Modin considered he himself had considerable expertise.[6]

They met once a month, but this was stepped up to each day in a 'crisis' such as the Western conferences over the Marshall Plan, or when the problems in Berlin became more urgent. The data Burgess was stealing grew to such proportions that he ended up carrying it in a regulation-size suitcase, Modin told me with a smile.

Modin gave him money to buy a car, so he would not have to lug around the pilfered load. Unlike Cairncross, Burgess didn't need further encouragement. He bought a second-hand, yellow Rolls Royce, which added to his outrageous image. In its own way, it was a clever cover for his clandestine work.

Yet his double role was also nearly discovered. Once, after Control Boris Krotov had met Burgess in the Grove Tavern, Krotov was walking to the door of the pub to leave when the suitcase snapped open and documents marked TOP SECRET were strewn over the floor. Burgess bounced from his chair and helped Krotov and other customers to pick up the documents.

'Thank you, old boy, very kind of you,' Burgess repeated to the other drinkers as they stuffed the papers back in the suitcase. His cheerful, polite manner distracted attention from the terror on Krotov's face.[7]

On another occasion, Burgess was strolling with Modin on Ealing Common, suitcase in hand, when a policeman approached them.

'I'll have to have a look in that, if you don't mind, sir,' he said.

'Of course. Not at all, officer,' Burgess replied, placing the suitcase on the ground and opening it. Modin began to shake with fear. The policeman took out all the papers, some of them again marked TOP SECRET, gave them a cursory glance and ran his hands over the suitcase's lining, looking for hidden compartments. He placed the papers back and nodded respectfully.

'Thank you, sir,' he said and marched away.

Modin was incredulous.

'Don't worry about it old boy,' Burgess said with a nervous grin. 'These suitcases are similar to those used by London burglars. There's been a spate of break-ins recently. He would have been looking for stolen goods — important things like watches, money, jewellery . . .'

Burgess looked at Modin's drained expression and laughed.[8]

BURGESS THE BELLIGERENT

Matters became more problematic during 1948 as Burgess began drinking more heavily. He picked fights with colleagues at the Foreign Office, his friends and even Modin.

'We forgave him,' Modin recalled, 'because he delivered. His brawling and nastiness still worked as a front. He was the only spy we had who made a public spectacle of himself regularly. No one, not a friend, not a superior, absolutely *no one* suspected him.'

The incidents increased but his boss, the Under-Secretary of State, Hector McNeil, was reluctant to reprimand Burgess, whom he relied on as an adviser who wrote brilliant reports. When he was finally forced to get rid of him, he helped him into the Far East Section of the Intelligence Service.

Burgess was downgraded, but still managed to furnish the Russians with important analysis of the attitudes of the Americans and the British towards China.

'The quality of his work never dropped,' Modin said, 'and I think he was happiest sitting down and analysing things. But when he wasn't, he got into trouble. His nerves were beginning to fray. He had become a chronic alcoholic. On top of that he had been under excessive pressure for nearly fifteen years playing a role.'[9]

Burgess's bravado, his skill at presenting a front, had taken its toll.

'It was partly my job, to encourage him, give him moral support,' Modin went on. 'I kept reinforcing his importance, the value of his espionage and his reports. He was very flattered when I told him how good I thought his writing was. I used to say he should write novels. He liked that idea, and I think dreamed of retiring to do so.'

Modin's youthful tenacity, sensitivity and genuine respect for Burgess and his work for the cause kept him running years longer than Krotov, Rodin, Miloszorov or even the tenacious Gorsky could have managed. But there was a limit. It was reached in 1949.

During the summer Burgess managed to get into brawls with other MI6 officers in Tangiers and Gibraltar over American Intelligence officers from the OSS and the newly-formed CIA, whom he abused. In August, while drunk and driving through a village in Ireland, he ran over and killed a pedestrian. His passenger, another Intelligence man, ended up badly injured and in hospital. Once more, Burgess was able to use his contacts in high places to cover up his lapse.

'I was under some pressure over all this,' Modin remembered, 'because the Chiefs in Moscow were becoming scared. They worried about his atrocious behaviour and such incidents, but were silenced by his magnificent reports. Yet there was always the fear, with all of us, that he would do something completely over-the-top and expose the other key agents in the Cambridge Ring.'

A SMOOTH BEGINNING

Rodin introduced Blunt to Modin soon after Burgess and they also found a certain rapport, although Blunt was less friendly. The Palace's art expert had been the key conduit to the Controls for Burgess, Leo Long, another Cambridge man and Bletchley Park Intelligence supplier, and most importantly, Rothschild. Blunt also had to steal the diplomatic correspondence of foreign governments, such as the French and the Poles, in exile in the UK. This allowed him to inform the KGB what these politicians were thinking about the English, the Russians and the Americans.

'We could then take advantage of their differences,' Modin remembered.

'Whatever the data (bomb technology, Bletchley Park decrypts, confessions of interrogated Nazis and so on),' Modin went on, 'Blunt brought all the skills of the mathematician and artist to his reports.'

The Control explained further that this meant he would often assist the other agents in the presentation of their espionage material by applying his drawing skills to help the Centre and Russian scientists understand new material. This applied, for instance, to bomb technology, which he would attempt to comprehend, using his knowledge of higher mathematics, in conjunction with the supplying agent.[10]

Blunt was also adept at gathering information from informal chats, not just Whitehall gossip, with contacts in the Intelligence services.

'Rothschild introduced Blunt to Dick White [one-time head of both MI5 and MI6] and Guy Liddell,' Modin said, 'and Gorsky directed Blunt to cultivate these relationships.'[11] During the war this not only led to employment in Intelligence for Blunt, but the continuous flow of secrets to Russia. Modin wanted to open up those spying channels again.

'During impromptu discussions [in the post-war years] on art and politics with White and Liddell,' Modin revealed, 'Blunt quite effortlessly picked up a lot of information. He learnt, for example, everything that English counter-espionage was doing against the Soviet Union or against the Communist Party [of the UK]. White even told him where the telephones were tapped, who the agitators attached to Soviet diplomats were.'

Agitators were Russian double agents placed by MI5. White also told him which of the Russians based at the Embassy MI5 aimed to turn into its spies. 'White and Liddell continued for a number of years to tell Blunt a great deal, without any reservations.'

This unrestrained 'unburdening' of secrets to both Blunt and Rothschild continued in the atmosphere of the leading London Conservative clubs such as Pratt's and the Athenaeum long after the war. Everything of interest was passed on to Modin.

Even Blunt's early tasks at MI5 continued to be useful to the Russians for decades after he had carried them out. For instance, he organized the operations of the watchers.

'He had to go out with them and follow *us*,' Modin said with a wry grin. 'Then he wrote a sort of handbook on how they should do it, and how to better their operations.'

Blunt's handbook was used by British agents.

'It was also used by the KGB,' Modin remarked with a chuckle.

Blunt made the KGB believe that he could be of use at the Palace after the war when he became 'keeper of the King's paintings.' But Blunt over-played his connections in the Royal household and in reality interesting information dried up. The main problem was the neglect of this special agent after the war by successive Controls.

When Modin was first introduced early in 1948, he was not KGB 'operational'. Modin decided to reactivate him. The Russian felt more 'secure' meeting Blunt, compared to Cairncross who was forgetful, and Burgess who was careless. Blunt had literally written the rules on the watchers. He knew exactly how MI5 operated, and even who might be assigned to follow Modin. They never had any problems with shadows.

However, Blunt was not an easy assignment. The aloof Englishman had become sceptical of Marxist dogma and Soviet 'imperialism'. He hated the repression in Hungary, Poland, and
Czechoslovakia.

'At an early meeting, I was told to inform him about Soviet
foreign policy,' Modin said. 'I probably went on too long, but he
listened to my exposition politely without saying a word. When I
had completed what I had to say he looked up briefly – he wasn't in
the habit of looking people in the eye – then glanced away.'

'Have you finished?' Blunt asked.

'Yes.'

'Peter [Modin's alias], I don't want you to lecture me on Soviet
foreign policy again,' he told him coldly. 'I don't believe it, I don't
care for it. I don't see it as much better than ours. I think it's an
aberration. The imperialist attitude in Eastern Europe will no doubt
pass, therefore I will look ahead, knowing it will improve.'

When Modin protested his analysis, Blunt became angry.

'Your current regime is not only imperialistic,' he said, 'it's Tsarist.
Its actions are not in the peoples' interests.'[12]

Blunt knew this was insulting to the young agent and his bosses.
'Tsarist' and 'imperialist' were epithets reserved for those attacked
in the Stalin-instigated show trials in the 1930s in Moscow, and in
Eastern Europe in the late 1940s. The latter had upset Blunt by
their transparent falsehood.

After this, Modin knew where he stood with Blunt, whom he
admired more than any other agent – except for the Fifth Man – for
his cool nerve. He remained a 'faithful servant' of the cause.

Blunt's status in Britain also improved when he was appointed
Director of the Courtauld Institute, one of the world's finest schools
for training art historians. Modin felt Blunt was inspired by his new
missions, which included exploiting the quarrels between MI5 and
MI6. Blunt pretended to side with MI5, his old employer, and
delighted in hearing gossip and intrigue about rival agents in MI6
and their operations. He would use this in discussions with MI6
contacts and learn more about MI5 business. As MI6 was largely
responsible for operations run against Soviets outside Britain, such
as tracking submarines or bugging Communist embassies, the KGB
wanted anything on what MI6 agents were up to.

It was not difficult for Blunt. That MI5 and MI6 hated each other was ackowledged by many in the services, including David Cornwell, alias John Le Carré, who worked for MI5, and later MI6.

'A sister service existed, I was told,' Le Carré wrote in *The Times* in August 1993, 'but it spied abroad and was full of shits. We called it "Six", or "The Friends", or more amiably "Those Sods Across the Park". We never called it the Secret Intelligence Service, which was its name.

'And in a way it was natural that we should affect to hate our sister service, because "Six" was trying to do to other countries what the Reds were trying to do to us: subvert, seduce and penetrate. Quite soon, a custodian's indignation infected my approach to SIS and, without knowing anything about them, I shared the common view that they were an untrustworthy, godless crowd . . .'[13]

The conflict within the Intelligence Services brought out the 'bitchiness' in Blunt, according to another contemporary of his connected to MI6. 'Anthony loved gossip, especially if it could be damaging.'[14]

Burgess influenced Blunt into returning to the Intelligence world.

'Burgess had an enormous hold on him,' Modin explained. 'It continued until Burgess's death.'

The Russian asked Burgess to 'work on' Blunt and make him feel it was his duty to continue his 'great' effort from the war.

The combined effort of Modin's cajolery and Burgess's urging succeeded. Blunt was fully reactivated a few months after meeting Modin in 1948. The Russians again began using him as the liaison dealing with the other key agents, including Burgess, Maclean, Philby, Rothschild and Cairncross.

Modin did not meet Philby or Maclean in this period, but he still acted as their Control, however remote at times. He was in direct contact with Rothschild, sometimes at official Soviet functions.

There was a long-standing KGB protocol involved with handling agents, which included making the covert relationship between the agent and his Control an overt one, if possible. According to former KGB agent, Oleg Gordievsky, who gave evidence in a Canberra committal hearing against a former ASIO (Australian Secret Intelligence Organization) officer, George Sadil, in February 1994, this 'could be done by keeping in regular contact with the agent through the Russian Embassy and social functions to take the suspicious element out of the relationship.'[15]

As Rothschild publicly lobbied the Soviets for support in helping create Israel, his meetings at Soviet events in London, even at the Embassy, did not arouse suspicion. Rothschild was well-known as a Jewish activist since his Lords speeches before and after the war. His leftist, socialist politics were also well known. Although Rothschild spoke with Modin about his concerns over Palestine, he dealt directly with Rodin when he lobbied for support.[16]

18. MASTER OF THE BACK-CHANNEL

MIDWIFE TO A NATION

Late in July 1993, I had interviews with ex-KGB Colonel 'F',
including one at the Kasbah of the Intourist Hotel, which was not a
top quality place like the Metropole or Savoy. Russians and those
from the newly independent Republics frequented it more than
foreigners. The bar area had a sleazy ambience, the atmosphere
enhanced by the hazy light which was all that could penetrate
through a high windowed dome, especially when it was pouring,
which was often.

It was private enough for meetings, with tables placed at discreet
distances from each other, and was known for its coffee, the best in
Moscow. London papers came in late in the afternoon, when the
interviews were conducted.

The Colonel, who preferred not to have his name mentioned, was
heavy-set and of medium height. He would not say his age, but
looked to be in his mid-seventies. Like Modin, he was polite and
well mannered, but with less of a sense of humour. He had worked
abroad for the KGB and had held a senior position at the Moscow
Centre, characterizing himself as 'a demanding chief'. He had
specialized in KGB Middle East operations.

The Colonel smoked Western cigarettes, and had two whiskies,
which he described as 'medicinal', before joining me for coffee. Like
Modin, he seemed to be ailing, and was brought to and taken from
the hotel by a figure who did not appear in my presence.

Again like Modin, and some of the other five key interviewees
from the KGB, the Colonel knew much about Rothschild. He was
familiar with his career since the 1930s, and there was a pronounced

respect for him in his rasping voice, as there was with Modin and the others.

'No one worked harder [in support of Israel] than Lord Rothschild,' the Colonel remarked. '[The rest of] his family were active in several countries and more public. But he knew the proper back-channels to reach decision-makers in Moscow. And he did.'

Whom did he reach? Beria? Gromyko? Stalin?

'Let us just say he got things done,' the Colonel replied. 'You only did that if you reached the top. He was very persuasive.'

How?

'He and others reminded us that any Jewish State would be strongly socialist. We would have another supporting state in public forums, such as the United Nations. He also reminded us of Great Britain's pro-Arab policy in the Middle East. If Israel was formed it would upset [Britain's] Imperialist activity in the region.'

This naturally pleased the KGB?

'It was an interesting development, which fitted Soviet foreign policy at the time . . . Lord Rothschild asked for our support in the United Nations [regarding Israel's formation]. We were the first nation to vote in support of it, with certain conditions.'[1]

Andrei Gromyko, Soviet Ambassador to the UN in 1947, made a speech supporting a Jewish State. This helped lead to the formulation of Resolution 181, which decreed the partition of Palestine into two states, Jewish and Arab.

On 29 November 1947, the General Assembly of the UN voted on the partition and it was accepted by 33 votes to 13, with ten abstentions – Britain being one of them. All six Independent Arab States voted against the plan, as did Afghanistan, Cuba, Greece, Iran, Pakistan and Turkey. Amongst those who favoured partition were the USSR, the US, Australia, Canada, France, The Netherlands, New Zealand, Poland and Sweden.

The situation brought great joy to Jews everywhere and no one expressed it better than a young Palestinian-born Jew, Moshe Dayan, who wrote in his memoirs:

I felt in my bones the victory of Judaism, which for two thousand years of exile from the Land of Israel had withstood persecutions, the Spanish Inquisition, pogroms, anti-Jewish decrees, restrictions, and the mass slaughter by the Nazis in our own generation, and had reached the fulfilment of its age-old yearning – the return to a free and Independent Zion.

We were happy that night [of the UN vote], and we danced and our heart went out to every nation whose UN representative had voted in favour of the Resolution. We had heard them utter the magic word 'yes' as we followed their voices over the air-waves from thousands of miles away. We danced – but we knew that ahead of us lay the battlefield.[2]

That battlefield, in fact, lay all around Israel as the Arab nations surrounding it – TransJordan, Lebanon, Syria and Iraq – erupted in hatred. Months of vicious killing followed as all its hostile neighbours acted independently in attacking the 'aliens' attempting nationhood in their midst. The Jewish pre-Independence Army – the *Haganah* (defence) – hung on in the first four months of 1948.

Iraqi troops cut off Jerusalem's water supply and random attacks from both sides claimed four thousand lives. In the full-scale battles that developed during April between Arab and Jewish armed forces, Tiberias, Haifa, Acre, Safed and Jaffa were occupied by Jewish forces between 19 April and 14 May. In Jerusalem, Arab troops were driven from many suburbs.

The shortage of men and arms became critical. Behind the scenes, Rothschild, Chaim Weizmann and others connected with Jewish Intelligence networks, pushed for more refugees to be allowed to leave Russia and the Eastern Bloc.

'I remember Victor taking Chaim and others to the Soviet Embassy for discussions during this period,' a relative of Weizmann, recalled. 'He had the contacts. It wasn't always the Ambassador they saw.'[3]

Rothschild brought Rodin information about a proposed British withdrawal from Palestine, ending its thirty-year rule there, which pleased the Russians, and vindicated their actions in support of Israel. Rothschild kept urging Moscow to ease restrictions on Jews wishing to emigrate from Russia's satellite countries.

In those early critical months of 1948, Romania, Hungary and Poland permitted Jews to emigrate, adding to Israel's manpower. Since late 1947, Rothschild had also helped persuade the Soviets to sell arms to Israel and was able to specify sources, particularly in Czechoslovakia where he had discovered the abandoned supplies at the end of the war.[4]

The cost to the Jewish military was low. It was a buyer's market with war surplus material cached in about twenty countries. Until Rothschild interceded, the only buyers not allowed into the market were Zionists. Czech rifles, machine-guns and ammunition were bought and smuggled into Palestine in March by merchant ships, despite a British naval blockade.

'Some arms were flown non-stop from Czechoslovakia by a chartered American DC4 aircraft,' according to Gordon Levett, an ex-RAF pilot who fought in Israel's War of Independence. 'They landed at a secret strip in Palestine at night.'[5]

The Israelis did not have one military plane, and they became alarmed as the Syrians, Iraqis and Egyptians build up their airforces to more than 130 planes between them.

Thousands of aircraft, from Spitfires going for £200 to Lockheed Constellations at £8,000 were being auctioned worldwide, sometimes to souvenir hunters. But not to Zionists. In response, Mossad had made a secret deal with some Mexicans to smuggle P47 Thunderbolts from Panama, but it seemed to be floundering.

Ben Gurion, the Jewish elder statesman and guiding light for Israel, became impatient three weeks before the British were due to leave in mid-May. He approached Weizmann, who informed Rothschild who in turn relayed the need to Moscow. Once again the Czechs came to the rescue with an offer of ten Czech-built Messerschmitt 109G fighter aircraft, including guns, ammunition and spares for $44,000 each, with an option for a further fifteen.[6] Zatec, in Czechoslovakia, was to be the base for the airlift.

The operation had to be totally secret so as not to offend the US, who would have stopped the sale, especially as the situation in Berlin was threatening to spill over into conflict. Ben Gurion cancelled the Mexican negotiations for P47 Thunderbolts to be airlifted 9,000 miles from Panama. Instead, lighter, smaller Messerschmitt 109s were to be flown 2,200 miles under the cover of darkness.

The actual British withdrawal on 14 May encouraged the Arab nations. The armies of Egypt, TransJordan, Syria and the Lebanon massed on the southern, western and northern borders, prepared to invade the moment the British left. However, with an influx of volunteer soldiers from several countries, including Jews from Britain, to swell the Israeli army, a raw fighting spirit emerged. It had not been seen since the defeat of Simeon Bar Kokhba, the leader of the Jewish resistance, by the Roman forces more than 1,800 years earlier. The Jews were at last able and prepared to defend their sovereign rights.

On the morning of 14 May the last British High Commissioner left Jerusalem. In the afternoon, Ben Gurion, the new nation's Prime Minister and Minister of War, announced the birth of the Independent State of Israel.

Days later, there was a clandestine airlift from Czechoslovakia to the besieged fledgling nation, which flew in war material, including guns and dismantled Messerschmitt 109s. The offer for fifteen more planes was taken up and Zatec became the secret centre for collecting aircraft, spares and arms being smuggled from all over Europe.

In his book, *Flying Under Two Flags*, Gordon Levett wrote:

'The hotels, bars and cafés in the small square [of Zatec], which had echoed to the sound of *"Horst Wessel"* and *"Deutschland uber Alles"* when the Luftwaffe were at play, and the airfield down the road where they flew their Messerschmitt 109s into combat, were now the European base for the despised *Juden*.'

ANOTHER VOICE FOR THE
INTERNATIONALE

Rothschild's argument to the Soviets concerning why they should support Israel proved accurate. The British were forced out of the Middle East in another post-war recognition that the once mighty Empire did not have the will or resources to stretch to an influential presence in a troublespot.

Furthermore, Israel began life as a socialist state and was dominated by left-wing parties, which pleased the Soviets and made the US uneasy. The political complexion of the country was a natural reaction to fascism, which had set out to destroy the Jewish race. There was a bias towards the Soviet Union despite its long history of anti-Semitism, because in the final analysis, it had been the nation to sacrifice most in destroying Hitler, thus saving Judaism.

The kibbutz, the unique Israel farm cooperative, was based on the principle of sharing assets amongst members according to their needs. It was the embodiment of the communist dream never seen anywhere else in any advanced nation or country with socialist regimes, particularly Russia. 'Capitalism' and 'free market' were considered dirty words in the new state.

As Moshe Dayan had predicted, Israel's formation was just the beginning of the real fight for survival – a struggle which would draw Rothschild even closer to the aspirations of his race.

19. A BOMB FOR
THE FIVE

THE MISCALCULATION

The Soviet Union detonated its first atomic weapon – a plutonium
bomb – at a test-site in Kazakhstan on 29 September 1949. Now it
was the West's turn to feel the pressure of knowing that the enemy
had the power to obliterate it. The two-year-old CIA had predicted
it would be at least mid-1953 before the Russians could explode a
bomb, and the Agency became the initial scapegoat, though not
even the FBI escaped blame, as Hoover announced that the Russians
had only been successful because of spy-rings inside the US. In a
news conference in December 1949, he told reporters that the spy
rings had 'stolen the most important secrets ever known to mankind
and delivered them to the Soviet Union'.

Hoover was guessing. He had no way of knowing then that the
cumulative Western espionage data passed to Moscow from 1943 to
1949 had indeed led to Russia's first Western-style plutonium bomb.
Nor would he have been aware that the Soviet Union's physicists
were only a few years from developing their own fusion bomb,
which would put their destruction capabilities on a level with the
US.

The FBI Director caused panic in his nation, and other Western
countries, and transformed routine investigations into a spy-hunt. It
was his way of increasing his power, for as the chief spy hunter
inside the US he needed funds, expansion and more personnel, and
he got them.

In early October, the brilliant American cryptanalyst in the
US Army Security Agency (ASA), Meredith Gardner, furthered
Hoover's cause when he deciphered a KGB message of 1944, which

provided the first clue to uncovering the double agent Klaus Fuchs. The FBI passed the information on to British Intelligence.

An investigation began, which led by December to Fuchs, the then deputy scientific officer at Harwell. He confessed in January 1950, giving justification to Hoover's attempt to cause hysteria in the US. Full-scale spy catching had begun on both sides of the Atlantic.[1]

THE MENTOR AND FRIEND

It was in this suspicious, dangerous atmosphere that Kim Philby arrived in America in November 1949, to take up his new role as MI6 representative in Washington. He wasted no time in renewing his friendship with James Angleton, just turned thirty-two, at the CIA, and they lunched three times a fortnight.

'I was more than content to string him along,' Philby wrote in his memoirs. 'The greater the trust between us overtly, the less he would suspect covert action.'[2]

Angleton was still learning much from Philby, or so he thought. After every meeting or lunch Angleton would dictate a memo to his secretary, which detailed all the matters discussed. This way, over about eighteen months, Philby fed the unsuspecting American with disinformation, which built up to a large file and misled the CIA on every facet of Soviet espionage.

In return, Angleton informed his mentor about current CIA operations including those in Albania, the Baltic, the Ukraine, Turkey, West and East Germany. According to Leonard McCoy, former CIA deputy chief of counter-intelligence: 'We had agents parachuting in, floating in, walking in, boating in [to these countries]. Virtually all of these operations were complete failures. After the war we had also planted a whole stay-behind network of agents in eastern Europe. They were all rolled up [by the KGB].'[3]

Philby also monitored what amounted to a time-bomb for the Five and other Soviet agents, which was *Venona*, the Russian code-name for the several thousand KGB messages from the last year of the war being steadily deciphered by Gardner in Washington.

He had managed the breakthrough because of a combination of factors starting with the discovery of a cipher code-book left behind when Finnish troops attacked a Russian base in Finland in 1944. The retreating Russians had attempted to burn anything secret, but the charred remains of the book were found and ended up with the OSS.[4]

Secondly, also in 1944, the Russian KGB Resident in the Soviet Embassy in Washington had sent a telegram asking if they could use their secret 'one-time pads' more than once when sending messages because they had run out. A ship carrying fresh supplies from Russia across the Atlantic had been diverted by German submarines.

KGB messages were encoded by replacing each word by a five-digit number group obtained from the code-book. A cipher clerk would then add to each group of numbers (formerly a word) another five digit number obtained from a series of randomly generated numbers in the 'one-time pad'. If – as its name implies – the 'one-time pad' was used once only, the coded message was unbreakable.[5]

'The Resident was allowed to use the pad more than once,' Modin explained. 'The information concerned Anglo/US talks on the atomic bomb, but it wasn't urgent. It could have waited several months.'

In 1949, Modin and the Centre had known about Gardner's breakthrough for a year. They couldn't prevent it but they kept watch, hoping that agents such as Philby could warn others and save themselves before detection. The MI6 liaison officer would visit Gardner in his ASA office. Gardner remembered him smoking his pipe, looking over his shoulder and admiring the progress he was making with his deciphering of Russian messages.[6]

It was a matter of when, not if, the bomb would go off for at least one of the Five, which could lead to the exposure of them all.

COUNTDOWN

Modin had used Blunt to brief Philby before he went to Washington that an agent code-named HOMER had been detected. Blunt and Rothschild had learnt this from Dick White and Guy Liddell at MI5. At first it wasn't known if he was British or American and the British Intelligence chiefs had no idea yet that HOMER was Maclean.[7]

He had been given the code by a chief at the Moscow Centre because, according to Modin, he was 'a good, prolific writer', which was vague enough to give no clues whatever to HOMER's identity, although it became a whispering point in the British Intelligence services.[8]

'There were more than 200 suspects to begin with,' Modin recalled and added with a laugh: 'The FBI were investigating charladies and flunkeys and sending huge files of information to London. They seemed a long way from finding HOMER, but it was worrying. Then suddenly we learned it was down to thirty. That was right at the end of 1950. Three months later it was down to nine or ten. We had to make plans.'

Philby, at Modin's indirect suggestion via his Control in Washington, fuelled misleading speculation by referring to evidence of a pre-war defector – Krivitsky – which suggested there was a well-bred and educated (Eton and Oxford) agent in the Foreign Office. Suspicion eased away from Maclean (Cambridge) and towards Paul Gore-Booth (Eton and Oxford), a future Permanent Under-Secretary at the Foreign Office.

In mid-April 1951, Gardner came up with another important decrypt. It revealed that for a time in 1944, HOMER had met his KGB Controller twice a week in New York, travelling there from Washington on the pretext of visiting his pregnant wife. This conformed to only one profile – that of Maclean.

Philby was the first of the Russian network to know (Blunt had been unable to learn if the suspects had been narrowed to less than nine). He decided to send Burgess from Washington back to London to warn Maclean and Modin. Maclean had been posted to Cairo in 1948. Successive drinking bouts led to a nervous breakdown early in May 1950, when he was sent back to London for treatment. After six months, he was made head of the FO's American department in London.

Burgess had arrived in the American capital in August 1950 after a string of outrageous incidents in Britain, Ireland, Africa and Gibraltar. If he failed again, his career in the diplomatic service would be over. Now Philby (at whose home he had been staying) was asking him to leave and warn the beleaguered Maclean.

Burgess suggested there was only one way to go back and be above suspicion, and that was to be 'true to form'. He went out, got drunk, sped around Washington and Virginia and made passes at the police who chased his vehicle. When caught he rudely waved his diplomatic pass under the noses of the police, who complained to the State Department and the British Ambassador.[9] Burgess's car was taken from him and he knew he would soon be dismissed.

He had to take taxis while waiting for an official verdict on his behaviour. Once, when trying to hail one in Massachusetts Avenue on his way to the British Embassy, a car pulled up. It was driven by Michael Straight, the American Cambridge man whom Blunt had courted for the Soviets in the 1930s. Straight gave him a lift. Burgess was quick to explain that he had been arrested three times for speeding. Each time he had claimed diplomatic immunity. The Governor of Virginia had protested. The Ambassador had impounded his car.

'What are you doing in Washington?' Straight asked him.[10]

'I'm working on Far Eastern Affairs.'

Straight was concerned. In the time Burgess had been in Washington, the Korean war – primarily between American and South Korean troops on one side, and Chinese and North Korean on the other – had begun. South Korean and American troops had crossed the 38th Parallel and had advanced to the Yalu River. There, troops led by US General Douglas MacArthur had been ambushed by 400,000 Chinese soldiers. After heavy fighting, thousands of American soldiers were left dead. Many more were wounded, captured and tortured.

Straight realized Burgess would have known about US plans to advance into North Korea. He would have sent that information to the KGB Chiefs at the Moscow Centre, who in turn would have sent it to Beijing.[11] His expert reports would have led to the deaths of many American soldiers.

During Straight's undergraduate toyings with Communism in the 1930s he had never envisaged that his contemporaries' endeavours would lead to this. But the world had changed. The game had turned serious. It was now a question of ideology versus patriotism. Straight, it seemed, had chosen to support his country.

'You must have known about our plans,' Straight said, in reference to Korea.

'Everyone knew about them!'

'Including the Chinese?'

'Of course! They did their best to warn you not to get too close to the Yalu River. We [the KGB] passed the warning along to you;

so did the Indians. No one here would listen. MacArthur said that the Chinese were bluffing. [Dean] Acheson [Secretary of State] and the CIA agreed with him.

'Acheson sees himself as another Metternich. He thinks he can prop up every rotten dictator in the world with American power. Well, he can't! I tell you that as a friend of the United States. If you try it, you'll fail.'

Straight became angry.

'You told me in 1949 that you were going to leave the Foreign Office,' he said. 'You gave me your word.'[12]

Burgess fumbled a response, attempting to explain why he had stayed on.

'You broke your word,' Straight replied.

Burgess asked him to pull over. Straight obliged.

'We're at war now,' he said. 'If you aren't out of the [UK] Government within a month from now, I'll turn you in.'

'Don't worry,' Burgess smiled as he got out of the car. 'I'm about to sail for England and as soon as I return, I'm going to resign.'[13]

Soon after this encounter, the Ambassador dismissed Burgess. He was sent home on the *Queen Mary*.

Burgess made contact with Modin, who noticed the stress that he was under.

'I told him Maclean would have to go,' Modin said, 'and that he should tell him a plan was in hand. However, he [Burgess] was unnerved, but trying to hide it. He was more often drunk than normal. He knew his career at the Foreign Office could be over. His career with us would then be over too.'

If Burgess was nervous, Maclean looked close to having another breakdown as the net closed. First, he was not allowed to have top-secret papers. Then he noticed he was being followed to Charing Cross station from his office. The watchers were not on the Sevenoaks train Maclean took each night on his way home to Tatsfield in Kent, but the experience of being followed confirmed his worst fears.

'They even bumped into the back of my cab when I stopped suddenly yesterday,' he told Burgess.[14]

The pressure caused Maclean to drink excessively. It made him loquacious. What should have remained on his mind, was on his lips. More than once at his club, the Travellers, he declared to friends: 'I am the English Hiss.'[15]

The American, Alger Hiss, who was suspected of being a Soviet agent, had been sent to jail in January 1950, for five years on a perjury charge. Hiss held similar positions to Maclean in the US State Department. Hiss had attended the Yalta Conference in 1945 as an adviser to President Roosevelt when he met with Churchill and Stalin to complete plans for the defeat of Germany and the foundation of the UN.

In many ways, their careers were parallel. Hiss was a brilliant, Harvard-trained diplomat involved in Roosevelt's New Deal in the 1930s. He held Communist-leaning views at a time when it was fashionable in the State Department. Like Maclean, he was caught in an ideological time-warp after 1945 when the former Soviet ally became the enemy in the Cold War.

The publicity surrounding Hiss and his suspected role as a Soviet agent, had haunted Maclean and Burgess because of their similar work feeding the Russians everything of importance at the Foreign Office.[16]

Modin was aware of Maclean's deterioration. He got a message to him via Blunt: Maclean had a few weeks' grace while Intelligence searched for evidence with which to interrogate and perhaps charge him. However, as Venona decodes would not be admissible in court, it was most likely that no damning evidence would be found.

In a poignant meeting with Blunt, Modin spoke about the strong possibility of Maclean being forced to defect, and soon. Modin warned Blunt that there could be repercussions for him. He would have to be prepared for questioning by MI6.

'Would you be able to stand that?' Modin asked.

'Absolutely, of course,' Blunt replied.

Modin believed him. He had read Krotov's reports about the great stress Blunt was under in 1945. But Modin was convinced he had recovered from the strain of the espionage overload of the war. Blunt impressed him with his cool nerve.

Modin was certain that British interrogation methods would not lead to a confession. Besides that, the Russian realized that the art expert had no intention of living in the Soviet Union. He detested the place, and preferred to continue his career amongst London's upper classes. Blunt was too fond of the privileges, comforts and pleasures to be had in Britain to consider a five-room 'luxury' apartment in Moscow.

Modin, in his polite yet dogged way, suggested that Blunt could continue his art work with access to the great Hermitage Museum in Leningrad.

'Could you ensure access to the Palais de versailles as well?' Blunt inquired.[17]

That final riposte settled the matter of his defection for the moment.

Of the top Five agents, the Fifth Man was the least likely to be implicated. The Russian felt that they did not have to worry about him.

'Like Blunt, the Fifth Man had officially left MI5 in 1945,' Modin observed. 'He had such a high public profile and was achieving some success in other areas after the war that he would not initially be investigated. At least, that was our assessment.'[18]

Since Israel had been created, Rothschild had kept himself busy on several fronts. In addition to his BOAC directorship, which guaranteed him free flights overseas, in 1948 he had been appointed chairman of the Agricultural Research Council, and in 1950 had become Assistant Director of Research at Cambridge's Department of Zoology.

He had kept close to Guy Liddell and Dick White, who was Director-General of MI5 from 1952 until 1956 when he took over as head of MI6. White had him running agents in the Middle East, notably in Iran. With such a respectable image in public, business, science and politics, and with friends who actually ran the Intelligence services – people who would decide on any questioning of suspects – the Russians seemed justified in not worrying about the Fifth Man's vulnerability.

He would not be a part of Modin's contingency plans for escape. Of course, the desperate flight of the other four could be avoided if Maclean were able to stay and withstand interrogation.

20. END OF A NETWORK

THE FLIGHT

Modin sent a message via Blunt to Maclean. Could he stand an inquisition? The stressed agent sent back word that he didn't think so. Modin telegrammed to the Centre. The KGB Chiefs said Maclean should prepare to run, and this message was passed on, again via Modin and Blunt.

Maclean's wife, Melinda, was expecting a baby in a few weeks.

'I can't leave her until the child is born,' he told Burgess.

'By then it will be too late . . .'

Maclean was in despair.

'You would have to face interrogation,' Burgess reminded him.

'I couldn't do it, I told Peter [Modin's alias] that.'[1]

Burgess reported this to Rodin. It was May and the Russians were meeting their agents every day.

'We were in stalemate and time was running out,' Modin recalled. 'I suggested that he ask Melinda if she would let him go. She had known all along – since before they were married – that he was a spy [Melinda has always denied this]. Melinda told him: "Go, go, it's fine." We of course would make arrangements for her to follow him to Moscow later.'

Modin consulted with Rodin. It was decided that Burgess should help Maclean escape, because in the diplomat's present state of mind they could not trust him to do it alone. He might disintegrate at the last moment or get blind drunk.

There were also worries that if he made it to Paris he might go on a sentimental binge, for it was his favourite city. He had been posted there with the Foreign Office in the late 1930s and it was where he had met Melinda and they had married.

In mid-May 1951, Modin met with Burgess near the toilet block in the park close to Ealing Common underground. The Russian remembered the meeting well. It was one of the most critical in his entire career as a Control. The following is a reconstruction based mainly on the Modin interviews:

'We wish you to go with Donald,' Modin explained.

'The Centre . . .?'

'Yes. They and we fear Maclean, will not get past Paris. He has too many fond memories there. You must go with him, guide him . . .'

Burgess was confused.

'I can't go, I really cannot. In fact, I *must* not.'

'Why?'

'Because of Kim. If I leave, the trail will lead back to him. Everyone knows about our friendship here, and in Washington.'

'If you have a good alibi, there will not be a problem.'

'What if the plan fails?'

'I can only pass on what the Chiefs demand,' Modin replied. 'My suggestion is that you take Maclean to Prague, and then come back slowly, via Scotland, where you will let people know you are planning to go.'

'Kim would kill me.'

'Not if you cover yourself and you're careful. We will help with passports.'

Burgess pondered his dilemma for a few moments.

'If I do leave with Donald, perhaps I shouldn't come back at all?'

That gave Modin pause. He knew this would displease the Chiefs in Moscow and Rodin. For one thing, Burgess was not yet considered a burnt-out case. His brilliant – in the espionage sense – reports on the lead up to the Korean War had given the Communists a great initial advantage in the conflict. Modin felt there was still mileage in this outstanding agent, *if* he remained somewhere, anywhere, in the FO, and *if* he could stand the pressure.

'You want to go to Moscow?' Modin asked.

'I've been thinking about it. Perhaps I should retreat there for a while, until it all blows over.'

'Then return here?'

'Yes.'

'No, I would doubt this would be acceptable. Perhaps you should consult Rodin.'

Burgess took his advice. The KGB Resident was adamant. Burgess should escort Maclean to Prague then return to London. He was not to go on to Moscow. Rodin flattered Burgess by saying that he was still very important to the Centre. His spying was 'exceptionally valuable'. What he didn't tell the Englishman was the fact that he, Rodin, received much kudos as the Resident running him. If he left, Rodin could no longer bask in this reflected glory.

'By 1951 he had become a lazy Resident,' an ex-KGB Colonel and contemporary of Rodin's recalled. 'Modin's reactivation of key British agents and his endeavours had made Rodin look good. If they were broken up, he would have to work harder. He wasn't up to it. He himself was becoming burnt-out. It [spying, brushing off the Watchers and so on] was physically and mentally demanding. Better to be young and fit. Rodin was neither.'

Most importantly, Rodin worried that Burgess's defection would ruin Philby's career and possibly lead to the exposure of the rest of the Ring, and other agents.

Philby was now the last of the Five left in the pivot of British espionage, although there were others well-placed. The Centre still had high hopes at that moment that he would rise to be head of MI6. Maclean's defection would not affect Philby because they were not in the same branch of Government. But Burgess's connection to Philby was well-known. The fact that Philby had played host to him in Washington DC just before Burgess's defection would create suspicion in the US and Britain, and he would be interrogated.

Burgess had no choice but to go at least to Switzerland with Maclean. He had begun to seriously consider defection, despite Rodin's instruction. He was still naïvely thinking that if he did go to Russia he could return to London after the whole affair had blown over.

'He had it in his head that he could say he had disappeared to Africa or something like that,' Modin recalled.

He made plans for a two-week trip to Scotland, making sure that friends at the Reform Club saw him with maps.[2]

Then on Wednesday, 23 May, Blunt and Rothschild heard from their contacts in Intelligence that the Foreign Secretary, Herbert

Morrison, would be sanctioning Maclean being called in for questioning by MI6. Nothing was firm but an investigation might just
start as early as next week, Monday 28 May.[3] Morrison would have
to sign a document to make it official, a formality that would be
completed by the end of the week.

Blunt told Modin and Burgess direct. It was time to leave.

Modin prepared their flight. He told Burgess to hire a car – an
Austin A40 – for the proposed Scottish holiday and then the Russian
bought two return tickets for St Malo, France, aboard the *Falaise*. It
would leave Southampton in two days' time, at midnight on Friday
25 May.

This particular boat was chosen because passengers did not have
to show their passports until the ship had sailed. If they had return
tickets for a weekend trip only, which would dock back in England
early on Monday morning, they did not have to present their
passports at all.

Under instructions, the two men did nothing out of the ordinary
during their last day in England, 25 May. In the evening Burgess
arrived at the Maclean home for dinner to celebrate Donald's
birthday. They both consumed a lot of champagne.

At 9 p.m. Burgess drove them at high speed to Southampton and
they just made it on board the *Falaise*, which sailed at midnight.
The two men collapsed in their cabin and did not emerge until the
boat docked at St Malo.

It was pouring when they stepped on to French soil around
midday. They took a taxi to Rennes, a train from there to Paris, and
a train to Geneva. They then caught another train at midnight to
Berne, which arrived at 6 a.m. on Sunday 27 May. Mid-morning,
they presented themselves at the Soviet Embassy and were given
two false passports.

'Their pictures were changed a little bit to disguise them,' Modin
explained. They were tired but anxious to escape the West. However, they had to wait nervously until a suitable flight two days
later.[4]

On Tuesday 29 May, the two fugitives flew from Berne to
Stockholm, with a stopover in Prague where they left the flight and
went to the Soviet Embassy, where they had to wait to be
'processed'.

Burgess was in touch with Rodin by telegram. Blunt had informed the Resident that there was an alert out for both men in the UK and across Western Europe.

The days slipped by as the two men waited idly and impatiently in Prague. After the terror, excitement and rush of their departure, Burgess at last had time to consider defecting with Maclean. He ruminated on Straight's warning that he would report him if he wasn't soon out of the FO. It might have been a bluff but it made Burgess wonder how many others might come forward to settle old scores once he was under interrogation.

Events in Britain settled the decision for him. Rodin had now realized that it would be impossible for Burgess to make his 'holiday in Scotland' alibi stick. The French taxi-driver who took them from St Malo to Rennes had already been interrogated by MI6 agents.[5] Rodin had no choice but to agree to Burgess's departure.

When their flight touched down in Moscow early in June, Burgess and Maclean had left behind a mess that both sides of the espionage war would take the next three decades to clean up.

THE TIDY-UP

The first person with his hands on a broom to effect a tidy-up for the KGB was the fastidious Blunt, who had a key to Burgess's flat in Bond Street. Contacted by Rodin on the day it was decided Burgess should defect with Maclean, Blunt was asked to check the flat to make sure nothing incriminating had been left.

When he got within a hundred yards of it, he noticed a police car and turned away. The spy had to wait until it left before venturing in. The flat didn't appear to have been searched yet by the Intelligence people. Blunt rifled through Burgess's untidy rooms, grabbed letters and documents and left.

Meanwhile, Philby in Washington heard the news and was stunned to learn that Burgess had gone too. He returned to his home, collected his copying camera and other equipment and buried them in a wood at the side of the Potomac River.

Philby waited for an official summons back to London, but was surprised to receive a tip-off in the form of a hand-delivered letter from Jack Easton, assistant chief of MI6. The letter said he would soon receive an official recall by telegram.

Philby considered the tip-off was a ploy to make him run and so incriminate himself. Or was it a real chance to run to Moscow? It crossed his mind that the British Government and MI6 actually wanted him to leave to save them the embarrassment of a revealing public trial and inevitable newspaper inquiries.

He decided not to run. He was hoping that he could squeeze through an interrogation and remain in the service, albeit in a reduced capacity.[6] But his and the Centre's dream that he would one day run MI6 were over.

On his return to Britain, Dick White at MI5 gave him a grilling. He made a point of questioning him about having been in Spain before he became a *Times* correspondent, which fitted the information given by pre-war Russian defector Krivitsky. This included a description of a young English journalist sent to Spain by the Russians.

White compiled a dossier. It highlighted Philby's leftist politics early at Cambridge; his visit to Vienna; his marriage to Litzi, a suspected Comintern agent (they divorced in 1940); his sudden move to the political right including his membership of the Anglo-German Fellowship; his tardiness in the Volkov affair, when the Russian defector was about to expose a key double agent; the circumstances of the Burgess–Maclean defection.[7]

White told the CIA that he had totted up the ledger.

'The debits outweigh the assets,' he said.

Intuition, suspicion, feeling, a list of fairly damning circumstantial evidence, and Philby's stammering demeanour during questioning, convinced everyone involved in his interrogation that he was the so-called Third Man. Almost. Weighed against the views of White and Arthur Martin at MI5, and many at MI6, were attitudes in England.

It was 1951. McCarthyism – the witch-hunts named after the US Senator, Joe McCarthy, for his zealous pursuit of communists – was sweeping the US, and already causing a backlash in Britain, where many in positions of influence in society were sympathetic to socialism and not against communism.

A perhaps misplaced British sense of fair play, especially as Philby was from the upper class, overruled logic, instinct and White's thick dossier. Yet even fairness could not save Philby's career. MI6's Chief, General Sir Stewart Menzies, called for his resignation. Philby was to get £4,000 instead of a pension; £2,000 down and then four half-yearly instalments of £500.

He was thirty-nine. In a period of weeks he had tumbled from being the rising star of MI6 to an out-of-work ex-spy. It was a tragedy for him and the Russians.

Philby was shunned by all but a few close friends – none of them from Intelligence. Instead of a thick in-tray on a neat desk in a quiet office and staff and secretaries to give orders to, he had a clear desk in his study, an alcoholic wife who felt estranged from him, and five young children to worry about feeding.

He felt he had been ruined long before his professional prime. No one, for the moment, would employ him. The stigma of being a suspected double agent and traitor seemed attached to him like a label, which he felt destined to wear forever. His prodigious energies went into joining Aileen in devouring bottles of Scotch.

There was much consternation at the suddenness of it all at the Soviet Embassy. Three members of the most effective spy ring in modern history were finished only a year or so after the loss of the atomic agents Fuchs, Nunn, May and Pontecorvo. Only the Fourth and Fifth men remained undetected out of the top Five, and their effectiveness was expected to be reduced.

The Russians had many British agents still operational but they had to be used with even more caution than before. Cairncross, for instance, worried that he might be followed since the defections. He arranged for a meeting with Modin in the public toilet near the Ealing Common underground. The Russian opted for a night rendezvous.[8]

Unbeknownst to them, MI5 had Cairncross under strict surveillance. They followed him to the meeting place. Cairncross had documents for Modin, which meant he would descend the steps into the toilet area and wait.

Modin arrived at 10 p.m. as planned, but stayed in the shadows eighty yards from the toilet. He could make out at least three people who to his trained eye were suspiciously-placed. One sat on a bench; another stood across Gunnersbury Avenue at a bus-stop; a third man had stationed himself along the Avenue on the Ealing Common side.

Modin was certain they were watchers. Instead of turning, he walked past the toilet, as if intent on a different destination.

The next day at the Embassy, Rodin berated him for being a coward, and threatened to inform the Centre.

'He had important material for us,' Rodin said angrily.

'There were watchers,' Modin replied. 'All my training and instincts . . .'

'You are scared, that's all. Just because of what happened to Burgess and Maclean.'

'Cairncross thinks he may be followed.'

'You are both acting cowardly! I'm going to report this.'[9]

Rodin wrote a damning letter to the Centre, which went in Modin's file. Rodin accused his star Control of 'behaving in a cowardly fashion'.

On the other side, MI5 reported that Cairncross had gone to a prearranged meeting place, but that his Control had failed to show up. Weeks later, the Scot was called in for questioning by MI5.

Under interrogation, Cairncross admitted passing 'confidential notes' to the Russians during the war, which he considered were 'most helpful, if not vital to the Allied effort against Hitler'. He denied spying after the war or passing documents to Burgess.

MI5 officers accused him of giving Burgess notes 'about confidential discussions in Whitehall' just before and at the beginning of the Second World War. The notes were unsigned but were supposedly in Cairncross's hand-writing. MI5 claimed that the notes had been left in Burgess's flat after he fled the country. This alleged evidence was not enough with which to charge him but Cairncross was forced to resign from the Treasury.

Modin was sceptical that Blunt had over-looked the notes when he went to the flat.

'Blunt would never have missed such information,' the Russian told me adamantly. 'I do not believe they existed. Would Burgess have kept such notes lying around for twelve to fourteen years in his apartment? I think not.'

Then why did MI6 suspect him?

'It was because we [the KGB] had become, careless – slack – in our methods. Rodin was at fault. He was not well. He took short-cuts, literally, when meeting our agents.'

He would have been seen meeting Cairncross?

'Exactly.'

Then MI6 trumped up the allegations about notes in Burgess's flat?

'I think so, yes. They had to salvage something [from the Burgess defection].'[10]

The series of agent exposures did not curtail Soviet penetration efforts. It simply meant that Modin and the other Controls would step up their recruitment of people such as George Blake at MI6. Espionage would go on. The Russians were also fortified by the knowledge that they still had moles well-placed in MI6.

In addition, Blunt and Rothschild could, through their links to White, Liddell and others, monitor the key attitudes, policy and decisions at the top of British Intelligence.

Over a drink at Rothschild's club, Pratt's, soon after the Burgess and Maclean defections, White expressed his suspicions about Alister Watson, who had been 'friendly' with Burgess at Cambridge. Rothschild recalled his Marxist fervour and that Watson had been, like him, an Apostle, but put it in the context of the time. He made light of Watson's enthusiasm for Marx, which he made clear to White had not impressed him, even at Cambridge.

White at the time was busy building dossiers on scores of possible spies, including Philby.

'Could you remind me to investigate him?' White asked. 'Could you write down a few things about him for the file?'[11]

Rothschild obliged. He wrote a general note, which was even less specific than his responses in the conversation with White. The MI5 man read the letter, filed it and took no action.[12]

THE BETRAYED

On the other side of the Atlantic, the cousins were just as angry about the Burgess/Maclean treachery, and less concerned about sparing Philby any embarrassment. The CIA director, General Bedell Smith, asked all senior Agency people to write a memorandum on the suspected Englishman.

Most wrote damning reports, more about what Philby knew than of the man himself. Bill Harvey, a rugged, former FBI man, tried to deduce where Philby would have been dangerous and highlighted the disastrous Albanian operation, in which MI6-sponsored agents infiltrated that country and were caught and executed. Philby, he deduced correctly, had informed the KGB.

One CIA person to be more shocked than angry over the Burgess/Maclean defections and the suspicions about Philby was his former pupil and friend, Angleton.

His memorandum to Bedell Smith showed that he still trusted the Englishman. It was a defence rather than even a mild attempt to create leads to his possible betrayal. Angleton wrote that he thought Philby had been 'honestly duped' by Burgess. The defector had acted alone, without Philby's knowledge.

Angleton was convinced that Burgess's 'aberrations were exploited without reference to Philby'. He refused to believe in his great friend's duplicity and treachery. In those tumultuous months of mid-1951, his only emotion was sadness at how such a fine, loyal and well-bred operator could be treated so shabbily.

The CIA man was to have many more deep and painful thoughts about Philby, Rothschild and other British agents, which would strongly influence world Intelligence for the entire Cold War.

The face of the Fifth: Victor Rothschild at fifty-two in 1963 – the year that Kim Philby, the Third Man, defected to Russia and Anthony Blunt was detected as the Fourth Man in the Cambridge University ring of Soviet spies. (*The Hulton-Deutsch Collection*)

Above: Marxist missionaries: some of Cambridge's Marxist Apostles after they had 'captured' the society in 1932. From left to right: Richard Llewelyn-Davies, Hugh Sykes-Davies, Alister Watson, Anthony Blunt, Julian Bell, Andrew Cohen. (*Peter Lofts*)

Inset, left: The First Man: Donald Maclean at Cambridge in 1934, about the time of his recruitment to Russian Intelligence. In 1951, he became the first of the ring to be detected as a KGB spy. (*The Hulton-Deutsch Collection*)

Inset, right: The Second Man: Guy Burgess at Cambridge in 1934. He joined Maclean when he fled to Russia, thus exposing himself as the second in the ring. (*The Hulton-Deutsch Collection*)

Left: The Kapitza connection: talented Russian physicist Peter Kapitza influenced Rothschild and recommended his recruitment to Russian Intelligence. (*The Hulton-Deutsch Collection*)

Top: The family man: Rothschild with his first wife Barbara in 1936, soon after the birth of their son Jacob. (*The* Illustrated London News *Picture Library*)

Above, left: An appealing lord: Rothschild, now the third Baron, speaks at the Mansion House on 9 December 1938, asking that Britain support the Lord Baldwin fund for German refugees. (*The* Illustrated London News *Picture Library*)

Above, right: MI5 to motherhood: three years after leaving MI5 with Victor, his second wife Tess is pictured here in 1948, shortly after the birth of their first child Emma Georgina. (*Cambridgeshire Libraries*)

A defector in waiting:
Donald and Melinda
Maclean with their sons
Fergus and Donald
in 1948, a few years
before fleeing the
West in 1951.
(*Popperfoto*)

An exile emerges:
Burgess in Moscow
with *Daily Express*
journalist Terry
Lancaster in 1957.
A year earlier the
Soviet government
officially acknowledged
that Burgess and
Maclean had defected
– five years after
the event.
(*The Hulton-Deutsch
Collection*)

Masterspy Modin:
Yuri Modin, in his
cover as press attaché,
with his wife Anne
at a media reception
in London in 1957.
He was the Control
of the Cambridge
ring post war.
(*Yuri Modin*)

A smile of clearance:
Kim Philby at a press conference
in his mother's London flat in 1955,
after the British government had
cleared him of being the Third Man.
(*The Hulton-Deutsch Collection*)

Gambling man: Rothschild, now
sixty-seven and still in the clear,
chairs a Whitehall press conference
on gambling in 1978.
(*The Hulton-Deutsch Collection*)

Keeper of Secrets, and the Queen's
Pictures: Blunt with a picture by
Velasquez in 1962, the year before
MI5, via the FBI, discovered
that he was a Russian spy.
(*The Hulton-Deutsch Collection*)

Above, left: A Blunt outing: the Fourth Man at a press conference in 1979, after Prime Minister Thatcher had exposed him in Parliament as a Russian agent. Rumours then began about the Fifth Man. (*The Hulton-Deutsch Collection*)

Above, right: Hollis the red herring: MI5 Director-general Roger Hollis was suspected by Peter Wright and the CIA's James Angleton of being a Soviet spy. He was used by Rothschild to divert attention and suspicion from himself. (*The Hulton-Deutsch Collection*)

Below, left: An agent of confusion: former Treasury official and Russian spy John Cairncross in 1990 at St Antonin, his home in exile in the South of France. Modin used his name to hide the identity of the Fifth. (*Popperfoto*)

Below, right: Mired in the maze: Angleton pictured in 1975 soon after losing power at the CIA. He never recovered from being deceived by his friend and mentor Kim Philby. (*Associated Press Photo*)

Lois and the Spyhunter:
Peter Wright and his wife arrive at
the Supreme Court, Sydney, to attend
the *Spycatcher* trial. The book, which
Mrs Thatcher tried to suppress, wrongly
claimed that Hollis was a spy.
(*Associated Press Photo*)

The fall guy: Cabinet Secretary
Sir Robert Armstrong arrives at the
Supreme Court in November 1986 for
the first day of the *Spycatcher* trial.
(*Associated Press Photo*)

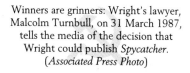

Winners are grinners: Wright's lawyer,
Malcolm Turnbull, on 31 March 1987,
tells the media of the decision that
Wright could publish *Spycatcher*.
(*Associated Press Photo*)

Left: Until death do us part: Modin – loyal to his top agents to the end – at Philby's Moscow funeral in May 1988. Within months, Modin retired after forty-five years service in the KGB and a record second to none as a Control of Western spies.
(*Yuri Modin*)

Below: A spy in profile: Rothschild in the early 1980s smoking one of his favourite Balkan Soubranie cigarettes. The shot was used in his *Times* obituary.
(Times *Newspapers Ltd*)

PART FOUR

THE SHIFTING
ALLIANCE
1952–1963

21. LEGACY OF A DICTATOR

BERIA'S BLUNDER

Stalin's death on 5 March 1953 ended nearly thirty years of his personal control over the USSR. He had set up such a brutal system, run by people prepared to murder their way to power, that it would be another three decades before a more humane leadership would emerge. His immediate legacy had to be more totalitarian dictatorship.

Beria, the most scheming and vicious of Stalin's henchmen, moved quickest. He had a running start. In the months before Stalin's death, Beria had discovered that the leader was planning to 'make an example of him and remove him', which meant he would be executed.[1]

Beria toadied even more than usual to Stalin, while lobbying support should the dictator move against him. When Stalin had a stroke in the middle of the night on 1 March, Beria went further and prepared to succeed him. By the day after Stalin's death, he had amalgamated the KGB and the MVD – Ministry of the Interior – under his control.

It gave him great initial power. He had 'embarrassing' dossiers on every member of the Presidium and kept each one under surveillance. But he began making mistakes.

The first was to recall many KGB Residents and senior operatives such as Modin to Moscow in order to assert his increased authority. In the battle between East–West Intelligence, this was a blunder. Western agencies were able to calculate who was who in the KGB by noting the travel movements during the recall period.[2]

If the suspected Residents returned to their embassies it meant they would not have been demoted; if they did not return, their replacement would probably be the new KGB boss in the country concerned.

Stalin's death and Beria's haste set the KGB back in a similar way to the 1936–38 purging of Comintern agents and created a disconcerting period for both Controls and agents. With Modin temporarily back in Moscow, Blunt and Philby had little or no contact with the KGB, while the Fifth Man felt temporarily estranged from the Russians for the first time.

Rothschild had observed with sadness but not surprise the purging of Jews in Soviet society and the administration, which peaked in the eighteen months before Stalin's death. The KGB was harshest amongst it own. It sacked all Jewish employees, even those such as Gorsky, who were experienced abroad. Then it created the so-called Doctor's Plot.[3]

Aware of Stalin's acute sensitivity to Zionism, which stemmed from his fabricated image of former arch-foe Trotsky, Beria, in late 1952, arranged for a disgruntled junior Kremlin doctor, Lydia Timashuk, to write to Stalin.[4]

Her letter accused her mostly Jewish superiors of a conspiracy to shorten the lives of Soviet leaders, including the entire Presidium, by 'sabotaging' their medical treatment. The hoax showed Beria's cunning, for Stalin and his cohorts were ageing, ailing and fearful of losing the power they had so thuggishly aggrandized over the decades.

The leader always acted if his paranoia was fuelled. This nonexistent plot fed on several of Stalin's fears. He hated Jews in general, feared hospitals, distrusted doctors and was terrorized by the mostly imaginary schemes of his enemies to kill him.[5]

The brave young Lydia was rewarded with the Order of Lenin for her exposures. Beria used the KGB's puppet news organ, *Pravda*, to attack. A lead editorial began a campaign against the 'monsters' and murderers [who] trampled the sacred banner of science, hiding behind the honoured and noble calling of physicians and men of learning'.[6]

Pravda 'revealed' that the doctors concerned were British Intelligence agents, whose vehicle was a 'corrupt Jewish bourgeois nationalist organization'.

'Stalin was crazy with rage [when he read the *Pravda* revelations],' according to Krushchev, 'yelling at [the then KGB head]

Semyon Ignatyev and threatening him, demanding that he throw the doctors in chains, beat them to a pulp and grind them into powder.'[7]

Stalin made sure that Ignatyev's more murderous deputy, M. D. Ryumin, was in charge of interrogation. Most of the doctors confessed to the crimes, which was 'no surprise', Krushchev noted.

The crude anti-Semitism went on. Ironically, the name Rothschild, in reference to the Bank and its international links, was mentioned as a key member of the Zionist plotters who were trying to control the world's finances.

In this atmosphere, relations between the Soviet Union and Israel cooled and helped push the Jewish State more towards the US, increasing American influence in the Middle East.

OUR MAN IN IRAN

Iran had been politically fragile during the war and the head of state, the Shah, installed by the British in 1944, was nothing more than an Anglo-Soviet puppet. The country had been 'ruled' by the Pahlavi dynasty since 1925 though nominally it was a constitutional monarchy with political parties in the legislature. Political tensions were caused by the pressure from the Russians, who had effective control in the north, and the British who controlled the south.

Shortly before his death, Stalin predicted Iran would fall 'into Soviet hands like a rotten apple'. This might have been the case if he had not died, and had there not been some enmity between the Soviet Union and Northern Iran which began in 1944 when the Soviets tried to obtain oil concessions.[8]

In October 1946 the lower house, the National Asembly, decided to declare any former Soviet oil agreements null and void. It forbade more oil concessions being given to foreign governments. A year later the Shah influenced the signing of an Iranian–US military agreement. Stalin reacted by boosting the strength of the communist-backed Tudeh Party. In 1949, one of its members tried and failed to assassinate the Shah.

The leader of Iran's National Front, Mohammed Mossadeq, a lawyer and son of a wealthy landowner, had resisted the Soviet efforts. By 1950, Mossadeq wanted Iran to be neutral, that is, independent of both the West and the East, which was extremely ambitious, considering his country's geographic location and its geology. The nation was oil rich, but the wealth had been controlled by the British via the AIOC, the Anglo-Iranian Oil Company.

Since the end of the war, the US had been arguing for a piece of that control, for its leaders saw the importance of fuelling the nation with an uninterrupted oil supply. In addition Iran was viewed as a useful buffer in the Middle East against Soviet expansionist aims.

Britain and the US feared Mossadeq, who wanted to nationalize the oil industry. By 1951, the AIOC's concession payments to Iran were not seen as enough.

In March, a prime minister who Iranian nationalists considered too close to British interests was assassinated. The Parliament (Majles) approved nationalization. Mossadeq became Prime Minister, much to the chagrin of the Shah, Mohammed Reza Pahlavi, who was losing power and influence to him.

Nationalization brought immediate financial hardship when AIOC stopped all payments to the Iranian treasury. Many public servants and workers received no pay. The dispute widened in 1952 and Iran became poorer. American oil men began arriving in Iran to see if they could take over from the British, but soon the UK Government had engineered the US into a worldwide boycott of Iranian oil. The economy began to collapse.

Mossadeq appealed to the US for loans, but it refused, saying the dispute had to be settled first. He told his nation it was better to proceed as if it had no oil so as not to be exploited. The Prime Minister proclaimed an 'age of austerity'.

Rothschild was by now a frequent visitor to the fledgling Israel. He often made a stopover in Iran in his agent running for MI5 chief Dick White, who, in effect, was straying outside MI5's brief, which was the defence of the realm. Foreign countries were supposed to be spied on by MI6. However, because the Shah was a British puppet some members of MI5 gave a liberal meaning to the concept of 'the realm'. Perhaps more importantly, White was reporting secretly to Churchill since he had been reinstated as prime minister in 1951. It meant that both MI5 and MI6 were monitoring events in Iran.

Rothschild was also reporting to Mossad, which wanted Iran in 'friendly' hands because of its oil supply to Israel's armed forces.

Rothschild's activities were very much of his own volition; he was the one who suggested agent running, not White. But the latter was only too pleased to have Rothschild operating. He had the pull to see anyone he wished, and he always got good information from the top. He never failed to see the Shah, with whom he had built a strong rapport, and Sir Shapoor Reporter, a mutual friend who was acting as an agent for MI6 (and indirectly for MI5).

Reporter was an Iranian with a British passport who spoke fluent Farsi, English and French. He worked as a 'translator' on the staff of Anthony Cuomo, the CIA man attached to the US embassy as political secretary. Reporter had a strong network of contacts throughout Iranian society, including politicians, royal court officials, newsmen, bank officials, military officers, both active and retired, and members of the Islamic religious orders. These links made him the best agent in the country. He was able to give Rothschild information on several areas, including what the CIA was up to.

Rothschild reported back to White on the political situation, the Shah's 'state of mind' and the growing American influence.

'There were plenty of cowboys in town,' White was told, 'all bearing gifts and wanting to knock on the Shah's palace door.'[9]

Some [American oil men] claimed [in discussions with Rothschild] that they were urging him to take over from Mossadeq. Rothschild saw the 'merchant-class' becoming dissatisfied with Mossadeq's 'fierce nationalism'. But it pleased the poor and the clergy.[10]

'I fear the Shah is heeding the cowboys and may do something precipitate,' Rothschild reported in May 1952. Two months later the Shah tried to remove Mossadeq from office, using more or less legitimate means through the parliament, but it failed and brought the Prime Minister's wrath down on the Royal Pahlavi household. Mossadeq's own spies told him that the Shah was weak and that it was his mother and sister, Princess Ashraf, who were influencing him. The Prime Minister had them banished from Iran, so that he could more easily manipulate young Mohammed Reza, who was then not quite thirty. He also broke off diplomatic relations with Britain.

About the time of Rothschild's May meeting, the Pahlavis set up the Bank of Omran to finance the development and sale of crown lands, and to collect crowns debts (twenty years later, it became a property developer, making fortunes for royal family members). It was clear that the Shah, or at least the women around him, expected to have continuing interests in Iran. However, the Shah himself appeared indecisive.

Rothschild informed MI5 that during a lunch they had the Shah seemed 'preoccupied with his political problems'. He needed repeated reassurances that they would not last and he had to be encouraged. The Shah was not convinced he could cope. An American businessman and his wife, also at the lunch, kept telling him to stand up to Mossadeq, who was 'threatening' the Pahlavi family.[11]

Rothschild's less than comforting reports to MI5 were backed up by British Embassy officials who in late 1952 suggested Mossadeq should be removed from office. Month by month, he was taking more power for himself while the economy continued to decline. The 'age of austerity' was turning into months of misgivings.

At MI6's instigation, the CIA was enlisted in a plot to remove Mossadeq. The CIA sent Kermit (Kim) Roosevelt, grandson of President Theodore, the head of its Middle Eastern operations, to London to discuss a British plan, to which Rothschild was privy.[12]

At first, MI6 was strongly in favour of orchestrating a coup but Roosevelt was cautious.

'Kim was a positive guy but not really a gung-ho type by nature,' a fellow CIA man involved in the coup recalled. 'On top of that we were nervous about the Russians. We knew Mossadeq had upset them but this lack of rapport did not necessarily mean that Uncle Joe would not move in. We calculated he might move troops into the north and occupy it. We had intelligence that there were troop movements, which could have meant just a show of strength.'[13]

The British wanted to make moves by Christmas, 1952. They sent a delegation, including MI6 operatives, to Washington to meet with Secretary of State John Foster Dulles and his brother, Allen, the CIA director, Roosevelt and Angleton. Again, the CIA stalled. They used the excuse that General Eisenhower would not like anything to distract from his inauguration as President in January.[14]

The British, however, did not leave empty-handed. They had an agreement that Mossadeq must go, and to keep the CIA involved it was suggested that Roosevelt should head up the planning for Mossadeq's overthrow. This would also help Britain overcome its lack of representation in Iran since Iran had broken off relations. All activity could be focused through the US Embassy, which was already being used by the nervous Shah in his strained communications with the British.[15]

MI6 suggested Roosevelt send two Iranian agents to the US for training so that plans for subversion could be set up in preparation for a coup. Yet still the CIA would not commit itself. It was aware of the Russo–Iranian Treaty of 1921, which gave the Russians the right to send troops into Iran 'in certain circumstances', which in diplomatic parlance meant for any reason that would be half-way legitimate in the eyes of the international community after the event.[16]

The Americans were doubly cautious because they were then busy disentangling themselves from Korea after a bloody war. New President Eisenhower was not enthusiastic about taking on the communists in another remote conflict, especially as it would mean a more direct confrontation with the Russians with a greater threat of nuclear weapons being introduced.

Stalin's death in March initially put any coup in Iran on hold as the world waited to see what and who would emerge in control at the Kremlin. Would it be a hard-liner? Probably. Would he want to show strength early and confront the West? Possibly.

Western intelligence services worked overtime in conjunction with journalists trying to find out what was happening in Moscow. But the Kremlin remained silent. It was a news-free zone as the power struggles began behind the scenes. Rothschild and other KGB agents failed to get their warnings about the possibility of a CIA-backed coup to the right people for action at the Moscow Centre.

Meanwhile, the oil crisis in Iran escalated. March, April and May passed without anything definitive coming out of Moscow. The CIA and MI6 began to think they should move quickly before the new Soviet regime regrouped and acted. They started organizing support for 'spontaneous' demonstrations against Mossadeq but were upstaged early in June by anti-Shah mob gatherings in Teheran. The Shah was urged by Roosevelt to encourage the army to appear in the streets to demonstrate support, which it did.

'A trigger [for a push by the CIA and MI6] was what happened in East Germany in the middle of June,' the ex-CIA man suggested. 'Workers revolted spontaneously by contrast with what we were doing in Teheran. This was real. It gave the Agency activity impetus. A few of us thought, hopefully, that it might start riots everywhere in the Soviet bloc. But we had to wait . . . (laughs) about thirty-five years! At any rate, it was a challenge to Communist rule – the first big one. The Russians had to smash it with tanks. They killed about twenty demonstrators before they put it down.'[17]

On 22 June John Dulles allowed Roosevelt to proceed with Operation Ajax (MI6 called it Operation Boot). He flew to Teheran and went to the Palace hidden under a blanket in the back of a non-diplomatic car. The Shah was nervous about 'Palace spies' so he ordered the car to a garage area, where he climbed in beside Roosevelt.

The CIA agent outlined the plan, in which the Shah would issue two *firmans* – decrees – dismissing Mossadeq and installing a royal supporter as prime minister. The Shah then had to fly to a hideout in a town on the Caspian, where he would await further instructions. Roosevelt said he would give the two Washington-trained Iranian MI6 agents $400,000 out of a big slush fund set up for Operation Ajax.

'This money was to go to athletic club members and poor folk from the slums of South Teheran,' the ex-CIA man said. 'It was bizarre . . .'[18]

However, while the city was about to erupt, the Shah still hesitated. Roosevelt had to meet and encourage him again. A referendum to dissolve parliament was held and it was claimed that 'a vast majority' wanted it. On 12 August the Shah issued his firmans.

But Mossadeq called his bluff by arresting the messenger delivering the decrees and issuing orders for the further arrest of the Shah's nominated prime minister, General Zahedi. He appealed to the army, which supported the Shah.

In the street, Mossadeq seemed to hold sway, with the most vocal demonstrators being the communist-backed Tudeh Party. Mobs brandishing red flags rampaged through the streets, smashing cars and shop windows. They stopped at graven images of the Shah's father, Reza Shah, and to chants of 'Yankees go home', destroyed them.

The Shah lost his nerve and fled the city with his wife, Soraya, not for the nominated Caspian town, but Baghdad in Iraq. The US ambassador in Baghdad was taken by surprise and had a fruitless meeting with the Shah. Not getting any answers to questions on what he should do, the Shah panicked and flew to Rome.

He found less than royal accommodation in the Excelsior Hotel. The US Ambassador, under Roosevelt's instruction, told the Shah to hold a press conference. Yet still he dithered about going back, when everyone from Kim Roosevelt to Churchill in dispatches were urging him to be bold and act. At that critical point Angleton, who was handling relations with Israel, was in touch with Rothschild who was in Tel Aviv at the time.

'They were discussing the Shah,' the CIA man claimed. 'I don't know who suggested what, but it was very much in Israel's interests that someone like the Shah was in power. He could guarantee oil supplies. Also our [American] sway with him meant that Iran would not side with the Arabs in any conflict with Israel. However, Rothschild backed off helping. Jim was disappointed.'[19]

It's not surprising Rothschild decided to do nothing. He would have been in one of the most conflictual political dilemmas of his clandestine life. The Soviet Union's power struggle temporarily paralysed its foreign decision-making, but still he would not want to be seen by his friends in the Kremlin as helping the Americans achieve their aim of reinstating the Shah. Rothschild could have used the excuse with Angleton that it was a CIA operation not controlled by British Intelligence. On top of that, he could have argued, MI6 would object if he, with his stronger MI5 connections, were to interfere.

The next day, the Shah started giving one-on-one press interviews using his greatest asset, his charm, to win support. He stressed his desire to go back to Teheran and said that he had always stayed within his constitutional rights, whereas Mossadeq had acted illegally.

'It seemed that someone, probably Roosevelt, had said something that influenced the Shah to at least look like he had leadership skills,' the ex-CIA man noted.

How did Roosevelt influence him?

'Well, it wasn't cajolery! He would have been saying what everyone else [the US Ambassador and the British] was saying. They were trying everything from flattery to inducements. It was as much about wealth as anything else.'

The Shah's press conferences and interviews made the news in Teheran and inspired some support for him. After a few days, reportage became circular. In a near ritual at each midday conference, the AP correspondent would read the latest dispatch from Teheran. The Shah would then put on his glasses, and comment. His manner was calm, firm and very respectful to the assembled scribes, not used to such engagingness. Once or twice his attractive wife, Soraya, was in attendance and this gratified the journalists further.

The reporting was sympathetic and gave the Shah a voice. The mere fact that he was saying *something* and indicating that he would like to take power, boosted his popularity with the Iranian army and what support he had in the parliament, where Western agents were lobbying hard.

The mobs, which had been all anti-Shah, began to change. The army, which had been waiting impatiently in barracks, started to have a greater presence in the main city streets, showing that they were still loyal to the Shah and the designated prime minister, Zahedi.

Roosevelt's paid demonstrators, the unlikely combination of the slums' poor and fitness clubs' muscular freaks started marching from South Teheran.

'It was the craziest, weirdest, procession,' a retired Texas Oil executive, Chuck T. Holloway, who was in Teheran at the time, recalled. 'I'll never forget weightlifters walking along pumping dumbbells as they went. Some guys were doing handstands – real athletic types making people clap and cheer. They first amused the crowds building in the streets, then they shouted "Long live America". The watchers didn't respond at first. There was a lot of anti-Shah shouting going on. But the procession had a kind of fascination for them.'[20]

Brawls started in the main streets, which was what Roosevelt had hoped for. It meant that law and order were breaking down and Mossadeq had lost control. The army under Zahedi restored calm.

Each day brought more demonstrators out for the politely smiling Shah back at the Rome Excelsior. 'Long live America' began to prevail over the 'Yankee go home' refrain.

Early on the morning of 19 August Mossadeq was overthrown and Zahedi used the army to take over.

Back in Rome, the AP correspondent came in before another midday conference began and read out a wire from Teheran, which told of Mossadeq's fall.

'I knew it,' the Shah exclaimed. 'I knew that they loved me!'[21]

Soraya burst into tears. That afternoon the Shah flew home with journalists on a champagne flight and reached the city to see supporters trying to re-erect a toppled statue of his father. Late in the evening, he met Roosevelt at the Palace.

'I owe my throne to God, my people, and to you,' the Shah told him.[22] Perhaps it was the reverse order, for without the CIA, and to a lesser extent, MI6, Reza Pahlavi would have been a mere footnote in history, rather than a figure of power and wealth for the next quarter of a century.

Zahedi promised to end the oil dispute with Britain, and the US promised loans which it had refused Mossadeq. The ousted leader's foreign minister was executed and many supporters were jailed. Mossadeq's house was bulldozed to the ground so that it would not become a focus for opposition. After this, he turned himself in at a police station and was put in prison (He remained incarcerated for five years and died soon after his release.)

The US Embassy, rather than the Palace, became the real seat of power as Roosevelt and assistants such as Richard Helms took up residence there for a time.[23] Within a year, a new consortium to manage Iran's oil emerged with US companies owning 40 per cent, the UK 60 per cent.

The Shah set up a new secret police force – SAVAK – with advice from the CIA and Mossad in order to control or destroy all opposition. The KGB had lost the initiative in the Middle East, partly due to CIA action, and also the inertia in Moscow. Rothschild and others had sent their warnings, but none had been heeded.

MR K. TAKES POWER

Meanwhile, the minor uprising in East Germany sealed the fate of the Soviet leadership. It was blamed on Beria, whose rush to reorganize the KGB after Stalin's demise had left it weak in Berlin. Beria flew from Moscow to investigate but had to rush back prematurely because of a meeting of the Presidium.

In a typically crude and thoughtless fashion, Beria made disparaging remarks at the meeting about East Germany – the GDR – implying that it was just a Soviet puppet state, which was an accurate assessment delivered to the wrong audience. His failure to be diplomatic about East Germany engendered a feeling of indignation in the hypocritical Presidium.

Beria's insensitivity gave Nikita Krushchev his chance, but he had to move fast. He lobbied key members, namely Bulganin, the minister of defence, Marshal Zhukov and foreign minister, Molotov.

A special meeting of the Presidium was called for 26 June 1953. Krushchev arrived with a gun in his pocket ready to defend himself should Beria pull a surprise. In the thuggish atmosphere in the Kremlin, a legacy of Stalin, there was no sense of the rule of law. Unelected, undemocratic power was left to the bold and the brutal.

According to Krushchev in his memoirs, 'Beria sat down, spread himself out' and asked what was on the agenda for the unexpected meeting. Krushchev jumped up and said:

'There is one item on the agenda: the anti-Party, divisive activity of imperialist agent Beria. There is a proposal to drop him from the Presidium and from the Central Committee, expel him from the Party, and hand him over to the court martial. Who is in favour?'

Molotov and Bulganin took the floor in turn and attacked Beria, who squirmed and protested. First Secretary Malenkov pushed a secret button. Zhukov entered with armed army officers, arrested Beria and removed him.

Zhukov moved a tank division and a motor rifle division into Moscow to combat any possible moves by the KGB's armed unit to free Beria. Troops surrounded the Lubyanka building. Orders were given to remove all images of Beria from KGB HQ. All portraits in foyers and offices disappeared.

'Each day, someone close to Beria would not appear at work,' former KGB Colonel 'F' recalled. 'Then we heard rumours the boss was in an army prison cell and we wondered if he would end up in the Lubyanka. We didn't anticipate how quickly Krushchev would move.'[24]

On 10 July Beria's arrest was publicly announced and Krushchev rode to power on the back of his swift move against the hated secret police chief. In September he replaced the comparatively meek Malenkov as Party First Secretary and quickly drew up charges for a compliant Supreme Court, which said that Beria had led 'a plot to revive capitalism and to restore the rule of the bourgeoisie'.

The Court heard in secret other charges of mass murder, rape and torture. Beria was found guilty and executed. On 24 December, scanty details were released about the trial and Beria's liquidation. His main crime, trumped-up for public consumption, was that he had been a British agent – a charge levelled at two other KGB heads in the 1930s.

After such upheavals, it took another six months for the KGB administration to settle down on a Krushchev favourite, 49-year-old General Ivan Serov, who took command. He was best known for the vicious, efficient way he crushed opposition to communist rule in the Baltic States and Eastern Europe.

At last, the KGB could make decisions concerning its operations and agents abroad. High on its list was Philby, who had become an alcoholic as well as running out of money.

22. THE VISITOR
FROM NORWAY

Modin contacted Maclean and Burgess while in Moscow in 1954 and found both men were working in his early vocation at the KGB: translating. Maclean was making an honest effort to learn Russian so he could contribute to turning Russian works into English. Burgess's usefulness was more limited, for he was not attempting to immerse himself in Soviet culture. He didn't care to learn the language except for a few survival basics and picking up boyfriends.

'I warned him it [homosexuality] was against Soviet law,' Modin recalled. 'If he was caught consorting with young men again, he would be prosecuted, severely.'

It didn't stop the promiscuous Englishman. The KGB solved the problem by finding him a suitable partner, a guitar-playing electrician named Tolya, the same name as Burgess's Alsatian guard dog.

Burgess's work was restricted to helping determine which English language books might be suitable for translating into Russian. It was a dead-end job but the alcoholic Burgess didn't care anymore. He believed he would eventually go back to London, cleared of all charges.

Maclean seemed disinterested in building any relationship with Modin, whom he had never met, even in the hectic days of his departure three years earlier. The former diplomat was concerned to put that part of his life behind him and to look forward to a job teaching in international relations.

He remained aloof, and even disdainful, of his espionage days.

By contrast, Burgess was very pleased to see Modin, for whom he had great affection. They had developed a curious bond because of their great dependence on each other. Their meetings in London had been in secret and often in the dark of night. It was an excitement-charged liaison, where the two men relied on the caution, courage and punctuality of the other.

Modin was the near-perfect Control, always discreet, on time and calm, and while Burgess was a notorious rogue, he was the most professional of agents on the job. He also brought humour to every incident, however dangerous, which the youthful, yet mature Modin appreciated.

There was also the nature of their intelligence exchanges. Everything provided was intellectual, layered and profound. He had the knack of delivering key information about foreign affairs, and Modin over time began to understand the scope of this exceptional agent's capacities as a thief of pertinent data. His reports were appreciated in the highest echelons of the Centre and Presidium. This also heightened the vitality of their liaison and made their reunion a pleasant, if not joyous occasion, as Burgess insisted on plying the visitor to his modest Moscow flat with drink.

Burgess was interested to hear in mid-1954 about Modin's report on Philby, who had passed on via Blunt to the Centre that his MI6 pension, or pay-off, had run out. Modin explained he would be returning to London in disguise to help Philby.

Modin was not allowed to meet Philby directly, so contact, encouragement and a cash payment to him had to be made through Blunt. Burgess suggested *he* write a London meeting place on the back of a painting postcard.[1]

It said: 'Outside The Angel, Caledonian Road, tomorrow, 8 p.m.'

A few days later Modin, in disguise as a Norwegian Jewish businessman and with a false passport, arrived in London. He booked into an obscure hotel near Marble Arch and did not make contact with the Soviet Embassy. Modin was acting as an illegal, which meant that if plans went awry and he was detected by the watchers, he would not be able to find sanctuary at the Embassy.[2]

But Modin, never one to lack front, turned up at an art lecture by Blunt at the Courtauld Institute. At the end after the audience had left, Modin went up to him and showed him the postcard.

'He did not recognize me,' Modin said with a hearty laugh. 'But he did know his great friend's handwriting. Then he looked at me and realized who I was.'

They met the next night as planned. Modin inquired about

Blunt's well-being, for they had not spoken for two years. Then Modin noticed someone lurking in the background.

'Were you followed?' the Russian asked.

'It's Kim.'

Modin was nervous and surprised.

'Could you speak with him,' Blunt asked. 'His spirits need lifting. He has no money. He wants to know where he stands.'

Modin took a paper bag from a briefcase and handed it to Blunt. It contained £5,000 in cash.

'This should help. It's his pension,' Modin explained. 'It has been accumulating since 1943.'

'He will be most grateful,' Blunt responded, 'but if you could . . .'

'I cannot. The Centre forbids it.'

'But he doesn't know what you wish of him.'

'He is still operating, as far as we are concerned. Tell him we think he is still most valuable. Most valuable.'

Blunt held Modin's gaze for a rare moment and looked relieved.

'Tell him things will settle down in Moscow soon,' Modin added. 'We will be in touch.'

'He is very worried about this Petrov business [the defection in Australia in 1954 of KGB Resident, Vladimir Petrov, and his wife, Evdokia]. How much do they know?'

'They provided some intelligence on Burgess and Maclean,' Modin replied, then he added with a laugh. 'They've confirmed that they are in Moscow.'

'Did they know about Kim?'

'Not a thing. Reassure him. There is nothing, *nothing* on him.'

'Are you coming back to London?'

'I think so. Next year.'

Blunt looked around at Philby, then tried once more to have them meet. Modin repeated he could not and they parted.[3]

In reference to Modin's contact, Philby later said:

'I received, through the most ingenious of routes, a message from my Soviet friends, conjuring me to be of good cheer and presaging an early resumption of relations. It changed drastically the whole complexion of the case. I was no longer alone.'[4]

A year later in 1955, when Modin had taken up his position at the Embassy as acting Resident, still with his useful cover as press attaché, Philby was accused by an MP in Parliament of being the

Third Man. The Foreign Secretary, Harold Macmillan, was forced to dismiss the charge. The British Government, as Modin had informed Philby, had no evidence.

Philby gave a press conference in his mother's London flat. He was smiling and ebullient.

'The last time I spoke to a communist, knowing he was one, was in 1934,' Philby told the journalists and TV cameras.

The problem had been aired, faced and defeated. It gave great relief also to the Fourth and Fifth men, for if Philby remained uncharged there was a low probability of any evidence being presented about their Soviet allegiances.

23. THE SEVERAL FACES
OF VICTOR

MASTER OF ONE

By the mid-1950s, observers attempting to pin down the ubiquitous Victor had trouble in pigeon-holing him. In Cambridge, where he lived half the time when in Britain, he was seen as an academic recluse. In London, he always appeared the busy action man in the corridors of parliament, or in his various executive offices round the West End and City. He maintained interests from the 1930s such as collecting old manuscripts, which saw him browsing in musty bookshops, and collecting art, which caused him to haunt St James's up-market galleries.[1]

But these were just surface images of Rothschild's eclectic life as he went about his main aim of establishing a career to match his enormous talents. So far his depth of genius, his administrative capacities, his perfectionism had been demonstrated in the service of three Intelligence agencies simultaneously. His skills and energies had been taken underground and diverted to silent, unpublic achievement.

By the mid-1950s, Rothschild had established a second family with Tess and their three children – Emma, Victoria and James Amschel. Yet while anchoring him more than he had been in the 1930s, it did not stop his drive for the Intelligence game or to find a challenging work niche. Miriam Rothschild remembered Victor in this period as a genius in search of a discovery. He busied himself in many fields but she sensed he was frustrated.[2]

Although he felt his own brilliant research days were virtually ended, Rothschild maintained his work in Zoology at Cambridge. It allowed his continued links to the scientific community, and its secrets, which he had a unique and experienced way of prying from it.

He was in his mid-forties and wondering how long he could stand the tedium of science labs, where after two decades he was becoming viewed as a freak, an eccentric with peculiar habits.

'Victor wasn't just unorthodox,' one of his colleagues at the Zoology Department, Dr Sidney Smith, remembered. 'He was absolutely *sui generis*. At one stage he was dieting by trying to survive all day on two oranges. Then he would work half the night, eating a tin of chocolate biscuits to give him enough carbohydrates to starve next day. Victor was a man driven by ideas.

'He could afford to employ his own research assistant, a marvellous man called Hubbard, one of the best people ever trained by the Cambridge Instrument Company. Victor would sometimes allow us to borrow Hubbard for our experiments. In the 1950s and 1960s, when he [Victor] was assistant director of research, he was able to divert his own money to the Department to buy apparatus that the University couldn't afford. It was a hidden subsidy. He was an extraordinary man, a good friend of the [Zoology] Department, very sensitive, and not too corrupted by money and power.'[3]

Also less enchanting after nearly two decades were the interminable committees in Parliament, and uninspiring directorships, which by now he was using for contacts as much as anything.

Rothschild had taken on another part-time post as a member of the BBC General Advisory Board, which he occasionally found stimulating. But he was 'noticeably bored' with his limited work at the Agricultural Research Council, which he had kept up for a decade.[4]

He had developed an autocratic style, which could be traced back to his early spoilt years at Tring, where the only males in the vicinity were a sick father and a painfully shy uncle. The women in the family tended to dote on him and put up with his cheek and pranks.

Later, during his university cricketing days, he found it difficult to take orders. He made a dashing century in his first game for Cambridge but was soon dropped for insolence to the captain. The freshman undergraduate kept telling him who should bowl next and how to place the field.

Even when the Comintern was after his services in 1934, he was only going to join the clandestine service on his terms. His connection had to be secret even to the other members of the ring, although in reality the Five and others knew who fellow members were. It developed a brotherhood. Rothschild only took this underground camaraderie seriously when the war began.

Every position he had in wartime, whether at Porton Down or within MI5, gave him autonomy. While investigating Nazi commercial espionage, he had his own little team. When Guy Liddell took him on in his counter-espionage section at MI5, the over-indulged yet deserving Victor – a favourite of Liddell's amongst the brilliant young spies he was commanding – was given his own section, the small yet important counter-sabotage unit. There were just six members at the beginning and Rothschild was boss.

Yet he never shirked his responsibility. The boss was first to risk life and limb. As MI5's security inspector turning up on secret research doorsteps, he worked solo and effectively. With SHAEF on the Allied thrust into the Continent, it was Rothschild who took command of the Ring of Five and even directed the KGB Controls who he had running to Paris to receive espionage data. Rothschild was the dictator of which intelligence should be purloined and from where. The KGB Controls kept their complaints to themselves.

By 1943 Rothschild, the KGB men realized, was indeed a one-off. He, more than any other agent, had the power to collect vital information for the Centre. He and they knew he was in a better position to determine what espionage was useful in the struggle against the Nazis. Yet still he cooperated if what he considered important requests were made.

Not surprisingly, he upset people when he took on the Chairmanship of the Agricultural Research Council in 1948. This was a much bigger, bureaucratic show, where one paid due deference to officialdom and the pace was slow. He no longer had the pressure and excitement of rushing the Soviets something they should know about a German tank division. There was not even the driving force of a profit motive, which the disdainful young Victor had briefly experienced at N. M. Rothschilds.

He had dealt with the slow grind of the civil service and government institutions before, but not from the inside as at the ARC, which he thought was an apt acronym.[5]

Rothschild, as everyone from his wife to his various intelligence networks knew, liked to get things done by the fierce and energetic application of reason and logic, which he was certain was the solution to all problems. It could apply to defusing a complicated bomb, or understanding the making of a nuclear weapon, or the mechanics of reproduction. He worked best on his own, and found fellow human beings occasionally difficult and often not governed by the laws of physics. They had ideas, admittedly often moribund and unimaginative ones compared to his, but minor intellectual inspirations nevertheless. These people would insist on airing their views or voicing opinions. If they were irrelevant to the way he wanted to go, he would ride roughshod over them. Former employees at ARC recalled that Rothschild was 'impatient', 'insensitive' and, on occasions, 'intimidating'.[6]

Some claimed he treated people like fools unless they could prove they were not. When they could not present evidence to the contrary, he would not suffer them. This upset and angered subordinates and colleagues.

'He would do drastic things without consultation,' an ARC executive recalled. 'He could be very persistent in trying to get his own way even against the majority of the Council. The Secretary, Sir William Slater, found him a great *trial*, interfering in things that were in the realm of management, not policy.'[7]

At heart, Rothschild was more an active governor or manager, not a policy-maker floating above the action and destined to create guidelines and stay aloof.

Whether he appreciated it or not he was trapped in areas that didn't suit him. He certainly understood that after twenty years his clandestine world, the extent of which only he knew, was still the field that extended his mind and diverse skills more than any other. This was because his espionage work was linked with survival, which had been his motivation during the war and after, when he was helping create and defend Israel. Consciously or unconsciously, Rothschild was clinging to the secret world for succour, and the intermittent sense of achievement, which he craved.

THE SURVIVAL COMPLEX

Months after Israel was formed, Rothschild was involved with Chaim Weizmann in setting up a special nuclear physics department in a scientific institute in Rehovoth. The establishment was named after Weizmann, the nation's first president and himself a distinguished biochemist.

Its aim even in those heady days of 1948 was to build nuclear weapons for Israel. It became the nation's best kept secret and the most fervent desire of the new nation's founders. They never wanted their race to be threatened with another Holocaust. Atomic weapons would be the ultimate deterrent to future Hitlers.

Yet when the idea for an Israeli bomb was first conceived, the Soviet Union was still a year away from its own first trial blast. The Russians were expecting to detonate, literally after seven years hard labour, when it should have taken perhaps a century of normal research. They had thrown enormous resources, thousands of scientists and strong spy networks at the problem. Israel would have to copy that approach from a standing start. It had limited resources and a trickle of Jewish technicians. But it did have espionage networks.

The dream of an Israeli bomb was ambitious indeed, but it spurred Rothschild to keep abreast of all things nuclear so he could pass on data to the Weizmann Institute, which was planning a nuclear reactor at Dimona in the Negev Desert. Under a modified guise of concern about the spread and dangers of nuclear weapons, he was able to keep contact with appropriate scientists around the world. He began this official and legitimate process at the end of the Second World War by becoming an expert on fallout, which allowed him to monitor the Manhattan project. He continued in the 1950s, even on occasions attending informal conferences on controlling nuclear weapons held by leading British atomic scientists, who were beginning to comprehend and assess their creation.

The Dane, Niels Bohr, had stimulated consciences post-war by arguing that nuclear matters belonged to an 'open world', with which the Russians – desperate to build a nuclear arsenal – agreed wholeheartedly. He had plenty of support from the scientific community in the US too, but Washington was never going to support 'the free interchange of ideas' with those dangerous Russians, even if it had nothing to do with detail about bomb technology.[8]

Bohr's idea was taken up by mathematician and philosopher, Bertrand Russell, Albert Einstein and the British Atomic Scientists

Association, many of whose members Rothschild knew well. They set up their first conference at Pugwash, Nova Scotia, in 1955.[9]

Rothschild assiduously kept contact with the key organizers so that his involvement always seemed natural.

Correspondence with Russell in early 1955 was typical:

Dear Russell,
  I would like to present the manuscript of your recent broadcast dealing with the Hydrogen Bomb to Trinity. Can you suggest any way in which I might acquire it?
  Yours Sincerely,
    Rothschild[10]

The so-called Pugwash Conferences emerged as the scientists' response to the arms race between the US, USSR, China, Britain and France, and the dangers of fallout.

Scientists from twenty-two nations turned up and problems concerned with peace and the impact of atomic weapons on humankind were discussed.[11] Rothschild later floated ideas about how to harness the nuclear genie for 'peaceful purposes' and not war. He urged the idea of breeder reactors for energy, of which he was a long-term supporter. What he avoided mentioning was the ease with which breeder reactors could be adapted to extract weapons-grade nuclear fuel.

Everything he learnt ended up at the Weizmann Institute, which was in part his creation. (His secret support of it with information and finance was rewarded publicly in 1962 when he was made an Honorary Fellow of the Institute.)[12]

Rothschild was not a technician like Klaus Fuchs. He could not create the weaponry for Israel. But he could inform its Intelligence leaders (with whom he was very close as an important, secret member of Mossad) which scientists might be helpful, where the available technology might be and how it might be obtained and funded.

The Israelis sounded out several possibilities. In 1956, Shimon Peres, then director of the Defence Ministry under Moshe Dayan, had many meetings with ministers in Guy Mollet's French socialist government as they prepared for the Suez Canal operation. The French, British and Israelis planned to wrest back the Canal from President Nasser of Egypt, who had nationalized it.

Peres first gained the trust of the French, then he struck a deal with Defence Minister, Bourges Maunoury. In return for Israel's help over the Suez Canal, in which it would make the initial attack on Egyptian defences, the French promised to consider supplying nuclear plants at Dimona. Israel carried out its part at Suez, and fortuitously Maunoury replaced Mollet as prime minister. Maunoury and his foreign minister signed a top-secret agreement with Peres and Asher Ben-Natan, a Mossad agent at Israel's Defence Ministry.

In it, the French promised to supply a powerful 24-megawatt reactor, the technical know-how to run it, and some uranium. The secret deal was only known to about a dozen individuals, including Rothschild, and with good reason. The fine print of the document allowed for the inclusion of equipment which would permit the Israelis to produce weapons-grade nuclear fuel.

In 1957, French engineers began building the two-storey reactor facility at Dimona on the edge of the Negev Desert, which secretly went down six levels below ground. The subterranean construction would be the place where nuclear weapons would be built. With several Mossad officers in attendance, the engineers also dug an 80-foot deep crater in the sand. In it they buried Machon 2 – a unit which would allow the Israelis to extract weapons grade plutonium, the fuel for the bomb.[13]

THE WRIGHT STUFF

In July 1955, Peter Wright joined MI6 as the agency's first full-time scientist at a starting salary of £1700. He was approaching forty and like Rothschild, in search of a true career path which had been interrupted by war. He had an atypical background for the old-boy networks that made up British Intelligence, having been educated in Chelmsford and Bishop's Stortford before working on a farm and then taking an unfinished degree in Forestry at the School of Rural Economy in Oxford. From 1940, he worked in the Royal Navy's scientific service, and later in the war took a job with Marconi, the electronics company which was creating various technologies for eavesdropping on enemies.[14]

It seemed that the talented Wright had found a niche in keeping with his pedigree, for his electronics engineer father, Maurice, had made a name for the family by inventing an antidote to Satyr, a brilliant Russian bugging device that did not need wires or batteries. Maurice built an equally ingenious piece of equipment which could scramble voices. It became a standard installation at US and British embassies.[15]

Technically, Peter was already in the spying business without being in the Intelligence services. In 1950, he was edged closer by Sir Frederick Brundrett, the chief scientist in the Defence Ministry, who set up a committee to improve science at MI5 and MI6. Wright, at the Marconi Laboratory at Great Baddow, in Essex, went the opposite way to his father and developed better listening devices.[16]

By 1955, British Intelligence needed to be dragged into the scientific age as espionage was rapidly moving beyond the straight human skills of thieving, agent-running and watching.

Wright was chosen to facilitate the change, cautiously. But he ran into problems of background, attitude, class, style and ignorance. He was a technocrat, the first at MI5, and this generated suspicion. Wright had power over the gadgetry, the new-fangled devices of the Intelligence war. For men who hitherto had considered even the secretary's typewriter a mystery, there were inherent difficulties in learning the new technology, which in the 1950s was as much scorned as feared.

At first, the new man didn't really seem to have hardened political allegiances, which was also a worry for those around him. He knew little about politics and cared less, for he had a disdain for parliament, which he viewed as over-run by people of little competence. Wright's only apparent ties to the vague notion of 'Monarch and Country' appeared to others in the Intelligence services as not grand but naïve.[17]

The scientist protested that he had no left- or right-wing leanings, which made him a sort of bureau-ostrich, who nevertheless saw enemies in the Moscow Centre and the Kremlin. They were the most powerful communists, who had openly stated their desire for the spread of their false doctrine, which Wright viewed as merely a vehicle for cruel, thuggish men to dominate the planet.

This rarely stated but clear belief of Wright's made him seem unsophisticated to others in the service. These men and women considered themselves more subtle. They never railed against the enemy, or mentioned it as such. Somehow, breeding didn't allow it. They just went about their business of combating it in espionage games, and surviving in a bureaucracy run by strict rules of engagement and procedure.

Wright suspected from the beginning that this meant the Establishment was soft and weak. He saw his role and those of his colleagues in more black and white terms, a little like the Americans did. It was no coincidence that he got on with them from the beginning of his career.

Wright could also be dismissive of those who merely shuffled paper. He was a doer, who could set up a bugging device and gather hard evidence. He felt he was in the service for a purpose, not a fat pension or a gong. Wright was vigorous and very ambitious in a way altogether different from long-term seekers of honours. He actually took his endeavours very, very seriously. This translated as hard work and drive, characteristics not altogether in keeping with long lunches gleaning data at one's club. It was at times unsettling for those above and around him.

Wright was seen as lacking tact, even uncouth. His will to succeed came to concern all in British Intelligence and at the Soviet Embassy. He actually desired to catch spies.

24. THE GOOD ACTING RESIDENT

IVAN THE TERRIBLE

Modin returned to London late in 1955 as acting KGB Resident, which was in part a promotion for his fine work when running several important agents from 1947 to 1953. It also came on top of his disguised entry into Britain in 1954, which proved to be Philby's temporary salvation.

However, Rodin was expected to return in mid-1956 to take over again as Resident. He had delayed his return so that he could avoid the major problem of looking after Krushchev and Bulganin on their proposed 'goodwill' visit to Britain by ship in April 1956.

'It was going to be a very difficult time for the Resident,' Modin recalled with a rueful grin. 'Apart from Krushchev and Bulganin, Ivan Serov [the KGB chief] was coming to personally oversee security on the ship, and in London. He was very demanding and never easy. Also, he had never travelled outside Russia. Serov had a terrible reputation with the Western press.'[1]

The KGB head tried to soften his image by allowing *Sunday Times* journalist Richard Hughes (later a character model for Craw in John Le Carré's book, *The Honourable Schoolboy*), Reuter correspondent Sydney Weiland, and the Russian representatives of *Tass* and *Pravda* to meet Burgess and Maclean early in February. There was no actual interview, and the reporters were handed a signed, three-page statement which was straight propaganda.[2] However, in the Cold War freeze operating at the time, Prime Minister Anthony Eden, the Foreign Office and the press took it as a sign of a possible thaw.

Serov arrived in London in March and sent a team of surveillance experts through the rooms at Claridges Hotel where most of the Krushchev party were due to stay. The Russians began by upsetting hotel staff with their brusque manner, which was reported to the press.

Serov blamed Modin, still the Embassy Press Attaché, for 'incompetence' because of the reports. The KGB chief was soon in a second argument with his acting resident concerning how the press should be handled.

One morning when several popular papers sent reporters and photographers to the Embassy, a disagreement developed over how they should be treated.[3]

'I shall go down and talk to them,' Serov told Modin as they looked down from a second storey window to the Embassy gates.

'I don't think you should,' Modin responded.

'Why not? I do this in Moscow. The press must be told our views, the way things are . . .'

'With respect, sir, the media here are very different.'

'Rubbish!'

'I deal with them daily. Those reporters are from popular papers.'

'So, Comrade? You are wasting my time.'

'You don't understand. They are known even here as the gutter press. I personally deal with the more responsible journalists from papers like the *Financial Times*, the *Observer*, *The Times*, and the *Daily Telegraph*.'

'Then get them here too.'

'We cannot *order* them to come. There is a different attitude to the media in this country.'

'I've had enough of this,' Serov said and accompanied by an interpreter marched downstairs and along the path to the front gate. A nervous Modin hurried out, trying in vain to stop him. A surprised press pack gathered round.

Modin was forced to introduce Serov, who began to dictate remarks through the interpreter to the astonished scribes. They looked at each other and Modin.

'Can we ask questions?' one reporter asked, breaking into the Serov monologue. Serov shook his head.

'You were responsible for butchering Estonians, weren't you?' a journalist asked. Photographers began taking shots. The interpreter looked nervous and said nothing.

'No photos!' Serov demanded, taking a step towards the assembled press people.

He glared at Modin, and demanded to know what had been asked. The interpreter stumbled over his words. Serov went white, then red.

'Is is true that you had dissidents shot in Poland and Hungary?' another reporter asked.

Serov turned on his heel and angrily marched back along the drive to the Embassy building. Inside, he fumed at the hapless Modin, who had tried to warn him.

The next morning several tabloids had screaming headlines such as:

'Serov Butcher Lies', and 'The Butcher is Here Giving Orders!'

The stories were tirades against the KGB head. He was furious at Modin and again abused him.

'You should control this!' he yelled. 'Ring up their editors! You must order a retraction, now!'

Modin tried to explain that the media was free to write what it wished.

'Would they write this about the head of the British Secret Intelligence?' Serov bellowed.

Modin was left speechless and humiliated. Now he understood more fully why the wily Rodin had stayed in Moscow.

The press reports reached Krushchev that night and he immediately sent a message to Serov, demanding that he return to Moscow on the next available flight.

It was the KGB chief's turn to be humiliated. In a desperate move to save some face and return with a minor strategic coup, Serov approached the British Foreign Office and asked if the KGB could establish a facility in Hong Kong which would allow it to technically 'eavesdrop' on China.[4]

The astonished FO flatly refused the request within hours of receiving it and Serov returned to the Centre empty-handed, much to Modin's relief.

MR K. COMES TO TOWN

In April, Krushchev and Bulganin arrived in Portsmouth aboard the big cruiser, *Ordzonikidze*, to be feted by Eden, who was keen to improve relations with the communists and so help thaw the Cold War. Eden banned any Intelligence operations. He feared that if the Russians found out relations with them would be damaged.

'We knew MI6 would try something,' former KGB Colonel 'F' remarked drily in one of our interviews. 'We would have done something too [if the British had been visiting the USSR].'[5]

Did the KGB know in advance about any MI6 operations?

'Yes, but I cannot say what they were, except that we were aware that the ship would be under radar surveillance. The British also sent out submarines to check our ship's technology.'

You learnt this from an agent – a double agent – within British Intelligence?

'I cannot say.'

MI6 did, in fact, run a low-level technical operation with the Navy, in which a radar image of the *Ordzonikidze* was acquired from the time it entered the Channel. A British submarine did tail the ship and actually sat on the sea bed under it to monitor the screw vibrations.

I asked him if the KGB had prior knowledge of other MI6 operations, such as those carried out by frogman Commander Buster Crabb. He refused to answer. Modin claimed there was none.

Crabb thought he could measure the screw's pitch and was told to go ahead and do it, but that it had to be a deniable operation – in other words, if he were caught the Admiralty would make out he was an adventurous freelancer. Either way, it was foolhardy, danger-ous and bound to upset Eden if he found out.[6]

Crabb and another MI6 agent booked in at a Portsmouth Hotel. At dawn on 19 April Crabb swam 300 yards underwater to the cruiser and then got into difficulties, either on his own, or because Russian frogmen were waiting for him in an unseen chamber below the water line.

'One of our sailors saw a frogman surface,' Modin claimed. 'He seemed to be in trouble.'

Crabb was never seen alive again. His headless body was found washed up a year later. Foul play or otherwise, the incident increased tensions between the Soviet Union and Britain, and made espionage operations by either side riskier.

The Russians made the incident public and Eden was furious after being embarrassed in parliament by the Labour opposition. The Prime Minister sacked MI6's director-general and replaced him with Dick White from MI5, which in itself was a further reprimand for MI6 because of the rivalry between the two services.

The top MI5 job was now vacant. White recommended his deputy, Roger Hollis, whose official task was 'the defence of the realm' from sabotage, espionage and subversion 'from within or without the country'.

Hollis was born in Taunton, Somerset, the son of the local Anglican bishop. He went to Oxford's Worcester College, but dropped out and went to China and worked for British Tobacco. He had quite a reputation as a womanizer and in China met Ursula Kuczynski Hamburger, alias Sonia Werner, a Soviet agent who was later a Control for Klaus Fuchs in Britain.

His main claim to fame during the war was the bugging of the British Communist Party. In the decade after, he seemed to have climbed to the top of the MI5 tree by misadventure rather than talent. He was certainly no meritorious rising star as Philby had been at MI6, or a genius like Rothschild. Hollis was the bureaucrat's bureaucrat, with nothing to distinguish him. Yet he was now the most powerful spy looking after Britain. Questions would arise later about his turbulent tenure as MI5 director-general from 1956 to 1965. The most pertinent queries surrounded whether or not he was a Soviet agent.[7]

MODIN'S MASKS

After Krushchev and Bulganin departed, Rodin returned to London as Resident. Modin, however, had gained the respect of fellow staff for the way he handled both the fearsomely ignorant Serov and the British press. It forced Rodin to give ground to Modin in terms of KGB power and scope in Britain.

In fact he was quite happy to delegate and let subordinates do the heavy work, such as the endless meetings with agents. They had taken their toll on his nerve and health, especially after the Fuchs, Burgess, Maclean, Philby and Cairncross affairs. In effect, the MI5 watchers had got the better of him, and he wanted others to shoulder the responsibility.[8]

Modin, now thirty-three, was still energetic and inspired enough for the demands of Control work. It was less taxing and even at times made 'most enjoyable' by his front as Press Attaché. He and wife Anne were invited to many social functions, including a Garden Party at Buckingham Palace.

'We joined the guests in morning suits and top hats, and uniforms, who queued at the Palace Gates,' Modin recalled with curious pleasure. 'Tents in the Palace park served tea and biscuits as the Queen roamed amongst the various groups. Then our delegation was lined up to meet her.'

Who arranged this? Your very good friend Sir Anthony Blunt?

'I don't know,' Modin laughed. 'Maybe! After all, he was related to the Queen Mother! Anyway, the Queen, Princess Margaret and the Duke of Edinburgh shook hands with everyone, starting with our Ambassador, Yakov Malik, and his wife. When Princess Margaret reached us [Modin and Anne], she stopped and gasped. Her eyes widened. She stared at Anne.'

Anne, an attractive brunette, was about the same age and size as the Queen.

'Anne and the Queen looked very much the same, down to the wide smile and charming eyes,' Modin added. 'She did not move on as quickly as expected, and the Ambassador bent forward at the front end of the reception line, frowning. He didn't know what had happened. The Queen and the Duke of Edinburgh also reacted. They didn't remark about Anne's similar appearance, but it was clear that they were intrigued. She and the Queen were practically doubles.'

The next morning, the Ambassador summoned Modin to his office.

'He wanted to know if we had any special relationship with the Royal Family,' Modin recalled with a chuckle. 'I tried to explain about Anne's similarity to the Queen, but he was suspicious.'

'He asked me if I knew the Royal Family,' Modin went on, roaring with laughter. 'He thought we might be running a KGB operation!'

Did he suspect Blunt had linked the Modins to the Royals?

'I don't know, but he didn't believe me!'[9]

The Ambassador could be forgiven for wondering. Modin was being seen around London with the nation's elite. David Astor, the editor of the *Observer*, invited him to dinner parties and even to watch test cricket at Lords in 1956 between England and Australia.

Modin (as, coincidentally, did Rothschild) spent a Saturday pre-lunch session watching Australian all-rounder Richie Benaud belt a whirlwind 97, which the Russian found enjoyable though incomprehensible. Over lunch, Astor lobbied him for access to interviews with Soviet leaders.

By day, the attaché presented a smiling public face, and enjoyed his prominence as the only conduit to Soviet information at the Embassy. If the press wanted to know about anything from Soviet foreign policy to sport he was the man with the contacts. By night or at obscure meeting places during daylight hours, he turned clandestine, operating in his prime role as a Control – now the most important agent-runner in Britain. Almost all his journalistic contacts had no idea of his importance within the KGB. His friendly, warm and intellectual air gave him a near-perfect cover.

'Yuri was popular,' ex-Fleet Street journalist Christopher Dobson recalled. 'Everyone [at the broadsheets] knew him. He had to lie often, that was expected and part of his job. But he was a likeable liar.'[10]

Modin was a frequent visitor to the restaurants round Fleet Street usually in the company of political and defence correspondents.

Which papers did he target?[11]

'I was very close to the *Observer*. I was once invited to their weekly boardroom luncheon. This paper was very well informed. There were also journalists at *The Times*, the *Daily Telegraph* and the *Economist*.'

Modin's press role gave him the best possible opportunities to turn journalists into Soviet agents. It might begin with someone wanting information from him, or he might seek out a particular reporter because it was known he had money problems or was a big spender. On occasions the candidate was simply sympathetic to the Soviet cause.

'Writers covering politics and defence were of particular interest because they had access to people, data and facilities,' Modin said.

He was the most successful of all Controls at 'turning' British journalists. He had access to a sizeable slush fund for pay-offs.

Sometimes such agents would be paid on an irregular, piecemeal basis to keep them supportive. This kind of access ensured that the diligent, hard-working Modin kept a steady supply of data flowing from the Embassy to the Centre from at least twenty spies, with some of them being controlled in rotation by other Russian agent-runners.

The loss of the key agents such as Philby was a blow to the Soviet network, but by mid-1956 Modin and his fellow Controls had restored British espionage networks to their greatest effectiveness since the 1930s.

The Russian learned from Blunt in July that Philby's MI6 friends had found an Intelligence job for him in Beirut. His cover was as a stringer for Modin's favourite British news outlets, the *Observer* and the *Economist*.

Yet there was still great suspicion surrounding Philby, and MI6 at first did nothing with him, which left him with the low-key role of gathering what he could as an Arab specialist with good contacts in the Middle East. This limited his usefulness to the Centre, which decided to make little contact while encouraging him to pass on whatever he thought would be of use.

The region had become of extraordinary interest with the growing strength of Israel, the coup in Iran and the emergence of President Nasser as a fierce Egyptian nationalist. Modin continued to monitor the position of one of his best agents from the original ring, to which he held strong allegiance. Gradually Philby's position was restored within MI6, until he was of value to the KGB once more. They began increasing their contacts.

ALL GOOD THINGS

By 1958, the spying game had taken its toll on Modin. Yuri was thirty-five, and had been an active Control in London for a decade. He was not exactly burnt out, but he had been working hard, at times under enormous stress. There had been pressure over the loss of atomic spies such as Fuchs, then the Maclean/Burgess defections, the clandestine return to see Philby, the Serov incident . . . The list went on.

As the years slipped by, the watchers and British surveillance technology – thanks largely to Peter Wright – were getting better. Agents inside, and close to, British Intelligence had been able to warn the Russians of most developments in advance, but there was always the worry of the next threat.

Modin had also been disillusioned by the ineptitude of Rodin, who had become sicker and more careless than ever. This had put Modin, the other Controls and the agents they were running in jeopardy.

MI5 was closing in. The watchers were taking photographs and building quite a file on him, to the point where he suspected his cover may have been blown.[12] He was no longer seen as the smiling, agreeable Press Attaché. In fact, by 1958, MI5 viewed him as a Control, although they were not sure of his importance.[13]

Modin told Rodin he wanted to return to Moscow, citing the education of his daughter, Olga, as the reason. She was due to go into the Soviet middle school in 1958, and both parents did not want her to miss a year. Furthermore, Anne was expecting their second child.

Rodin refused his request at first, saying that his work was 'too vital' at the moment. Training a new Control who would then have to gain the confidence of his agents would be too difficult.[14]

In reality, Rodin knew that the burden of agent-running in London would fall to him once Modin left. The Resident knew he was not capable of it.

Modin applied again and Rodin refused again. They argued. It developed into a violent confrontation with Modin accusing the Resident of causing the detection of Soviet agents. Modin said he was lazy and undisciplined in his job. After the blazing argument, Rodin had no choice but to agree to release him.

The family relocated to Moscow at a time when there was some excitement amongst Western journalists over Russia, with Krushchev in power and scientific achievements like the Sputnik satellite flights appearing to set the pace in the East–West technological race. The Soviet Union was the place for leading correspondents, especially if they were left-leaning, and Modin's initial work was in dealing with some of the Moscow-based journalists. He had received a glowing 'characteristic' – the report on his work in London – from Rodin, who had still not lost hope that Modin would return.

Normally when Controls returned to home base, they were

required to write an extensive report about all their foreign operations. Modin was frank. He spoke his mind as diplomatically as
possible, but could not resist an honest analysis of Rodin. Modin
wrote about his inefficiency and inadequacy. KGB Chief Serov, a
close friend of Rodin, received the report. He had always blamed
Modin for his own disastrous attempt to handle the Fleet Street
press in 1956 before Krushchev's visit.

Serov contacted Rodin to tell him of Modin's negative remarks.
Rodin was furious. He immediately wrote a new, unflattering
characteristic, which blamed all the KGB's London failures, such as
the defections, on Modin. Serov decided to send Modin to Siberia.
The conflict was common knowledge throughout the KGB. When
Burgess heard of it, he wrote a forceful letter to Serov defending
Modin's great work as his Control from 1947 to 1951. He made
special reference to his 'controlled, professional behaviour' and
courage in masterminding the departure of himself and Maclean
from Britain.[15]

The Burgess testimony stopped him from being sent to Siberia
and held up action against Modin for some time, but eventually he
was demoted.

25. MOVES AND COUNTER-MOVES

DAY OF THE TECHNICIAN

Peter Wright and his technical equipment had an immediate impact at MI5 and in an effort to improve relations with the FBI and the CIA, he was sent to the US in 1957 to explain his new bugging techniques to them. FBI director Hoover was more interested in lecturing his visitor, but Angleton, now the CIA chief of counter-intelligence, gave him a more sympathetic ear.[1]

The American had become an important figure in espionage after obtaining the secret text of Krushchev's 1956 denunciation of Stalin from Israeli agents. Wright counted him as a friend and encouraged him to believe that they could 'do business together'.[2]

Angleton was as fervently anti-communist as Hoover, but he was smarter, more sophisticated, and his education in the UK had given him a greater rapport with the British. Over a convivial lunch in Georgetown, Angleton asked about Philby and Wright told him he thought he was a Soviet spy.[3] The American listened without defending his mentor. Angleton had stopped doing that since about 1952, but he remained noncommittal about his own feelings.

Wright got the impression that Angleton still wanted to believe Philby was an innocent victim of circumstances – namely his connection with Burgess and his follies. Wright divulged some of his London Soviet Embassy bugging plans to a receptive and intrigued Angleton. Apart from their common work, the two men saw in each other an unequivocal desire to defeat communism, which might develop into a cross-Atlantic bond. For the first time since the Burgess/Maclean defections, Angleton felt there was someone he could possibly trust within British Intelligence.[4]

Back in London, Wright began expanding the use of his bugging techniques, in particular Rafter, a method of monitoring radio wave transmissions which could tell if MI5 watchers were themselves being listened to, and Engulf, an operation to read machine-generated cipher messages. For example, Wright asked his MI5 boss, Roger Hollis, for extra funds to buy a house in the middle of a cluster of Soviet diplomatic buildings and installed Rafter receivers in the loft.

Not only the Russians were targets. Embassies across London, from the French to the Greek, were put under surveillance.

As Wright noted in his book, *Spycatcher*, 'we bugged and burgled our way across London at the State's behest, while pompous, bowler-hatted civil servants in Whitehall pretended to look the other way.'

But it didn't stop at London. As a result of his inventions, GCHQ (the Government Communications HQ, which had originally resided at Bletchley Park and was later moved to Cheltenham) presented MI5 with a 'mammoth' list of overseas targets.

Although Wright failed to amalgamate the research and development of surveillance technology by MI5 and MI6, he found himself frequently involved in foreign operations. His expertise as British Intelligence's top bugger was in demand.

For instance, despite the disaster of Buster Crabb's demise in the *Ordzhonikidze* Russian cruiser operation, MI6 was determined to continue monitoring it and tracked the ship to Stockholm. In 1959, Wright was called in to run an Engulf operation against the cruiser's cipher machine. He and others from GCHQ set up secretly in a warehouse on the docks and intercepted cipher messages.

They failed to break the cipher codes, but it was the beginning of a huge escalation in bugging and listening, the new dimension of espionage. In a few years' time the human element would be augmented by special equipment, which could hear and record every word, and photograph everything from satellites.

Wright had reached a position of influence within the services at the right time. GCHQ operations were expanded up and down the country via Post Office towers topped with microwave dishes, which the public were told were for relaying TV and radio signals. The towers formed a network for secretly passing on military Intelligence data to GCHQ from the many British and US installations in the UK.

By the late 1950s, Britain had become a floating aircraft carrier for the US in its Cold War activities, providing bases for electronic surveillance and for a rapid military response to conflict with the Soviet Union. The Americans had major bases, minor reserve bases, depots, Intelligence stations, Thor missile sites and communications links running from Thurso-Forss in the north of Scotland to Ringstead in the south of England. Every base was prepared for war and on the alert for warnings of a possible first strike by the Russians.

Wright as a techno-spy had an important role in the expanded, clandestine espionage battle against the enemy.

THE BUREAUCRATIC WAY

Like all scientists, he thrived on research and he knew that MI5 could not hope to compete with friends or enemies in the spy world without proper facilities. He applied for funds, but was told – in true bureaucratic style – it would be better first to produce evidence that KGB scientific and technical developments were ahead of British Intelligence in specific areas.

Budgets always had to have a well-researched and written justification, so the canny Wright set out to provide one. He began by delving through the debriefings of so-called 'Dragon Returnees' – German scientists captured by the KGB after the war, who had been forced to work in the Soviet Union to gain their freedom.

'The debriefings,' Wright noted, 'provided much useful intelligence about the state of Soviet rocket, jet engine, and nuclear research.'[5]

He followed up with a trip to Germany to interview specific scientists further and then compiled a paper which, on shrewd advice, he submitted to MI6 as well as MI5, so that he would have joint support for a research facility. The idea was rejected by the Defence Research Policy Committee, but it made everyone aware that the KGB had advanced ahead of Western Intelligence in several areas. This applied especially to the field of electronics and surveillance devices, including the use of infrared systems, which had put them in a commanding position since the 1940s.[6]

Wright still had to apply for specific programme funding, but his submissions had stimulated the government into responding with some budget increases. This, and the expansion of the Anglo-American surveillance capability throughout Britain via Post Office towers and military bases, helped escalate the weapons/technology race with the Soviet Union.

The Russians' British spies were keeping them informed of all Wright's activities and the general increase in the West's capacity to listen to and watch the enemy. The KGB and the Soviet military intelligence arm – the GRU – had to find ways to combat these new Western advances. The London Controls, led by Rodin, were instructed to ask their key agents, such as Blunt, to use their contacts to supply information which would enable the KGB to counteract the bugging and do some eavesdropping of their own.

If the KGB knew in advance about an MI5/MI6 operation it could take steps to nullify it. Similarly it had to find a way of countering the huge build-up of American forces and bases on the British mainland.

The problem was how to spy on and be ready to destroy the Anglo-American bases when war started. The KGB and the GRU had to create an organization which would have outlets all over Britain without creating suspicion. It seemed impossible because the bases were often in remote places off 'B' roads in the country.[7]

None of the handful of existing Russian companies in Britain was suitable. It taxed the brains at the Moscow Centre for some time after it first learned that the British Department of Defence was planning to build Post Office towers up the spine of the country to communicate defence information. Finally, an ingenious report came from one of Blunt's connections.[8] It suggested that the Russians should attempt to set up an oil company with retail petrol outlets throughout the UK as a cover for spying and potential sabotage operations. It would be the biggest capitalist business venture the Russians had ever created in the West.

The special agent's report noted that the Soviet Union could offer a trade *quid pro quo*. For instance, increased access to Soviet crude oil (it was the world's biggest supplier) might be an incentive to the British since the shock over the Suez Canal Crisis. In exchange the Russian commercial venture inside Britain might be allowed.

The ever-available excuse for the Russians wanting to set up the company would be that it wanted to generate much-needed hard currency.

KGB sources refused to say from whom the daring report came.[9] They were coy about the agent in question, but there was no one amongst the British spies with the technical skills, access and brilliance to create such a plan – with the exception of one agent.

THE HUMBLE RESEARCH ADVISER

Late in 1958, Rothschild became a part-time adviser to the research organization of the Shell Corporation, after leaving the chairmanship of the Agricultural Research Council earlier in the year. The new job raised many eyebrows. At the age of forty-seven, this open socialist and member of the Labour Party was making his first major move into private enterprise, if his youthful, short foray into the Bank in 1931 is discounted.

Why, it was asked, would such an exalted individual take a lowly position with a commensurate salary? It was whispered in Shell's corridors that this might be one of those positions where a 'personality latched himself on to the company and no one quite knew why'. This was an indicator that he could be there for anything from influence in business to 'doing something for the Foreign Office', which was a euphemism for spying.

There was an unwritten policy at Shell to call on the old-boy network for 'personalities', such as Douglas Bader the wartime ace fighter pilot. If these characters fitted in or did well they were moved on from being part-time appointees to something bigger (which occurred in Rothschild's case).[10]

Certainly, with Shell's thirty laboratories worldwide and its production facilities in the Middle East, it was a good cover for his agent-running for Dick White, which Rothschild continued into the 1960s. But it was also a perfect opportunity for him to deploy his skills in commercial counter-espionage, honed for Guy Liddell and MI5 during the early part of the war.

This spying experience would be useful to the KGB, especially if he was helping to create a Russian company – one which wished to copy the main aspects of Shell business in Britain from its oil products to its research, marketing and distribution operations.

On 30 September 1959, a year after Rothschild joined Shell, a wholly-Russian-owned company was registered to operate in the UK. It was called Nafta Great Britain.

AN INVESTIGATIVE DIVERSION

I stumbled across Nafta two decades later in 1978 when the KGB and British Intelligence probably considered it a blown operation. An MI6 contact, one of three I knew in the 1970s, met me for lunch in the usual cavernous wine bar off Northumberland Avenue, Whitehall, near the Ministry of Defence building in which he worked.

It was frequented by smart-suited civil servants and their secretaries. The cubicles allowed for private conversation.

I had first been introduced to MI6 people via an executive at the then US-based Univac Computer company late in 1974, before my first trip to Russia in the summer of 1975. I had maintained contact ever since. They were an important source as background for several articles, books and documentaries.

'You never met me', was their refrain at each rendezvous as it has been with most agents East or West. Their information had been useful for background, perhaps a contact in this country or that, but rarely provided revelations. Secrets were not divulged.

However, at this particular lunch, at which rich Bulgarian red wine flowed, I asked for something sensational I could perhaps use in a book, a newspaper article or a documentary. The MI6 man – bright and Oxbridge educated – mused for a while before suggesting I check the different types of wholly-owned Russian companies in Britain.

'You might look into their economic viability,' he said, 'especially those operating outside London.'

The tip was the beginning of many elliptical clues. My contact refused to spell things out. I would have to do the heavy research, so as to cover the source. In effect the oblique directions cut the research time from twenty years to one, part-time.

A contact at the British Department of Trade sent me a list of twelve Russian companies registered in the UK. They included banks, a finance house, a watch company, a TV, radiogram and refrigerator distributor, a company which imported Soviet cars, an insurance group, Intourist and a farm equipment company.[11]

Only one of any significance operated around the country: Nafta. The Department of Trade document showed that in 1976 it generated £345,643,150 turnover, indicating that it was a substantial and legitimate organization. It ran about 150 retail petrol stations, mainly in London, Yorkshire, the East and West Midlands, and the home counties. It was registered as company number 643351 at 11 Moorfields, High Walk, London EC2.

Its one million shares were 100 per cent owned by Russian companies: Anglo-Soviet Shipping Company (1500 shares, same address as Nafta GB), Arcos Ltd (1500 shares, same address), Russian Oil Products (47,500 shares, same address) and V/O Sojuznefteex Port of 32/34 Smolenskaja Square, Moscow, which controlled the group with 949,500 shares. Its directors – all Russian nationals – were listed as V. A. Arutunian, O. A. Kourenkov, and V. A. Boonin, who was the managing director.

The company's employees were mostly unsuspecting British nationals. Russians were not allowed to travel beyond a 25-mile radius from the centre of London. Officially Nafta was to trade 'as an exporter, importer, distiller of crude oils and petroleum, including gas, oil and Derv – diesel engine fuel oil'.

Yet under the auspices of the KGB and GRU some of the outlets could be built on obscure 'B' roads and be uneconomic as long as they were close enough to spy on important US/UK/NATO bases and intercept communications.

In October 1978, I contacted Nafta and said I was writing an article on the success of Russian companies in Britain. They checked my credentials. I was allowed to meet a manager who reported to the Russian directors.

'They are shy about publicity,' he explained over a lunch interview. The manager was defensive about working for a Russian group, but was not an agent himself. The KGB and GRU used British agents from outside the company to find suitable sites and run the intelligence operations.

Without prompting, he said Nafta offered him the opportunity to sell its products uneconomically.

'I guessed they wanted to get some sort of niche in the market and cash flow to establish themselves,' the manager remarked.

He spoke of the company going 'over the top' to buy stations at Ironbridge near Uxbridge and Luton. In other words, it paid exorbitant prices to acquire certain sites. These two stations cost more than £500,000 in the 1970s – well over the going market price each time.

The two were in a direct line (as was the Soviet Embassy in London) for data pumped out of the hub of the Post Office tower network off Tottenham Court Road en route to Bristol. This was the most vital NATO defence link of all – to the US via the satellite communications station at Goonhilly Downs in Cornwall. In addition, an important RAF station at Uxbridge protects Autovon, a worldwide military communications system set up inside a former British army anti-aircraft operations bunker.

Apart from the prices paid, the profitability of each station had to be checked by obtaining an economic assessment of Nafta from a rival company, Esso. A woman in the research department sent me a computer printout of Nafta station locations and how much petrol they sold monthly. As MI6 had indicated, many outlets in out-of-the-way places were losing money for the organization. At least twenty of them were located where Shell, Texaco, Esso and others had not bothered to venture.

I approached the MI6 contact for more clues.

'Work a little harder,' he advised. 'Take a trip into the countryside and observe. There is a 1971 *Sunday Times Magazine* article you might want to use as a guide . . .'[12]

The article in question, which upset the Department of Defence, showed the major UK and US military bases around the country. It led to me spending many weekends in the winter of 1978–79 touring round England with a camera and a bored girlfriend searching for the bases, often discernible by the huge golf ball dishes which picked up a steady flow of data from satellites.

Once discovered, it was a matter of referring to the Nafta printout and a map to find the right petrol station nearby. During this period, while producing a documentary with Jon Lane, a former ITN cameraman, I came across a Nafta outlet in the heart of the Yorkshire dales near the quiet hamlet of Otley, birthplace of Thomas Chippendale. On the horizon was a Post Office tower – one of the 200 placed 30 miles apart, which transmitted the ultra-high-frequency radio waves. Over the decades, phone, telex, computer and (later) fax information were to be added to TV and radio signals, and secret military data.

The Otley Nafta station and the tower were filmed. The next day the documentary crew began a search around Yorkshire. We came across the US National Security Agency-run Menwith Hill in Yorkshire, where there was a 6,000-strong US army contingent based underground. It was one of the most important communications Intelligence bases in the world.

After a few minutes driving round the area we found a Nafta station over a nearby hill. At 6 p.m. that evening we drank at the local pub where about twenty young crew-cut American military personnel were enjoying a break from their subterranean world.

Nafta hunting had become an obsessive sport. I found clusters of them around the Russian Trade Mission at Highgate, London, which were in line with post-office towers to Dover and, across the Channel, to the North Atlantic Treaty Organization's military HQ (SHAPE) at Chievres, near Mons, Belgium, and administrative HQ in Brussels. (NATO was set up in 1949 as a defence against the USSR and was dominated by the US.) After knocking out UK installations, NATO facilities on the Continent were the next target for destruction by Soviet special forces in the build-up to war.

Towers also formed a line to Birmingham, a so-called 'back-bone' route set up as a defence warning system against a Soviet nuclear attack.

The stations were further positioned to pick up data from towers linked towards Norwich, which were part of the RAF network carrying radar pictures from Britain's three east coast, early-warning radar stations to defence chiefs in London.

A few weeks later, I took cameraman Lane and a crew to Paris to make another documentary and we diverted via Belgium to shoot Nafta stations sited close to NATO links to the UK.

In all, I visited about forty British Nafta stations and estimated that at least thirty of them were in locations of dubious profitability near important military bases and communications links.

Interception equipment could easily be set up in the stations to spy on bases and, as MI6 explained once I had mapped the correlations between petrol stations and military bases, the stations could be used to destroy the bases in war.

'Using petrol stations was ingenious,' one Shell executive noted when I interviewed him in March 1994. 'You might have 100,000 gallons of fuel in storage which would make a hell of a bomb with which to sabotage those bases.'

I assumed that MI6 eventually discovered the clandestine activities of Nafta hidden behind its normal commercial business. Some of the 105 Soviet personnel expelled from Britain in 1971 would probably have been involved with it.

The development of medium-range missiles by both sides in the 1970s may have partly usurped the role of Nafta as a first-strike weapon in war. In the late 1980s, the company sold out and the Soviets retreated with the end of the Cold War and the disintegration of the communist bloc.

Yet in 1958, the setting up of the petrol chain in Britain was considered by the KGB and GRU as one of their most vital foreign operations.

26. MAKING FRIENDS

THE INTRODUCTION

Wright was surprised and pleased to be invited for supper at Rothschild's St James's Place flat in late 1958.[1] Wright, the ambitious techno-provocateur had not made many friends at work and it was rare for a star from the upper reaches of the British firmament to invite someone in his position to a meal at home.

The scientist had always had a grudge against his superiors from the educated Oxbridge ranks. His poor background had prevented him from entering a major university, and he felt their attitudes were antiquated and snobbish.

Rothschild was probably operating in response to a request from KGB Resident Rodin.[2] Blunt informed Rothschild that the Russians were concerned with the efforts of MI5's surveillance team.[3] The KGB needed to monitor Wright's work more closely.

Before supper, Rothschild took the scientist to his study . . .

'. . . a light scholarly room overlooking Green Park, and stamped with his extraordinary character – paintings, scientific diagrams, musical instruments, books ancient and modern, and on a wall a huge, self-designed slide rule. There was also a piano, on which Victor played jazz with great skill and élan . . .'[4]

Rothschild had a plausible excuse for making contact via either Roger Hollis (according to Peter Wright) or Dick White (according to Rothschild himself).[5] He told Wright a fellow Shell scientist might be useful to MI5.[6]

Showing magnanimity in keeping with a fine fellow still wedded to British Intelligence's success, he was offering this man for secondment or joint work with Shell. Rothschild was aware that

MI5 had limited resources and the gesture seemed generous to Wright.

'Rothschild was fascinated by my plans for the scientific modernization of MI5,' Wright recalled, and admitted being particularly garrulous in his company. '[He] offered me many suggestions of his own.'[7]

After dinner they talked until late into the night.

'I soon realized that he possessed an enormous appetite for the gossip and intrigue of the secret world,' Wright said, ' and we were soon swapping stories about some of the more bizarre colleagues he remembered from the war.'

Rothschild was in full charm mode from the beginning with Wright, whose deference to his friendly lordship left him gullible and open to manipulation. Wright came away 'feeling for the first time that, with his backing, great achievements were possible.'

This demonstrated Rothschild's pervasive influence from outside British Intelligence, thirteen years after he had officially left MI5. The Intelligence services' key scientist in the now dominant techno-war could only look forward to continuing achievement, developing operations using modern techniques, if Rothschild supported him.

Wright looked up to him, not only socially but professionally and intellectually. He was also in awe of his subtle power and influence:

'I doubt I have ever met a man who impressed me as much as Victor Rothschild,' he commented in *Spycatcher*. 'He is a brilliant scientist, a Fellow of the Royal Society, with expertise in botany and zoology, and a fascination for the structure of spermazotoa. But he has been much, much more than a scientist. His contacts, in politics, in intelligence, in banking, in the Civil Service, and abroad are legendary. There are few threads in the seamless robe of the British Establishment which have not passed at some time or other through the eye of the Rothschild needle.'[8]

Wright was very proud of the relationship. It showed that he was not neglected by the amorphous establishment after all. On the contrary, one of the greatest amongst its ranks was fulsome in his recognition of the scientist's skills. He was even patronizing him and willing to become friends.

It gave Wright a certain sense of his own importance and power. He could pick up the phone to the high and the mighty and say with increasing confidence, 'Victor . . . er . . . *Lord* Rothschild said I should speak with you.'

Rothschild also showed he was a man of action as well as talk by putting some Shell laboratories at MI5's disposal, which made everyone happy. The meagre MI5 budget was augmented by Shell's generosity, and Rothschild was able to keep abreast of everything MI5 was doing.

He went further and began work himself on 'a variety of technical developments, including a special grease which would protect equipment if it was buried underground for long periods'.

The grease was developed. British Intelligence used it 'extensively' as they did other of Rothschild's inventions. Not only was he aware of and knowledgeable on everything from British Intelligence bugging techniques to surveillance operations, he was creating the technology himself and overseeing many new developments.

THE CONTINUING NUCLEAR CONNECTION

Rothschild went further in his lordly patronage of Wright. He had kept abreast of nuclear weapons progress in Britain and was a close friend of Sir William Cook, then the deputy head of the Atomic Weapons Research Establishment (AWRE). He suggested that Wright should approach Cook for resources.

'His well-timed lobbying made my visit much easier,' an ever-grateful Wright remarked.

Wright told Cook of his approach to counter-espionage, which was to develop technical ways of attacking Soviet spy communications. Communications were the only vulnerable point in an agent's cover, because he had to send and receive messages to and from his controller.

Wright said in *Spycatcher*:

'I explained to Cook that Rafter already provided us with the most valuable weapon of all – an entrée into Russian radio communications – but that we urgently needed new techniques to attack their physical methods of communications as well, such as secret writing, microdots, and dead letter drops. Progress on these would vastly improve our chances of counter-espionage success.'[9]

Cook responded by providing MI5 with thirty people at AWRE including top scientists, and resources. AWRE paid for everything for two years before the UK Defence Research Policy Committee took over the funding.

This example demonstrates Rothschild's power to instigate developments which embraced so many people and resources that it hid his action as the trigger of the expanded activity. Yet with his great capacity and passion for absorbing all matters scientific, he kept intellectually on top of all these new activities.

AWRE's people devised four programmes. The first was a chemical agent which used radioactivity to detect any secret writing. Secondly, AWRE produced a neutron activation process for detecting microdots — photographs which were reduced to microscopic size, making them virtually invisible and easily concealed under stamps, on top of punctuation marks in typed letters, or under the lips of envelopes.

The third programme encompassed a counter to the success of dead letter drops — so called because instead of dangerous face-to-face meetings, an agent could leave espionage material in containers in, for instance, a tree trunk, where it would be picked up later by the receiving spy.

The KGB treated their containers so they could tell if they had been tampered with by MI5. AWRE came up with a special X-ray technique, which allowed MI5 to inspect containers without tampering with them and fogging unexposed film inside.

The fourth programme caused ecstasy among MI5's buggers. It developed an X-ray method of reading safe combinations from the inside which, according to Wright, 'gave MI5 potential access to every safe in Britain.'[10] Thanks to Rothschild the KGB knew of every development and were able to take steps to counter them. Furthermore, they used the technology themselves against Western agents.[11]

MI5 inventions and technical advances went on, while Rothschild kept in contact with the key figures and digested the reports. This, coupled with his close contact with Dick White, other intelligence chiefs, Wright and the heads of the key research facilities in everything from weapons to radar, meant that Rothschild understood better than anyone in MI6 or MI5 every aspect of British Intelligence, from technical developments to their application in the field.

By comparison, Roger Hollis, MI5's head, had the power of veto on operations but he did not comprehend the detail of the technology or its application. He would have known when, where and why an operation was being run, but would have had little knowledge of how. Hollis's attention to them would have been at times scant, given his key function as an administrator. Even then, according to most, he was at best a competent paper shuffler.

He was not atypical of the underwhelming civil servants in the British bureaucracy, who had risen to prominence due to diligence rather than talent. His background – Oxford undergraduate, with a serviceable, unspectacular intelligence record – rather than his brilliance had seen him rise with little trace to a top job, which really needed someone as safe but with more intellect and flair. The same limitations applied to Graham Mitchell, Hollis's deputy, although he was sharper and more cunning than his boss.

Rothschild made a point of keeping strong contacts with them both, so that if he was in the MI5 building, seeing Peter Wright or someone else, it would seem natural. There were many ex-service officers who visited the offices from time to time, but never with the frequency and interest of Rothschild.

His role was unique in the annals of British Intelligence, and he was welcomed as a VIP, a vital friend with the whiff of power, money and influence, always used to the good of the Secret Service.

It was an overwhelming front, used creatively during the war when research facilities opened up to him unquestioningly. After all, he was a peer of the realm, a man of enormous wealth, great intellect and at times an imperious manner which if anything boosted his overall image.

From the doorman to the director, everyone showed the highest respect to the busy lord, who often seemed to be in a rush from a meeting in Whitehall or the Bank, or on his way to Cambridge.

Until 1962, little Rothschild did was questioned. He had information, access and the best understanding of the espionage war of anyone, including Wright. The scientist may have known as much about what was going on in the research laboratories, although even this is doubtful. Rothschild himself was creating and directing some of it at Shell.

Yet Rothschild also knew the information that counted, which Wright would never be privy to. This was the vital data, including secrets, discussed at the top of the Establishment in clubs and at dinners held by Rothschild and his peers.

This information on the espionage demi-monde would filter down to Wright only if it were necessary. The data in question was not only concerned with this operation against the Russians or that versus the French. It might be about a new appointment, the cutting of a budget, the boosting of another and the power-plays in politics and business, all of which affected the shape and destiny of British Intelligence.

Everything of importance was passed on to Sir Anthony Blunt for consumption inside the Soviet Embassy and the Centre in Moscow.[12] He had not been entirely above suspicion since the Burgess/Maclean defections, but nevertheless he had near-impeccable credentials as the Queen's art surveyor and expert. What's more, Her Majesty liked him. He had been a favourite of her father's and he had done an important service for the Royals during the war.

It all added up to Blunt having an excellent cover. Even though his own direct spying days were over, he was still an important conduit for others and the KGB could rely on him. It meant that the Controls had steady, fast access to the important operational secrets.

Over a period of time, Wright began to notice that every single counter-espionage operation run against the Soviets was failing. He began to wonder why.

27. ALIBI FOR A SPY

IN FROM THE COLD

In mid-December 1961, a stocky, Ukrainian-born KGB major defected in Finland and set up a chain of events which would eventually lead to exposure of the complete Ring of Five. Anatoli Golitsyn was not running for ideological reasons. He had been caught in a typical Soviet Embassy power struggle between the Ambassador and the KGB Resident. Golitsyn had sided with the Ambassador, who had lost the battle. Golitsyn thought he might be murdered, so he defected with his family and was happily accepted by the CIA.[1]

The KGB major was in such a hurry that he departed empty-handed, with no files or stolen documents. But the determined, tough son of a peasant carried much information in his head. He doled enough out to the CIA to encourage them, particularly Angleton, to persevere with him. The head of counter-intelligence was most interested to hear what he had to say about a Ring of Five spies recruited in Britain in the 1930s. This was the first confirmation from Russia of rumours circulating in the West since the Burgess/Maclean defections in 1951 that there was a Cambridge Ring of Five Soviet agents.

Golitsyn claimed they were close to each other, close enough to know that each had been recruited by the Comintern as dedicated, secret communist agents. The bonding had made them a formidable combination.

Golitsyn could give no names, except that one of them was code-named STANLEY and had been connected with recent KGB operations in the Middle East. It stunned Angleton. Philby was in Beirut at the time working for the *Observer*.

'Jim had been pondering the subject of Philby's betrayal since 1951,' former CIA operative 'I' claimed. 'I would say that he had at first rejected the idea and then had gradually, slowly come round to the idea that Kim could have been a traitor. But it was hard [for Angleton], very tough. Not just because he had looked up to him and had been trained by him. Jim was one very proud *Chicano*. To have been conned like that was not palatable. Now there was a pretty goddamn strong indicator that Philby was a traitor.'[2]

It preyed on Angleton's mind. He began to wonder about others he had met in London in 1944 and 1945.

'He had a little list,' the CIA man recalled. 'It was the other suspects among the British.'

Was Rothschild on that list?

'He wouldn't show the list to anyone. But he was already suspicious of Rothschild. He had first annoyed Jim on his patch. Jim had special connections with Israel and he felt the British [Intelligence] through Rothschild were interfering. He had the same doubts about Philby that he had about Rothschild. They never uttered sentiments [one way or the other] about the communists.'

Angleton also took note of Rothschild's maverick attitude and subsequent behaviour in dealing with Israel. In the 1940s it ran contrary to British interests. He was serving two masters with a conflict of interest: MI5 and Mossad. If he was capable of serving two, could he secretly serve a third?

'Jim worried about Israel's left-wing politics when it was formed. He was concerned that some of the British agents [including Rothschild] had been happy with that. But not Jim. He wanted them to be a wholesome [laughs] anti-communist US satellite. That took a little time [laughs].'

Angleton let British Intelligence know of Golitsyn's revelations. He encouraged them to investigate further.

'The Philby and Blunt cases were exhumed,' Peter Wright recalled, 'and a reassessment ordered. MI5 and MI6 came quickly to the conclusion on the basis of the new leads that Philby was the Third Man.'[3]

British Intelligence was abuzz with the new data. Meetings were held. Key MI5 people like Dick White were keen to move against Philby immediately. It soon became a matter of not if but when something would be done. But the Intelligence chiefs and their masters in Whitehall decided as early as February 1962, that Philby would *not* be charged.

Instead he would be offered immunity in exchange for disclosing all. It was thought that it would be far better to interrogate him in depth to drain from him as much information about the KGB as possible. He would have been the best placed of all foreign spies to explain Soviet operations abroad.[4] According to a former senior MI6 officer:

'If he didn't accept that [immunity], the general feeling was that it would be better if he defected, though the former was preferable to the latter. We had kept such situations quiet before. The last thing we wanted was a scandal.'[5]

Former KGB Colonel 'F' was in agreement:

'Philby was a major prize for them [MI6]. We were informed that they wanted very much to question him, but without fuss – without trouble.'

Philby and his biographer, Phillip Knightley, considered it more likely that British Intelligence wanted to engineer his defection:

'My view, and that of my superiors in Moscow,' the spy told the writer, 'is that the whole thing was deliberately staged so as to push me into escaping, because the last thing the British government wanted at that time was me in London, a security scandal and a sensational trial.'[6]

Modin agreed with this assessment. 'They didn't want him back,' he told me adamantly. 'The publicity would have been damaging to MI6. The Government would have been in trouble.'[7]

It *was* a difficult time. George Blake, another of Modin's former agents working for MI6, had been arrested and charged under the UK Official Secrets Act. Blake confessed, was tried at the Old Bailey and given a forty-two-year jail sentence, the longest term ever imposed under English law. The British Government would have been upset by another public airing of the poor security in British Intelligence, especially as Philby was a far bigger operator, and someone viewed as part of the ruling class. It would have been a severe embarrassment for Prime Minister Harold Macmillan, who seven years earlier had announced that Philby was not the Third Man. He would be made to appear either a liar or unable to control British Intelligence if Philby now confessed.

Early in 1962, there were also calls in Whitehall for an inquiry into

MI5's failure to detect another spy, John Vassall, at the Admiralty. Fleet Street was making matters worse by catching spymania.

Under instruction from editors, journalists were looking for any new angle on espionage, no matter how thin or hoary the story. They were picking up on rumours and scurrilous tales such as the one about the senior member of the Cabinet who was sharing a girlfriend with a Russian from the Soviet Embassy. In fact, it was later discovered that this triangle involved John Profumo, Secretary of State for War, Christine Keeler and GRU officer Yevgeny Ivanov, whose cover was Soviet Assistant Naval Attaché.

It all added up to the KGB having the luxury of time to examine its options and cover the tracks that might lead to the Fourth and Fifth men, should Philby defect. According to several sources in the KGB, MI6 and the CIA, Modin planned and executed the whole operation.

Although Modin admitted a 'knowledge' of what was happening, he refused to speak of his involvement. It was 'a KGB operation matter' he couldn't discuss. Yet fellow officers, Colonel 'D' and Colonel 'F', were less reticent.[8]

'He lectured about defection [at the Andropov Institute in Moscow in the 1980s],' Colonel 'D' recalled. 'While he never mentioned his own part [in the Philby affair], he seemed to be an expert. It is unlikely that the Centre would have given that [operation] to anyone else. Modin had been the Control for the Five. They knew and trusted each other.'

In fact, Modin travelled to Beirut in May 1962 to warn Philby via the local Control of the evidence against him and to explain that a decision not to prosecute had been made.[9]

How were the Fourth and Fifth men involved?

'They were the two left in the ring. He [Modin] couldn't just leave them without some contingency.'[10]

Colonel 'F' suggested that Blunt was again asked if he wished to defect. But the KGB still couldn't offer him access to the Palais de Versailles.

'We wanted to know how he felt now,' he said. 'It was a decade since he had refused to leave with Burgess and Maclean. But he was sure, still. He would stay in London and face the situation.'

And the Fifth Man?

'He was not directly under suspicion. I don't believe there had been any thought of him defecting.'[11]

But the KGB still had to cover the Fifth Man's tracks or create an alibi for him, something that would put him above suspicion at a critical time. Modin was in touch with Rothschild and a scheme was hatched.

It was also decided that Rothschild, who had been monitoring the attitude to Philby by talking to Dick White, Hollis and Wright, was to get a message to Philby warning him that British Intelligence were prevaricating over his fate. He should be prepared to face interrogation and make contingency plans for escape.[12] However, Rothschild was to make it clear that Moscow preferred he stay in place for as long as possible. Defection was to be a last resort.

PLAYING JUDAS

In August 1962, a few months after British Intelligence planned to move against Philby but not put him on trial, Rothschild was in Rehovoth, Israel. He made contact with a fellow Mossad agent, who was despatched to Beirut to contact Philby and brief him on the latest attitude of White and Hollis towards him. They were now planning to interrogate him in Beirut. He would probably be offered immunity in exchange for a full confession.

Rothschild was visiting the Weizmann Institute, to take part in a ceremony at which he was made an Honorary Fellow. He went to a party at Weizmann's house afterwards and met Flora Solomon, 'a Russian émigré Zionist' and former friend of Philby's, who was an executive at department store group, Marks and Spencer. She had introduced Kim to Aileen and had been a witness at her wedding.

'She had obviously been in the thick of things in the mid-1930s,' Wright recalled, 'part inspiration, part fellow accomplice, and part courier for the fledgling Ring of Five, along with her friends Litzi Philby, and Edith Tudor Hart.'

Now Solomon and Rothschild were claiming that she had come forward to denounce Philby. The reason? Philby's pieces in the *Observer* about Israel. She was saying that their anti-Israel slant had 'angered' her.

'It is simply not true that Philby's articles showed any bias against Israel,' Knightley noted in his Philby biography. 'True, he wrote favourably about Nasser, who was getting a bad press in Britain in the wake of Suez, and he believed the Palestinians had a genuine grievance, but Philby was a stringer, not a commentator, and if any of his articles were blatantly slanted against Israel, the *Observer* would not have run them.'[13]

After more than twenty years this was supposedly enough for her to turn on her old friend. Solomon claimed to have asked Rothschild why the *Observer* used a man like Kim. Didn't they know he was a communist? Rothschild said he questioned her further and then asked her to see MI5 with him back in London.

'With great difficulty,' Wright noted in *Spycatcher*, 'Victor managed to persuade her to meet [MI5's] Arthur Martin in London, to tell her story. I was asked to microphone Victor's flat, where the interview was to take place. I decided to install temporary SF [special facility – a phone tapping device], which made Victor nervous.'

'I don't trust you buggers to take the SF off!' Rothschild told Wright and made him promise to personally supervise the installation and its removal.

'Victor was always convinced that MI5 were clandestinely tapping him,' Wright said, 'to find out details of his intimate connections with the Israelis, and his furtiveness caused much good-humoured hilarity in the office.'

Wright gave Rothschild his word and supervised the work of the Post Office technicians. In between, he monitored the interview back at MI5's Leconfield House. Now recorded on tape was Solomon's testimony. Philby had taken her to lunch in 1937 before he went to Spain and told her she should 'work for peace', as he was then doing.[14]

In 1938, Philby had said that he was in 'great danger'. Solomon told Arthur Martin that she thought this meant Philby had kept his links with communism, which started at Cambridge. It was tissue paper thin and would have had no weight in a trial. And Solomon wasn't going into any court.

'I will never give public evidence,' she told Martin. 'There is too much risk. You see what happened to Tommy since I spoke to Victor.'

Tommy Harris, a friend of Philby's, had recently died in a 'mystery' car accident in Spain. She feared KGB reprisals, or so it seemed.

Wright, his earphones on at Leconfield House, was absorbing her intermittent 'agitation' and 'screeching voice'. He noted remarks which indicated she had 'ambivalent' feelings towards Philby. Very much the amateur psychologist, Wright deduced that she and Philby must have been lovers. This denunciation was 'her revenge for the rejection she felt when he moved into a new pair of sheets'.[15]

Was it all a Rothschild/Modin-generated scam to put MI5 off the scent of the Fifth Man?

In effect, Solomon's evidence contained less information than Golitsyn's leads and was not as important. It added nothing to the sum total of data in Philby's file, which included his links to Burgess and Maclean.

Even though MI5 pounced on the admissions, Wright found her 'a strange, rather untrustworthy woman, who never told the truth about her relations with Philby in the 1930s'.[16]

Knightley, more objectively, was puzzled by the timing of her actions against Philby.[17]

'At first she says it was because he was writing anti-Israeli articles in the Observer,' the biographer wrote, 'but when she complains to Rothschild about him she says it is because he is a communist. Since she had known this since at least 1938, why did she wait until 1962 to say anything about it?'

Knightley tried to clear up the confusion when he interviewed Philby in Moscow in January 1988 for the Sunday Times. But the puzzle seemed to widen. Philby was surprisingly forgiving of his supposed Judas.

'Flora was an old family friend,' he said. 'I had known her since I was a boy. My father used to take me to see her. I met her several times when I was in the period of my fascist front. Sometimes I'd catch Flora looking at me with a wry look as if to say that she knew exactly what I was up to. She was hard left herself, you know. Then in her later years she became very pro-Israeli and seemed to change.'[18]

Instead of the expected bitterness, Knightley was presented with a sentimental old man speaking of a past friend who had perhaps strayed off the ideological rails.

And what of the apparent arch-Judas, the true betrayer – his once good friend Victor Rothschild? Surely Philby would have said something that would demonstrate anger? Again, the opposite reaction came from the cunning old spy.

'Here's a little story about Rothschild for you,' he said. 'Make of it what you will. We were talking one day in 1946 and Victor suddenly said: "And how long have you been a member of the Communist Party, Kim?" I said: "Me, Victor!" And he said: "Just a little joke. I try it on everyone."'

Knightley again wasn't sure what this was meant to convey.[19] But Philby was foxing again, obliquely trying to give the impression that Rothschild was always at heart a commie baiter and chaser – someone who had tried to catch him out in 1946 and had finally snared him in 1962.

Yet this didn't gel with any aspect of Rothschilds' lifetime of true beliefs, actions and friendships, or even his marriage. A quarter of a century after the event, Philby was still in full operational mode for the KGB covering up for his great – still living – unexposed partner in the Ring of Five.

OUT FROM THE HEAT

By September 1962, Philby was in a living hell in Beirut as his two opposing spy masters held their positions, waiting for the other to falter. British Intelligence, under guidance from their political bosses, were working out how they could force him into a secret confession. This, it was hoped, would be kept quiet for a long time so as not to cause a political furore which would engulf the Macmillan Government.

If that didn't succeed, Philby would be given every opportunity to run.

The Moscow Centre knew – from Rothschild, who was kept informed by Wright and Hollis at MI5, and Dick White at MI6 – every move British Intelligence was making concerning Philby, including its list of other possible KGB agents, headed by Blunt. Rothschild, via Mossad, kept Philby informed that there was still no danger he would be forced to return to Britain to stand trial, or even be interrogated. Any questioning would be in Beirut, far away from the inquisitive British media.

The KGB would have preferred to have left Philby in place. To arrange his defection would be to admit defeat to British Intelligence and his operative days would be over. Judging from the Maclean/Burgess defections, a witchhunt, probably of unprecedented proportions, would commence inside British Intelligence in search of other double-agents.

The Fourth Man, possibly the Fifth, and definitely several others, would be in danger. On balance the KGB would prefer to avoid this, though if it happened there was always the satisfaction of anticipating the disarray in which MI5 and MI6 would be left.

In the meantime, Philby was left with only alcohol for solace. His nerves began to fray as London and Moscow spy chiefs waited.

'Just as in the case of Burgess in 1951,' KGB Colonel 'F' commented, 'we [the Centre] underestimated the pressures on our agent. Philby's father had died the year before, and this had shaken him. He had enormous love and respect for him. He was not in the best state of mind – given his drinking – to prepare for pressures to come.'

The Centre made contact with him?

'Yes. Then we realized the problem. He claimed he could control himself. We took him at his word, but we weren't sure.'

Despite his demotion, Modin was chosen by the Centre to organize a contingency escape route for Philby. The Russian visited the Cairo station of the KGB then flew on to Beirut in early September.[20]

He was once more ordered not to meet Philby face to face. The local KGB Control passed a message to Philby asking for a night-time rendezvous. At the meeting, Philby was informed of Modin's plans, based on the tardiness of British Intelligence in making a decision on how to act. It was stressed that he should hold out as long as possible.

'Philby was reassured that MI6 were not going to put him on trial,' KGB Colonel 'F' remarked. 'But Blake's long sentence was on his mind.'

So were the numerous Western agents his spying had caused to be executed. Although he saw them as an inevitable consequence of the great ideological struggle for supremacy, Philby knew that if his informants were wrong and there was a trial, he would not be forgiven for honestly-held beliefs. There would be recriminations. He would suffer more than the indignities of being paraded in a British show trial as a traitor.

Despite his fears and the KGB's worries about him, Philby still had a reserve of strength, which was once more fortified by Modin's firm but sensitive handling of one of his great agents. He would be protected and he would be welcome at home in Russia, if necessary.

'Philby's predicament was understandable,' Colonel 'F' commented. 'He had spent thirty years meeting his Centre contacts. He wanted to know that we still cared, that we would really help him and look after him.'

The British agent's long view that no matter what, communism eventually had to triumph over capitalism for humanity's sake, had carried him forward until now. It had also bound the Ring of Five for those three heady decades. Burgess and Maclean had brought their faith into the open by running to the bosom of the cause in 1951 and, in a way, this had excited and inspired the other three, and the secret movement as a whole. The Five had believed implicitly, since their recruitment, that they would see communism rule the planet. The defections were just a premature relocation to their true masters and the eventual centre of world power.

The Five had acknowledged blips on the screen of Soviet advance, such as Stalin and Beria's excesses, the brutal takeover of the Eastern Bloc and the 1956 crushing of the uprising in Hungary, although even this was excused by a fantasy that the CIA had provoked it. Yet they adhered to the Marxist view that the demise of imperialism and capitalism was inevitable. They saw themselves as very much part of the vanguard of a great historical development.

Instead of dwelling on what they perceived as negative propaganda, they were inspired by other events, such as Soviet achievements in science and space, which were evidence of a growing superiority that would emerge more in the coming years.

Now Philby was facing a test of faith. The KGB had come through in support by expressing its appreciation of his outstanding work for the cause. Modin was demonstrating that he would not be left to rot and suffer.

His timing was good. In November, MI6 and MI5 prepared a case against Philby. Nicholas Elliott, who engineered Philby's job at the *Observer* and had been MI6's man in Beirut, volunteered to return there to confront Philby. Several delays, possibly intended to induce Philby to defect, meant Elliott did not make the trip until 10 January 1963.

Elliott angrily presented Philby's spying to him as a *fait accompli* and grilled him about others suspected of being Soviet agents, including Blunt. Philby nearly buckled. He was stunned by Elliott's words and shocked by the names on the list.

MI5 was closer to the mark than he had anticipated or perhaps Blunt, the conduit for all the key agents in Britain, knew. Philby would have reasoned that Blunt may not have been aware that the net was closing in. The Fourth Man was no longer in contact with old friends such as Dick White.

Philby gave a stuttering admission to having worked for the KGB before 1946, which would allow him to admit that his work was dedicated to helping the Soviet Union defeat Hitler. This was the standard morally defensible position that both the Fifth Man and Blunt could also claim with even greater credibility since they had both officially stopped being British spies for MI5 in 1945.

Elliott offered Philby the expected immunity from prosecution. In return he would have to make a full confession and come back to Britain with Elliott. Philby procrastinated by accepting the deal in principle but then declaring that he needed time to think things over. Elliott wanted him to start writing it all down immediately. Philby stalled, saying that he would resume discussions the next day.

He then moved the pot-plant on the balcony of his Beirut flat, a sign to his KGB Control that he wanted an urgent meeting. They met that night and Philby was advised to take the initiative by writing up a 'confession', which he did, ignoring Elliott's accurate list of Soviet agents and naming ten others as fellow KGB spies. In fact, each person on Philby's list was innocent. The 'confession' also attempted to clear Blunt of any KGB links, stating that the art curator had nothing to do with the Russian Intelligence. It was an attempt to confuse and distract British Intelligence, which would have to investigate every Philby claim, just in case Elliott's confrontation had panicked him into naming real Soviet spies.

Philby told his Control he couldn't accept the terms of the immunity deal which would have meant a prolonged, disturbing debriefing, in which he would have been expected to name others as spies. The game was over. He wanted to defect.

However, before telling his Control this, Philby wanted it confirmed that he would have a suitable office at the Lubyanka. The Control said that this had been agreed. Philby asked if he was going to be made a general. The Control replied that this had not been confirmed but, because of Philby's great service, it was most likely. With these assurances, Philby informed his Control that it was time for him to *go home*.

The next day he met Elliott and gave him the two-page confession. Elliott returned to the British Embassy and contacted White and Hollis, who told him to persuade Philby to return. Elliott obeyed instructions, but Philby stammered an invitation to dinner in order to meet his third wife, Eleanor, an American whom he met in Beirut and married in 1959.

Elliott accepted and the stalling went on another few days until 17 January, when he returned to London empty-handed except for the confession, which was not a detailed factual admission of guilt.

Even in his near breakdown state, Philby held the upper hand knowing that he would never have been brought to trial. Elliott had failed to bring the immunity deal to fruition, so White and Hollis decided to do nothing for the present. If Philby stayed in place, they planned to interrogate him more professionally in Beirut or, better still, in England, if he dared return.

In effect, they were opening up the possibility of option 'B' for both sides: his defection. Philby tacitly accepted this alternative.

He disappeared from Beirut on 23 January 1963, and headed for Moscow via a Modin-instigated escape plan. The move solved a mutual problem for British Intelligence and the KGB, but left the Fourth and Fifth men extremely vulnerable.

PART FIVE

☭

THE LAST OF
THE RING
1963–1975

28. A PREDATORY
ENVIRONMENT

WRIGHT'S CASE – WRONG
INVESTIGATOR

Philby's departure caused the expected paranoia inside British Intelligence as every member began to suspect others of tipping him off on every move against him. Peter Wright felt particularly aggrieved and desperate for revenge.

Each operation he had been involved in, whether it be bugging a room in a Soviet Embassy or monitoring a ship, had been a clear failure. Cumulatively, it was reflecting on his competence. Wright became fearful that he would be fired.[1] It was important to find a reason, someone to blame for Soviet victories in the espionage game. He was determined to make a case for a mole in a position of influence at the top of MI5.

His sharp, scientific brain reasoned that there could be no other possible explanation, and it was important for his own emotional satisfaction and fluctuating self-esteem that he at least make a case against the most likely person he could find *within* MI5.

'Peter was fine at the technical stuff,' a former MI5 officer noted. 'But he had no idea how to handle people. He had not been trained in dealing with human beings. He had spent most of his life in hands-on activity dealing with the wires, bugs and tapes. This specifically avoided human contact. They were only useful in increasing budgets and approving operations . . .'[2]

His less attractive character traits – arrogance and abrasiveness – were reinforced by the class-layered structure in British Intelligence, where he was uneasily lodged because of his expertise. But his command of the special equipment, which didn't appear to be doing its job, was no longer enough to maintain his position. He could sense the disdain behind the managerial reserve and politeness of his superiors.

Only his great friend Victor was sustaining him and staying close in his hour of frustration.

Wright began at the beginning for him: 1955. The mole, if there was one inside, had to be someone in a position to wreck the operations he had been involved in against the Soviets for eight years. He checked and cross-referenced eight years of files and came to the conclusion that there was not just a mole, but a super-mole, who had burrowed deep since about 1942.

He narrowed the suspects down to five men: the director, Roger Hollis, his deputy, Graham Mitchell, Colonel Malcolm Cumming, Hugh Winterborn and Wright himself. Perhaps because of a combination of naïvety, lack of people skills and investigative talent, or because it would have destroyed his own self-esteem, the scientist never seriously considered that he might look wider for someone officially outside MI5.

It would have been too much at that point for him to suspect Rothschild — the one individual in contact with all of the five suspects; the only person next to Wright who had a complete command over the technology and the operations in which it was being used. Just as Angleton had been deceived by Philby, and to a lesser extent Rothschild, Wright had not even begun to comprehend how he was being used.[3]

Wright dismissed Winterborn and Cumming as not fitting the profile he spent months building. That left Hollis, Mitchell, and Wright himself.

'Was it Hollis, the aloof, pedestrian autocrat with whom I enjoyed a civil but distant relationship?' Wright wondered. 'Or Mitchell, his deputy, a man I knew less well?'[4]

Mitchell was his first choice because of his 'secretiveness' and 'slyness'. The scientist found him 'a clever man, clever enough to be a spy', which was an odd remark about the deputy head of an espionage outfit.

The self-appointed internal investigator naturally dismissed himself. 'I knew it wasn't me,' he noted. He was only half right.

THE UNRAVELLING

Modin's position in the KGB was restored with the successful defection of Philby to Moscow and he was at last made a full Colonel. His duties included special trouble-shooting abroad and looking after defectors in Russia. Modin had remained close to Burgess.

'He was not well when Philby arrived in Moscow,' Modin recalled. 'He was told at first that Philby was not in Russia, which he relayed to the *Daily Mail*. However, when he learned from Maclean that Philby had arrived, he desperately wanted to see Kim. But Kim would not see him. He blamed Burgess for his own fall and believed that if he had not run with Maclean in 1951, he [Philby] might be still be in place.'[5]

Modin and the Centre were deeply disappointed by the ending of Philby's career, for they had had high hopes that he would rise to be the head of MI6, the most important position in British Intelligence.

Burgess was ailing by mid-1963 and he became desperate to see his close friend. He pleaded with Modin and anyone who would listen to intercede for him. Philby's cold neglect of the sick man's plea was a blow from a near-perfect spy to an imperfect one, who nevertheless had been a great agent for the Russians. It was also the first unharmonious act inside the Ring of Five.

Burgess had been trying to return to Britain for the last few years. Once, while dining in a Moscow restaurant with Modin, he had collapsed with what seemed at first to be a heart attack. It wasn't. He had been over-drinking. When he recovered, he was 'very emotional' and told his friend 'he did not want to die in Russia'.[6]

However, in his beloved England there was no desire to have Burgess back. He had made vague and veiled threats about what he knew and how much embarrassment he could cause. It was enough to give the Government and his close friends the jitters. Blunt and Rothschild worried that he would get drunk and talk indiscreetly.

But on 19 August 1963, at the age of fifty-three, he solved the problem by dying, the years of hard, debauched living having caught up with him. The Ring of Five was now four.

Blunt, Rothschild and a dozen other spies could not rest easily for long. In January 1964, Arthur Martin, the bland, self-made, earthy MI5 officer, was sent to the US to interview John Cairncross in connection with the Burgess/Maclean/Philby defections. Martin was surprised to be introduced to Michael Straight, the American Cambridge graduate who had been part of the circle of communist supporters in the 1930s.

Straight had been offered the chairmanship of the Kennedy administration's Advisory Council on the Arts in June 1963. He felt he could not take the job without first confessing to his communist past, in which he had been recruited by Blunt. The White House called in the FBI.

The American repeated his story to Martin, who at last had something concrete on Blunt. Like his friend Peter Wright, Martin had little compunction about tackling an Establishment figure.

In London, on 23 April, he visited Blunt at his apartment at the Courtauld Institute in Portman Square and told him he had evidence that he was a Soviet agent during the war. Blunt denied it. Martin told him of Straight's testimony.

Blunt then demonstrated a trait that had impressed Modin over the years – he kept ice cool and in control under pressure. He almost certainly would have been forewarned by Rothschild via White or the garrulous Wright, which would have helped. He stared at Martin and did not respond. The MI5 man then hurried into offering him protection:

'I have been authorized by the Attorney-General to give you a formal immunity from prosecution.'[7]

Blunt diverted his eyes to a Scotch bottle on a tray near a window in his living room. He went over to it, poured himself a double and then turned to Martin.

'It is true,' he said, again without any apparent emotion.

The two men talked for a few minutes and Martin added a condition. The immunity deal stood if he had not been a spy recently. In other words, he would not be prosecuted if, as Straight had indicated, he had only been a spy until 1945, the end of the Second World War.[8]

Philby had taken the same misleading line in Beirut and now Blunt was using it too. He also slipped into semantics, saying that he could not have been a spy recently since there had been nothing for him to spy on. In fact, Blunt, since he left MI5 in 1945, had been the key middleman for a range of agents including Rothschild, who was passing on information to the Embassy Controls. In a technical sense he had probably not been in a position to steal classified information himself. But in reality he had been solidly involved in espionage for the Soviets. His role was important.

An excited Martin returned to MI5 and told everyone, including a delighted Wright, of Blunt's confession. Hollis congratulated Martin.

A few days later, Wright was asked to come up to Hollis's office. It was evening. Present were Hollis, another MI5 officer, Martin Furnival Jones and Rothschild, whom Wright was surprised to see because he assumed his powerful friend would always let him know if he were visiting MI5. Rothschild looked distraught.[9]

'I have just told Victor about Anthony,' Hollis informed Wright.

In *Spycatcher*, Wright remarked that there was 'little wonder Victor looked devastated'. He and Blunt had been close friends for nearly thirty years.

'Like Blunt,' he said, 'Victor also fell under suspicion after the Burgess/Maclean defections . . . But while the suspicions against Victor swiftly melted, those against Blunt remained . . .'

Wright added that Rothschild's main concern, as soon as he was told the truth, was how to break the news to his wife, Tess.

'He knew as well as I did that news of Blunt's treachery would, if anything, have a more traumatic effect on her than on him. I had got to know Tess Rothschild since first meeting Victor in 1958. She was a woman of great charm and femininity, and was closer to Blunt in many ways than Victor had ever been. She understood the vulnerable side of his character, and shared with him a love for art.'[10]

Wright could not hide his contempt, not for Tess but for what he viewed as the privileged group she was a part of, when he added pejoratively:

'In the 1930s she moved in that same circle of gifted left-wing intellectuals who studied at Cambridge, partied in London and holidayed at Cap Ferrat, as the world tottered into the Second World War.'

According to Wright, Tess was 'well aware' of MI5's doubts about Blunt after the Burgess/Maclean defections, but she 'defended him' to the hilt. Both she and Rothschild 'knew how it felt to be innocent, yet fall under suspicion' through having been friendly with Burgess.

Tess always found Blunt a 'vulnerable and wonderfully gifted man, cruelly exposed to the everlasting burden of suspicion by providence and the betrayals of Guy Burgess.'

Tess was going to have to discover a new dimension to Blunt, more in keeping with his name. As Modin came to realize, his inner character was as invulnerable as that of the toughest espionage agent. His clandestine gifts, such as they were, extended to the uncompromising, tense world of espionage as one of the foremost traitors of the era.

He would never have been in the same class as the Fifth Man as a procurer of espionage information, but Blunt had no peer as a conveyor to the agents' Soviet masters of a range of data from several sources.[11] He was the safe linkman everyone trusted and looked up to.

Tess remembered fondly that Blunt would come back so 'tight' to Bentinck Street that she had to help him to bed.

'I would have known if he were a spy,' Wright claimed she remarked.

She was in for a rude reassessment of her judgement of character, or perhaps she had been deceived by Blunt, just as Wright had been by Rothschild.

'Victor realized that we would need to interview Tess now that Blunt had confessed,' Wright recalled, 'but he dreaded telling her the truth.'

Wright then reported Rothschild as saying: 'That is why I asked you up to Roger's office. I think it would be better if the news came from you.'

This was part of the continuing deception. First there was the inveigling of Wright and MI5 by Flora Solomon. Now Rothschild was asking the most zealous of the mole-hunters into his home to inform his wife about a spy they both knew intimately. Emotionally and intellectually Wright and British Intelligence were being artfully drawn into what seemed a growing cover-up.

'I knew he needed to get away from Leconfield House, and gather his thoughts alone,' Wright remarked of Rothschild, for once with some perception.

Looking back twenty years, Rothschild characterized his reaction to Blunt's confession in a less than convincing, perhaps disingenuous manner:

'Many people, I suppose, suffer blows which seem devastating, crushing and beyond belief,' he wrote in *Random Variables*. '[One occurred] when I was told by "the authorities" that a former close friend of mine, Anthony Blunt, had confessed to having been a Soviet agent for many years.

'I found it almost impossible to believe and childishly, felt like telephoning Blunt to ask him if this appalling news was true. But there *was* no doubt; and why should "they" wish to play a cruel and meaningless practical joke on me? What might I be stimulated to confess in return? The short answer was: nothing. As "they" knew, I was not a Soviet agent.'

In this over-protestation of his innocence, Rothschild proceeded to distance himself from Blunt, adding:

'Blunt joined the Security Service during the Second World War some time after me, and our paths rarely crossed because I was concerned with bombs, whereas he, after a brief incubation period, became involved in highly secret work, so secret that the "weeders" will see that it is not disclosed, even after thirty years.'

The reference to clandestine work would have been, among other things, a reference to Blunt's work for the Royal Family, but his other remarks were misleading. Rothschild was very close to Blunt and saw him often – before, during and after the war.

The passage went on:

. . . the crushing blow about Blunt had destroyed my confidence. For whom would I put my hand in the fire? I can still name a few and among them would, undoubtedly, be Guy Liddell.

The 'authorities' knew, of course, that many years before, I had been a close friend of Blunt, though we drifted apart in about 1950; and they were therefore interested in anything, anything, I could tell them about him, his friends and acquaintances.

So appalled was I by their news, as I am sure they expected, that I felt it essential to help them in every possible way; and this I did within the limits of my imperfect memory.

Curiously, perhaps, this did not make me cast doubt on any of those for whom I was already prepared to put my hand in the fire.[12]

Curious indeed, except for the fact that the Fifth Man would have known the other traitors. There would be no need to doubt anyone else.

THE TESTING

A few days after first hearing about Blunt, Wright took Evelyn McBarnet, an MI5 research officer, to see Tess. According to Wright, Rothschild was – no doubt genuinely – ill-at-ease. So was Tess.

'I could tell that Tess sensed something was wrong. After a few minutes, Victor said I had some news for her, then slipped out of the room.'

Wright told her that Blunt had 'confessed at last'.

Tess appeared incredulous and wanted to know to what he had confessed.

'You are not saying he was a spy?' she asked.

Wright, the compassionate conveyor of bad news replied that, yes, he *was* saying that.

'For a second she raised her hand to her mouth as if in pain,' Wright remembered. 'Then she let it slip gently onto her lap.'

Wright then told her how he had admitted being recruited in 1937 (which was incorrect) a year or two after Philby, Burgess and Maclean (which was again misleading – Blunt was making out that he was a lesser agent, who had been recruited later).

Wright also informed Tess how Blunt had given a long and detailed account of his espionage activities throughout the war (which in fact was a demonstration of thriftiness with the facts). Again, like Cairncross, Philby, Burgess and Maclean, Blunt was admitting to helping the Soviets defeat Hitler. It was a defensible, arguably laudable position, even though the law frowned upon it. After all, even Churchill had passed on espionage material to Stalin in order to help him fight the Nazis. Like the others, he was making out that he had suddenly stopped spying for Russia once Hitler was defeated. British Intelligence appeared to be buying this line, mainly because it was convenient and less embarrassing.

'Tess did not cry,' Wright observed. 'She just went terribly pale, and sat hunched up and frozen, her eyes staring at me as she listened. Like Victor, she was a person for whom loyalty in friendship was of surpassing importance; to have it betrayed shook her, as it had him, to the core.'[13]

'All those years,' Wright reported her as saying, 'and I never suspected a thing.'

Wright claimed to understand for the first time the 'intensity of feelings which had been forged in the crucible of those strange, long-ago years in Cambridge in the 1930s.'

JOKERS IN THE PACK

Once Blunt had confessed and taken the generous immunity card, everyone under suspicion expected to receive the same offer. Martin used it to make a difficult job easier and most accepted a deal. It began to irritate Hollis, who saw a huge problem emerging for him and the Government, should the secret arrangements ever become public.

How would they explain doling out no sentence to men like Blunt from the upper class, and slamming the lowlier-born Blake with an extremely harsh forty-two years? It seemed like one rule for the privileged, and another for the rest, and it became a political time-bomb for the Government. Once the cover-up began it was a case of the longer it lasted the better, so as to make it less of a disaster for some unsuspecting future prime minister, who would be left with damage control should the secret ever leak. Just how far the immunity scheme was extended developed into one of the British Government's greatest cover-ups.

Did the Fifth Man do such a deal? I put this to several people, who may have been in a position to know.

'I think so,' Modin said. 'He was uneasy in that period [1964]. He wasn't alone. There were many other former communist students, who had risen to be senior civil servants. They defended themselves by claiming they had stopped working for the KGB at the end of the war. Cairncross was among them. Their excuse was clearly untrue. As far as the Fifth Man was concerned, he never confessed to anything. I think the British Secret Service had strong suspicions that he worked for the KGB but could not prove it.'[14]

A former long-serving MI5 officer expounded on the immunity business:

'There were two camps,' he recalled. 'First there were those who made a deal to escape prosecution and then admitted having passed data to middlemen or Controls.

'Then there was another group, who treated the immunity offer like an American might take the Fifth Amendment. They said, "Yes, thank you very much", and then proceeded to hide behind the arrangement by confessing absolutely nothing – except that they might have known someone from the Comintern during university days, or that they had once been members of the Party.

'This way, if the connections ever became public they could say with impunity: "There was never a shred of evidence that I was ever a Soviet agent." '[15]

Rothschild appeared to have been in the second group. He was interrogated eleven times.

Commenting much later, he said:

> I was questioned very extensively. The authorities, as I call them, said that they wished to talk to me and they talked in quite a friendly way.
>   I have a feeling that they believed in me. I was quite happy to tell them everything I knew. We had a very long talk. I was quite happy to tell them how well I knew Burgess and Blunt. I have no recollection [of] anyone asking me if I was a Soviet agent and it would have been naive for a professional interrogator to do that. I think they were more interested in who were my friends. I know all sorts of people who were questioned in the same way. I know people of great distinction, greater distinction, who were also questioned. All sorts of people. There really was an investigation. And I don't object to that. You have to help your country and I think all the people concerned did that.[16]

According to former MI6 agent James Rusbridger, Peter Wright and another MI5 source, Rothschild was fed information in 1962, which ended up 'in the wrong place' – namely with the KGB inside the Soviet Embassy in London. This did not prove he had spied, for the data just conceivably could have been stolen from him. Yet it raised suspicions. However, Rothschild still managed to convince people that he and Tess were victims by association. Their friends, Guy, Anthony, Kim, Michael, Leo and so on, with whom they dined, drank, studied, lived and worked, had duped them.

So believable was Rothschild that his links with MI5 in 1964 did not diminish. In fact, while Blunt took the brunt of the on-going inquisition, and others were hounded, transferred to unclassified work, even forced into suicide, Rothschild intensified his MI5 connections, as if he were making amends for ill-advised, always innocent past friendships.

29. WILSON AND OTHER WITCHES

MOLES TO THE LEFT OF ME . . .

The first day Wright took over the interrogation of Blunt from Martin, his tape recorder broke down. He knelt to thread the loose tape spool which had jammed it.

Blunt remarked to Martin: 'Isn't it fascinating to watch a technical expert do his stuff?'[1]

Blunt had never met Wright before and was supposed to know nothing about him. The remark told Wright instantly that someone had briefed him about his new inquisitor. According to KGB sources, it would most likely have been the Fifth Man.

'Who else would it have been?' Colonel 'F' remarked. 'He was a friend, still in contact, and the Fifth Man was the only one of the ring left unexposed. Logically he would have been concerned to help Blunt.'[2]

It added to Wright's confusion as he began a monthly questioning of Blunt. Each session drifted into drunken reminiscences and the interrogator walked away with nothing, except well-honed disinformation. Blunt was surviving where Philby had feared to tread. He was fortified by the knowledge that he would never be charged and secretly informed by the Fifth Man of every reaction by Wright.

His work at the Courtauld and the Palace continued, allowing him to keep his respected public status, and sustaining his air of superiority.

It added to Wright's perturbation. Not only were his technical operations against the Russians a failure but he could not elicit the vital information from Blunt that would have directed MI5 to the Fifth Man. Frustration led to anger and a growing desperation to find someone, anyone that would even vaguely fit the profile of the mystery mole within.

Wright's initial, unauthorized investigations failed to find any evidence remotely connecting Graham Mitchell, Hollis's deputy, to the Soviets. Furtive eyes began to turn towards Hollis himself. Meanwhile, spurred on by Philby's duplicity, the CIA and MI5 turned their attention from deeply burrowed moles to witches.

If they couldn't find Soviet agents *inside* British Intelligence, why not look outside? The ensuing witchhunt even pointed to the new socialist prime minister, Harold Wilson.

In the US, Angleton's disappointment over his former friend Philby's betrayal had led to a determination to exact revenge. He would help, push, even force British Intelligence into divulging or disgorging other key spies. If Angleton couldn't have Philby himself, he could still thwart and destroy KGB aims, which he saw as the vanguard for attempted Soviet world domination.

Angleton worried about Wilson with his Fabian Society membership, his trade deals with the Soviets and, in the CIA man's eyes, his strange assortment of Eastern European émigré businessmen friends. These factors added up to the absurd rumour that Wilson might be a Soviet agent.

Angleton and Wright's continuing rapport was based on an increasingly common goal. When they met on either side of the Atlantic, they fuelled each other's doubts, fears, paranoias and complexes, which ranged from superiority over their enemies to inferiority about their backgrounds.

The American often asked about Rothschild and Wright obliged by talking about his great companion. Angleton could never be convinced about him. His suspicions grew.

'He could never get over Victor's closeness to Philby, Blunt and Burgess,' Wright told me in a 1988 discussion. 'I tried to reassure him but the same doubts surfaced. He would tick off a list of links . . . This included Cambridge, his, shall we say, quiet membership of the Communist Party in the 1930s . . . he was an Apostle, he had [Soviet] agent friends, and so on.'[3]

Rothschild managed to partly allay those doubts by alleging, for instance, that he supported the Shah in Iran in 1953. Furthermore, his work for Mossad drew him on occasions close to Angleton, who had encouraged close CIA–Mossad links. In fact, at one point in the 1960s, the American was so keen to keep British Intelligence out of his cozy US/Israel intelligence link that he complained to Wright's superiors about his closeness to Rothschild.

In 1964, Rothschild told Angleton an Israeli agent had 'hinted' that Wilson could be a Russian agent. Wright remembered Rothschild telling him something similar but couldn't recall if it were in 1964 or later. Rothschild was busy deflecting scrutiny from himself by spreading unfounded innuendo. The fact that Wilson was a Socialist gave the rumour greater credence.

'Victor didn't seem to have much time for Wilson,' a former business colleague recalled. 'It may have been because Wilson was seen as a "soft" liberal and not a tough enough Socialist. Victor liked his Socialism undiluted. He was interventionist in his mentality and much influenced if not by Marx, then Keynes. He wanted governments to step in and take charge to stimulate the economy and achieve things. He was an ideas man, who liked to see them come to fruition. It didn't seem to matter if the state or a corporation was involved.'[4]

A far-fetched conspiracy theory emerged from the Israeli source. Wilson had taken over the Labour Party leadership after the former right-wing leader, Hugh Gaitskell, had been murdered by the KGB. Gaitskell had died from a rare tropical disease – *Lupus disseminata erythematosis*, or something like it. After discussing it with Rothschild, Wright checked with scientists at Porton Down, who had been working on quick-action biological toxins, which could be used for assassination.[5]

Wright then asked Angleton to comb all Russian medical literature to see if there were any mention of the disease. Angleton sent him a translation of an article in a 1956 Moscow journal. A drug – hydralazine – had produced *Lupus*-like effects in rats. Porton Down scientists informed Wright that the Russians could have refined it to a one-shot drug, but it seemed unlikely. The inane conspiracy theory fizzled, but only fired the Angleton/Wright desire to score a victory in the real or imagined intelligence war with the KGB.

So far both men had been outsmarted by their Soviet agent counterparts.

THE WITCHHUNTER-GENERAL

Wright formalized his witch-hunting role when he became chairman of the so-called Fluency Committee, a small joint MI5–MI6 group

set up to find the elusive mole inside MI5. Its initial key suspect was
Deputy director Mitchell. Hollis reluctantly approved a secret,
internal inquiry, mumbling something about the Gestapo as he
did so.

The most memorable thing about the investigation was that
Mitchell had been seen picking his teeth in front of the two-way
mirror the Fluency team had set up in his office. 'We got to know
his tonsils well,' Wright joked.[6]

Apart from that, he was responsible for a poorly written, mistake-
ridden white paper explaining, or not explaining, how Maclean and
Burgess managed to defect.[7]

A year or so after its inception, the Fluency Committee really
only had one suspect, Roger Hollis. Wright and Martin, who was
now at MI6 after being fired by Hollis, were planning to spend years
attempting to create a case against him. Fluency identified 28 leads
or allegations by Russian defectors, which could have applied to
many people within British Intelligence. Wright was particularly
concerned with the evidence in September 1945 of Konstantin
Volkov (mentioned earlier), who tried to defect from the Soviet
Embassy in Istanbul. His claim that there was a spy inside MI6 or
MI5 was vague, and could have meant Philby, Blunt, Rothschild or
someone else. Philby made sure that the Russians caught and
executed him, so his information remained meagre and confusing to
analysts.

The Fluency Committee spent even more time dwelling on
information from Igor Guzenko, who succeeded in defecting and
was questioned fully.

He spoke of a spy code-named ELLI.

'He said he knew there was a spy in "five of MI",' Wright recalled.
'He had learned this from a friend, Luibimov, who had worked
alongside him in the main GRU (Soviet Military Intelligence) cipher
room in Moscow in 1942 ... There was something Russian about
ELLI, and Guzenko, either in his background or because he had
visited Russia, or could speak the language. ELLI was an important
spy because he could remove from MI5 the files which dealt with
Russians in London ... Guzenko said that when ELLI's telegrams
came in there was always a woman present in the cipher room who
read the decrypts first and, if necessary, took them straight to Stalin.'[8]

Again, this was imprecise and could have applied to several

people including Hollis, Blunt, Liddell and Rothschild. Oleg Gordievsky, in his collaborative book with Christopher Andrew, *KGB*, claims ELLI was Leo Long.

'That codename appears in large letters on the cover of Long's KGB operational file,' Gordievsky says.[9]

Cambridge graduate Long was a second-rank spy who during the Second World War supplied Blunt with data from MI14 in the War Office, which collated and analysed German battle order Intelligence. He, like several agents at MI6 and MI5, had access to Ultra Intelligence from Bletchley Park, which deciphered German military Enigma machine codes.

Wright was excited by the mention of the GRU. After looking into Hollis's background, he concluded that he may have been recruited by the GRU in China, where Hollis once worked for the British Tobacco Company in the 1930s. But ELLI, or the spy inside MI5 for whom he was searching, was recruited by the KGB not the Soviet's military arm. The fact that a GRU cipher clerk picked up the data in Moscow and gave it to Stalin was irrelevant. The GRU office at the Centre would naturally have seen all military data coming in from KGB agents via Blunt.

Fluency latched on to the 'something Russian in his background or he had visited Russia or he could speak the language' and took note that Hollis had once taken a train from China to Russia. It was inadequate, as was most of the evidence, and the committee was unsure and insecure because of it.

Realizing he was the target, Hollis began parrying their moves, which was a natural reaction to a team trying to destroy him. But everything Hollis did only inflamed their fervour, until it spiralled into an obsession which overtook and consumed Wright. He was unhappily wandering in an espionage maze, with only a very few companions who really understood the dilemma, to offer sympathy.

'It's startling,' Wright would tell them, 'there's a clear chronological pattern from 1942 to 1963 concerning serials [leads or allegations].'[10]

It meant that this spy had been connected with MI5 for at least those twenty-one years. The information was not specific enough to 'point in the direction of any one officer, beyond the fact that it had clearly to be a high-level penetration to account for the allegations.'[11]

One of Wright's confidants, who stayed close, listened intently to his problems and offered calming, sensible advice, was his now close friend, Victor. They had known each other seven years and Rothschild knew all Wright's secrets. But Wright knew very few of his.

INTO HIS SHELL

During the period of their friendship, Rothschild had been at the Shell Corporation proving that he was far from just an imperious face, or a lightweight front-man used to impress the natives at home or in foreign parts. From his lowly role as part-time adviser, he had become vice-chairman of Shell Research in 1961. Two years later, he was chairman overseeing a budget of £34 million and in charge of 5,000 scientists. He had also taken up a directorship of Shell Chemicals UK.

The timing for his increased activity with Shell – 1963 – was significant. The Fifth Man's major spying days for the KGB *inside the UK* were over. The scrutiny by British Intelligence after Philby's defection would have limited his opportunities, while Blunt's exposure finished them. It would have been too dangerous to carry on. Unlike Burgess, Maclean and Philby, Rothschild could concentrate on building another life and career in Britain. When the crunch came, he had much more to lose than the other four in the ring, with his name, background and position in politics and business. He would rather not cause an international scandal by being forced to defect to Moscow. In short, his ideological commitment was found to be less than the other four when it came to the critical point.

From now on, he would spend more time in damage control, attempting to cover the trails that could lead back to him. It would mean continuing his relationship with MI5 to make sure he knew the scope and findings of internal investigations. His wedding to British Intelligence had to go on.

Simultaneously, Rothschild decided to build his image away from espionage areas, which would make it appear unlikely he could be involved in anything so grubby and clandestine. This saw him applying his talents more at Shell, where he went into over-drive devouring every aspect of the corporation's business with an astonishing hunger that impressed and alarmed his fellow executives.

'He had been busy in the early years,' a senior Shell executive recalled, 'but quite suddenly he was into everything. He upset some, by insisting on sticking his nose everywhere. But he was hard to resist. He came up with some terrific research and even marketing ideas that led to products, which put Shell ahead in many areas in that period.

'He certainly stimulated everyone that came into contact with him. I got to know him well enough in a work environment. His intellectual energy and range had no peer in my time in business. But there was still a closed side to Victor. He would disappear somewhere in the world on some mysterious mission that no one dared ask him about.'[12]

Not surprisingly, his capacities came to the notice of the Wilson Government, and he was appointed in 1965 to the Council for Scientific Policy. His performance there caused Wilson to offer him the post of Minister of Technology.

Rothschild's public reason for rejecting the offer was that he had 'a larger budget and a freer hand at Shell'. Privately, he probably wanted to distance himself from Wilson to preserve his image in the eyes of Wright and Angleton, who were feverishly trying to prove the Prime Minister was a Soviet agent. Failing that, they hoped to remove him from office.

Hollis also continued to be a target for destruction.

In order to rid British Intelligence of real or imagined double agents, Angleton guided the CIA into attemptimg a takeover of British Intelligence operations inside Britain itself. The Agency had become concerned that US secrets shared with British Intelligence were being betrayed by British agents. Angleton and CIA Chief, Richard Helms, were not going to sit idly by while secrets in everything from submarine detection systems and eavesdropping tunnels under Berlin, to missile and nuclear weapons developments, ended up in the Moscow Centre.

Moreover, satellite spying technology was about to transform espionage. Everything the prying eye in the sky picked up would pass through the British defence and Intelligence systems. The Americans wanted to 'clean out' MI5 to make sure KGB access to the new developments was limited.

The CIA engineered for two representatives from President Johnson's Foreign Intelligence Advisory Board (PFIAB) to be sent to

Britain and shown into every secret establishment by the resident CIA liaison officer who had a pass everywhere.

Even Wright became nervous.

'No one in British Intelligence was told that the review was even taking place,' he claimed. 'In any other country, the review would be known by a cruder name – espionage.'

The report, predictably, was highly critical of British security. It recommended a greater US presence to ensure its secrets were better protected. Hollis was attacked for failing to implement effective counter-espionage.

It seemed that the CIA was looking at Britain as it did every other country from Iran to Vietnam. In order to create a political climate suitable to US interests, the CIA would bolster its local station, take control of the local secret police, use espionage and other methods to remove hostile politicians, and replace them with puppets. Hollis was so enraged by this American interference that he approved Wright's own ideas for strengthened MI5 counter-intelligence operations, which partially thwarted the CIA takeover. Wright also placated Angleton by convincing him that when Hollis retired at the end of 1965, he would be replaced by a suitable hawk – Martin Furnival Jones.

Consequently, Wright's power was elevated. He had a stronger counter-intelligence operation and less opposition to his forceful, obsessive and maverick ways. He decided to investigate Soviet rings at Oxford and in the scientific community, particularly at Cambridge's Cavendish laboratories. He became interested in Peter Kapitza. As usual, Wright turned to Rothschild for help. He knew Kapitza and it was important for him to cover his links to him. Rothschild organized a dinner party so that Wright could meet Lord Adrian, Cambridge University's Chancellor and President of the Royal Society.

Wright was overawed. At the party he was able to 'guide him gently on to the subject of the Russian scientist.'[12a]

Adrian recalled Kapitza, for whom he had a high regard, but did not have a clue about espionage. It was not his field. He gave Wright the names of people who had worked with Kapitza.

'More names for my black books,' Wright noted wearily in *Spycatcher*. 'More names to be checked in the registry. More names to be traced, interviewed, assessed, cleared, and in one or two cases, removed from access [to classified material].'[12b]

In reality, no one was removed from any major British project. No spies were caught. Rothschild's diversion had sent Wright up another score of back alleys leading nowhere, except into the espionage wilderness. The ever grateful Wright was thankful to Rothschild for his introductions to an Establishment figure. He would mark it down as another example of his friend doing the patriotic thing.

CHINA SYNDROMES

Also in 1965, Rothschild was elevated to director of Shell International, and he acted as research coordinator for the Royal Dutch Shell Group. In short, he had taken charge of all Shell research whether it be for the Dutch, which owned 60 per cent of the group, or the British.

It allowed him to roam the world and was convenient as a cover, when he needed it in the Middle East or even China, where his agent-running took on an intensity with the build-up to the Cultural Revolution.

His secret work for Dick White and MI6 included running agents who were monitoring political events and the mood of Chairman Mao and his administration. As the Russians were even more nervous than the British and Americans about China's intentions concerning military expansion and weapons development, it's most likely that Rothschild's assessments of events would have been passed to the Moscow Centre. But Wright linked Rothschild to a bizarre plot that may have been based on some fact. Wright claimed to close confidants that by the early 1960s the Chinese had frightened the Russians and the Americans with their development of nuclear and biological weapons, which they seemed willing to use.[13]

Chairman Mao Zedong had told India's Nehru in the late 1950s that nuclear war would be no bad thing. Even if half of mankind perished, the other half would survive and imperialism would vanish from the face of the earth.

The KGB knew the extent of Chinese germ warfare research, partly because it had given some of the technology to them. Furthermore, the Chinese had taken over a huge biological weapons centre at Harbin, Northern Manchuria, which had been run by the Japanese during the Second World War. Japanese doctors and scientists had used POWs as guinea pigs in hideous experiments, which rivalled those in Nazi concentration camps.

Now Chinese scientists had begun experimenting. According to Wright's wild theory, the Asian and Hong Kong flu viruses in the 1960s were part of that experimentation.

This, the strange story continued, caused alarm in sections of the CIA and KGB. They then combined to run agents in China who encouraged Mao to purge the intellectual class, which would include the key scientists, particularly in the area of biological weaponry. Mao was apparently convinced that he could be murdered by 'a drop of invisible poison on his skin'.[14]

In fact, the KGB and the CIA did draft in more Chinese experts and built up their Embassies in Beijing. The numbers increased further in 1966 at the beginning of the Cultural Revolution, when Mao unleashed unprecedented terror across China. He stirred the youth of the country into forming Red Guards who were encouraged to root out 'bourgeois and revisionist tendencies'.

If the KGB did encourage the Cultural Revolution, the plan backfired on them a year later when families of Soviet diplomats and KGB officers were manhandled as they tried to escape at Beijing airport. However, during the terror, 'intellectuals' – which meant anyone qualified and working in a major university – became targets for assassination. About 50,000 of them were killed, including those working in important scientific research and development, such as biological weaponry. Mao boasted about this, comparing himself to previous emperors, who had butchered intellectuals.

But was this part of a combined CIA/KGB project? Such operations are known to have occurred in a very low-key way over the decades. Yet I found no evidence to support Wright's erratic claims.

However, KGB personnel – including Modin – *did* have something to celebrate with their CIA counterparts in October 1993. During our Moscow interviews in July and August 1993, Modin told me he was flying to Washington 'soon' for a 'get together' with CIA agents. I was in correspondence in September with him asking follow-up questions. He replied in one letter from Washington DC.[15] The unusual rendezvous of supposed 'enemies' was, according to a CIA source, to celebrate a 'joint operation', yet its nature was not specified. Whether it concerned the prevention of China's advances in germ warfare is speculation.

Wright did not elaborate on Rothschild's or Modin's links to the Cultural Revolution, although both of them were agent-running in China at the time.

The only other thread which could be remotely connected was the expertise that both Rothschild and Wright had in biological and chemical weapons. Rothschild had built up a vast knowledge since the late 1930s, particularly from Porton Down in 1940, where he garnered much for the Russians.

'The whole area of chemical research was an active field in the 1950s,' Wright wrote. 'I was cooperating with MI6 in a joint programme to investigate how far hallucinatory drug lysergic acid diethylamide (LSD) could be used in interrogations, and extensive trials took place at Porton. I even volunteered as guinea pig on one occasion. Both MI5 and MI6 also wanted to know a lot more about the advanced poisons then being developed at Porton, though for different reasons. I wanted the antidotes, in case the Russians used a poison on a defector in Britain, while MI6 wanted to use the poisons for operations abroad.'

Wright was at one stage the only British Intelligence operative who had quick access to antidotes for various poisons.

He was at least indirectly involved in plots to assassinate foreign leaders as he pointed out in *Spycatcher*:

'[Two MI6 agents] both discussed with me the use of poisons against Nasser, and asked my advice,' Wright said matter-of-factly. 'Nerve gas obviously presented the best possibility, since it was easily administered. They told me that the London Station had an agent in Egypt with limited access to one of Nasser's headquarters. Their plan was to place canisters of nerve gas inside the ventilation system, but I pointed out that this would require large quantities of the gas, and would result in massive loss of life among Nasser's staff.'

According to Wright, Prime Minister Anthony Eden, who had first called for Nasser's assassination, later 'backed away from the operation'.

The remarks, however, demonstrate the mind-set within sections of British Intelligence. Sources close to Wright claim it wasn't the only time he was involved in plots to kill with such weaponry.

30. WARS SILENT
AND SHORT

STANLEY, I PRESUME

Six months after Philby arrived in Moscow he was well into his debriefing by KGB agents when he received word that a person from the Centre who was important to his career would be coming to the apartment to meet him.[1] Philby thought it might be former KGB Chairman, Alexandr Shelepin (1958–62) and hoped it would not be 'cold-blooded' Ivan Serov (Chairman 1954–58), who was hated throughout the KGB. He was nervous with anticipation.

Philby had become disheartened after the promised office at the Lubyanka and the accompanying status failed to materialize. In fact, he had no office, just a very modest flat, even by Moscow standards. He certainly was not going to be made a KGB general. Philby was also disillusioned by the reality of the Soviet Union. It was not the paradise painted by the Comintern's Deutsch and Maly in the 1930s. International Marxist agents from the Comintern had not endured Stalin's repression until he recalled them to Moscow for execution. They had not informed him of the brutality that kept the citizenry in fear and under control. Now he was at his spiritual and ideological home, he was finding it more like the state portrayed in George Orwell's classic 1984 than Karl Marx's promised land.

'Kim asked me not to open the door,' his wife Eleanor recalled, 'to please keep away from the living room windows and, above all, not on any account to disturb him in the study. He was terribly excited.'[2]

No car pulled up at the central Moscow apartment. There was a knock at the door. A tall, handsome man of about forty was standing there. Philby's face dropped. It wasn't a KGB chief, but nevertheless an important figure in his professional life as he had been forewarned.

'I'm Yuri Modin,' the man said, with a grin. 'You know me as "Peter", I think.'[3]

Philby recovered quickly and ushered his visitor in, offering him a vodka. They chatted for some time before Modin informed him that he would be suggesting 'writing assignments' from time to time.

Once his debriefings were completed in 1964, Modin suggested he ghost the memoirs of Soviet spy, Gordon Lonsdale. Philby virtually edited them because Lonsdale 'wasn't much of a literary man'.

Modin continued to give his former star agent assignments, from political pieces for Russian magazines, which the Control enjoyed translating, to reports advising the KGB how it should react to international events. Philby was not impressed, for instance, with the KGB's reaction to President Kennedy's assassination.

Modin, however, noted that these writing assignments were not allowing Philby to show how important he could be to the KGB. The Englishman was a good writer, but he felt he had much more to offer, and was keen to be given some overview of operational matters in the West.

But the KGB would not allow it. Modin thought that this was a waste of an enormous resource. Colonel 'F' agreed:

'On reflection, he should have been used better. But it was the time. His superiors knew what to do with him when he was in place, but finding a position in Moscow was a different matter. There were many who resented a foreigner telling them how to run things. It was ignorance in most cases, it has to be said.'[4]

Philby was given a token elevation in 1965, when he began advising KGB section heads on operations, but his abilities and directness were resented. At this time he also began complaining about the treatment of writers such as Solzhenitsyn.

'He wasn't always as diplomatic as he could have been,' Colonel 'F' commented. 'But I doubt he would have managed anyway. In the end he was seen as a foreigner, no matter how experienced.'

Philby found that his advice was being ignored. For instance, he warned the Russians not to get too involved in Africa in the mid-1960s, but they overdid their financial and military aid and it cost them dearly.

The lack of appreciation for the skills he could offer made Philby second-guess himself for the first time in his career. He was well into his fifties and didn't seem to have a useful professional life ahead. For a man who had put communism above everything, including his loved ones, it was depressing. A sense of uselessness enveloped him.

Philby began drinking more. He started an affair with Maclean's wife Melinda when Eleanor was visiting the US. It was yet another betrayal by a man who had made it a habit. Eleanor realized that there was no future for her in Russia and she returned to the US for good. Philby's affair with Melinda was happening long after her marriage to Maclean had been reduced to a sham, yet it did not help the relationship between the two men, who became estranged in Moscow.

Despair drove Philby to slit his wrists one drunken night. The suicide attempt failed, but it marked a low-point in his life.[5] Modin understood Philby's despair.

'He needed motivation,' he said. 'He had to be given more effective work – assignments which would give him a sense that he was defeating the enemy again. I asked him how he felt about writing his memoirs. He wasn't sure at first what this would achieve.'

The two men had several meetings to discuss it. Philby began to realize the value of a book by him in propaganda terms. He would explain – as far as he could – how he had fooled the British and American intelligence world.

'No one in the mid-1960s outside [the CIA and MI6] knew how much damage Philby had done,' Modin recalled. 'His revelations would drive this home to the public.'

The British Government had tried to play down Philby's importance and the damage he had done to the West. The memoirs would be a way of giving the KGB an image of superiority, while at the same time reducing morale inside British Intelligence. Philby could also cause some trouble by naming names.

He warmed to the idea and agreed to start writing, with Modin acting as an adviser and an editor in the censorial sense. It gave Philby a new zest for life. He was back causing turmoil inside MI6 and double-crossing his old colleagues.

He had some perverse fun, with Modin's careful scrutiny, in mentioning most of them. In one passage he judged the intellectual endowment of Felix Cowgill, the head of Section V of MI6 during the war as 'slender'.

'Unfortunately, Cowgill was up against a formidable array of brains,' Philby noted on page 55 of *My Silent War*. 'Most of our dealings with GCBCS [Government Code and Bletchley Cypher School] on the subject of German intelligence wireless traffic were with Page and Palmer, both familiar figures in Oxford. RSS [Radio Security Service, which intercepted enemy Intelligence signals] presented the even more formidable Oxonian combination of Trevor-Roper, Gilbert Ryle, Stuart Hampshire and Charles Stuart.

'Herbert Hart, another Oxonian, confronted him [Cowgill] in MI5, though here Cambridge too got a look in with Victor Rothschild, the MI5 anti-sabotage expert . . .'

A publisher's footnote about Rothschild on that page added to the intrigue: 'Also at Trinity College, Cambridge, in the 1930s. His mother employed Burgess soon after he left Cambridge – to report on her stock holdings, and later Burgess took over his flat in Bentinck Street. Later on in the war he trained Allied saboteurs for operations in Nazi-occupied Europe.'[6]

This would later cause Philby-watchers and espionage commentators to go into a frenzy of analysis. If he left out a colleague, did that mean he was a fellow double-agent? Surely, he would have to mention everybody? If he was disparaging about a British spy, would that mean he just might be representing the KGB too? And what if he were effusive or flattering about someone? Was this honest, or an attempt to whitewash them?

On page 73, he remarked:

'The quality of MI5 in wartime owed much to its temporary recruits. There was a particularly good haul from the universities, Hart, Blunt, Rothschild, Masterman, and others, and the law also made a substantial contribution . . . at the top of B Division [of MI5] there were two professional intelligence officers who contrived throughout the war to retain the respect of their brilliant subordinates . . .

'The head of B Division was Guy Liddell. "I was born in an Irish Fog", he once told me, "and sometimes I think I never emerged from it." No self-deprecation could have been more ludicrous . . . behind the façade of laziness, his subtle and reflective mind played over a storehouse of photographic memories . . .'

The mention of Blunt in this passage was particularly mischievous. He had confessed to being a double agent and had been blithely
grouped with several other names. Modin and Philby anticipated
this would cause apoplexy amongst MI5 and MI6 ranks when the
book was published in Britain.

Later in the book, Philby delivered the most damaging cut of all
to Angleton. The words were bound to have repercussions in the
brutal intelligence world for a long time to come:

'Our close relationship was, I am sure, inspired by genuine
friendliness on both sides. But we both had ulterior motives . . . by
cultivating me he could better keep me under wraps. For my part, I
was more than content to string him along. The greater the trust
between us overtly, the less he would suspect covert action.'

Philby would have had his tongue firmly in his cheek when he
added:

'Who gained most from this complex game I cannot say. But I
had one big advantage. I knew what he was doing for the CIA and
he knew what I was doing for SIS. But the real nature of my interest
was something he did not know.'

The exercise of writing lifted Philby's spirits, and though his
heavy drinking continued, he had a renewed sense of importance.
Perhaps once his masters at the Moscow Centre had read his story,
they might reassess his capability.

COMING OF AGE

While Philby was using Rothschild's name to stir up his adversaries,
the man himself was causing trouble for Israel's enemies in the
Middle East. Rothschild had long urged Mossad to use as much
modern technology as possible in preparation for probable war with
its hostile neighbours. He had informed Mossad chiefs of the need
for computerized data in intelligence work, even introducing them
to contacts in the CIA via Angleton and Helms, who could secretly
assist in the electronic upgrade.[7]

Since the early 1960s, Rothschild had pushed for the use of
electronic listening devices (thanks in part to what he had learned
from Peter Wright) to replace human agents as guards on Israel's
vulnerable borders.[8] Consequently, Mossad developed the signals

side of its Intelligence operations so that it could intercept enemy communications.

By the mid-1960s, masts, antennae and radar discs began to appear on Mount Hermon above the Golan Heights. They allowed military Intelligence to listen to phone and signals traffic in Damascus, which was only forty-three miles away. The listening system was a replica of the one developed in Britain for use by America's National Security Agency, the CIA and British Intelligence in their techno-battle and war defence against the Soviet Union.

Israel was using the information captured by its giant border ears to computerize data about every enemy officer in the armies of Egypt, Jordan, Iraq, Syria and Saudi Arabia. By 1967, every Israeli Field Commander had a dossier on his potential opponents in the field, down to the military qualifications of each opposing platoon and company leader.

On the eve of the Six Day War, Jews worldwide prepared to rally to Israel's cause. For many who had, in the two decades since the Second World War, settled as refugees in new countries, the horrors of the Holocaust were still stark. They would do everything to avoid a repetition.

Among the deeply concerned was Miriam Rothschild, now sixty and recovering from a major operation. She had to be restrained by her brother from rushing to the airport. Victor had just donated a million pounds to Israel on behalf of the family, but Miriam was not satisfied. However, he managed to make her see she might be a hindrance rather than a help.[9]

Besides, Victor pointed out, a Rothschild would be there. Baron Elie of the French house was flying out in his own private plane. Victor was also confident that Israel would cope. He more than anyone knew the preparation that had gone into the country's military.[10]

Yet Rothschild still looked on with nervous anticipation and a sense of *déjà vu* on the eve of the Six Day War with the Arabs as Israel's Signals Corps cracked enemy army codes, intercepted messages and transmitted false ones, in much the same way that British Intelligence did against the Nazis in the Second World War.

Israeli and Egyptian troops massed on either side of the border. Nasser delivered an ultimatum demanding the removal of the UN buffer force in Sinai. The force left. Nasser's troops occupied the

region of Sharm-el-Sheikh, which threatened to blockade the sea
route to the Israeli port of Eilat. The move made war inevitable.

Israel's Intelligence readiness was now to be tested. The large
amount of data gathered indicated how vulnerable and unprepared
the Arab armies and airforces were. Once the Egyptians made their
anticipated moves in Sinai, the Israeli air force mobilized and carried
out pre-emptive air strikes.

The Israelis boldly sent false messages about Egypt's success in
Sinai to Jordan in order to draw that country into the conflict. Later,
the Israeli Signals Corps cheekily demonstrated its skills by eavesdropping on a radio conversation between Egypt's President Nasser
and Jordan's King Hussein.

Israel's superiority in the techno-war allowed it to win a quick
and resounding victory. Their spectacular success caused Jews to
hope that the homeland's troubles might be over, especially as
Jerusalem was a united city and a safe border had been established
on the River Jordan.

Yet Israel's Intelligence chiefs were already considering the consequences of humiliating its neighbours. They did not anticipate the
response of dejected Palestinians, who had hoped Israel would be
defeated and banished from their region and whose guerrilla groups
would join forces for a new kind of conflict, which would be harder
for Israel's technology to monitor and control. Instead Mossad chiefs
were expecting that regrouped and improved Arab military forces
would again try to destroy Israel.

When Rothschild flew to Israel not long after the Six Day War,
uppermost in the minds of his friends in the military and Intelligence
was an enhancement of the nation's nuclear weapons programme.[11]

In the decade since the Dimona Plant had been completed,
Israel's leaders had felt some measure of comfort in knowing that
they had the technology to develop a nuclear arsenal as an ultimate
deterrent to aggression. The Six Day War was an urgent reminder
that they still needed access to the nuclear weapons' raw material:
uranium.

Israel had been supplied with uranium partly thanks to the efforts
of Zionist Dr Zalman Shapiro, a research chemist who had worked
on the Manhattan Project. Shapiro set up an Israeli-financed
corporation called Numec, which handled nuclear materials and
equipment.

Over the next decade, 206 lb of enriched uranium disappeared from Numec's Pennsylvania plant and ended up in Israel. The corporation was investigated by US authorities and fined a million dollars, causing it to shut down.

Along with the cutting of this supply, US regulations safeguarding uranium supplies were tightened after the Six Day War. Some in the State Department feared Israel's aggression and Arab revenge could see an escalation of war to a nuclear conflict in the Middle East.

Now Rothschild's expertise in both banking and bombs was needed in a more complicated plot to acquire uranium. He was consulted by Intelligence chiefs and became privy to a plan to set up a European operation – codenamed Plombat – involving dummy Israeli companies and shipping, which would eventually see a large amount of uranium being hi-jacked to the Israeli port of Haifa and transported to Dimona.[12]

Scientists at the plant were thus able to prepare a 'substantial number' of atomic devices, which were stored in tunnels under the Negev Desert.

According to both CIA and Mossad sources, Rothschild was also useful to the Israelis in 'mending fences' with some neighbours in the Middle East after the disruption of the Six Day conflict. For instance, he called on his old friend the Shah of Iran and suggested several 'crop breeding' ventures, which had been perfected in Israel and elsewhere. Some were adapted in Iran.[13] By 1968, he had put his money, exceptional know-how, contacts and influence at the disposal of the state he had helped create and protect.

31. BLUNTED

THE POSSIBLE APOSTLE

Blunt had proved as resolute and steely as Modin expected under the constant nightmare of his interrogation by Peter Wright. By 1968, after four years of meetings, Blunt had not given MI5 one important lead. Those he identified as fellow Soviet agents were already known.

Rothschild had been questioned about his links with communism, such as his membership of the Party while at Cambridge, but this was dismissed as the mild misadventure of an exuberant youth caught up in the undergraduate passions of the time.[1]

Now Rothschild was giving the impression that he wanted to help Wright open files on former communists working in sensitive areas of Government, including Intelligence, military, defence and weapons.

He offered to assist Wright to meet those who warranted investigation. Sooner or later Wright would have got around to seeking them out, but this way, Rothschild could manage the direction of the inquisitions and prepare those who would be subjected to them.[2]

Rothschild knew all the Establishment figures under suspicion. Without his intervention these men and women might have incriminated themselves. On the other hand, Wright was most grateful for Rothschild's diligent assistance, for it seemed easier to make contact once he had smoothed the way. Rothschild arranged lunches, dinners, even parties so that the MI5 investigator would think he was making subtle contact with targets and leads to possible spies.[3]

High on the list was Alister Watson, the Apostle, Marxist expert and close friend of the Ring of Five since Cambridge days. As head of the Submarine Detection Research Section at the Admiralty, he had risen to 'one of the most secret and important jobs in the entire NATO defence establishment'.[4]

Wright pursued him and reported back to Rothschild after every encounter, expressing his frustration and contempt for the suspect.[5] After interviewing past and present members of British Intelligence and considering evidence given to me by other sources, I believe Watson was innocent of any spying. He endured a brutal interrogation, which was like a scene out of *Ipcress File* or *The Manchurian Candidate*, and according to former British Intelligence contacts, was drugged with LSD without his knowledge. It left him in an extremely confused state. MI5 investigators hoped this would cause him to confess to spying. These claims are in part supported by Wright himself (see page 287), who had experimented with LSD for interrogation purposes.

In *Spycatcher*, Wright noted that during questioning Watson was '*too far gone . . . He seemed unable to even understand the offer that was made to him.*'

He was hallucinating according to his wife Susan, whom I interviewed at her Surrey home in October 1994. His behaviour during the interrogation period was consistent with having been given LSD.

'Alister was incoherent and lost his memory,' Mrs Watson said. 'I recall him flicking through diaries from the 1930s, trying to find people who may have been spies. He was searching for appointments at regular intervals and places. At one point he announced he had found someone, which proved he [Alister] and the other person were spies. Later he realized the person was his dentist.'

All through the ordeal, Watson was bullied into confessing things he had never done. In a disorientated state, he was shown thirty photographs spread out on a table. They contained portraits of some of the KGB's leading agents based in Britain since 1940. After several hours, Watson groggily selected three, including Modin. However, when he recovered from the hideous grilling, Watson recalled having been shown these photos during his last vetting by Naval Intelligence in 1952.

Wright claimed that Watson admitted meeting the three dubiously selected agents, '*sometimes close to the Admiralty Research Laboratory* [where the scientist worked] *at Teddington during his lunch hour, but he denied passing any secrets*'.

Mrs Watson refuted this.

'Alister was a man of meticulous habits,' she said. 'he *always* came home for lunch to our house, which was five minutes away, for the whole hour he had off.'

The claim that he had met Russian controls so close to his work is also disputed by Modin. He denied he had ever met Watson or that he was a Soviet agent.

'We would never, *never* meet an agent so close to his place of work,' Modin, said with a laugh. 'It would always be a long distance away. That is why we more often met at night, so that an agent could spend time reaching a rendezvous point and making sure he was not followed [by MI5 'Watchers'].'

Blunt and Rothschild tried to deflect guilt from themselves and on to the innocent Watson, but he never confessed to spying.

Wright continued his zealous hounding of suspects, who included Leo Long, John Cairncross and highly-placed civil servant, Dennis Proctor. Often he took them back to meet Blunt in harrowing encounters, at which much alcohol was consumed but no new or surprising secret connections were divulged.

Wright felt he had found his true niche as a spyhunter. He widened his brief to several scientific and academic institutions. But, it seemed, each time the ruthless investigator came close, the pressure on suspects caused tragedy. While he was probing an Oxford University spy ring, Sir Andrew Cohen, a diplomat who had been an Apostle at Cambridge with Rothschild and Blunt, died of a heart attack soon after he learned he was to be questioned. Bernard Floud, a proposed junior minister in Wilson's cabinet, committed suicide after tough questioning by Wright and before he had to endure another interrogation. A few days later, Phoebe Pool threw herself under a tube train. She had been a courier for Blunt in the 1950s and a colleague of his at the Courtauld Institute.[6]

Wright's relentless pursuit of those he envied for their privileged education of three decades ago was causing a spiralling despair among the former ideological students from Oxbridge. The fear generated would touch everyone involved for the rest of their lives.

All during this time Blunt anaesthetized himself with alcohol and stood firm. He insisted there had only been a ring of four at Cambridge – himself, Burgess, Maclean and Philby – with second-rank spies, such as Cairncross and Long, existing independently of the central ring members. There was no Fifth Man, Blunt insisted. But the more he protested, the more Wright became suspicious that there had to be a key figure he had missed, someone who could even be right under his nose.

He complained to Rothschild that it could be the only reason that all their investigations led to dead spies or those who were already under suspicion. For once, his genius companion seemed perplexed. Not even he could offer a plausible explanation.

DAVID AND ROSA

Anatoli Golitsyn, the defector, addressed a conference of counter-intelligence officers from Canada, Britain, the USA, Australia and New Zealand in Melbourne in late 1967, and made a convincing case for there being a lack of understanding of his methodology – the way he went about searching for Soviet spies.[7]

He had bounced back and forth across the Atlantic maintaining his marketability with 'new' information about Soviet penetration of Western Intelligence. But until that conference, he had slipped in credibility because many of his leads were too general and proved fruitless. MI5's chief, Martin Furnival Jones, Hollis's successor, was impressed and offered him the files on all MI5 personnel.

From the spring of 1968 Golitsyn was given £10,000 a month to peruse the files in a safe house near Brighton. The defector concentrated on Venona – the several thousand KGB radio communication messages, which had been partly or completely decoded. Eight codenames had been found.

Two in particular interested him: DAVID and ROSA. The messages decoded indicated that they had worked together, most likely as a married couple. Golitsyn asked for the files of all MI5 officers who had been working for British Intelligence at the time of the Venona traffic. He studied the files and after a week asked Wright to come and see him in Brighton.

Wright arrived at the safe house excited about a break-through. Golitsyn pointed to two files on the desk in the study.

'I've discovered DAVID and ROSA,' he said excitedly. 'My methodology has uncovered them.'[8]

Wright glanced at the name on the files. He knew them well. They belonged to Victor and Tess Rothschild.

Wright told him not to be absurd. Rothschild, he informed the Russian, was one of the best friends this Service ever had. Golitsyn, however, was emphatic and Wright asked how he came to such a conclusion.

'They are Jewish,' Golitsyn replied. 'DAVID and ROSA are Jewish names.'[9]

Golitsyn was guessing wildly and was incorrect. Tess was not Jewish. Nor did she marry Rothschild until 1946. Although they had worked closely during the war, they were not always together. Rothschild often went on assignments alone, such as when he acted as MI5's security inspector at weapons research facilities. Wright put the accusation down to typical 'KGB anti-Semitism', which had been rampant since Stalin's purge after the 'Jewish Doctor's Plot'.

Golitsyn could not give any further reason for linking David and Rosa with the Rothschilds and Wright dismissed his claim as another attempt to justify his importance and the money he was being paid, which irritated the MI5 man. In the bitter atmosphere of accusation and counter-accusation in the late 1960s, which had been in the main engendered by Wright himself, this appeared to be another hopeful, ill-founded guess.

'I could not help thinking that if this had been the CIA and I had been Angleton,' Wright remarked in *Spycatcher*, 'Victor and Tess would almost certainly have been listed as spies on Golitsyn's groundless interpretation.'

Fortunately for Rothschild, his close companion and confidant had been the one informed and there was no further investigation. Golitsyn had earlier informed Wright about a file marked 'Technics' in a safe at the Moscow Centre. It was basically a file on all MI5 technical operations against the Russians, which Wright and his team had initiated. This proved to him that a mole had indeed been spying on him and his activities. Wright never discussed with Golitsyn what he had told Rothschild. If he had, the Russian would have realized that his guess had been accurate.

Furnival Jones (FJ to everyone at MI5) had never disguised his contempt for Wright's witch-hunting – especially his unauthorized investigation into Hollis – which everyone inside, and Rothschild on the outside, were well aware of. FJ eventually reshuffled MI5's divisions to take away Wright's role as investigator of Soviet penetration.

It had been a long time coming. Wright, and his fellow spyhunters had been seen as a small, spiteful and disruptive Gestapo. Wright admitted that the Fluency team were viewed as men with grudges and obsessions, who were so convinced of Hollis's guilt they were unable to conceive of any other interpretation of the evidence.[10]

But he was not alone in suspecting the MI5 boss, who retired in 1965 to play golf in Somerset. Wright's successors in the reshaped MI5 came to the conclusion that the Hollis file was worth reopening. Reluctantly, FJ agreed that Hollis should be called in for questioning.

The 1969 interrogation took place in a safe house in Mayfair's smart South Audley Street, not far from the American Embassy in Grosvenor Square. Hollis stood up to several days of questioning, which Wright listened to at MI5, without missing a beat. There was no stuttering like Philby, or reaching for the Scotch bottle as with Blunt. He had a few justifiable memory lapses and was even caught out in a small lie: his failure to mention, on joining MI5, his friendship with a known member of the Comintern.

His answer was acceptable. He didn't want the link to ruin his chances of joining Intelligence. Even his remark that he would not have been alone in breaking the rule about the disclosure of such relationships seemed reasonable. Either Hollis was not guilty of being a Soviet agent, or he was one of the coolest, most nerveless performers under pressure ever seen on either side of the Iron Curtain.

Wright was crestfallen at the failure to make him confess. He wasn't part of the interrogation, which he thought was too tame.

'It was all shadow boxing,' Wright remarked. 'Somehow, he [John Day, the interrogator] never got close enough to street fight, to grapple and gouge him . . .'

Unless some new defector stepped forward with a conclusive piece of evidence, Wright acknowledged, time was against trapping Hollis. He would never be caught, if, in fact, he were a double agent. In the days immediately after Hollis's interrogation it appeared unlikely, even to Wright himself, that he would ever be cornered.

A few weeks later Hollis had a stroke, again demonstrating the impact of the witch-hunt on its victims. Hollis regained his health and was able to play golf again.

When Wright reported the result of the Hollis inquiry to the Americans Angleton was sceptical, although the CIA had no more evidence in its files about Hollis that would have suggested he was guilty. The end of another decade was upon them and both Wright and Angleton had yet to trap even one Soviet penetration agent.

This was after, collectively, forty years of trying.

32. NEW CHALLENGES, OLD ROLES

THE IMMERSION

The restless Rothschild was still, at the beginning of 1970, a genius in search of a genre away from the underground spy world. His more than a decade at Shell had served its purpose and he had made a point about his capacities. But if Victor was going to really prove something to himself away from the intriguers, paranoids, and keepers of espionage secrets, it would have to be in public life, not business.

He had been reluctant to leave Shell in order to take a job in the Wilson administration, but he had been tempted. Yet the 1966 offer of Minister of Technology involved more of the same work he was doing at Shell. Rothschild considered that he was a man with a vision that encompassed more than just the science world and he needed a greater challenge than boffins and budgets would offer. He wanted a role more in keeping with his own extraordinary skill at grappling the big ideas – something that tackled the major problems facing the nation, if not the world.

There was always the nagging, quiet problem of keeping up with developments in Intelligence. The job of Technology Minister would not have allowed him to stay in touch with MI5 and MI6, which he felt he had to do, just in case some defector, or a refreshed Peter Wright came out of left field with new evidence about the ring.

Changes were coming up in his private life too. The children of his first marriage were all adults and those of his marriage to Tess were maturing fast. The bright and precocious Emma was twenty-one and he had done everything he could to give her a fine education, even to the point of forming a private school at his home, which included the sons and daughters of various Cambridge dons.

She had not let him down, having won scholarships to Oxford and Cambridge at fifteen. Emma opted for Oxford, perhaps a wise decision given her parents' possibly stifling connections with Cambridge. She took a first in Politics, Philosophy and Economics, and won a Kennedy Memorial Fund Scholarship to the Massachusetts Institute of Technology (MIT), making her a frequent commuter between New York and London.

Her politics, in keeping with her parents', especially in their undergraduate days at Cambridge, would have brought quiet approval at home.

'[Emma] is a disciple of Tynan & Co and the glossy Left,' author Chaim Bermant wrote in his book, *The Cousinhood*, 'and she has been active on behalf of several of its causes.'[1]

Daughter Victoria, sixteen, and son Amschel James, fourteen, would be finishing school soon and no doubt looking for careers that would take them away from the Cambridge family home.

Victor, in his sixtieth year, was looking for change.

It came from an unexpected source when Conservative Party leader Ted Heath was elected Prime Minister, replacing Wilson, in 1970.

Heath's close advisers decided to set up a Think Tank, to guide the new prime minister and his cabinet on the big issues facing the rapidly evolving Britain in an even faster-changing world. The concept of using a team of brains to back up a new government was not new, for everyone in modern administration realised it was almost impossible to find time to strategize, conceptualize or reflect on major problems. Advisers, consultants and assorted well-paid academic hangers-on had been around for decades filling up quangos and soaking up the public purse.

But using outside, specialized sources of advice and information had never been institutionalized before. Heath did it in the form of the bland sounding Central Policy Review Staff, attached to the Cabinet Office.

When the feelers were sent to Rothschild to sound him out on becoming its first Director-General and First Permanent Under-Secretary, he replied that he was more than interested. In discussions it was agreed that he would have an overseeing role concerning British Intelligence.

Rothschild accepted the position. He had to go through a normal vetting procedure. Not surprisingly, after his great help towards the vetters' and their organization – MI5 – he was assured of clearance, especially as there was no evidence that he had ever been a Soviet agent. Had he taken the immunity card of 1964 it is unlikely that Heath and Downing Street would not have been told the details.

Victor was in. His appointment was greeted with glee, especially by a surprised Left. Richard Crossman, an ex-cabinet minister under Wilson, noted in the *New Statesman*:

> By persuading Victor Rothschild to leave Shell and head his new central brains trust, Ted Heath has accepted a rival's advice and put 'a tiger in the tank'. Here is a new type of Whitehall warrior who combines scientific eminence and managerial drive with a dialectical diabolism which whenever I meet him leaves me (nearly) speechless. He is a Lindemann and a Balogh rolled into one and stiffened with a strain of sardonic tycoonery. The furies roused by the 'prof' [Lindemann] under Churchill and by Thomas Balogh during his more recent stay at Number 10 were as nothing compared with the rows I confidently expect to erupt when Lord Rothschild really gets to work under the protection afforded by Sir Burke Trend's cabinet secretariat. I congratulate the Prime Minister on a really adventurous appointment.[2]

Crossman showed prescience.

TANKS FOR THE CONCORDE

Rothschild's first meeting with Heath did nothing to clarify and much to confuse his role at the Tank. The conversation at Number 10 was strained.

'It's funny we have never met before,' Heath remarked.

'Prime Minister,' Rothschild said after a pause, 'do you not think it would be better to have an economist in charge of this Unit?'

'I did Economics at Oxford,' Heath replied, implying that he could handle the Tank's economics thinking.

'Prime Minister, could you give me an example of the type of problem you want the Unit to tackle?' Rothschild said, rather desperately.

'Concorde.'

With that Rothschild 'detected some anguished vibrations' from Sir Burke Trend, the Cabinet Secretary, and Sir Robert Armstrong, Heath's Principal Private Secretary, 'who were hovering in the background.' When they briefed him before the meeting, Concorde was cited as an example of something the Tank would *not* be studying.[3]

The vague, *Yes, Prime Minister*-type situation was just right for Rothschild's ambitions, both overt and covert.[4] The Tank could be a creature of his creation, and his unofficial role with the Intelligence services would ensure there were no surprises concerning the past. Its lack of guidelines allowed Rothschild to emerge as the most powerful man in Whitehall, after Armstrong.

He fulfilled Crossman's predictions and cut a swathe through the bureaucracy like no one before him. He put his weight behind the Statutory Incomes Policy and attacked lame duck industry support, such as that given to the Upper Clyde Shipbuilders. Rothschild pushed for more funds for scientific research and development in industry and was attacked by universities for doing so. He used his considerable contacts and expertise in oil to predict price rises and the crisis.

Rothschild created discussion and support for a pet topic – nuclear reactors – and aired his great knowledge, which stretched back to his espionage work in 1942. He was against Concorde because it was a 'financial disaster' but recommended it to go ahead for political reasons. The 'flying white elephant' had been given such a big build-up by the Government that scrapping it would have been an embarrassment.

When Heath was at the Prime Minister's country retreat, Chequers, Rothschild and his brains trust at the Tank would lecture the cabinet, and answer questions – all with the use of charts and diagrams, of which Rothschild had been fond since his wartime espionage days.

It was refreshing for ministers, even if it ruffled them, for they were given 'elegant and ruthless' expositions on a variety of topics, regardless of the political pressures on issues. No cabinet in British history had received such wide-ranging, in-depth and honest advice, making the Heath government an informed and educated administration as far as the big issues were concerned.

Rothschild also turned the memo into an art form, firing pointed missives to startled bureaucrats, who were no match for him because of their training in circumlocution. This directness carried over into his speeches, which even hurt the government. On one occasion, he made a case for Britain reassessing its place in the world as a middle power. On another he was pessimistic about the economy. Both times Heath responded angrily and reprimanded him. Rothschild had over-stepped the mark by going public, and for a moment gave the impression of a de facto leader dispensing honesty, something intolerable in a Whitehall which had traditionally shadow-boxed with reality and hidden unpalatable truths. By telling the public that Britain needed an overhaul of its attitudes and institutions, he was expressing the views of a long-time, frustrated socialist. In the 1930s and 1940s, Rothschild had expected revolution. In the 1950s, it was still on the socialist agenda. The 1960s saw the hope of rapid change dissipate. Now he had to express warnings about where his country was heading since it seemed obvious his dreams were not going to become reality.

Perhaps these confrontations weakened Rothschild's later cases, for instance when he suggested that the government could justify giving the National Union of Mineworkers (NUM) a pay rise because of increased oil prices. Heath said no to this. His lack of compromise on this issue eventually brought down his government.

- - - -

33. THE CENTRE'S
MIXED FORTUNES

PHILBY'S SALVATION

As Rothschild was giving full rein to his exceptional talents, Philby was rediscovering his after a second period of KGB neglect in Moscow. The writing of his memoirs, published in the West in 1968, had at least given him a goal. Although Modin organized trips for him inside the Soviet Union to Siberia, Tbilisi, Armenia, Middle Asia, the Crimea and Azerbaijan, this had reinforced his isolation, both geographically and within.[1]

While he enjoyed seeing these places as a tourist, it was a long way from his work as a journalist in Spain, a spy in London or both in Beirut.

Modin thought it might be useful for him to gain accolades from within the Communist Bloc. He was sent abroad to Czechoslovakia, Hungary, Bulgaria and Cuba – where he was fêted quietly among espionage agencies, which temporarily restored his self-esteem.[2]

But the reality back in Moscow was that by the end of the 1960s he felt useless. The KGB had disliked his hard advice on world affairs and some KGB operations. For instance, in 1967, in a break from his memoirs, he had worked on an espionage dirty trick with Modin which failed.

Modin had flown to Bombay in an attempt to discredit the anti-communist candidate, S. K. Patil, in an election by circulating a forged letter from the US Consul-General in Bombay, Milton C. Rewinkel, to the US Ambassador, Chester Bowles. The letter suggested that the US had backed Patil's campaign with 'half a million rupees'.

Modin also circulated a false telegram from the British High Commissioner, 'Sir' John Freeman, which reported to the British

Foreign Office that the Americans had donated vast sums to the election funds of right-wing parties and politicians.

At the time Freeman had not received a knighthood. MI6 knew that Modin was in Bombay and guessed he had been responsible. The Russian was forced to make a hurried departure. The mistake was thought within KGB ranks to be Philby's, although he denied it.[3]

Coupled with the KGB's negative responses to his advice on political issues, the former double agent's credibility slipped. The KGB stopped sending him papers to work on and no longer sought his opinion.

There was also disquiet in the KGB about his affair with Melinda Maclean. Philby turned again to alcohol for comfort and seemed to be literally drinking himself to death. He told friends that he was miserable and he struggled with the language. His driver and secretary were removed.

However, in 1969 Modin and others lobbied Yuri Andropov, the KGB head since 1967, for Philby's reinstatement as an esteemed adviser. Andropov read some of Philby's analysis on the Middle East and the Six Day War, and listened to views on the importance of Philby's memoirs as an effective disinformation document in the West. The KGB Chief decided he should be given more work.[4]

By late 1970, his secretary and driver were restored to him. The papers began arriving at his Pushkin Square flat once more and his 'doubt and depression vanished'.[5]

A year later he met Rufina ('Rufa') Pukhova, a friend of British spy George Blake.

Philby's first words to her were: 'Take off your spectacles. I want to see your eyes.'

Her initial impression of the 'great KGB Cambridge spy' were not flattering.

'He was just an elderly man with a flabby face.'[6]

However, using a bit of romantic subterfuge, Philby contrived to meet her several times and fell in love with her. They married in December 1971, and Philby, at fifty-eight, was 'content' with most aspects of his life for the first time since he had defected. Yet he was still suffering some mental anguish and drinking too much.

'I got a glimpse of how tortuous life was for him,' Rufa told a friend, former KGB Colonel Michael Bagdonov. 'Sometimes he would painfully exclaim: "You can't imagine how unhappy I am!"'[7]

She discovered the wrist scars from his attempted suicide and he angrily ordered her to never again ask him about it.

Rufa spoke also of a period of extreme tension when the KGB feared that someone – the rumour was a Russian working for MI6 – would attempt to assassinate her husband.[8]

'We were sent to Armenia with two bodyguards,' she recalled.

Early in the marriage her main goal was to attempt to cut Philby's excessive alcohol intake, which 'turned this cleverest of men into a fool.'[9]

His drinking made life very difficult for her as 'he used to begin his day with wine and then it went on and on eternally, until it became a nightmare'.

Philby feared he would lose her.

'One morning in winter when we were going for a walk,' she recounted in a summary of her seventeen years with him, 'I discovered that one of my boots was missing. We looked at each other in surprise and began a long search. Suddenly Kim struck himself on the forehead. Then he went to his study and returned with the boot. In a drunken moment the night before, he had hidden it so that I could not run away from him. It was funny, yet sad.'[10]

OPERATION 105

In May 1971, MI5 officers under Martin Furnival Jones' leadership used a honey-trap – where sex is part of an entrapment – to turn a middle-level sabotage operator, Oleg Lyalin, working for the KGB in London. Lyalin was a killing machine, who had been trained to murder by hand, with weapons, poison and bombs. He was a part of a big sabotage team in Britain, which had a plan to assassinate leading British figures such as the prime minister, top ministers, and heads of the military, in preparation for conflict with the West.[11]

Other plans for these saboteurs targeted public services, such as water and power, transport, communications and the nerve centres of government. This is where Nafta, the well-placed petrol station chain, would be used by Soviet *Spetsnaz* (special forces) to smash and blow up the major US and UK military bases throughout the country, as part of a wider operation to immobilize Britain as the floating aircraft carrier for a US-led NATO assault on Russia.

Apart from plans to obliterate bases by mortar, missile and fire-bombing attacks, Lyalin disclosed more James Bondian plots such as flooding the London Underground, and sending agents posing as messengers to scatter colourless poison capsules along the corridors of power, which when crushed underfoot would release deadly toxins.

MI5 gathered details from Lyalin on these plans for six months and they gave Furnival Jones and Wright a perspective on the wide scope of KGB operations in Britain. They had a fair idea before Lyalin fell into MI5's clutches, based on information from Venona radio communications traffic, defectors and double agents captured, which together indicated that there were about twenty-five Russian intelligence officers running about 400 agents. Many of these were low-level spies in the Communist Party. A few were high-penetration agents in powerful positions.[12]

Furnival Jones, Wright, Dick White and others had long been concerned that there was a huge imbalance of spies in Russia's favour in Britain, which put too much pressure on MI5 and its watchers, who could not hope to cover every known enemy, let alone uncover those unknown.

The Russian numbers had swollen during the 1960s. Now MI5, with a Conservative prime minister in power, decided to redress the imbalance. Furnival Jones put the case to Heath and he reacted by saying MI5 should 'throw out the lot of them'.[13]

Lyalin defected in September 1971, and then MI5 swooped. It expelled 105 Soviet agents. The Moscow Centre was shocked. The London station had been its great haven in the West, and vital in its preparation for war, thanks largely to the performances of Modin and a couple of other Controls in the 1950s. But even Modin recognized KGB numbers had grown too large.

'There were just too many by 1971,' he commented. 'They were too difficult to control and there were bound to be errors. You only needed one agent to make a mistake or be lazy and an operation would be finished.'[14]

This unwieldiness had caused vital operations such as Nafta to be blown, and expert observers such as Modin and Oleg Gordievsky (who defected in 1985) could predict that the KGB's London operation might never recover from the blow.

The reduced numbers of KGB and GRU agents were suddenly under far greater pressure from surveillance. The MI5 watchers had taken the ascendancy for the first time since the war. The mass expulsion gave Wright and others more than a flicker of hope that they could again target high-penetration British agents.

PASSPORT TO TRAGEDY

Modin continued to monitor and assist Blake, Philby and others in the close coterie of former foreign spies in Moscow. But in August 1972, the highly regarded former Control suddenly needed their support. His daughter, Olga, then twenty-five, had flown to see relatives in Kurzastan, but had trouble getting on a return flight to Moscow. She rang her influential father and asked him to help. At first he refused to use his KGB weight to get her home, but she cried and pleaded with him.

'All the time she was trying so hard to get me to intervene,' Modin told me, 'I had a strong feeling that something would happen.'[15]

Modin relented and sent his passport to her via his KGB contacts and she used it to arrange a seat on a flight. The plane crashed. All on board, including Olga, were killed.

Modin's passport was found in the wreckage. For a day the Centre assumed that he had died and that sabotage might be involved. However, Modin turned up at the Lubyanka and was shattered when he was told of his daughter's tragedy.

George Blake came round to his flat immediately he heard the news and was one of the first to offer his condolences, as was Philby. Modin had offered all his defector agents full back-up as both adviser and friend in their difficult readjustments and work in their adopted country. Now it was their turn to repay the debt.

34. THE PM'S EYES
AND EARS

THE BACK-CHANNEL MANIPULATOR

The Heath Government and certain key Whitehall civil servants saw the Think Tank as a vehicle for taking control of and changing British Intelligence, which they considered dangerous to British democracy. However, Rothschild was the wrong choice to implement such a move, for it allowed him to manoeuvre himself into a position where *he* had power over Intelligence, which meant that the *status quo* would remain. He had a vested interest in making sure that his cronies of the last thirty years in MI5 and MI6 held sway, and not new appointments who would try to change the services.

Part of the strategy for maintaining the strength of MI5 was to demonstrate that there were still major threats to Britain from agents, such as those within the communist movement.

The continuing red menace in the trade unions had to be presented to Heath directly and not via Philip Allen, Permanent Secretary to the Home Office, whose department took reports from MI5's 'F' Branch. The Wright-led faction inside MI5 considered these reports weak, so it wished to present its own and used Rothschild as a back-channel to Heath.[1] Rothschild gave Wright a perfect opportunity to beef-up the government's perspective on the continued Soviet threat by complaining to him that 'F' Branch was 'pulling its punches' over the issue and asking for 'something better'.

It was also a good opportunity for Rothschild to again present himself as being tough on communism without compromising any of his own former KGB operations. This in turn would assist him in covering any trails that could still, because of some unforeseen incident, expose him to accusations of being the Fifth Man. New leads in the early 1950s and Philby's defection in 1963 had put him under scrutiny and made him alert to further possible problems.

In 1972, Rothschild reported to Wright that Heath had been 'appalled' at a recent cabinet meeting, which had been addressed by Jack Jones and Hugh Scanlon, the two powerful trade union bosses. Rothschild implied that Heath was concerned that the unionists 'talked like communists'. (This was unlikely. Heath would have known that Scanlon was not a left-winger.)[2]

Rothschild had long discussions with Wright and pumped him for details on recent Czech defectors, who were providing information about trade union and Labour Party subversion, which gave him a broad idea of the strength of the material. Wright asked Rothschild to 'minute him formally' with a request for analysis on Jack Jones.

The request began: 'The Prime Minister is anxious to see . . .', which was probably inaccurate. It's more likely that Rothschild suggested that he might be able to provide information and Heath, not suspecting he would upset the Home Office, had probably nodded his agreement. Its 'typical Victor style' was designed to thwart any Home Office protests that they were undermining its role in channelling MI5 intelligence to the prime minister.

Wright took two days to trawl through the files and wrote an inaccurate, misleading report, turning supposition, smears and innuendo into 'fact'.[3] He characterized his actions thus in 1980, in a special report for Rothschild when they were composing a list of Rothschild's achievements or actions, which were meant to demonstrate that he could not have been the Fifth Man:

At the height of Heath's trouble with the Unions, the PM was not satisfied with the Security Services reports on Jack Jones . . . The reports only gave the subversion information. The PM discussed the matter with Rothschild. Rothschild said that he might be able to get more information. He consulted Peter Wright, who knew the case. Peter Wright consulted DG (FJ) who told him to 'give Rothschild what he wants'. Wright gave Rothschild a note summarizing the evidence of Jones' Soviet connections, which were damning (but not legal proof).

Rothschild was attacked by the Permanent Secretary, Home Office, for going outside his terms of reference, despite the PM's request.[4]

Whitehall reacted strongly. Wright was given a dressing-down by Sir John Hunt, the Cabinet Secretary, who 'asked what on earth I thought I was doing passing material about an opposition party into the government party's hands at such a delicate time'.

Wright defended himself by saying Rothschild had made the request. Rothschild and FJ supported him.

'Victor relished the row,' Wright recalled, 'and composed a series of elegant memorandums which winged their way through Whitehall defending the Security Services' right to provide intelligence requested of it by Number 10 Downing Street.'

Philip Allen was so angry he hardly ever spoke to Wright again. He sent a note to Rothschild, which said: 'Keep off the grass'.[5]

In *Spycatcher*, Wright showed the extent of Rothschild's influence when he introduced Wright to Heath (in a chance encounter in the Cabinet Office) as 'one of the stranger phenomena in Whitehall'. Heath asked Wright where he worked. Rothschild told the prime minister that Wright was responsible for the briefing on subversion which was causing the problem between MI5 and the Home Office.

'You should not be indulging in politics,' Heath admonished Wright. 'There are mechanisms for this sort of material.'

When Heath left them, Wright protested that Rothschild's mischief had put him in trouble. Rothschild assured him that he would smooth matters over with the prime minister by showing him the report.

THE ANOINTING OF 'JUMBO'

A major worry for MI5 spies in the early Heath years was the imminent retirement of their boss Martin Furnival Jones. Key figures in the civil service, particularly the Home Office, had heard at least rumours in the past few years of the activities of MI5 figures like Wright in their traumatic mole hunts. People such as Philip Allen began to push for a clean-out of British Intelligence. The way to achieve it was to appoint a like-minded civil servant to run it.

Wright, Rothschild, Dick White (the newly installed Cabinet Intelligence Coordinator since his retirement from MI6), Furnival Jones and others inside MI5 were concerned that an Allen-backed appointee would uncover the big secrets, such as the over-use of the immunity card and MI5 dirty tricks against leaders such as Wilson. Once discovered, MI5 would be in for an overhaul which would end its unauthorized autonomy in dealing in everything from political smears to assassination abroad.

A power struggle between the would-be new cleaners and the old spies began. Rothschild had most to lose from the cleaners taking over, so he joined the old spies to support Michael Hanley, a big florid-faced man, nick-named 'Jumbo' in the prevailing boarding school tradition. Hanley was Deputy director when the battle started. The cleaners wanted Sir James Waddell, a dependable mandarin, in his place.

When the lobbying started FJ asked Wright: 'Is there anything you can do with your powerful friend?', meaning Rothschild.[6] Wright approached him and Rothschild replied that he and Dick White were already plotting the succession. Rothschild was in his element with his methodical lobbying. He planned to attempt to sway Heath, if the moment was propitious.

Rothschild insisted on meeting 'Jumbo' first, after Wright had briefed him in detail. Wright told him how he and the mole-hunting Fluency Committee had once tried to prove Hanley was a double agent. Jumbo had come through the inquisition to FJ's, and even Wright's, begrudging satisfaction.

Wright arranged a rendezvous with Hanley at Rothschild's St James's Place flat and during drinks made a 'tactical retreat'. The meeting with Victor, the new Intelligence king-maker, and the candidate, was vital for both men. Each knew about the 1960s mole-hunting inquiry into the other, so that in an unspoken way they had a common bond. It was in both their interests that the past remain buried and not exhumed by some meddling bureaucrat, who couldn't understand, who would never understand, how spies operated and why.

The next day Rothschild rang Wright to tell him he thought Hanley was a 'very good choice'. The old spies made their moves and used their huge advantage of having access to the security files. Wright spread rumours about the 'Leighton Group', a 'nest of 1930s communists', inside the Home Office, to which Waddell was falsely linked. It was enough to make Hanley the favourite.

The Permanent Secretaries led by Allen were further out-manoeuvred when Rothschild cornered Heath alone in the garden

at Chequers in a break from a didactic chart session. The boys in
MI5 would resist an outsider being appointed, the PM was told.
Heath was sympathetic but wary of rejecting unanimous civil service
advice. Rothschild shrewdly suggested that Heath meet both candidates. The old spies were sure the forceful, weighty personality of
their character, and his experience in the espionage game, would
impress the prime minister more than civil servant Waddell.[7]

But the Permanent Secretaries didn't get to be portrayed as
Humphrey Appleby for nothing.[8] They were able to predict the
outcome of the Heath interviews. Even though they felt Waddell
was the better man for the job as they saw it, they felt out-
manoeuvred. They opted for another candidate.

Rothschild heard the news first and phoned Wright, who was
buying cows in Wales as part of his plan to retire to a farm in a few
years' time, or sooner if the cleaners were to win. The name of the
new candidate for Director-General of MI5 was Graham Harrison.

'They will never accept him,' Wright said. 'The man was a friend
of Burgess and Maclean.'[9]

This, by implication, made the innocent Harrison seem a security
risk which he was not. Hanley was appointed MI5's Director-
General at the end of 1972. The old spies had won and the secrets
that would have damaged them remained buried for the time being.
Instead, they were able to continue on as before. Wright was even
to be rewarded for his secret work.

THE WRIGHT HONOURABLE

Rothschild made sure that Wright remained under his influence by
putting his name forward for an honour – Commander of the British
Empire.[10] A Heath aide wrote the customary confidential letter to
Wright, indicating that the prime minister wished to give him a
CBE. Wright accepted the honour, the motto of which is *For God
and Empire*. The MI5 officer no doubt felt it was his due, but it was
also a sop for his troubles and lack of success in obtaining a suitable
pension.

'I had been discussing retirement with Victor,' he said. 'In 1972 I
finally learned that the promise MI5 had made to me in 1955 about

my pension was not to be honoured. In order to join the Service I had to give up fifteen years of pension rights with the Admiralty.'[11]

In 1955 officials, he claimed, had talked about ex-gratia payments, and the ways the 'Service could iron out the problems'.

According to the rules, Wright had no case for a pension, even though the fifty scientists who joined the Intelligence Services after him were able to transfer their pensions, 'largely through my pressure to rectify the inequity.'

Wright began grumbling about his future. He was disgruntled about what he had seen as over-payment for information to agents such as Golitsyn, which proved of minor importance. It had dismayed him a few years earlier to see the cunning Russian receive £10,000 pounds. Wright would have been happy to see that figure for the whole of his retirement. But it wasn't going to come.

The Spyhunter grew disillusioned, then bitter, which concerned Rothschild, who knew Wright's character well. He had a vindictive streak and would have been his well-placed friend's last choice of enemy. More vitally, Wright knew many secrets and, after a sixteen-year relationship, even *too many* concerning Rothschild. The Spyhunter had to be kept on-side.

35. GHOSTS AND WRITERS

KILLING TWO BIRDS

In keeping with his manipulative and diplomatic skills, Rothschild asked one of his best journalistic contacts, Harry ('Chapman') Pincher of the *Daily Express* to do him a favour in early 1972 concerning the Shah of Iran, who intended to make a State visit to Britain in June.

Rothschild had a strong rapport with Pincher for many reasons, not the least being the journalist's training in zoology and botany. He had also been a specialist writer on science, medicine and defence, which gave the two men further common ground. Moreover, Pincher had joined the Military College of Science in 1943 and taken a defence course in ammunition and explosives. Rothschild had once lectured at the College, from which Pincher graduated as a Technical Staff Officer. Their first meeting was twenty years later at a dinner at the home of Lord Sieff, then chairman of chain-store Marks & Spencer (Flora Solomon's employer). Other guests included Tess Rothschild.

Pincher had been at the *Daily Express* since 1946, and in 1967 won an ITV award for *Reporter of the Decade*. Pincher loved defence and espionage intrigue and had written innumerable front-page stories, which had built his formidable reputation. He had few peers amongst the more right-wing investigative journalists.

The Left attempted to denigrate him. Left-wing historian Edward Thompson called him the 'pissoir of Whitehall' because he was regarded as a repository for leaks from right-wing civil servants. Yet Pincher acted in what he saw as the national interest, which was often opposed to the extreme left. Nevertheless, his scoops did not always make him the darling of the Establishment in the civil service or the military.

Rothschild and Lord Sieff had cultivated him on occasions.

'On visits to Israel as a guest of Lord Sieff and Lord Rothschild,' Pincher wrote in his book *Inside Story*, 'I have been afforded special facilities to see the astonishing development in that basically arid and stony country.'[1]

It was time for a return favour for Rothschild. Pincher was asked to fly to Teheran and interview the Shah. The resultant article would be a nice piece of public relations for the Shah, and indirectly Rothschild himself.

'The Shah felt he had been subjected to unfair criticism by the British media and wished to give an interview that would present his aims and attitude to Britain more favourably. I learned that the most important part of his visit would be an attempt to pave the way for very large arms sales; being then a Fleet Street defence correspondent, I was particularly interested in that. I agreed to go.'[2]

Pincher received a message 'that His Imperial Majesty was well pleased' with his efforts, 'as was the editor of my newspaper.'

Rothschild was even more satisfied. It was confirmation to him that Pincher was a useful contact in the press and a collaborator. He regarded the newspaperman as someone to be trusted. For his part, Pincher regarded Rothschild as an 'old friend', a strong source on a variety of areas including Intelligence. He was the kind of contact any worthy journalist would give a lot for.

Yet he was not close to the laconic, dry lord. Despite their growing friendship, Pincher also found him somewhat of an intriguing figure.

In 1973, Roger Hollis, the man to whom the two of them were destined to be drawn, had a second stroke and died at the age of sixty-seven. Dick White wrote a small obituary notice for *The Times*. Hollis's death, which had to be partly attributed to the hounding he received, inspired Wright and others to pursue him beyond the grave.

HAROLD BE THY NAME

Rothschild discussed Wright working in security at N. M. Rothschild but, according to Wright, Hanley's unhappiness about the proposal acted as a veto. Rothschild then introduced him to someone Wright claimed was a shady businessman wanting access to MI5 files for alleged nefarious reasons. That proposal for work also fell through.

In 1974, Labour seemed likely to win a general election, which would place Wilson in Number 10 once more. Plotting within MI5 against the probable new prime minister began in earnest again, this time with Wright as a ring-leader.[3]

'The devil makes work for idle hands,' Wright recalled, 'and I was playing out time before retirement. A mad scheme like this [to bring down Wilson] was bound to tempt me. I felt an irresistible urge to lash out. The country seemed on the brink of catastrophe. Why not give it a little push? In any case, I carried the burden of so many secrets that lightening the load a little could only make things easier for me.'

In addition, Angleton was urging Wright to take action.

Rothschild talked him out of it. He told Wright that he didn't like Wilson any more than he did, but that Wright would be prosecuted if he went ahead with plans to 'get rid of' Wilson. It would put even his half-pension in jeopardy.[4]

Wright persisted and Rothschild kept urging caution, telling him it wasn't the 'right time' to re-open the Wilson file with the intent of destroying him politically. Wright took his powerful companion's advice, but it showed Rothschild the extent of the MI5 man's dangerous intent and capabilities. He had to be kept content so that he would stay quiet. If not, many people, including Rothschild himself, were bound to suffer.

Hanley solved the problem temporarily by sending Wright around the world chasing Venona traffic in 1974. He saw Angleton at the end of the year for what was to be the last time. He too was bitter and defeated. New CIA director William Colby was about to remove him. They had quarrelled over the conduct of counter-intelligence, especially in South East Asia, where Colby had specialized for the CIA.

Soon after the Wright/Angleton meeting, the American was named in a big *New York Times* investigation which accused him of masterminding a huge domestic mail surveillance programme. Americans didn't like the idea of a spy using his government office to read their mail. It created an excellent opportunity to dislodge Angleton.

Simultaneously, two important players in key Western Intelligence Services on either side of the Atlantic had been replaced.

The two men were left with obsessions and bleak futures dwelling on their failure to capture one enemy spy between them. But they had yet to stop trying.

A PREMATURE PREMONITION

Rothschild's worst fears resurfaced in 1974 when he learned that Blunt had cancer and might die from it. He worried that his old companion might just leave a will or written revelations about the past.[5] Blunt was the most likely to do this of the handful of individuals – in Britain and Russia – who knew about his secret life, at least as it pertained to his spying for Russia. There were just two or three KGB agents who were fully cognisant of the facts about him, plus Maclean, Philby and Blunt.[6] The KGB had too much to lose by his exposure and none of the others would have a motive.

Would Anthony expose something after his death? Would he perhaps leave information about the immunity deal or the real extent of his spying? Would he name names? They had remained close, but there was always that nagging doubt about the old aesthete. He too could be vindictive. Would some guilt mechanism cause him to name himself and the Fifth Man, which would complete the exposure of the century's most important spy ring?[7] Rothschild would take no chances. He needed to know how much damage Blunt could do and how far he would be implicated.

At this time there was increased agitation from Wright and others to re-open the Hollis investigation. This created an atmosphere of fear and suspicion, which gave Rothschild room to manoeuvre. He helped feed a worry about moles and scandal, and how they had troubled, even ruined previous governments. Concerns about Hollis and the Soviet spies he may have appointed to succeed him once more deflected the spyhunters away from the scent of the Fifth Man.

Heath decided there should be an investigation to see if British Intelligence had been penetrated. At first it was thought that an independent body should review the matter. Eventually it was decided that it would be wise to choose just one non-political privy councillor with experience and integrity to do the probing. While Whitehall pondered who this impeccable individual should be, Rothschild adopted the useful guise of concern about the damage revelations would do to the teetering Heath Government. He checked with Wright. What did he think about the possibility of any revelations by Blunt?[8]

Wright had often asked Blunt whether he had made a complete confession in a will, but he had denied making such preparations. Then again, Wright made the point that he had never quite trusted Blunt. This was not surprising considering that after a decade of interrogation, the Fourth Man had revealed nothing of substance to MI5.

'Ted is worried that we could have another Profumo-type scandal on our hands,' Rothschild inaccurately claimed. He went further, suggesting that Blunt might delve into a range of secrets in a last testament or memoir, which would go beyond the immunity deals and the naming of other agents and into the 'sexual peccadilloes' of famous people, such as former prime ministers.[9]

Rothschild then 'pressed' Wright for a full brief on the damage Blunt could do if he told all. He wanted the fullest assessment possible, stretching even to the unprovable. Wright obliged and yet again pulled the files for his great friend. He drew a complete picture of the history — as far as it was known — of the Ring of Five.

The web of their connections reached out to forty names.

Rothschild had the Intelligence he wanted, which amounted to a full understanding of what MI5 knew and, more importantly, didn't know. If Blunt was leaving a tell-all document, Rothschild was as prepared as possible for its ramifications.

In June 1974, a Fluency Committee representative knocked on the door of the new prime minister, Harold Wilson, in order to keep the pressure on a government investigation into Hollis and his appointees. Privy Councillor Burke Trend was chosen as the independent prober.

Trend spent about a hundred days over a year quietly interviewing all key witnesses to major espionage events since the war and reading the files at MI5's Curzon Street offices. Even Wright thought he was thorough and fair.

Trend concluded that there was no evidence that Hollis was a spy. The Fluency Committee was informed without being shown Trend's report, which would remain on file. Wright and the other committee members were far from satisfied. Rothschild feigned dissatisfaction too. As long as suspicions remained about Hollis, they would stay away from him.

Fortunately for Rothschild, rumours of Blunt's impending demise were exaggerated and he recovered from cancer.

36. IMPRESSIONS OF A KNEE-JERK BANKER

CZECHMATE

Despite the Trend report, Wright would not give up plotting against Wilson. In July 1975, he was given a tip-off by his now deposed CIA soul-mate Angleton that a defector from Czechoslovakian Intelligence, Frantisek August, was due to visit Britain from the US under a false name and on a secret mission for the CIA.[1]

August was being prepared for a US Senate hearings investigation into Soviet Bloc intelligence penetration in America, which would commence in a few months' time. Angleton had told Wright that August's information included something about British Labour MPs, who had been recruited by Czech Intelligence.

Wright couldn't wait for the US Senate hearings. He wanted to put pressure on Wilson immediately. He met Rothschild to discuss tactics, but the latter was reluctant at first to be involved. He had been out of the Think Tank for several months, and had no real enthusiasm for intrigues against the prime minister.[2] However, when Wright pressed him Rothschild asked for more details. August had information on former Labour MP John Stonehouse, who had disappeared off a Miami beach in 1974, in a presumed suicide. Rothschild checked the so-called new information. It was nothing more than a re-hash of accusations by a previous Czech defector, Josef Frolik.

Rothschild agreed to help Wright and summoned his journalist friend Harry (Chapman) Pincher of the *Daily Express*. Rothschild, dripping with his usual intrigue, intimated to him that he was giving him a real scoop.[3] In his book *Inside Story*, Pincher did not mention Rothschild by name and referred to him as 'a former MI5 Officer'.

'I was given the name of a man in Wales he [August] was to contact and told that if I could induce August to talk he could give me a most interesting story concerning the espionage activities of a well-known Labour MP who, for libel reasons, must be nameless. It was said that this MP was not just an agent of Czech Intelligence but "an officer of the KGB".'[4]

Pincher contacted the Welshman, 'who was highly embarrassed to learn that I knew of the impending visit'. The journalist had him 'watched for a while in the hope that August would appear on his doorstep'. When that failed, Pincher had an MP ask a parliamentary friend to question the Home Secretary, Roy Jenkins, about August's visit. Jenkins's reply revealed that the Czech had already completed his visit and was back in the US.

This was another example of Rothschild's apparent help in ferreting out communists, which he would later add to the growing list of evidence that he was not a Soviet agent. His misleading cooperation with Wright and involvement of Pincher added to their conviction that their well-placed friend was a pillar of steadfast loyalty, who was always prepared to help in the destruction of the red menace. Rothschild successfully gave the impression of being, at times, a knee-jerk anti-communist.

FROM THE TANK TO THE BANK

In 1975, several months after Rothschild had resigned from the Think Tank in the wake of Heath being replaced by Wilson, he was appointed Chairman of N. M. Rothschild after his second-cousin Edmund Rothschild's retirement. Victor felt he was well-qualified after his seventeen-year stint at Shell and then The Tank. Besides, he was the titular head of the family and arguably entitled, if qualified, to take the Bank over.

The maintenance of his golf handicap of just 1 could wait. Victor at sixty-four was not ready to retire for some time yet. He was also conscious of needing to keep his exceptional mind occupied.

He ran into a family feud, partly of his making, which stretched back to the end of the war when the Bank was in trouble. Some revenue sources, especially on the international scene, had dried up because of the five years of hostilities in Europe, and there did not seem to be anyone with a modern approach to lift and develop the Bank in the new post-war environment.

In 1974 it was changed from a partnership into a private company with a new capital structure. Victor had been busy with everything except the Bank and he was not interested in fighting to control it. His disdain for capitalism had reached a peak, and he was sure then that sooner rather than later communists would rule Britain. Capitalism and private wealth would be consigned to history, as predicted by Marx and preached by many of Rothschild's friends since their Cambridge days.

Proof of great change to come seemed everywhere, especially in the minds of the Ring of Five, and a socialist government had just won an historic victory in Britain. Victor turned his back on the opportunity for pre-eminence at the Bank, and although he put funds into it to revive its flagging fortunes, he refused to invest enough to give him control. This gave his cousin, Anthony, a chance. He put up most of the money and took 80 per cent of the shares, leaving Victor with just 20 per cent.

The ramifications of Victor's misguided neglect became apparent in 1975 when a power struggle developed between Anthony's son, Evelyn, who had a 40 per cent share and Victor's son, Jacob, who had just 10 per cent. Victor stepped in to placate the warring factions at New Court, who were putting the organization under unprecedented scrutiny in the City of London. Fleet Street's business pages were taking an interest in the squabbling, much to the very private Rothschild family's distaste.

The well-rounded Jacob, who took a first in history at Christ College, Oxford, felt his record in banking, quite apart from his position on the Rothschild family tree, qualified him to control the Bank. He was a throwback to his great-great-grandfather, Nathaniel ('Natty') Mayer, who advised Disraeli, and financed – and made a fortune out of – the Battle of Waterloo. He carried the gene for entrepreneurial flair, the necessary inheritance for success in the furious banking era of the 1960s, where the faint-hearted and the traditional faded, and the takeover merchants began operating and creating high profiles. The profits were huge.

Jacob ran the finance department and took stakes in companies from the Savoy to the *Express* newspapers. He created deals like a magician producing rabbits from a hat. There was big money to be made and he was not afraid to advise the controversial movers and shakers of the new era in a changing Britain, people such as Robert Maxwell, Jimmy Goldsmith, Jim Slater and James Hanson. Yet, his breeding, background and intellect allowed him to slip back into the Establishment City with ease.

Evelyn, too, was no slouch as a banker, but not quite in Jacob's class.

Jacob was peeved when his father took over. The son knew he was far better suited to the banking environment than his genius yet out-of-touch father, who loathed the business as much as he had during his abortive stint in 1931. Now here was this domineering, moody, quirky, secretive old man, coming in and ruling the roost. They had always had a mixed relationship because of Victor's failed marriage to Jacob's mother. Now it would be put under a spotlight. Father and son quarrelled. Much to Jacob's chagrin, Victor appeared to quickly lose interest in the job, and the running of the bank fell to Evelyn.

Victor became distracted by other matters, not the least being two unusual items which appeared in the press. *Penthouse* and *The Times* carried articles in 1975 about the possible existence of the Fourth and Fifth men. The stories were scant on fact, and high on speculation, but even that was a worry. However, the profile of the Fourth Man was a little too close for comfort.

Rothschild wondered if the stories had been planted by someone – an adversary, an enemy agent, perhaps someone who really knew something. He had made his share of enemies over the years, and this made it difficult to judge who the source was, if, in fact, it was more than investigative journalists beating up an unprovable sensation.

HORSE SENSE

Wright had a share in an Arab stud in England and he spoke often about his desire to farm and raise horses. Rothschild encouraged him to do so. Wright thought Australia would be a fine place to fulfil this last dream, and again his long-standing friend encouraged him to make the break a complete one by distancing himself from the spy world both mentally and geographically.

He should go out to the sun and get fit, Rothschild urged. Someone else could take the strain of mole-hunting. Wright hesitated. At what was to be their last meeting for some time, at his Cambridge home, Rothschild told him he had done the work of three men.[5]

They related well to each other's problems – both knew too many secrets. This condition manifested itself in Wright's moods and stress-related illnesses, just as it had on a different level with Philby, Burgess and Maclean. The strain was showing and Rothschild told Wright it was time to let go.

Wright complained that he would not be receiving a £5,000 lump-sum payment from MI5 until August 1976. The sooner he had that, the sooner he would leave the country. The ever-generous Rothschild promised him a £5,000 bridging loan until he received the MI5 pay-off. This immediately allowed Wright to consider going to live in Tasmania, which was as far south as one could go, short of Antarctica. He said he didn't want to cut himself off completely. It would be nice, he told Rothschild, to pick up some Intelligence work out there.[6] Rothschild said he would see what he could do through his contacts. Wright left for Tasmania early in 1976, much to his friend's relief.

GAMBLING ON THE GOVERNMENT

Soon afterwards, Rothschild resigned as chairman of N. M. Rothschilds and sided with the more private Evelyn (with his 40 per cent interest) and against his own, more financially high-flying son Jacob (holding just 10 per cent) in the resultant power struggle for the vacant chairman's position. If Jacob felt cheated by his father's inaction in the 1940s over his side of the family's share in the Bank, he would now have felt more than a twinge of betrayal. Others close to the family judged that Victor could have been more loyal.

Victor's reasoning was that the imbalance in the shareholding would have seen more damage being done in a continuing internal squabble. Better to end the power plays now and let the Bank settle down. A disappointed Jacob left soon afterwards, determined to create his own merchant bank (which he did with Charterhouse J. Rothschild).

The enmity between son and father was strong. A close friend of Jacob's said that he 'hated' his father. Miriam Rothschild said that this was an exaggeration. Once when the two men were quarrelling, Miriam told Jacob to stop bickering and phone his father in order to patch up the difference over lunch, which she claims he did.[7,8] However, the rift between Victor and Jacob would remain.

Victor stayed on in 1976 as non-executive director of the Bank and chairman of the holding company, Rothschilds Continuations. He also later became chairman of a new company, Biotechnology Investments Ltd.

Now out of full-time work, Victor let it be known around Whitehall that he was available. Roy Jenkins, Home Secretary in the Labour Government, appointed him chairman of the Royal Commission on Gambling in Britain. This was not demanding by Rothschild's standards so he began thinking about another book – a compilation of essays on his wide experiences, which would range from his counter-sabotage heroics in the Second World War to his role with the Think Tank.

He liked writing and had produced several works before, including publications such as *The History of Tom Jones, a Changeling* in 1951; *The Rothschild Library* in 1954, which was a catalogue of his collection of eighteenth-century books and manuscripts; *Fertilization* in 1956 – a definitive text on the subject; *A Classification of Living Animals* in 1961; *The Rothschild Family Tree* in 1973.

The new work, to be entitled *Meditations of a Broomstick*, would also be a much-needed exercise in public relations and an attempt to distance himself from a murky past and any association with the other four. This might just be needed soon.

Rothschild had received a letter from Wright, which enclosed a cheque for £5,000 pounds – the amount loaned to him and now paid out by the government. However, the government was still only prepared to pay him a £2,000-a-year pension, which would not go far even on a poor stud farm. Wright was bitter again. He was thinking about a way to force the government to pay him more. Perhaps he would write a book, he suggested, which would expose the whole Blunt affair.

37. AN EPOCH OF DISILLUSIONMENT

DECADE OF BROKEN DREAMS

Modin's concern for Philby re-emerged in 1975 when he learned from Rufa that he was starting to drink wine from early in the morning again. Modin thought it was time to inspire the Englishman once more and he mentioned the idea of a school for young KGB agents.[1]

The subject had been broached before, but Philby had been dismissive. To become simply a teacher, he felt, was like a race-horse being put out to stud. Philby had always considered that he had many more miles to run. But after twelve years in his adopted country he began to accept that he would never be given the sort of Intelligence assignments or position within the KGB of which he was worthy.

The written analysis and advice he had been asked to provide again since 1971 was encouraging, but not enough. Why, he asked Modin bitterly, wasn't he asked to KGB HQ to meet, dine, drink and plot with the Big Chiefs? Didn't they comprehend how import-ant he could be to them?

The KGB proffered unsatisfactory excuses and reasons. Modin flattered, encouraged and praised the agent. But the fact was that one of the greatest spies of all time had been left to moulder in cold comfort.

The Russian broached the teaching idea in subtle ways. One was to moan about the quality of the Controls, their British agents and the material they were producing in the 1970s since the bombshell of the dismissal of 105 agents in 1971.

It was appalling. The Russian Controls needed special training, Modin repeatedly complained. Would the Masterspy please help?

Philby's earlier resistance melted. He said he would consider the proposal.

A few realities, quite momentous ones, had been taken in by Philby in his more sober moments, since the Soviet invasion of Czechoslovakia in 1968. Philby had always defended such actions as necessary in the Cold War struggle with the West. He had spoken of the big picture of history as the most important consideration. In other words, no matter how brutal the Soviet dictatorship, it was all part of a grand evolutionary communist plan to consign capitalism to the dustbin of history, as Krushchev had succinctly put it. Then Communism could begin a new, more humane world order. At least, that was the crude theory, which had been about since Marx had first propounded it in 1848.

Since the Russian Revolution in 1917, Lenin had excited the imagination of supporters like Philby enough to excuse the excesses of the country's secret police. Although Stalin had left 30 million Soviet citizens dead in the brutal, devastating wake of his 'communism in one country' concept, Joe again could be excused by Philby. He had, after all, given firm leadership in the war against the Nazis, and the Soviet Union had won, at a cost of between 20 and 40 million dead, depending on whether Stalin or some Russian historians are to be believed.[2]

Nikita Krushchev came next. He was bellicose but believable and more liberal than his predecessors. He was big on real science as opposed to Stalin's Marxist fantasies, and in the late 1950s gave a glimpse of a communist future that just might be.

Then came Leonard Brezhnev, who emerged as the nation's leader in the mid-1960s. Philby found him a huge disappointment. He seemed no more than a corrupt, anti-intellectual thug. He was too much of a cowardly bully to lead the Soviet Union into a war with the US, but his rigidity could cause the nation to stumble into one. During his first decade in power, Philby grew to hate him.

'He would shake with rage and run from the room when Brezhnev appeared on TV,' Rufa recalled. 'The Brezhnev epoch and corruption enraged him.'[3]

Philby was also disillusioned. The Brezhnev era made him face the certainty that in his life-time he would not see communism, in its ideal or in any other form, as the dominant political force in the world. He had held on to this dream since the 1930s, when it had to be the answer to fascism and would replace it as the main world ideology. During the war, communist domination had been the promise for after the war. In the late 1940s it was just around the corner. In the late 1950s it was a decade away. But in the 1960s, the dream evaporated. It wasn't a struggle of ideologies any more, but a battle of military machines boasting new and more deadly weapons.

By 1975, Philby, who had regarded himself as an important figure in the struggle, was nowhere with the military chiefs. He was a battler from another era which had relied on stealth, intellect and ideas. The era had passed and his ambitions had died with it.

Philby, now in his early sixties, as usual immersed himself in alcohol to forget the disappointment, the rage and the pain. He would see out his days doing the odd analysis for the KGB and reading *The Times*, which came from Embassy Newspapers at Notting Hill. He would complete its crossword to keep his brain functioning between hangovers. There were also Western books and correspondence with old friends such as Graham Greene.[4]

SPY-TRAINER

Now he was being offered a lectureship. He was not impressed. But Modin didn't give up easily. He knew how to massage British egos. Finally Philby relented. He gave a seminar to a group of men and women doing KGB training and education. The subject was trade-craft in the West, and covered how to become acceptable to the right people in England.

'I suppose it was a lesson in "do's", "don'ts", and etiquette,' ex-KGB Colonel 'E' recalled. 'Kim was attempting to indoctrinate us in ways to ingratiate ourselves with British society. At first, we were perplexed at the subtleties. I personally learned an enormous amount, but the real weight of what he was saying didn't strike home until I was part of the London Residency [Colonel 'E' was thrown out of Britain with eighteen other agents when Oleg Gordievsky defected to England in 1985]. After that, I sang his praises. He was a great teacher.'[5]

Philby was imparting three decades of unsurpassed spying experience in the West, and enjoying it.

'He definitely warmed quickly to this work,' Colonel 'E' noted. 'It drew him closer to his own strengths . . .'

In deception?

'Yes . . . in deception. He was instructing these young people how to make the British, and Americans, like them. [chuckles] Do not forget how he worked with the Americans.'

In order to suborn them?

'Yes. Each Control had to find his own agents. It was never easy. But Kim showed them the problems.'

The seminars became regular and Philby began giving extra lessons at his home and elsewhere. They were popular. The young KGB agents were tutored in how to behave in everything from dinner parties to dealing with the media. They were trained how to educate their own Western agents.

'Of special interest,' ex-KGB Colonel 'E' remembered, 'were the instructions to our agents should they be caught. He impressed on us that they should never, under any circumstances, admit to spying, even if overwhelming evidence was put before them.'[6]

Philby liked citing the cases of Allan Nunn May and Klaus Fuchs, the atom bomb spies, which he had observed at first hand. He wrote up the examples, which were presented 'like detective stories'. Philby made the point that the American and British Intelligence agencies had great difficulty in mounting a legal case against these two spies.

'The eventual success of both cases [for the Western agencies],' Philby told them, 'was based on getting the suspects to confess. In each instance, the Soviet agent probably would have been found not guilty, or there would have been no court action against them, if they had not confessed.'

Colonel 'E' remembered Philby trying to explain that the KGB's anti-Zionist fervour would be disastrous if expressed in Britain.

'I worked with one agent,' Colonel 'E' said in an interview at the Intourist Hotel's coffee shop, 'who made the mistake of saying at a dinner party that he thought the West's economic problems were caused by a Zionist plot. The host and the other English guests politely ignored the remark and went on to another topic. A journalist from a leading British paper, who had invited him to the party, took the Russian aside and told him never to make such a stupid remark again. He then understood the gravity of Philby's instructions.'[7]

Philby worked on his agents' political manners and wrote reports on each undergraduate. For instance, ex-KGB Colonel Bagdonov, boasted to me how the Masterspy-turned-tutor had assessed him as potentially a top agent:

'Very high marks for general acceptability in British Society,' Philby wrote in a KGB characteristic concerning Bagdonov. 'More than once during our meetings, I thought that, but for an accident of birth, he might well be working in the British Foreign Office today ... My only doubt about him is reflected in the word "modesty". Our work sometimes requires a considerable degree of self-assertion on the part of controlling officers. So will he be able to cope with the agent who needs rough handling?'[8]

After meeting with Bagdonov and two other 'graduates' from Philby's school of deceit, espionage and subornation, I could appreciate that the Masterspy wasn't necessarily being flattering or disingenuous in his assessment. (However, I would disagree that their training would always cover their true intent, background or even beliefs. Their command of the English language was laudable, but an artifice was transparent in the way they spoke or wrote. The written information they gave me had phoney-sounding clichés such as 'let us be frank' and the occasional odd use of words. For instance, they wrote: 'materials we found in his personal archives', when they meant documents.)[9]

Kim Philby had at last found a niche in Soviet espionage. He was creating replicas of himself.

PHILBY'S LAST PENETRATION

Philby's new work as a minor Russian don was invigorating and successful enough for Modin to suggest to KGB Chiefs that he be allowed to visit the KGB First Chief Directorate's HQ at Yesenevo, south-east of Moscow, a half-mile beyond the outer ring road. It had been the home of the Directorate, which handled all foreign Intelligence operations, from 1972.

In 1977, after some lobbying, KGB Chairman Yuri Andropov

agreed he could visit HQ and deliver an address to senior intelligence officials. It was the most important speech Philby was to give in his life and he spent much time on it, rehearsing in front of the bathroom mirror in his apartment.

Philby was very nervous on the day, but in command, having downed only a double Scotch before being picked up by a chauffeur-driven vehicle. It took him on the short route to the Yesenevo compound with its Y-shaped office building flanked on one side by an assembly hall and library, and on the other by a polyclinic, sports complex and swimming pool. It was surrounded by a double ring of fencing with guard dogs in between. Armed guards patrolled the perimeter.[10]

Philby had mixed feelings as his credentials were checked by sentries at the front gates. He had served the KGB for forty-three years, the last fourteen of them in Moscow, and this was the first time he had been invited to formally meet the Chiefs, none of whom could boast his success, risks or achievements for the cause. He surveyed the faces in the audience and then began:

'During my lifetime I have held official passes to at least seven of the biggest special services in the world: Four British – SIS, COE, MI5, the Government School of Codes and Cryptography; three American – the CIA, FBI and the National Security Agency . . .'

Philby paused for the translator and then added with a wry smile:

'Now I can claim a successful penetration into an eighth major intelligence organization.'[11]

Modin smiled. He understood the nuance and irony in the remark, but most of the other Russian agents did not. Perhaps it was a fault of the translator's delivery but the comment caused some shock and confusion in the audience. Was Philby admitting that he was a triple agent still at root working for the British? There had always been such rumours inside the KGB. Philby had been extremely successful for such a long time that many wondered if he might be a plant. After all, the ease with which he left, or was allowed to leave, Beirut had worried some.[12]

Philby was, of course, exacting some satisfaction from airing his long-held grievance that he had been overlooked by the Chiefs. While his opening comments were not appreciated, the rest of the lecture was. He concentrated on the psychological aspects of being an agent, and the problems that went with it. He used his own experiences liberally, again making the point of his enormous achievement.

However, the opening salvo drew the most reaction. While his didactic skills were utilized more after the address, Philby was never again invited to HQ to fraternize with the Chiefs.

PART SIX

EXPOSURE
1976–1990

38. BEFORE THE STORM

THE DISGRUNTLED PENSIONER

Wright and his dutiful wife, Lois, paid about £5,000 for a former apple orchard in a valley a mile outside Cygnet, a country town 25 miles south of Hobart. The area had first been spotted by Europeans in 1793 when a French explorer landed nearby. It was used mainly for apple and potato-growing and timber-felling. Irish convicts in the early 1800s had been the first Europeans to settle the region around Cygnet. The town had remained predominantly Catholic, with about 800 residents, which would have seemed odd, even ironic to Wright, who had been involved in MI5 operations against the IRA in Northern Ireland. Yet this was Australia, which prided itself on being able to keep the political problems of other lands and times at bay.

The sleepy little hamlet was peaceful and uneventful, with the centre of activity revolving around its three hotels, three churches and the local Returned Services League (RSL) Club, which Wright joined. He seemed distantly cheerful to the curious locals as he trundled into town in his flat tray Land-Rover.

The local RSL members began to show him due deference, because of the inside knowledge he had of world events. Wright always said he worked for the British Government. He expressed right-wing views. No one guessed he was a retired spook.

The Wrights lived close to the poverty-line, in a shack – a couple of timber huts used by apple-pickers. They spent much money on fencing the place for their horses. A big early set-back was the death of a grey stallion, Pizzicato, which threw the Wrights into a financial crisis.

Wright kept up his correspondence with Rothschild, knowing he had some leverage with him because of his worry about the Blunt affair becoming public. He let Rothschild know of his continued disgruntlement about the miserly pension he had received. In a November 1976 letter, Wright wrote almost threateningly: 'He [Blunt] will have a special place in my memoirs . . . I've still got my notes of my talks with him . . .'

Rothschild was vexed, but played a double game to keep Wright's confidence. In a reply, he encouraged him to write his memoirs, then he wrote to Jumbo Hanley, the MI5 Director-General. His letter explained the potential threat and suggested a solution.[1,2] Wright was 'going bad' Rothschild remarked. The situation was dangerous. It would be wise to increase his pension. Hanley, however, didn't see Wright as a threat. The pension was not increased and MI5 sent Wright a standard warning about a former employee's obligation under the Official Secrets Act.[3]

Wright kept in contact with another pensioner, Angleton, in the US and their correspondence dwelled on their misfortunes and the ones that got away. Wright reaffirmed his obsession with the guilt of Wilson and Hollis. Wilson resigned as prime minister in 1976, which gave the two old spies some satisfaction, as they tried to convince themselves that they had won some sort of victory. The political world agreed that Wilson's resignation had been premature yet he had not been driven from office by MI5.

After being at the centre of the espionage business for decades, Wright and Angleton were still caught up in the past, re-living their problems and failures. Wright was even more out of touch than his American counterpart, who watched as his old power base at CIA HQ in Langley was steadily dismantled. Angleton had plenty of cronies with whom he could drown his sorrows. But for Wright there was no one close by. Victor, whom Wright knew was easily disturbed by the past, was 12,000 miles away.

With Wilson off the scene, Wright concentrated on the Hollis case, with a mixture of motives. He dreamt of writing his memoirs, of their devastating effect, and the money he might make from them. Yet the dreams quickly turned sour. An unsympathetic Labour government was in power. They would use the Official Secrets Act legally to prevent any publication. Besides, Wright was aware of his limitations as a writer. He could produce a fair technical brief, but he had little idea of how to construct a readable manuscript.

The Wrights struggled on in Cygnet but were hindered by Peter's run of illness, which saw Lois doing most of the heavy work on the farm, such as putting mares to the stallion, keeping the horses fit, mucking out stables and growing vegetables. Their future with Peter's meagre pension seemed bleak.

After the excitement of moving half-way round the world to start a new life, fresh worries nagged Wright. Had he done the right thing by isolating himself so far from the centre of British Government? It was impossible to fight for retirement security from such a distance.[4]

Wright had but one recourse. Early in 1977 he began to scratch out his memory of events from 1955 to 1976. But it appeared such a slow, laborious process that the sick man was quickly fatigued by even the thought of carrying on. It seemed hopeless. Labour would be entrenched for at least another two years. Thatcher was making the right political noises, but could a Conservative woman really become prime minister? Surely this was a desperate Tory gimmick that could not work. And while Labour remained in power, there was little chance that Wright could influence action over Hollis.

Wright considered that there was even less chance he could find a publisher brave enough to publish a book which would claim that British Intelligence could possibly be riddled with Soviet spies, or that Wilson might have been a Soviet agent of influence.

From a distance, the thin and infrequent newspaper articles on the old country seemed to be all about economic decline and inflation. The Chancellor, Denis Healey, had even gone cap in hand to the International Monetary Fund to beg for financial assistance.

In June 1977, just when Wright seemed to despair about his plight, Rothschild wrote one of his poignant, vigorous letters, with all the old lust for intrigue. It enclosed an article in *The Times*, which erroneously suggested that Donald Bevis, a former tutor at King's College, Cambridge, was the Fourth Man. Rothschild wanted to know, in his customarily direct manner, who had 'planted the evidence and why?' He added: 'It would interest me to know your reactions.'[5]

Wright replied that Bevis was innocent. The Rothschild demands made him feel as if they were back in Whitehall running things. For a day or two Wright felt wanted and important again. He was inspired. He wrote and told Rothschild that he was definitely going to pen those memoirs.

But it was clear that Wright would not be able to write a manuscript except under the auspices of his powerful, distant companion.

Tess wrote back: 'V. says he hopes you will write something but don't post it. He'll be in touch.'[6]

BOYLE'S BOMB-SHELL

In 1978, radio journalist and writer Andrew Boyle was busy on his third year of research for his book, *Climate of Treason – Five who Spied for Russia*. He contacted Rothschild by letter and they corresponded over the book. Rothschild gave away very little, doing his best to distance himself from the so far exposed spies from the Ring of Five – Burgess, Maclean and Philby. Rothschild made out that he was more interested in fast cars and women than communism in those long ago Cambridge days.

He could not really tell from their correspondence if Boyle was on to something but Blunt was worried that he would be exposed as the Fourth Man.

In October 1979 Tess wrote again to Wright: 'Boyle's book will have appeared by the time you read this and it is causing a good deal of anxiety to A. But neither V. nor I know what it's going to say. Nor does A.'[7]

When *Climate of Treason* was published, spies, politicians, journalists and an interested public combed through the pages trying to work out who 'Maurice' and 'Basil' – Boyle's Fourth and Fifth Men – were.

'Maurice' was named after the homosexual hero in E. M. Forster's last published novel and rumours quickly spread that Maurice was Blunt. But the Fifth Man was as much a mystery as ever. Boyle had been misled. He had a British scientist working in the US, Wilfrid *Basil* Mann, marked down as the Fifth. Angleton had used Boyle to fabricate a story within the book, which attempted to demonstrate that the American knew that Philby and Maclean were KGB agents long before Maclean's defection in 1951.

Angleton was trying to re-write events to make it appear that Philby had never duped him and that the reverse had occurred. According to Boyle, he had been running an elaborate scam to trap Philby and others.

Angleton confirmed to Wilfrid Mann himself in November 1979 that Boyle had him in mind when he spoke about the concept of the Fifth Man:

'There is no question that Basil is you,' Angleton told him.

In a book, *Was There a Fifth Man?*, which answered the accusation, Mann wrote: 'He [Angleton] was not making an accusation. Indeed, he had already offered to go to the UK to testify on my behalf should that be necessary. He was merely drawing a logical conclusion from Boyle's text.'[8]

Philby's biographer, Phillip Knightley, drew the same conclusion in a review of Boyle's book in the *Sunday Times*.

Mann confirmed that he had made low-level contact with Soviet agents in the US with the full knowledge of the CIA, but that was all. The chronology, location and activity of the Boyle/Angleton Fifth Man was easily demonstrated by Mann himself to be a Phantom Fifth. This Fifth never existed.[9]

First, Mann had not been in MI5. Second, his movements from Britain to Canada and the US during the war kept him away from the spying action – and off the suspect list. The exception was his work at Professor G. P. Thompson's laboratory at London's Imperial College. But even if Mann had given the KGB data about the plutonium bomb being experimented with at the time (1942–43) – and there was never any suspicion that he had – it hardly would have qualified him to rank as one of the KGB's top five agents of the war. Third, he showed by documentation that he was not in the US in the critical period in the late 1940s, when Boyle maintained his Fifth was supposed to have been operating. Fourth, he could never have had any knowledge of any of MI5's major operations run against the Russians from 1945 to 1963, which were all blown.

However, there were some disturbing references for Rothschild in *Climate of Treason*, which by chance paralleled a piece of his own profile.

Especially pertinent was the remark:

'Exactly how London-based Jewish intelligence dug out the original information, which eluded MI5, that at least one important British nuclear scientist in addition to Nunn May had undertaken to spy for the Soviet Union [was not known] . . .'[10]

As shown earlier, Rothschild had developed a general expertise in nuclear science and weaponry, and the Fifth Man had passed to the Russians important data in the field, much earlier than Fuchs and Nunn May.

In the same passage, Boyle quoted the CIA source (Angleton himself) who had given him this information:

'As part of the price for uninterrupted but informal cooperation with US Intelligence, a crucial necessity to the Jews by 1946–47 owing to the intransigent policy of Britain, two agents [members of Jewish Intelligence] passed on to Angleton the name of the British nuclear scientist whom they had unearthed as an important agent.'[11]

Rothschild was further shocked by the use of a photograph of him in the Boyle book, which was near three similar-sized photos of Burgess, Philby and Maclean. The caption under the surly, moody shot of the handsome young undergraduate read: '. . . Rothschild, while professing left-wing views, was more interested in entertaining and driving fast cars than in propagating, or listening to, his friends' Marxist convictions.'

The text linked him squarely for the first time with the other spies and he became agitated. He wanted to do something to cover himself before events got out of control. They seemed headed that way when, on 15 November, Mrs Thatcher (who had become the Conservative prime minister six months earlier) rose in the House of Commons to make a statement about Blunt, Boyle's Fourth Man:

In April 1964, Sir Anthony Blunt admitted to the Security Authorities that he had been recruited by, and had acted as a talent spotter for, Russian Intelligence before the war, when he was a don at Cambridge, and had passed information regularly to the Russians while he was a member of the Security Service between 1940 and 1945. He made this admission after being given an undertaking that he would not be prosecuted if he confessed . . .

Moments after Thatcher's statement, the Queen withdrew Blunt's knighthood, only the second time this had ever been done.

But it still was not quite enough punishment when compared with the many other spies who were languishing in Her Majesty's prisons for similar crimes.

Mrs Thatcher's statement, which partially broke the long conspiracy of silence, caused an inevitable furore and raised ten questions for every one it answered.

Rothschild was shaken by it, for now the media hunt would be on in earnest for the Fifth Man. At that time, he received more correspondence from Wright, who reported on his progress with his own book. Because of his illness, he had struggled to write, but had at last begun the laborious exercise. Lois was typing it up as he went.

Rothschild wrote back, encouraging him. A plan was beginning to formulate in his at times over-functioning intellect, that would prevent him being identified as the Fifth Man, once and for all.

ANGLETON'S INTERFERENCE

In December 1979, the spy world was abuzz with the Boyle revelations and it was in this atmosphere that British MP Jonathan Aitken met Angleton in Washington DC. Aitken's late father had been a friend of Angleton.[12]

The former CIA counter-intelligence chief had retired to tend his prize orchids, drink and reminisce. He still could not put his past failures, particularly his duping by Philby, behind him. The fabrications in Boyle's book which on paper restored his image in the eyes of the misinformed reader, had not been enough to salve his own bitterness.

Angleton wanted a British scapegoat for Philby's duplicity, and now that Harold Wilson had long retired, the ghost of Roger Hollis was the best target. The American had been in correspondence with Wright for several years after his retirement. They speculated on Hollis's guilt, and, armed with no more than new rumours and old insubstantial evidence, they dwelt on the need to see him exposed.

Now that Blunt's spying had been revealed, the feeling amongst the old spies was that at last there was a prime minister they could reach. Thatcher was seen as someone solidly anti-communist, who would be horrified to learn that there had been serious, red penetration in her Intelligence Services.

Aitken hastened back to London certain that he had information that the realm was imperilled. It was confirmed by contacts that Angleton gave him, namely Arthur Martin, ex-member of the Fluency Committee and also frustrated by not nailing Hollis.

Martin cooperated in background to a letter Aitken sent to Thatcher, which she received early in February 1980.[13]

Those venomous days of the 1960s had returned, thanks to the combined efforts of Wright and Angleton, with some of the former players such as Rothschild and Martin involving themselves.

Aitken's letter summarized the alleged 'new material' about Hollis and his deputy, Mitchell, and other Soviet penetration that these two organized to succeed them. In reality, the 'new material' was novel to Aitken only. His letter regurgitated all the grudges of the old spies. They had been given last gasp hope by the Blunt revelations, which had been served up by the strong new prime minister, whom they perceived as their Boadicea.

Aitken waited and waited. Day after day, there was nothing in the mail. He rang the prime minister's office to see if she had received his dire warnings. Days again slipped by. Eventually he was told by a contact at Number 10 that Thatcher was aware of the allegations.

Did this mean that she knew of them before Aitken had warned her? Or was she letting him know that he would receive a pat on the head for the information? Her response seemed a bit, well, tart.

In fact, Thatcher, a very quick study when she put her mind to it, was learning quite a bit about Intelligence after nearly a year in office. She was even beginning to form her own opinions. Yet she would still defer to the Chiefs at MI5 and MI6.

Aitken, catching the frustration fever which had been endemic in the old spies, decided to work on journalist Chapman Pincher, showing him the letter he had sent the prime minister. Soon everyone was alerting everyone else, including MI5. Even Duncan Campbell, as left-wing a journalist as Pincher was right-wing, was investigating Hollis.[14]

The fever didn't end with the late Director-General of MI5. The Blunt affair had inspired the ignorant, the informed and the stirrers of Fleet Street.

In June 1980, journalist Auberon Waugh wrote an article in *The Spectator* entitled 'Lord Rothschild is Innocent'. In an elliptical piece, Waugh at first linked Rothschild to Burgess and Blunt then proceeded to knock down any notion that the 'immensely distinguished spermatologist' was the Fifth Man.

The article referred to 'Andrew Boyle's cryptic revelations of last week that amongst those questioned by MI5 after the defection of Burgess and Maclean was a hereditary peer who worked in intelligence during the war and who later rose to great eminence . . . nobody who has followed the Blunt case at all closely can be in any doubt that this refers to Lord Rothschild . . . who sits as a Labour peer in the House of Lords . . .

'It would be most surprising if Lord Rothschild had not been asked by MI5 to help in their investigations into the disappearance of Burgess, since he was not only a colleague of Burgess's at Trinity College Cambridge, like everyone else, but also something of a personal friend, in whose London house Burgess lived at one time.'

Waugh added:

'Any suggestion which implied that Lord Rothschild could even have been under suspicion by MI5 as a Soviet agent or witting concealer of Soviet agents is so preposterous as to belong to the world of pulp fiction . . . My real purpose is to appeal for a general amnesty on all Fifth, Sixth, Seventh, Eighth and Ninety-ninth Men who may still be lurking as venerable septuagenarians around the portals of the Athenaeum.'

Waugh's piece worried Rothschild. In the intense media speculation created by Blunt's exposure and the revived Hollis business, Rothschild could see press hounds of different political hues beginning to sniff a possible story, which would mean trouble ahead for him.[15]

It was time for a deflection that would take the heat away from him, in much the same way as it had in the 1960s.

On 25 June, he wrote to Wright:

Things are starting to get rough. I cannot see that it would be a breach of the Official Secrets Act for you to put on a piece of paper but not to send to anyone, a detailed account of your relationships with me, including all details, and let me have it by a method which I shall let you know in due course. There is certainly a need to know and you would only be telling someone that, memory lapses apart, he could put down himself. I think it might be a good idea for you to come over to this country for a few days if you could bear it, but I shall think about it.[16]

This set up things with Wright, if Rothschild was to need him. But now he planned to make use of the Blunt affair at a dinner party given by Lady Avon, the widow of former prime minister Anthony Eden, to which Thatcher had been invited.

The social event took place on 11 July at the Cheyne Walk, Chelsea, home of Nuala Allason, the former wife of a Tory MP. Other notables and friends of Rothschild present included Lady Avon, Hugh Trevor-Roper (Lord Dacre) who had been in Intelligence with him during the war, Rothschild's lawyer, Lord Goodman, Lord Charteris and Sir Isaiah Berlin.[17]

Thatcher and Rothschild did not know each other well. However, she had developed a healthy respect for his intellect and ideas following their limited contact during the Heath Think Tank years when she had been Minister for Education. Despite the enmity between her and Heath, Rothschild thought she was a strong enough character not to bear grudges for his having served her rival.

He was right. She gave him a good hearing at private moments during the dinner party and listened to his request to be her special Intelligence adviser. Rothschild laid out his 'concerns' about the Blunt scandal blowing up because of the Boyle book and all the problems surrounding it.

A source who worked closely with Thatcher said that Rothschild wanted to be put in charge of 'managing the skeletons', which mainly related to the period from 1964 onwards, when several Establishment people opted for immunity from prosecution. Rothschild explained that he knew all about the problem. He had been there and had 'assisted MI5 in its interrogations'. He also reminded Thatcher that he had been the one to expose Philby.[18]

Thatcher said she would consult her Intelligence chiefs and think about his proposal. She was cautious, and he was disappointed but not surprised to be turned down.

That failure caused Rothschild to move quickly to his contingency plan involving Wright. They struck a deal: Wright would compose a 'detailed account of our relationship', which in effect would be a testimonial to the innocence of both himself and Tess should it ever be suggested they were Soviet agents. The testimonial would be a list of Rothschild's achievements at MI5, which would purport to show that he could not possibly be a Soviet agent. In return, Rothschild would assist Wright with his manuscript. Wright wanted it to go to Thatcher, whom he thought would take action.

Wright wrote to Rothschild saying he couldn't pay for a trip to London. Rothschild rang him and, in typically clandestine fashion, arranged for him to meet a courier at Hobart airport. The courier would exchange plane tickets and expenses (for him and Lois for the duration of their short stay in England) for the letter Rothschild had sent.

In the meantime, Pincher consulted his old patron, Rothschild, about the Hollis revelations and rumours, which were furiously circulating Whitehall and Fleet Street. Rothschild was well aware that Wright would be wanting to say something about Hollis in his manuscript, so he decided to stall Pincher in early July by sending him a sanctimonious note on the subject:

> Leaving aside a small number of people who have got the subject on the brain, to the extent of paranoia . . . I wonder whether the anxiety and mistrust caused by those with their own motives for discrediting people and institutions are not being successful if experts such as yourself take up the cudgels. I am inclined to think one should let the dogs lie without comment.[19]

It seemed that in the middle of 1980, every species of canine was lying, and plotting.

39 . VICTOR'S LIST

THE INTRICACIES OF CHANCE

As the pressure mounted during 1980, Rothschild decided to become an undergraduate again. He was in his seventieth year and aware that he was not quite as intellectually sharp as he had been a decade ago when he joined Heath's Think Tank. He was forgetting things, simple things such as where he had put his keys or the location of a book in his impressive library.[1]

Rothschild detested the idea of having his mind deteriorate even marginally or in a way most septuagenarians would consider normal. So he employed a Cambridge don every Friday afternoon for an hour to supervise him in statistics.[2]

Part of the inspiration for this late burst of learning was his long held fascination with probability, to which he had first been introduced at Cambridge when studying the movement of sperm. Such matters as the odds against sperm fertilizing one egg compared to another had captivated his attention in the mid-1930s. Rothschild's interest in the realm of chance had been rekindled during his recent three-year (1976–78) stint as Chairman of the Commission on Gambling. He aimed to be at about first-year Cambridge undergraduate level in a few years.

'My brain cells have been dying,' he told friends, 'but I feel immediate benefit. I intend to go on polishing the remaining functional ones.'[3]

Rothschild believed and, in fact, could demonstrate that he had improved his mind. He found it increased in agility as he tackled several work problems at once. Not the least challenging was the tactics to be used in continuing to cover his tracks from his earlier

life of espionage. As usual, the cerebral doyen of the spy world
would use reason and logic to influence the course of events.

He was beginning to plan a possible diversion. If the focus was on
the ghost of Roger Hollis, the chances were it would not be on him.

GAUGING MARGARET'S MOODS

Rothschild had another opportunity to gauge Thatcher's mood on
various issues, including the old spies-engendered crisis concerning
Hollis, during at least one other social meeting with her, although
there would not have been a moment to talk in-depth. If she was
concerned about events in the secret world, the prime minister
would have the opportunity to mention to him that she had
reconsidered his offer to manage the skeletons.[4]

Rothschild learned that Thatcher was scheduled to visit a Cambridge laboratory on 27 August. He invited her to 'drop in for tea'
at his nearby home and she accepted. She arrived with husband
Denis and her political assistant, Ian Gow, and chatted for about an
hour. But she did not mention anything about Hollis. Nor were any
other Intelligence matters raised.[5]

Rothschild, in turn, did not tell Thatcher on either occasion that
another special, secret guest – Peter Wright – would also soon be
visiting him in Cambridge.

Rothschild had received the message clearly without a word being
said. The prime minister was quite happy to have her current
Intelligence personnel look after the skeletons. This meant he could
not rely on a link with the government to help him avoid another
possible witch-hunt. This time it would be conducted not in-house
by spies, but in the public arena by investigative journalists. He
would have to fight words with words. It was time to call on old
friends from the Fourth Estate.

THE ACHIEVEMENTS

Wright and Lois arrived on 22 August 1980 and took a week off in
Yorkshire to see their daughter. On 2 September Wright then took

an early-morning train from York to Euston station and a taxi to Rothschild's flat at 23 St James's Place.

'We had some drinks and lunch,' Wright recalled. 'He explained that he needed a list of his achievements for MI5 because of the rumours circulating about him following the exposure of Blunt. I agreed to provide one . . .'[5a]

It was an uplifting moment for Wright. He felt that he was back in the action, near Whitehall, the centre of political power and involved with his great and influential friend.

Wright showed Rothschild his manuscript of 10,000 words, the latter part of which had been inspired by Thatcher's exposure of Blunt, which had excited him. Wright read her breaking of tradition as a sign that she was approachable on the subject of Soviet spies still unexposed. Victor, however, was gloomy about her responding personally.

'It's pointless giving it to her,' he said. 'She would pass it on to MI5, and you would be back where you started. They would simply find fault with it and it would be buried.'[6]

Wright replied that he wasn't so sure. He thought Thatcher was a genuine Cold War warrior, who would be tough enough to put the record straight and weed out any remaining moles.

'You know,' Rothschild responded, 'I was with her a few days ago. She doesn't understand about Intelligence matters.'[7]

Rothschild's observation may, in part, have been based on his social meetings with her in July and August when he had failed to convince her that he should manage the skeletons. Yet it may also have been a gratuitous remark to make Wright do things his way. Wright was about to argue further but thought better of it.

'Victor did not elaborate,' Wright said later. 'I knew him well enough to know the significance of what he had said and not to question him about it.'[8]

The next day they went to Cambridge, and Wright started compiling Rothschild's list of achievements for MI5 and by implication against the KGB, which would demonstrate that he could not possibly be a KGB agent himself. It took him a day and a half. Then Rothschild read it and added more of his anti-Soviet, anti-communist involvements, some undertaken before Wright joined MI5 in 1955, and some after.

The list covered three pages and was headed 'Victor Rothschild's help since 1951 to the Security Service'. It included Rothschild's 1951 letter to Dick White concerning Alister Watson being a communist; his 1962 presentation of Flora Solomon, who told of Philby being an agent; his assistance from 1964 to 1968, to British Intelligence (Fluency Committee) investigators in tracing communists from Cambridge University in the 1930s, including their links to Peter Kapitza; his part in the 1953 coup in Iran; his help, while at Shell (1958 to 1969) to MI5 in developing special technology to be used against the KGB; his 1971 suggestion to Heath that he could find more communist subversion information on Jack Jones; his 1975 tip-off – at Wright's request – to Chapman Pincher that Czech defector Frantisek August could tell him about Labour MP John Stonehouse, who was thought to be a Czech intelligence agent.

Other evidence purported to show that Rothschild always had the Intelligence Services' well-being at heart, especially in successfully lobbying for Michael Hanley as Director-General of MI5.

Wright wrote in the Achievement list:

'Victor Rothschild discussed the matter with Peter Wright, who said the service wanted Hanley. Peter Wright arranged a meeting between Rothschild and Hanley. As a result, Rothschild had a private talk with the Prime Minister.'

Another example was the way Rothschild passed on the untrue 'security doubts' about another candidate for the MI5 Director-Generalship, Francis Harrison.

Rothschild got Wright to complete the document with the conclusion: '*I do not believe it conceivable that either Victor Rothschild or Tess Rothschild have ever been Soviet agents . . . I am willing to testify to that effect in any way deemed possible.*'[9]

Rothschild was satisfied. The list was his insurance, his document of last resort should anyone uncover anything that might link him, however remotely, to the Fifth Man. He had constructed proof that any rational human being would consider adequate. That is, if they did not examine the list too closely.

With that done, they discussed Wright's 10,000 word manuscript. Rothschild removed a chapter about himself and said he was not to be mentioned in any documentation.

'It's very good,' Rothschild told Wright in reference to the other chapters, 'but it would be hopeless putting it through official channels.'[10]

The lord decided the dossier should be published as a book. 'But you'll need a ghost writer,' Wright was told. Pincher, the journalist Rothschild had dissuaded recently from pursuing a story on Hollis, was the best choice. He knew the subject and had strong background with this kind of material.

It was now 4 p.m. Rothschild telephoned Pincher and arranged for a chauffeur-driven car to bring him from London to Cambridge. Pincher arrived before 8 p.m. and was taken to Rothschild's dark study where he was alone, 'casually dressed without a jacket.'[11]

Wright was waiting, unseen, in another room.

'They were two old spooks playing silly buggers,' Pincher remembered. Both Pincher and Wright knew of each other, but Rothschild still insisted on introducing Wright as 'Philip'. Rothschild then left the room and let Wright tell Pincher his story.[12]

Pincher could sniff something huge. The former MI5 man spoke of a story concerning Blunt, Philby, Maclean, Golitsyn and Roger Hollis. Pincher was one of several top British journalists searching for a lead on Hollis. The veteran Fleet Street scoop finder knew from the sources and the way it was being presented that this was it.

Wright said he wanted 50 per cent of any net profits that the book might bring. A deal was struck.

The next month, October, Pincher flew to Tasmania to research the book, but soon found he would have to discard Wright's document of nine chapters – 9,000 words in all, after the removal of the chapter on Rothschild. The journalist, an experienced author, would have to start afresh.

Pincher had mixed feelings about Wright. He appreciated his high intelligence, 'exceptional' memory and genuine concern about Soviet penetration. But the journalist did not appreciate his personality, the traits of which were 'common to those who have spent too much time isolated in the secret world. He was calculating and intensely suspicious, with an air of cunning . . .'[13]

At the time, Pincher was happy to cope with Wright's foibles, for the journalist felt he was receiving the story of his life. No scoop or book he had ever dealt with in thirty-five years of journalism had come even close to this. He, or any other reporter, had never had such open access to someone who was not only close to the centre of espionage and major political events at home and abroad. Here was an individual who had driven some of them.

Pincher returned to Britain and got in touch with his publisher, William Armstrong, at Sidgwick & Jackson.[14] Armstrong was naturally most interested. This sounded like an important piece of modern espionage history, and a potential big seller. Pincher, as usual, did not disclose any confidential sources for the new book to be called *Their Trade is Treachery*. Nor did he mention the Rothschild connection.

Rothschild's contribution to the deal was to organize his bank to set up a company – Overbridge International, based in Curacao in the Netherlands Antilles. Wright's royalties would be paid into it.[15]

Rothschild now had both his precious list and the knowledge that the book Pincher would write would divert everyone – from nosy investigative journalists to righteous MPs – away from him and towards Hollis again. His old, dead acquaintance from MI5 was proving most useful indeed.

Rothschild now wished to withdraw from the scene, but he had to make sure Wright was getting his money. There are several references in the big file of private letters between Pincher and Wright to Rothschild's participation in the transfer of funds to Tasmania.

For instance, Pincher wrote on 7 January 1981, two months before publication of *Their Trade is Treachery*: 'Five is on the way through the V-Channel.' In a follow-up letter, Wright pointed out that another payment was due.

On 20 January, Pincher noted: 'Our mutual friend has just confirmed that the deposit of the mares is on its way to you.'

The journalist wrote a week before publication on 13 March: 'I have talked with our intermediary and he will see what he can do re your Swiss venture but rather regards himself as having completed his contribution.'[16]

Apart from this irritation, Rothschild believed that his two friends would produce a strong book, which would deflect suspicions about Soviet espionage agents away from him. Consequently he did not read the text of *Their Trade is Treachery* or even ask about its progress.[17] Nor did he have any contact with the government in what is known in Intelligence parlance as a deniable operation – that is, one which the government has sanctioned but will deny having done so should its role be questioned. Rothschild acted alone as a fixer. He was looking after his own interests in covering traces to the Fifth Man.

However, MI6, MI5 and the government were to get a look at the rapidly produced manuscript before publication and no action was taken to legally stop it. The book did not conclude with a plea for a public inquiry. Soviet penetration at the highest level of MI5 had been removed after the mass expulsion of Soviet agents in 1971. Yet it stuck to the point about Hollis being a likely Soviet agent.

Though the book – published in early March 1981 – was an irritation for the Intelligence Services and 'some official quarters', it was not a major bombshell like the Boyle book.

The Government handled the matter by first leaking to political correspondents and MPs that Hollis had been cleared by MI5 after his interrogation in 1969 and that this had been reviewed by Burke Trend's investigation in 1974–75. Then Thatcher got up in Parliament and reviewed Pincher's book with hostility, repeating the MI5/Trend conclusions that Hollis had not been a Soviet spy.

Thatcher said inquiries had decided that all those MI5 operations against the Soviets that had gone wrong (mainly in the period 1942–63) and 'other security failures' could be attributed to Philby and Blunt. This was nonsense, considering that Philby had been ineffective after 1951. Unbeknown to the government, Blunt *was* partly responsible for the British mishaps and failures, but as a receiver of espionage data, not as a spy himself. The agent responsible was the Fifth Man.

Thatcher had been, if not misled by her advisers, then misguided through their ignorance or failure to consider the simple chronology of events. How, for instance, could Philby possibly steal data from MI5 if he was out of Intelligence by 1952 and in Beirut from 1956?

However, Thatcher's advisers at MI6 were fairly sure of their ground concerning Hollis, at least. They had a double agent of their own, Oleg Gordievsky, inside the Soviet Embassy, who was adamant that the London Residency files indicated that the KGB had no high-level source inside MI5 since 1945.[18] (MI6 had George Blake, who only became a most useful Soviet agent once Modin took over as his Control in 1955. Blake was most effective in that year in compromising an MI6 operation in Germany, where it was attempting to tap telephone lines in a tunnel under East Berlin. But he had no idea of what MI5 was doing in anti-Soviet operations. Blake was apprehended in 1961.)

So Thatcher and her advisers were going on two sets of information – the internal inquests by MI5 and Trend, and also the Russians themselves through Gordievsky. Both indicated that the mole within MI5 could not be Roger Hollis. There was other peripheral evidence that pointed away from Hollis. For instance, in 1954 he was aware for at least three months before a KGB couple – Vladimir and Evdokia Petrov – defected in Sydney that they had been acting for Australian Intelligence, ASIO. Hollis would have had ample time to warn the Moscow Centre of the coming defection and at no risk, because the crisis was a long way away. But nothing happened. The Petrovs, who proved most useful to Western Intelligence, made the move successfully.

The prime minister's statement had been correct about Hollis, but wrong about Philby and Blunt.

Rothschild must have been most satisfied with the result of his fixing. There were now two schools of thought about high penetration Soviet moles within MI5, neither of which had any direct link to him. First, there was the Wright, Angleton, old spies and Pincher school, which was saying that Hollis was probably the big spy. Then there was the second school – Thatcher, her advisers and others – who were offering the opinion that it wasn't Hollis, but Philby and Blunt.

To add a third school after that and suggest Rothschild or anyone else was also an agent would have seemed frivolous in the heady early months of 1981. Rothschild's diversionary tactics had worked, getting the government and the nation in an unnecessary tizz over moles, while at the same time keeping his friends Wright and Pincher happy with money and work in their respective 'retirements'.

The media, not just in Britain but throughout the West, was abuzz with the name Hollis. Despite Thatcher's denials in Parliament, the word was that he *was* a Soviet agent, and that the British government was involved in a cover-up. This theory had particular credence in the US, where cover-ups had had much publicity since President Nixon made them a crude art form seven years earlier.

For the moment, Rothschild had won the main battle of words, innuendo, allegations and insinuations which had first threatened him less than a year ago when Auberon Waugh wrote his piece in the *Spectator*.

However, he was still being nagged by Wright through his correspondence with Pincher. Two months after publication, on 24 May, Pincher wrote: 'The Ks you requested immediately available. Held up only on advice our mutual friend.' On 4 June he informed Wright: 'After consultation with your adviser your Ks for the horses already sold on the way to you. No more may be expected for three months when your adviser may have organized a new arrangement.'[19]

Wright's bank in Cygnet, however, had not received the expected deposit. He complained. Pincher wanted to keep Wright happy in the hope of getting help on further publications, including the paperback edition of *Their Trade is Treachery*, and another book, *Too Secret too Long*. He responded on 22 July: 'I am appalled to hear that you have not received your stallion proceeds. I set this in motion a month ago and the failure is due to the mechanics at our mutual friend's end. Am doing all I can to expedite. Will see him.'

Then six days later, he informed Wright: 'Have seen our mutual friend who promises to pull out all stops. No problem my end re stallion Ks. Hope now with you.'

The payments became more reliable and Wright stopped pushing. But the financial success of the venture had inspired the old spy. The more Pincher pumped him for information, the more Wright began to think there was money to be made while pursuing his all-consuming passion to have Hollis condemned and MI5 fumigated to rid it of his protégés.

Rothschild was relieved to at last wash his hands of the affair, in which he had been ultimately responsible for organizing the publication of official secrets. It had been a mild and minor event compared to his activities during the war and from 1945 to 1963 when he had passed on far more secrets to the Russians at far greater personal risk. Rothschild would have considered it an easy and successful operation.

40. AND THEN THERE WERE TWO

ANDROPOV'S LEGACY

Modin rose to pre-eminence in the training of new KGB spies during the early 1980s. The venue was the Andropov Institute where he became head of Faculty Number One (Political Intelligence) and taught tradecraft. Modin's lectures were the most popular, mainly because he had been successful in the KGB's halcyon days during the 1950s.[1]

He drew on his experience when running the ring of five, which enthralled and inspired the students, who were expected to restore the KGB's position in London in particular, where espionage had been in the doldrums since the 1971 expulsions. For instance, Modin spoke with authority about how he masterminded the defections of Burgess and Maclean, and how he looked after a grateful Philby in 1954.

Thanks to the training and careful build-up of Controls in the London Residency, new hope reigned at the Moscow Centre that they could repeat their victory over British Intelligence.

The other two leading figures at the Institute were Ivan Shishkin, head of counter-intelligence, and Vladimir Barkovsky, head of scientific and technological intelligence. Illegals – those Russian agents insinuated into a country, but not connected with the Embassy – such as Konon Molody, alias Gordon Lonsdale, were also popular. Like Modin, they had had hands-on experience at out-foxing the enemy on its own soil. Their insights brought lectures alive and thrilled the eager listeners assembled, for one day they would be putting all they were hearing into practice.[2]

Every six months the students spent a week at a training centre in

Moscow called The Villa run by a KGB General. Teachers took them through traditional tradecraft, such as agent recruitment, rendezvous with agents, surveillance, and filling and emptying dead letter boxes. The students had to be taught about mortgages so they could acquire agents by offering to help them out with payments. Driving school for the KGB trainees was also essential. Soviet agents rarely owned cars in Moscow and they invariably had crashes on foreign postings, especially in London where cars were driven on the opposite side of the road.

The one notable absence among the lecturers at the Andropov Institute was Philby. His talents were being exploited in smaller tutorial sessions, which the undergraduates loved.

'Without question Kim would have been the most popular lecturer ever,' ex-KGB Colonel Bagdonov remarked. 'He was forceful, erudite, experienced and, at the appropriate time, amusing. He had such an acerbic wit.'

'He knew the British better than the British,' ex-KGB Colonel 'E' recalled. 'By that, I mean he had studied their mannerisms, habits etcetera – especially those of his own superior, privileged class. He passed on to us what he called their "fortes, foibles and frustrations".'[3]

Philby was responsible for selecting the students' reading list, which included Dickens, Fielding's *Tom Jones*, and everything Le Carré had written. Some of Graham Greene's books were on the list. Philby had been careful to leave off Greene's *The Human Factor*. Philby wondered if Greene meant him to be the model for the main character, Maurice Castle, the vacillating MI5 agent who defects to Moscow. Castle finds himself living in a drab Russian apartment. According to Modin, when Greene visited Philby late in 1982, he went out of his way to impress the author with his apartment and its mod cons, which included a video recorder. Philby made sure Greene realised he had his *Times*, *Observer* and *Private Eye* subscriptions, unlike the fictional Castle, who had to visit the Lenin Library to read the English papers.[4]

'We had to know Anthony Sampson's *Anatomy of Britain* inside out,' Colonel 'E' remembered. 'Philby and others would often question us about it and other references.'

Required reading included a classified thesis by Mikhail Lyubimov, who had been a Control in London in the early 1960s, and

V. V. Ovchinnikov's *Britain Observed, A Russian's View*. The latter
was a piece of quaint, over-simplistic KGB propaganda on everything in Britain from the art of conversation to the workings of the
House of Lords.[5]

Ovchinnikov noted:

'Lord Rothschild, the famous banker, warned his compatriots,
during his time as a government adviser . . . that if they did not rid
themselves of the antiquated notion that Great Britain was one of
the richest, most important, and most influential countries in the
world; rid themselves, in other words, of the notion that Queen
Victoria was still reigning, then by 1985 England could become one
of the poorest countries in Europe.'[6]

The book was 'condescending', and Philby warned that it should
be read and understood as a 'half-way book', something that
reinforced Soviet 'sometimes accurate, sometimes prejudicial views
about the UK', but which, 'if regurgitated out of context, would
cause antagonism within sections of British society'. He noted that
the book's thoughts could be used to suborn potential agents, but
that this had to be done subtly. Philby's constructive criticisms of
such works did not endear him to the hierarchy within the KGB,
especially if they had recommended such reading. He was kept at
arm's length for fear that his inside knowledge of how to operate as
an agent in the West would embarrass some of the less experienced
Chiefs.[7]

This continued to frustrate him, nearly as much as the problems
he had in publishing *My Silent War* in the Soviet Union. His book
had endured poor translations and severe editing, which he and
Modin deplored but could do nothing about. More than a decade
after it had appeared in the West, it had been distributed in the
early 1980s to the Central Committee of the Communist Party, the
GRU and selected sections of the KGB itself. Yet the tiny publication never reached the Russian public. This embittered Philby, who
had wanted to be given heroic status in his adopted country. It
would have given him immeasurable satisfaction. But the KGB
vetoed it.

Yet by early 1983, at the age of sixty-eight, he had come to terms
with the fact that his influence with the KGB Chiefs would be
minimal. However, he was gaining great satisfaction from the
knowledge that his students now in London were starting to

penetrate the British Establishment again via agents they were picking up. He delighted in hearing stories of acquisitions from agents who had trained under him and Modin. If he couldn't have a say in running the KGB, he was at least having some influence again at the point where he began – as the second most successful Russian agent ever in Britain.[8]

VALE, MACLEAN AND BLUNT

Moscow's long winter of 1982–3 bit its hardest in March and hastened the deaths of more elderly Soviet citizens than normal. Among them was 69-year-old Donald Maclean. He had died, after a prolonged bout of alcoholism, a convinced and content Marxist who did not wish to be reminded of his days with the Ring. Unlike Burgess, who had fallen apart in Moscow, and Philby, who had sometimes squandered his skills through alcoholism, frustration and depression, Maclean had constructed a new and modestly successful career as a teacher and analyst of British affairs.

In a way, he had been luckier than Philby by being a diplomat and not an Intelligence operator. He did not meet blocks in the Soviet Foreign Ministry to his mild aims to teach and advise, whereas the more ambitious Philby was never going to be allowed to reach the top of the KGB.

Maclean's death on 6 March caused a plethora of reports, obituaries, analyses and features in the British press, which were soberly absorbed by the Fourth and Fifth Men.

After twenty days of coverage, and just when the espionage articles seemed to have dried up, newspaper editors sent assistants to their library files again with the news that Blunt had died of a massive heart attack on 26 March.

That left the Fifth Man as the last member of the Ring in Britain. Journalists began phoning Rothschild's homes in the hope of getting a comment on the passing away of his friend. Some would also have had in mind the rumours that Rothschild was the Fifth Man – perhaps, in the emotion of the moment, he might let something slip. But the Baron was not available for comment. He waited in fear for news of any incriminating document to emerge from Blunt's papers, or in his will. There was also a 30,000 word autobiography,

AND THEN THERE WERE TWO

which he had abandoned because it was too depressing. Had Blunt destroyed this?

Blunt was the last remaining figure Rothschild had considered could just possibly betray him, apart from Philby, but even he had no idea of the extent of the Fifth Man's espionage. During the war, Philby had been busy setting himself up in MI6, and he would have had no knowledge of Rothschild's post-war efforts, especially after 1951 – except for his part in Philby's own defection. Blunt had been the constant factor in the Fifth Man's spying efforts as the middleman link to a string of Controls from 1940 to 1963.

After a few months, when nothing appeared, a thankful Rothschild began thinking about a new book of his 'experiences', in which he would meet the persistent media demands and comment on Blunt. Hopefully, this would bury the connection forever.

TAKING FEW CHANCES

Espionage fever was kept running through 1983 when MI5 officer Michael Bettaney was arrested in September for spying for the KGB. Bettaney was low-level, but his detection gave continuing credence to the theory that Hollis had been an agent who left a network of other operatives inside British Intelligence.

It was just the sort of story the media loved for it gave follow-up angles on espionage more currency. Retired or old spies, especially those with grudges, were inclined to talk, mostly off the record to newspaper journalists, but now some were induced to consider appearing on television.

A circular mini-industry on espionage information had developed involving the old spies and journalists. Following Pincher's book, *Their Trade is Treachery*, MI5 had meetings which ascertained that there were several old spies who may have contributed to background for the writer. Wright and Martin were at the top of the list.

The names of the old spies were then leaked to Rupert Allason, the son of a wealthy former Conservative MP, whose book *A Matter of Trust: MI5 1945–72*, had been published in 1982. The book's main source was Arthur Martin. Considering the secrecy surrounding British Intelligence, this book, along with Boyle's *The Climate of Treason* and Pincher's *Their Trade is Treachery* were breakthrough works, which were published within a few years of each other. They gave the public a sudden taste of cold reality. Until now this had been left to Le Carré, whose outstanding novels had captured the mood and atmosphere of the Cold War era.

Allason teamed up with the moustachioed, long-haired Paul Greengrass, who had the look of a barricade anarchist. He was a producer with Granada TV's *World in Action* programme. Although politically conservative and a begrudging admirer of Thatcher, Greengrass was not going to let his political leanings get in the way of a good story. He approached some of the old spies to see if they would be willing to appear in a documentary.[9]

Greengrass used the recent Bettaney case to mount an argument concerning the public's right to know about MI5 in order to persuade Wright to appear before cameras in Tasmania, which he did early in January 1984. (The film was not to be shown until six months later.)[10]

In May 1984, Rothschild's new book, *Random Variables*, appeared and his publishers asked him if he would do some promotional interviews. Several journalists lined up for a chance to put questions to him. Rothschild was reluctant, although he now felt secure knowing that no one in the West could accuse him of being the Fifth Man. It would have been a different matter if Blunt had been alive, because the ailing, disgraced art historian might have resented Rothschild producing a self-serving book, intended to increase his prestige and distance himself from the main activity of his life.

Blunt just might have said, 'Oh, come, come, Victor, own up as I, Donald, Guy and Kim have been forced to do.' But Blunt was gone and apparently his incriminating secrets were buried with him.

Rothschild had a minor dilemma. He knew his book would never be a bestseller. He just wanted it read by the governing powers, the British Establishment who read the top papers, formed key opinions and therefore shaped history. Their consumption of it would ensure that he remained an unsullied, respected footnote to British military, Intelligence, science, political and business history. But if he sat in his study in St James's Place and did nothing to help promote it, *Random Variables* might just go unnoticed, which would make it a wasted exercise.

The book – an eclectic compilation of snippets of his life, experiences, thoughts, reflections and humour – had a tantalizing, three-page essay on Blunt tucked neatly away at page 203. It was entitled, 'The File is Never Closed'. Taking care to appear off-hand, Rothschild misled his readers:

'I was very ignorant about politics and ideologies in those [Cambridge] days, being . . . too busy with my scientific work, sport and social life to have much time for anything else . . .'

It was a line he had fed Boyle for his book, and it contrived to make it seem he could not possibly have been caught up with communism.

'I remember, very vaguely,' Rothschild went on, 'once thinking that an article about porcelain by Anthony Blunt in the *Spectator* or the *New Statesman* – I forget which – dragged in Marxism in a way I thought unnecessary and irrelevant.'

In the end, he decided that he would do a few interviews with leading papers, such as *The Times*, which was running extracts of the book including the Blunt essay, and the *Sunday Times*. The reference to the Fourth Man, was enough to interest the *Sunday Times'* Simon Freeman, an experienced political journalist. He was well aware of the rumours about Rothschild's possible link to the Ring of Five. Freeman and Barrie Penrose were gathering research into a book on Blunt.

It was a strained interview, with no love lost between the two. Rothschild was prepared for the unnerving questions about Blunt, which Freeman introduced by bemoaning the fact that Rothschild had not, and would not, write an autobiography:

'It would reveal much about the development in Cambridge during the 1930s of that group of homosexuals and aesthetes who later spied for the Russians. Rothschild liked Blunt but found Guy Burgess a "fairly repulsive drunk who ate garlic, but who, despite all that, was quite amusing".'[11]

Freeman remarked that Rothschild was widely rumoured to be the Fifth Man.

'No,' the journalist wrote, 'he didn't particularly resent being suspected, but no, he was not a spy although he had been and still was, in a vague way, left-wing. He no longer blamed himself for not realizing earlier that Blunt had been a spy; after all, Blunt, Burgess and Philby were men whose very natures led them to the world of spying and were thus able to hide treachery from their closest friends.'

Freeman remarked that most people assumed that because Victor was a Rothschild he had to be 'fabulously' wealthy, and that 'like very rich people' he was preoccupied in keeping or expanding his fortune.

Rothschild disagreed and showed him the patched sleeves on his ageing suit.

'I come from a ghetto and that stays with you,' he commented without explaining that the Rothschilds left a German ghetto 200 years earlier. 'The English Rothschilds aren't very wealthy anyway. We've paid all our taxes and death duties and we definitely aren't very rich. I haven't paid much attention to it.

'As my great-grandfather said, it is ten times more difficult to keep a fortune than to acquire it. And I have been far too busy to worry about it.'

Rothschild may have had in mind the fact that he had not been a financial 'builder' of wealth like his forefathers and son. His destiny had been to move away from the family preoccupation with money and assets. Consequently, when he needed extra funds for himself or others he sold family acquisitions. Just two years earlier he had sent fifty-eight gold boxes to Christie's for sale. They had been part of a collection of 500 belonging to Baron Carl von Rothschild, of Frankfurt, in the mid-nineteenth century. Victor's boxes brought £750,000 at auction.

Rothschild finished his rare interview with an observation about his most important asset – his mind. He saw himself as a good analyst, but not a truly creative thinker, which he distinguished as a higher form of cogitation.

'People who think creatively hear the music of the spheres,' Rothschild commented. 'I have heard them once or twice . . .'

The two parted ways disliking each other. Freeman, who had secured one of the rare public interviews of any note with the secretive lord, felt more mystified by him than before the interview, which had been only a mild digging exercise. The meeting had left the journalist with more questions than answers, and a hunger to know more about this difficult and quirky figure of the Establishment.[12]

Rothschild, however, felt he had overcome the worst and vowed never again to take face-to-face questioning, no matter how it might help book sales. He preferred his journalists friendly and compliant.

MORE OF THE WRIGHT STUFF

Rothschild had been kept informed about Greengrass's documentary by Pincher, whose appearance on the programme Wright had objected to. He wanted centre stage and did not want to be contradicted by anyone. Furthermore he was just beginning to think about writing another book – without Pincher's help. Entitled *The Spy Who Never Was*, the programme was broadcast on 16 July 1984. Wright's main contention in the one-hour programme was that he was '99 per cent certain' that Hollis was a spy.

MI5 knew about the programme's contents in advance and discussed it with the government, in this case represented by the Treasury Solicitor. No injunction to prevent broadcast was taken out, presumably because part of its contents were about an MI5 operation in 1955 called Party Piece. This involved the burgling of a Mayfair flat and the photocopying of documents about the British Communist Party, which showed that several public figures, including top trade union officials and thirty-one MPs, were secret members of the Party.

If an injunction had been served it would have meant at least a part-explanation of this illegal operation in court. MI5 and the government decided it wasn't worth it. They were caught in a catch 22 situation.

Wright was encouraged by this inaction, for he had now spilled state secrets in a book, *Their Trade is Treachery*, and in a TV programme, and he had survived. He began to consider writing his own book. He had received more than thirty thousand pounds in royalties from *Their Trade is Treachery* which had supplemented his pension and kept him on the farm at Cygnet. Why not write his own exposé and make his retirement secure, even a little comfortable?

Rothschild, however, would have had mixed feelings about the TV exposure of Wright. On the one hand, it had helped to keep the Hollis affair bubbling for three years after it had first distracted everyone in 1981. But it also showed Wright as the maverick he had always threatened to be. Rothschild sensed the danger in this, especially as Pincher and Wright had ceased communication.

Within days of the broadcast, Arthur Martin became the second spook from within the old spies to go public. He wrote to *The Times* on 19 July, tempering Wright's '99 per cent' claim about Hollis.

'I think that was an exaggeration,' Martin said. '. . . while Hollis fitted the circumstantial evidence more closely than any other candidate, the case against him was not conclusive.'

But so as not to be seen to be attacking his old spy companion from the Fluency Committee inquisition days, Martin remarked: 'I remember Peter Wright as a dedicated officer, deeply concerned by the threats to his country.'[13]

The most important paragraph in his letter said:

'It was the evidence of continued penetration of the service after Blunt retired in 1945 until at least the early 1960s which carried complete conviction amongst those working on the case.'

The evidence against Hollis was far from convincing. Yet every dedicated officer knew that MI5's secret operations had been passed on to the Russians for about twenty years. Somebody had to have been acting as a double-agent. Perhaps the word penetration was the problem. It more than implied that MI5 had been infiltrated by the enemy. This had bred the frustration, paranoia, fear and suspicion within the British Intelligence network exemplified by the actions and utterances of the old spies.

In actuality, this had not been the case. The Fifth Man had remained on the outside.

41. A TRUE
BRITISH MOLE

A SHOCK FOR THE CENTRE

While the old spies were preoccupied with espionage ghosts, MI6 was receiving full benefit from running its own Russian agent, Oleg Gordievsky, inside the Soviet Embassy. Gordievsky had sought to become a British double agent after Russia's rough handling of Czechoslovakia in 1968 and was recruited by MI6 in 1972. Since then he had become a key agent in place passing on vital information, especially about KGB and Soviet leadership attitudes.[1]

Gordievsky reported some strange directives from the Moscow Centre, which would have been hilarious had they not been so dangerous. The most perilous occurred when Ronald Reagan became President early in 1981. KGB chief Yuri Andropov was then convinced that the US planned a first-strike nuclear attack on the USSR.[2] In an operation code-named RYAN, Andropov ordered all KGB stations to gather intelligence that would back this hazardous assumption. They didn't have to look far in Britain. The US had placed cruise missiles in the UK and were carrying out practice manoeuvres during the middle of the night. In 1983 Reagan was talking about the Star Wars concept to 'end the threat of nuclear confrontation', which was in reality an escalation of the arms race, while in the next breath speaking of the Soviet Union as the Evil Empire.

Gordievsky informed the West of the danger of feeding the Centre's obsessions, which led to Reagan toning down his speeches. He also communicated his fears about the KGB chiefs' paranoias to Modin, Philby and others in a position to influence trainee agents in their attitudes.

They spoke in private to students about the absurdity of 'Zionist plots' which were supposed to have removed Richard Nixon from the US Presidency and later put Ronald Reagan in. When some of the recruits became agents and reached the Soviet Embassy in London, Gordievsky reinforced the Philby/Modin lessons, by telling his new staff not to take too seriously some of the sillier directives from the Centre during the height of operation RYAN.

For instance, the London Resident was told to report any increase in the sale of blood. In Britain blood donation is free. Other agents were ordered to check a long list of buildings at night to see if their lights were on – which would have been a sign at, for instance, the Department of Defence in Whitehall, that something was being plotted. The agents were not given cars so they had to traipse around London on foot.

One agent caused alarm by noting that the top floor of a Foreign Office building in Carlton Gardens near the Mall had 'lights on until the early hours'. In fact, the agent had been spying on a building on the wrong side of the street, which housed the International Wool Secretariat.[3]

Gordievsky's peak as a double agent was reached in 1984 when he briefed Mikhail Gorbachev for his first London meeting with Thatcher. Gordievsky primed Gorbachev on Thatcher's attitudes, her government, the economy and British reaction to his London visit.

Thatcher prepared for her meeting with the Russian with information also supplied by Gordievsky. Gorbachev emerged from the discussions saying that the British prime minister was remarkably well-informed on his country. Thatcher responded by commenting that Gorbachev, then involved in a power struggle to take over as Russian leader, was 'someone she could do business with'.[4]

This was high praise indeed from the Iron Lady, who, until that point, had been a staunch anti-communist like her good friend President Reagan.

Her timely remarks were seen in Moscow power circles as an important endorsement of Gorbachev's claims to leadership. Gordievsky's indirect assistance was part of the KGB's push to put Gorbachev in as Soviet leader, which succeeded soon afterwards. He returned the favour immediately he took power by beefing-up KGB operations worldwide. In early 1985, their presence and effectiveness in London was at its strongest since 1971. Gorbachev's reasoning was simple and logical. If he was to survive politically he had to transform Russia's industrial base and make rapid changes in the economy. The fastest and cheapest way to do this was to steal secrets from the West, something Russia had done with great success thanks to the Fifth Man and others during the war, when it could not afford the time or funds to research and develop its own atom bombs, biological weapons or radar.

Gordievsky's impact on Gorbachev resulted in his promotion to London Resident in January 1985. But within two months, he was under suspicion at the Centre for being 'too soft' in his attitudes to the West, according to KGB sources. This would have been partly due to his playing down of the more ridiculous KGB directives to new Russian agents placed at the London Embassy. Any counter-manding of orders, however mild or sensible, would be reported back to the over-sensitive Centre eventually, and would put Gordievsky at risk.[5]

However, the main reason was the fact that the KGB had a mole inside the CIA, Aldrich Ames, who early in 1985 was a senior Soviet counter-intelligence officer. Ames – the CIA's Philby of the 1980s – had informed the KGB about eleven Russian double agents. Each had a code name with the prefix GT, which meant they were highly sensitive. Gordievsky was GTTICKLE.[6]

He was placed under surveillance and his behaviour, and that of his family, was noted. Over-fraternization with the West, real or imagined, was marked down against him. An example was Gordievsky's pride in his bright, six-year-old daughter's ability to recite, in perfect English, the Lord's Prayer.

In May 1985 he was summoned back to Moscow, drugged and interrogated. A shocked Gordievsky did not confess to being a British agent and instead hung on because his inquisitors had not presented substantial evidence against him. Nevertheless, he knew he was virtually under sentence of death.

MI6, knowing his immense value, wanted to save him, so they planned his daring escape, while under house arrest, with a dash in a van through Moscow streets. Gordievsky was smuggled across a border to the West, where he delivered to MI6 one of the most effective ever debriefings of any defector or former spy in place.

Once he had divulged the important information, thirty-one KGB espionage agents, who collectively had been running close to a hundred British agents, were expelled.

Among those thrown out of the UK was Colonel Bagdonov, who was retrenched when the KGB was reorganized in 1990. (He retains a link, as do all the others who have been fired in recent times, through a little-publicized reserve structure, which could be reactivated in an emergency. Bagdonov had, like several other ex-KGB people, set-up as a business consultant with the West. Some of them were finding it hard to make the adjustment which amounted to a complete ideological turnaround.)[7]

'I was acting Resident at the London Embassy when Oleg had to go back to Moscow,' Bagdonov told me. 'We didn't know what had happened. Later, I was most grateful when he did not mention me in his book.'

What happened to the 100 agents set up and controlled by Bagdonov and others?

'I ran five myself,' Bagdonov remarked. 'They would either break their connection (with the KGB) or wait to be reactivated, when a new Control was trained and inside the Embassy, or even via an illegal.'[8] (MI6 sources suggest that some of these British agents would have been padding by Bagdonov and his fellow KGB operatives, who were trying to impress their Moscow bosses. For instance, a handful of London journalist contacts would have been included to swell the numbers. Gordievsky seemed to back this up when, in December 1994, it was alleged in the *Spectator* magazine that Richard Gott, the literary editor of the *Guardian*, was on a KGB payroll. Gott resigned over it.)

KGB intelligence inside Britain was once more in disarray, and the ripple effect did not help friends of Gordievsky such as Philby back in Moscow. He had continued to be outspoken in criticism of the KGB, and was yet again out of favour.

Gordievsky's debriefing by MI6 reaffirmed what he had been telling them for a decade. There had been no KGB source inside MI5 since the war. It strengthened the British government's resolve to prevent Wright accusing Hollis of being a Russian agent.

42. THE DEVIL
IN TASMANIA

THATCHER-CATCHER

Wright's TV appearance in mid-1984 alerted the media and publishing world to one of the 'stranger phenomena' of Whitehall, as Rothschild once characterized him. Here was a spook who seemed to have all the answers to the post-war woes of British Intelligence, someone who was articulate and willing to talk. His brusque, intriguing personality told the media he was not the usual lip-sealed, pinstripe-suited civil servant. He was full of guile and bile, yet he was also somehow naïve and credible. There was something approachable about him, once you got over the barrier of suspicion. Wright had grievances, he would fight. The man had a massive ego, it had to be stroked. These were strengths and vulnerabilities that experienced media people could use to reach him.

Hundreds would try. He was, after all, the only one of his kind from British Intelligence this century. Circumstances had made him open for business, or so it seemed, *if* he could be reached.

Uppermost in Wright's mind immediately after the programme was not scrounging more money from his expertise – he wanted action. He was consumed by his sincerely held view that the realm was in grave danger. It was as real to him as Hitler's threat in the 1930s. Wright felt he was like Churchill in the wilderness years before he took power. No one in authority would take him seriously.

The ailing Wright was literally living for the 9,000 word document (with the Rothschild chapter out). After the TV programme, a contact told him that he could get the document to Thatcher. Wright said 'Do it.' The contact obliged. He claimed her reaction was frosty, even scathing. The document was old hat, and not accurate. Thatcher was adamant: there was no evidence that Hollis had ever been a Russian spy. What's more, if Wright pursued this project he would be prosecuted under the Official Secrets Act. Rothschild had been right after all, Wright thought. It *was* useless approaching her.[1]

Thatcher's response humiliated and confused him. Wasn't this the powerful leader who had just rolled up the National Union of Mineworkers? She of the hectoring manner seemed a highly competent and intelligent leader, the strongest Britain had had since Churchill, someone he felt certain he could reach intellectually. Yet she was rejecting him, when he was handing her evidence that the realm was being subverted! Why? It must be as Victor had warned, Wright thought again. Thatcher was ignorant of Intelligence matters.

It didn't occur to him that, firstly, it was unlike her to be ignorant of any major or even minor issue facing her government. Or secondly, that she might be right about Hollis, and that he might be wrong.

It was now a stand-off between two people with extraordinary wills. Both were dogmatic to the point of stubbornness. They were individuals who would not compromise when their intellects told them they were absolutely, categorically correct. This meant a legal, political, financial fight to the death.

Wright was now cut off completely from the government. There was no chance there, so he decided to revert to airing his views in public, through a book based on the existing document. He sent it out to British publishers.

There were sniffs of initial interest but excuses for not publishing trickled back to him. There was the geographical problem of Tasmania. Wright laughed that off, saying that it tested the other party's commitment.

He began to enjoy the offers he was receiving from the media and the hesitant, cautious interest from publishers. He did not reply to letters, and the keener among the suitors realised he could only really be communicated with over his book project. It was now his life.[2]

Wright wanted his document taken seriously as a starting point with British publishers. He had not been happy with Pincher's handling of the information in *Their Trade is Treachery*. The main problem for Wright was the conclusion, which implied there was no

penetration now and that there was no need for an inquiry into
MI5.[3]

Hamish Hamilton toyed with the document and decided to
approach the Treasury Solicitor, to whom it was sent. The Treasury
Solicitor's Office invited the publisher from Hamish Hamilton 'to
have tea'.[4]

The publisher expressed a desire to produce the book based on
the Wright document, which he assumed was part of the government's unofficial line, mainly because nothing had been done to
stop Their Trade is Treachery, and because Wright had made that
July 1984 TV appearance, again without hindrance.

An indignant Treasury Solicitor's Office representative put the
publisher straight. The document was not part of the government's
unofficial disinformation/information line. Hamish Hamilton was
advised to stop the whole affair immediately. It complied.[5]

The incident was more proof that Rothschild's actions were
independent of the government. On his own volition, he had put
Wright and Pincher together, and had set up the off-shore company
operation to send the old spy royalty payments, in order to produce
Their Trade is Treachery. Rothschild had not been involved in a
deniable operation.

The book was passed to Brian Perman, managing director at
publisher William Heinemann. He was more than interested –
enough, in fact, to pay a £75,000 advance for the world rights, a
hefty sum by English standards. A contract was signed in late 1984.
Perman came to Australia for a sales conference and slipped quietly
down to see Wright in Tasmania, taking with him Heinemann's
Australian managing director, Nick Hudson.[6]

Hudson, an Oxford-educated literary Englishman, had migrated
to Australia to 1958 and had been a publisher with Heinemann for
all of those twenty-six years. He struck up an immediate rapport
with Wright, who spilled his story. When he had finished Wright
remarked to Hudson:

'People are saying I'm mad. Do you think I'm mad?'

'No, Peter,' Hudson replied, 'you're not mad. You're obsessed.'

This pleased the king of the old spies. He then showed Hudson
his espionage memorabilia, including Gordon Lonsdale's camera.
Wright was in fine form and loving the attention. It brought out his
peculiar, very individual charm.[7]

Also visiting him at the time was Paul Greengrass, who agreed to collaborate on the project. He was not a writer, but a television journalist, which under the circumstances was near enough. He could tart up Wright's prose to give it life, atmosphere and readability. This was no short order, given the complicated material that was to come. Greengrass had the advantage of understanding the topic and its ramifications. He was a voracious reader of spy books. A deal was struck to give him part of the advance and royalties.[8]

On the way back to Hobart airport Perman told Hudson why he had been invited to meet Wright.

'If MI5 get tough, we'll get a criminal charge under the Official Secrets Act,' Perman said. 'We don't want to go to jail. So if they get heavy, you'll be publishing the book down here, if that's all right with you?'

Hudson loved the idea.

'I've even got the title,' he said shaking hands with Perman in the airport lounge as they prepared to go their different ways.

'What? We've been struggling with that.'

'Spycatcher!'[9]

TRIBULATIONS

A few months into 1985, Perman rang Hudson in Melbourne.

'MI5 are getting heavy,' Perman said. 'We would like you to take over *Spycatcher*, if that's still all right?'

Hudson was most agreeable, so Perman drew up a new contract between William Heinemann Australia, represented by Hudson, and Idiogram, the company name covering the Wright/Greengrass collaboration.

Wright began telling his story into a tape-recorder at home. Hudson's wife, Sam, transcribed the tapes in Melbourne before sending typed pages to Greengrass, who set up in Amsterdam in order to keep away from MI5's prying spies.

'Peter's tapes were not as bug free as you might expect from one of the world's best buggers,' Hudson observed. 'Sam kept hearing things such as Lois doing the dishes in the background.'[10]

In Tasmania, Wright had told Greengrass about Rothschild's role as the catalyst for *Their Trade is Treachery*, and Greengrass had urged Wright to add as much as he could about his relationship with Rothschild. Wright was reluctant and only wrote what he considered could do his powerful friend no harm. When the chapters touching on Wright's relationship with Rothschild arrived in Amsterdam, Greengrass decided to talk to a strong CIA contact about it the next time they met.

Despite the secrecy about the creation of *Spycatcher* (Sam Hudson's code-name was Rubber Duckie and Wright's was the Rothschild sobriquet, Phillip), word leaked that Wright was writing.

Thatcher, the impartial conqueror of such diverse characters as the Yorkshire Miners' leader Arthur Scargill and Argentina's Dictator, General Galtieri, sent in the legal paratroopers – Treasury Solicitor John Bailey, and Sydney Establishment law firm Stephen Jacques Stone James – to shake up the enemy. Perman in London, Hudson in Melbourne, and Wright in Tasmania received threatening letters – ultimatums to desist from scribbling memoirs or else.

Unless Thatcher's emissaries heard from Perman, Hudson and Wright within seven days, she would 'consider such action to protect the interests of the Crown as they may be advised'. It was just the sort of challenge Boadicea's reincarnation thrived on. She could not have her spies running off and supplementing their incomes with filthy fat contracts for publishing Crown secrets. That might do for Ronald Reagan's CIA. Its members were often disloyal. But the British had higher ideals. They did not sell their nation's hidden affairs for pieces of silver. It was as distasteful to Thatcher as treachery itself. She wanted to show Ron and the American cousins that the British government would not stand for it.

She met a little bit of resistance, just enough to show that the legal paratroopers had not had quite the effect intended. Her threats were officially acknowledged in a letter from Wright, but there was no word of capitulation. The government gained temporary injunctions on Wright and Heinemann Australia on 13 September 1985.

The pressures had some impact. Lawyers told Heinemann they couldn't win such a case. Hudson, who had taken up the challenge, left the company after a reshuffle by new Heinemann UK director, Nick Thompson.[11] Whatever the reason, Wright's small army was in disarray.

However, Hudson left one life-line legacy on file at Heinemann. He had recommended a young Sydney solicitor to represent them

and Wright. His name was Malcolm Turnbull. He had been
described by writer John Mortimer as 'chunky, dark-haired with a
falling lock of hair and the appearance of a young Oscar Wilde.'
This may have been unfair to both young Oscar, who was much
prettier, and to Turnbull, whose falling lock was due to macho
unkemptness rather than an effeminate touch. Hudson had also
mentioned him to Heinemann's UK management.

The first question was, is he silk? Well no, Hudson had told them,
but he was young and brilliant. He went on to explain how
impressed he was with Turnbull's representation of media pro-
prietor Kerry Packer, who had been subject during the Costigan
Royal Commission to inaccurate suppositions and conspiracy
theories concerning his involvement in murder, illegal drugs and
organized crime.[12] Hudson was ignored.

We want silk, was the order. In the end the QCs engaged were
not quite suited to this case. Heinemann went back to the idea of
Turnbull, someone with a bit of unorthodoxy, a capacity for hard
research, and more than a smidgen of drive beyond the call of duty.

Turnbull, thirty-two, had a rapport with Hudson's replacement
Sandy Grant, thirty-one, and not just because of their youthful
energy. Both had clocked up years of experience of the English
mentality – Turnbull at Oxford and the hirsute, bearded Grant at
Heinemann UK – which caused them to be under-awed by the
opposition, yet alert to the subtle tricks that would be played.
Grant's cynical humour and 'calm' complemented Turnbull's tough-
ness and ambition. Together, their personalities formed an unusual
but promising team with which Wright would now confront Her
Majesty's Government.[13]

Turnbull thought the dispute could be settled without resort to a
costly courtroom struggle. It didn't seem like an issue that Thatcher
would bother taking that far. But they had underestimated the
undercurrents and passions swirling around the case.

The British government's injunction action was set down to be
tried in the Equity Division of the Supreme Court of NSW in late
1986. In the meantime, Turnbull attempted to fix a settlement that
would avoid expensive litigation. In effect, this was a concession to
all the pessimistic advice he had been given: Wright could not hope
to win this case, not when the opposition had the near-limitless
resources of the government of a middle-power nation.

Turnbull tried reason, suggesting that the British government could oversee an edit of the book, which would remove contentious sections. That didn't work. On a visit to London, he met with the Treasury Solicitor John Bailey. The meeting ended in a confrontation, which drew out the two men's less flattering characteristics. Turnbull felt patronized and lived up to the meaning of his surname by becoming belligerent. Turnbull showed his hand in a precursor to any prospective trial strategy by offering to delete passages the government didn't like. Bailey said no, they objected to the whole book.

Turnbull asked why there could not be negotiation as there had been with Tory MP Rupert Allason (alias Nigel West) over his book, *A Matter of Trust: MI5 1945–72*, which Arthur Martin had helped him with with MI5 documents and information. In that example, the government had locked up publication with an injunction before sitting down with the author and throwing out offending paragraphs. After that, the book was allowed to be published. Feeling that Bailey was lecturing him rather than answering the query, Turnbull retorted that Bailey should seek advice from his client, meaning Thatcher, and Sir Robert Armstrong, the Cabinet Secretary and the prime minister's 'principal adviser on Intelligence matters', who would be expected to partake as the government's 'front person' in any trial.

Bailey responded by saying that he was in 'a special position', implying to Turnbull that he didn't need to consult them. Bailey then, according to Turnbull's account, said Wright should seek medical advice before he came to court, suggesting he 'would get no quarter in the witness box on account of his ill-health'.

Turnbull pawed the ground.

'You tell Armstrong from me,' he snorted, 'that whatever happens to Wright, he will be politically ruined by this case.'

'Well, young man,' he said, patting Turnbull on the back as he showed him out of his office, 'we'll see what you're like on your feet, won't we?'

The British government's message was uncompromising. The book was not to be published. It would tolerate, just, publications by journalists who had been fed information by insiders at MI5 or MI6. But it would not tolerate insiders putting their names to their own books. There had been precedents for this, but they had received full government approval or encouragement in advance.

It was a debatable delineation, but the Thatcher line seemed to be that no mavericks like Wright could be allowed to publish. It would mean other British agents might be encouraged to write also. She did not want British Intelligence acting like the CIA. Presumably this was because every insider in government – not just in Intelligence – might be inspired to scribble their version of the handling of every major issue from the sinking of the Argentinian ship the *Belgrano* in the Falklands War to selling arms to Iraq. If this was allowed, the prime minister's judgement and actions on everything would be queried as if Britain were some kind of unique perfect democracy.

How, Thatcher's argument seemed to ask, could a modern government perform with propriety under the pressures of such scrutiny? She was not running the US, which might believe in open government. This was Great Britain, which had managed extremely well as a great world power for 400 years, with conditions of secrecy paramount. The issue was now a matter of principle, and Margaret Hilda Thatcher had always been tenacious about principles, particularly hers.

THE DEFENCES

Thus rebuffed by Bailey and Thatcher, Turnbull began working on three defences. First that *Spycatcher* disclosed evidence of MI5's criminal activities, and that an Australian court could not suppress it. Second, that if MI5 was penetrated by the Russians in the way Wright was claiming, then the book would not be doing harm. On the contrary, it might be doing good. Third, and by far the strongest argument, was the fact that a great deal of *Spycatcher*'s information had already been published, particularly in *Their Trade is Treachery*. How could it then be considered confidential and worthy of protection? Heinemann were uncomfortable with this, for the lawyer would try to prove that *Spycatcher* offered nothing knew. However, the publisher bowed to the agreement to let Turnbull handle the case his way.[14]

All the time, Turnbull's senses of logic and instinct were working overtime telling him that the case, against everything he had been told, was winnable. He, too, got on with Wright and was impressed

by him. He was believable. He had a presence and a delivery on the
espionage topic that reeked of credibility and integrity. Like Hudson,
Turnbull was in no doubt that Wright sincerely believed he was
correct. His intelligence, vehemence, and obsessive nature were
infectious to the point that Turnbull was very keen to represent him
and win for him, even if he didn't share his passion for ridding
British Intelligence of moles working for the Russians.

The Australian lawyer also liked the idea of taking on Thatcher.
He had his lawyer wife Lucy (the daughter of top Australian QC
and ex-Liberal Attorney-General, Tom Hughes) and Greengrass
as invaluable support. The latter had devoured just about every
published tome on Intelligence, so Turnbull cajoled him into
cross-referencing *Spycatcher* with previously published works.[15]

The next six months were taken up with legal manoeuvring as
each party questioned the other side on points of fact (interro-
gatories) and attempted to get certain documents from the opposing
side (discovery of documents). During this period (in fact, throughout the case), Turnbull kept open the seemingly fair compromise
option of an offer to edit the book so that passages contravening the
Official Secrets Act could be deleted. But the plaintiff stunned the
defence by suggesting that only three chapters of the 100,000-word
Spycatcher manuscript would be allowable, apart from the odd
sentence in the rest. It was clear now to the defence that Thatcher
was serious about following through without compromise.

43. VICTOR THE VULNERABLE

INSURANCE AGAINST RISK

In September 1986, Greengrass was able to speak with his CIA contact about Rothschild's action in getting Wright and Pincher together so that *Their Trade is Treachery* could be written. Greengrass looked upon his disclosure as a sort of insurance policy. He did not know what was behind Rothschild's action, so he thought it important to tell someone else, particularly a figure in a position of authority. He could not go to anyone in British Intelligence, so he chose a foreigner he could trust, whom he regarded as a friend.[1]

The CIA man's reaction was one of amusement. He wondered if it was a deniable operation by the British Government. Greengrass was happy for the CIA to formally request an explanation from MI5.

Not long before the Sydney trial against Wright and Heinemann was to begin, the request from the CIA was seen by MI5's chief, who passed it to the government via Sir Robert Armstrong, now head of the civil service and Secretary to the Cabinet. Sooner or later, probably after the Sydney trial, Rothschild would be asked for 'a please explain'.[2]

Rothschild's prepared argument would be that he had been trying to avoid a potentially explosive situation with Wright if he had attempted to get published without someone like Rothschild himself, or 'the authorities', supervising the direction of his writings. He would say he had merely put Wright together with a writer (Pincher) who was safe from the government's point of view.

Had Rothschild breached the Offical Secrets Act? It was a question the government could not ignore. A police inquiry was possible.

Rothschild was shaken. His solo, covert action was now known by 'the authorities'. He would sweat over every aspect of the Sydney case, from discovery of documents to evidence that would be submitted by the defence. They just might include such things as private correspondence between Wright and himself, or Wright and Pincher, which could be damaging.[3]

Rothschild worried over the fact that his involvement in putting Pincher and Wright together would become public, thus exposing him to media and press questions about the reasons for such an action.

Furthermore, Rothschild's diversionary tactic had ended now in exactly the situation he had tried to avoid, a tell-all book with several embarrassing references to Rothschild. On top of this there was the nagging possibility of a police inquiry which he would not be able to cover up and which would raise further questions in the public mind. He could, however, be sure that the nature and content of the inquiry could be suppressed if, and only if, he could avoid having charges laid against him.

It was not yet a nightmare, but events out of his control in far-away Sydney were making him nervous. He probably regretted bringing Wright to Britain and introducing him to Pincher. If Wright had been appeased, perhaps by a private payment to him, or even an investment in his stud, would it have been a better proposition for Rothschild? Perhaps not, for then it would have looked like a cover-up.

Even Wright, in his adulation of his great and powerful friend, may have begun to reassess him and his motives. Rothschild was aware also that any payment would not have stopped Wright in his quest. His determination to correct the record on Hollis and Soviet penetration went beyond mercenary considerations. Even if hush money had been paid out, it may have leaked to the press, which would have led to further questions. Possibly, Rothschild mused, it would have been better to have left Wright in Tasmania. Then again, how could he have supervised Wright's compilation of that 'List of Achievements' at MI5, which was his 'proof' that he could not have spied for Russia?

Wright was the only person in British Intelligence who would have, or could have done that for him without questioning his motive. Without the list, Rothschild would have felt vulnerable to the media snipers who were suggesting by innuendo and clever devices to avoid libel that he was the Fifth Man.

The only consolation, so far, was that for six years he had managed to place the centre of attention concerning Soviet MI5 moles on Roger Hollis. While everyone concentrated on him, there would be less time devoted to considering Rothschild's own past. Even *Spycatcher*, from what he had gleaned about it, was focusing on Hollis, while attempting to show Rothschild himself in a good, positive, anti-Soviet light.

But, he wondered, had Wright in his naïvety gone too far in his references to him? If some of that original chapter on him had made it back into *Spycatcher* that could reflect badly on Rothschild, no matter how complimentary Wright might be.

He had removed the offending chapter in 1980, but that might not stop Wright and his collaborator. Rothschild, more than most, appreciated Wright's awesome, accurate recall. He had demonstrated this as early as 1958 at MI5, and nearly thirty years later he had shown it again in the minute detail he was able to provide in his original 10,000-word document, and in general conversation.[4] Wright would have no trouble reconstructing the information on Rothschild from the deleted chapter.

It all added up to Rothschild feeling increasingly vulnerable. For the first time since Blunt's admission to being the Fourth Man in 1964, he would not be able to control events. He had not contacted Wright since 1980 and did not intend to do so now.

He then considered whether or not his lawyers should make representation to the Treasury Solicitor's Office in order to suppress any references to him in court, or to at least keep them in camera, if that were possible. The drawback was that such action on Rothschild's behalf would make people more suspicious of his motives. Any move he made now would be scrutinized.

The revelation to the Government about his links to *Their Trade is Treachery* capped a bad year for him. Rothschild had been ill for most of it. The anxiety surrounding events about to happen in Sydney would only exacerbate his poor health.

THE LEAK

A valuable leak for the defence occurred in the pissoir of London's Garrick Club, and remarkably carried to Sydney only days before the trial was to commence. Attorney-General, Michael Havers, had apparently unburdened himself to companions concerning the case, and one of them had told a friend of Turnbull.[5]

Havers had said that he had persuaded Australian prime minister, Bob Hawke, that the Australian Government should 'give evidence in support of the UK'. It was even suggested that Australia might intervene in proceedings and 'take over the running' from the UK.

Turnbull was disturbed by this news. He soon found that Thatcher had been in touch with Hawke, who had agreed to see what he could do to help the British government's case. It was a tricky crossing of national boundaries, where governments were considering collusion. Hawke passed the problem with alacrity to the appropriate minister, Australian Attorney-General Lionel Bowen.

Turnbull followed the ball and wrote to Bowen saying that in his view Thatcher 'made a false statement to the House of Commons in March 1981 concerning the investigation of Roger Hollis'. Turnbull went on: 'In other words the efforts to suppress this book are essentially political efforts to prevent political embarrassment for the government and its advisers.'

Again, he was unwittingly running on the inaccurate premise that Thatcher had been misled into a cover-up.

'Your [Labour] government has built upon the achievements of the Whitlam government in showing the world that Australia is a truly independent nation,' Turnbull went on, banging a jingoistic drum. 'Australia should not run to Mrs Thatcher's whistle. It should not protect Britain from the consequences of its past crimes . . .'[6]

This bold Turnbullese was a bit rich but it seemed to work. The defence received an affidavit by Michael Codd, the Australian Cabinet Secretary. It was such a weak document that Turnbull realized the Australian government's support for Thatcher was going to be no more than window-dressing.[7]

Turnbull's journalistic background – primarily as a writer on legal matters for *Bulletin* – gave him another edge in the case. He was able to court the local and British press in a way that must have infuriated the plaintiff. The Australians would naturally support him against the British government, who were easily beat up as the bullying Poms, who were attempting to suppress freedom of speech. As it turned out, the British press were just as supportive. They loved, first, a spy story, and second, a chance to upset Thatcher, who had been in power for almost eight years.

Some of the journalists – from the *Guardian* (Richard Norton-Taylor), the *Observer* (David Leigh, who would be inspired by the trial's revelations to write the book, *The Wilson Plot*), the *Independent* (represented by Robert Milliken), and Channel 4 (David Walter and Trish Lawton) – were liberal to left-wing. The others from the BBC (Hong Kong correspondent, Brian Barron), *The Times* and *Financial Times* (represented by Stephen Taylor and Chris Sherwell respectively) were ready to fall in behind the Wright–Turnbull freedom of speech line.

Somehow, the UK government had managed to unite against it one of the strangest ever collection of journalistic bedfellows, most of whom had never before supported what was essentially Wright's far-right-wing, anti-communist cause.

Others such as the *Express* (represented by Ross Benson), and the *Sun*, predictably, were set to record the case as Aussie Pom-bashing, no matter how events unfolded. It made good copy and would be pro-Thatcher, more or less.

Turnbull had another advantage. He would not be afraid to be unorthodox and use a media conference, should the need arise. Such a tactic – legitimate but risky – for lawyers in Britain and Australia without strong media contacts or background would be unthinkable.

THE APPARENT MISSING LINK

Over a drink in a Sydney wine bar on the eve of the trial, Greengrass informed an astonished Turnbull about Rothschild's involvement behind the scenes in getting *Their Trade is Treachery* published.

Turnbull was concerned. He was trying to present Wright as an 'idealist', but the £30,000 deal to supply Pincher with information about Hollis and other matters seemed to the lawyer to make his client look 'rather greedy, if not grubby'.[8]

Greengrass explained the Rothschild/Wright connection. The 'incredibly socially insecure' Wright had never felt welcome at MI5 with its 'Establishment people', until Victor came along.

'He was very kind to Peter,' Greengrass told Turnbull. 'He introduced him to a lot of people, made a fuss of him. In return Peter kept Victor posted about what was going on at MI5.'

Turnbull asked if Wright was allowed to do this.

'Peter says that Furnival Jones authorized him to talk to Rothschild,' Greengrass replied. 'Victor was always part of that intelligence world, but a little outside of it. He seemed to have been close to everyone, but no one . . . When Blunt was exposed in 1979 everyone was looking for the next mole. Rothschild thought he might be accused . . .'[9]

Greengrass expanded on the Rothschild/Wright/Pincher links. Turnbull wondered if Rothschild could go to prison for his responsibility over *Their Trade is Treachery*. The lawyer's quick conclusion about Rothschild's behaviour was the most logical one, given what he had been told:

'I think it's a conspiracy,' he said. 'I think the government wanted *Their Trade is Treachery* published. I think Rothschild was given the job of organizing it.'[10]

This was Wright's strong belief, and Turnbull wanted it to be correct because it made his case stronger. Rothschild fitted beautifully as the missing link in Wright's claim that *Their Trade is Treachery* was a secret UK government deniable operation to 'get the Hollis business out in the open'.

Turnbull was acting like any good advocate should. He was taking his client's advice, when it seemed appropriate, to help win the case. But the advice and Turnbull's conclusion was wrong, as was Wright's obsession with Hollis being a Soviet agent.

The lawyer rang Pincher in London to test the conspiracy theory.

'How did the government get the typescript of *Their Trade is Treachery*?' he asked.

Pincher refused to tell him. They had a stilted discussion and in it, Turnbull revealed he knew about the Rothschild connection. He warned Pincher that 'Labour MPs would be calling for the prosecution' of Rothschild and him for 'corrupting Peter Wright'.

'That's not true,' Pincher replied. 'Wright approached me in the first place . . .'

'Rothschild organized it, didn't he?'

'Not Wright's approach. He did that himself. If anyone has been corrupted, it's me.'

'I can tell you there will be questions about it in Parliament.'

They rang off, tension thick across the long-distance line. Turnbull had got confirmation of Greengrass's tale, but not of a deniable operation. Once more, circumstances appeared to back Wright's conspiracy theory.

Turnbull's false assumptions seemed to have more weight. They helped propel the energetic young advocate into the courtroom. He was now convinced a victory for Wright was closer to a probability than a possibility.

44. CAUGHT WITHOUT EQUITY

THE TRIAL BEGINS

The packed gallery in the hot, bunker-like court 8D on 18 November, the first day of cross-examination in the case HM Attorney-General v. Heinemann and Wright, seemed bored. In the main, the audience included the usual run of pensioners, lawyers from other cases in the building on Queens Square, Sydney, journalists, and friends and family of the participants.

They were watching three Oxford graduates – Turnbull, the circuitous examiner, Armstrong, the circumlocuting witness in the box, and Theo Simos, QC, who was acting for the plaintiff. Simos seemed a first-rate choice by the British government. He was one of Australia's top equity lawyers, that part of the law which is not covered by statutes or Common Law. Simos had topped his post-graduate degree at Oxford with another at Harvard. They didn't come much brighter than this second-generation Australian Greek.

This day, all eyes were on Armstrong. He was an unusual animal, this head of the British civil service, not often seen in captivity, except as fictionally portrayed by Sir Humphrey Appleby in the television sit-com *Yes, Prime Minister*. Turnbull himself noted:

'In the flesh he looked fit and confident, but his face lacked the fine features one normally associates with a well-bred Englishman. He had none of the mannered effeminacy that is so common with Englishmen of his background. He looked and talked like a tough and practical man of the world.'[1]

In short, to Turnbull, Armstrong looked more like an Australian, and his actions in recently smashing a press photographer's camera were very Merv Hughes. But that is where the rugged Aussie comparison would end. Armstrong was the gracious, polite Eton-educated son of a head of the Royal Academy of Music. Sir Robert himself was a first-class musician, who had considered it as a career. He also wrote 'beautiful' prose according to critics and colleagues alike. He was particularly skilled at writing in a detailed, ambiguous way, which would allow different interpretations of meaning, depending on the moment and the reader.

It was a necessary asset for a civil servant wanting to rise in the bureaucracy's paper jungle. Armstrong had also built a reputation as the prime minister's fixer, someone who could do the difficult behind-the-scenes negotiation needed to settle an issue. He had done this on several occasions such as during the controversy over the banning of trade unions at GCHQ (Government Communications HQ at Cheltenham), and in organizing big pay rises for civil servants.

Armstrong was viewed in Whitehall and by impartial observers as one of the finest British civil servants since the Second World War. He had worked with equal dexterity for Labour and Conservative governments and was respected by all the leaders he had served. By necessity, Sir Robert was a secret manipulator *par excellence*. He also knew much about being the fall guy for Thatcher, especially in an incident, the Westland Helicopter contract affair, which had politically damaged her rival Michael Heseltine. He had then appeared before a parliamentary committee and acquitted himself well. Sir Robert would have fallen on his sword for Thatcher, although he didn't need to in the end. He had shown himself to be capable of handling cross-examination and therefore suitable for the *Spycatcher* trial.[2]

But the quizzing he had endured in the Westland Affair was fine for the confines of the Palace of Westminster where his courteous smudging of events were appropriate in achieving the exoneration of Number 10 in leaks that had wounded Heseltine. It was a long way from the court he was now in where inspired leaks, his verbal gift for ambiguity and gymnastic writing talents might not be so effective.

The outcome would depend on the flexibility of the court and the presiding judge, and most importantly the ability and determination of the examiner. He had to be able to find his way through the maze of double-meanings, obfuscation and doubt.

The observers in the court were confused at first by Turnbull's approach, which seemed esoteric and leading nowhere, and disappointed by Armstrong's cautious defence. After all, he was the plaintiff's key witness. He should be more attacking and forthright. What was going on here?

The early saving grace in the low-key drama appeared to be Justice Philip Ernest Powell, fifty-six, a Justice of the Supreme Court since 1977. The style of the Equity Court as opposed to, say, the Criminal Court in Britain and Australia was very different because there was no jury. This allowed the judge to throw off the normal restriction of having to take care not to sway a jury by dialogue with the opposing parties' counsels. Propositions could be questioned and argued. A smart, sharp, well-read judge could get involved. In fact, it was better if he or she did, so that complications could be ironed out and clarifications made in order to move proceedings along at a productive rate and so that the best final judgement could be made.

The Equity Court in a case like this was no place for a dilatory judge, or one that had done no homework or who understood little British history. Powell, known as Perc to friends, was no dill. No one in the courtroom on either side knew his British history better. Nor was there anyone, apart from Greengrass, who would have a better grip on espionage literature by the time he brought down his judgement. Powell knew his Le Carré, which would be mandatory for understanding the post-war mood and atmosphere that had led over the decades to this public explosion of frustration over Her Majesty's government's secrets.

In a broad sense, Powell was an Anglophile, who had another advantage in handling this case. He knew something practical about spying himself. As a citizen soldier in the 1950s, he had been a captain in the Royal Australian Intelligence Corps.[3]

Yet even he would have been hard-pressed to know where Turnbull's early meandering was heading. The defence lawyer deliberately started peripherally by discussing Catherine Massiter, a former MI5 officer who alleged in a 1985 TV interview that MI5 had been bugging left-wing trade unions, members of anti-war groups and civil libertarians. A UK government inquiry held by Lord Bridge investigated allegations of illegal phone-tapping and found there had been no breaches of the law. This conclusion had been reached without giving reasons, and without making public any evidence. Armstrong suggested the public had to accept that the government had come to the correct conclusion.

Turnbull used this opening to get Armstrong to agree that the public had to accept such government proclamations as a matter of faith.

TURNBULL: It is a matter of trust, isn't it?

ARMSTRONG: It's a matter of trust, to coin a phrase.

The defence lawyer then launched into an analysis of Rupert Allason's book, *A Matter of Trust: MI5 1945–72*. Turnbull aimed to challenge the government intention to disallow the publication of anything a former spy wrote or caused to be written on the basis it could damage national security. He eventually angled the debate to *Spycatcher* itself, but could not shake the dogged Sir Robert.

ARMSTRONG: I would argue that publication by Mr Wright, even of some information that is already in the public domain in other ways, could cause detriment to the national security of the United Kingdom.

TURNBULL: All of it?

ARMSTRONG: All of it could.[4]

After this exchange, the intercourse warmed up. Turnbull set out to show that when the government ran its blue editing pencil through *A Matter of Trust* it had not removed all data from MI5 informants. These MI5 characters, the most senior being Arthur Martin, had not been charged with breaching the Official Secrets Act. Turnbull got half way, squeezing an admission out of Armstrong that only those matters (in the original manuscript of *A Matter of Trust*) which the government and Allason's lawyers agreed should be removed were taken out. This meant that a lot of breaches of the Official Secrets Act – information from Martin and other agents – could have been left in.

Turnbull had an opening at last. But to win the case he wanted to lay bare not just the illogical anomalies in the way alleged breaches of the Act had been handled in the 1980s particularly, but also the character of the government which did the handling. Encouraged by Wright, and fortified by his own sense of logic, Turnbull felt certain that the British government had acted duplicitously over the publication of *Their Trade is Treachery*.

If he could prove that the government had been deceitful or

misleading he would strengthen his case that it was covering up 'past crimes', and that there was no reason why the old hat information in *Spycatcher* should not be published. It was a brash approach, not expected by the plaintiff.

THE PARTIALLY CLAD CIVIL SERVANT

Turnbull became sharper as the morning progressed. He forced Armstrong to deny on four occasions in the space of a minute that he had misled the court over what had been taken out of *A Matter of Trust*. With the witness thus exposed, the defence lawyer lifted the examination to a high plain, questioning the very integrity of the government.

TURNBULL: Sir Robert, how high in your scale of values is telling the truth?

ARMSTRONG: It reckons very high.

The cross-examination went on for a minute in this vein and ended with the witness saying that he had 'fortunately not been put into a situation' where he was forced to say something that was 'untrue'.[5]

Turnbull pounced. He showed Sir Robert a letter he had written to William Armstrong (no relation), the Sidgwick & Jackson publisher of *Their Trade is Treachery*. In the letter Sir Robert wrote that he wanted to read copies of the book when, in fact, he had already secretly obtained a copy of the manuscript.

The defence lawyer was now able to move powerfully along, showing with a concrete example that Armstrong was representative of a government which could mislead. In the history of any government this was not an earth-shattering revelation. In fact, it was merely demonstrating a seedy aspect of how most governments operate from time to time. But in the context of the case, it allowed Turnbull to throw doubt on the plaintiff's motives and actions.

Armstrong had been cornered. He became hesitant. He dissembled a little. The public gallery was stunned, while one or two of the British media shook their heads and laughed derisively.

Armstrong defended himself by saying that in formally asking for copies of the book from the publisher he was protecting the person who had secretly given the government the manuscript. Turnbull left no one in doubt that Armstrong had deceived and misled the publisher by writing an untruth.

The lawyer pushed, harried and shoved his way through a thesaurus of definitions covering what was meant by untruth. Just when Justice Powell was about to step in a second time to avoid getting bogged down in semantics, an extraordinary exchange took place.

TURNBULL: What is the difference between a misleading impression and a lie?

ARMSTRONG: A lie is a straight untruth.

TURNBULL: What is a misleading impression – a sort of bent untruth?

ARMSTRONG: As one person said, it is perhaps being economical with the truth.[6]

The gallery was amused. The remark eased the tension. It was not original, but Armstrong could claim it as his after this day. He would be remembered for it, and the phrase would become part of the English language. It would be repeated, with variations forever, and always with a little knowing chuckle – creating just the sense that the British civil service chief had intended.

But it didn't end there. In the exchange that followed, Turnbull seemed to be giving him every chance to say that he would not lie under oath. Armstrong avoided saying that, almost as if he was covering himself with this tricky advocate just in case he had another googly for him, which would expose his wicket once more. Perhaps the witness was, in a perverse way, being honest. He wasn't going to say he would never tell an untruth under oath, in case he was forced to protect a supplier of pilfered documents by telling, well, an untruth.

Just before the luncheon adjournment, Turnbull suggested that the Attorney-General, Sir Michael Havers, had *not* been advised that *Their Trade is Treachery* should not be restrained by an injunction (as *A Matter of Trust* was).

ARMSTRONG: Why are you putting that to me?

TURNBULL: Because if he received that advice he received it from somebody that should have not got through first year law.

The defence lawyer was now running on a tone of incredulity and the oft-stated haughty presumption rather than fact. He had no evidence that the Attorney-General had not received 'such patently mistaken advice'. In the back of Turnbull's mind was his Wright-influenced belief that *Their Trade is Treachery* had been a deniable operation, which he assumed had been organized at Thatcher's behest by Rothschild. Turnbull's logic said that Armstrong was now fulfilling this type of operation by denying it.

However, Armstrong made it clear that his own advice to Thatcher on the book was that it should not be published as it was. This hit the conspiracy theory for one bounce over the mid-wicket fence, if not six, so Turnbull did not pursue it. Instead, the defence lawyer conducted his questioning in such a way as to imply to the court that Sir Robert was the ignorant fall guy, who had been selected by the true plaintiff – Attorney-General Havers – to filibuster and dissemble through the case. Turnbull went back to his deniable operation theory.

TURNBULL: You and the Prime Minister and the Security Service agreed to let Pincher write the book about Hollis so that this affair would come out in the open through the pen of a safely conservative writer rather than some ugly journalist of the left?

ARMSTRONG: It is a very ingenious conspiracy theory and it is quite untrue.

TURNBULL: Totally untrue?

ARMSTRONG: Totally untrue.[7]

It mattered little that Armstrong's denial was factual or that he himself may even have wanted an injunction against the Rothschild-inspired Pincher/Wright tome. It was even of less importance that the Thatcher/Havers strategy had worked concerning *Their Trade is Treachery*. They decided not to stop it, and to instead have the Prime Minister comment on it in Parliament soon after publication. She gave it such a rotten review, by saying that her advice was that Hollis was not a spy, that the book did not have the sales success expected, although it remained 'high in the best-seller list for several weeks'. The publisher had to remainder 11,000 copies of the first edition hard-cover. Such was the relatively new Prime Minister's integrity in the eyes of the public that had she reviewed it favourably or neutrally it most likely would have been top of the best-seller list for some time.[8]

All this was lost in the mist of doubt and conspiracy in the over-heated Sydney court-room. Turnbull had set up such an image of dishonesty on the part of the British government that there was little apparent credit in Armstrong's responses. He fell back increasingly on the argument that the decision now to stop *Spycatcher*'s publication was not his but that of the Attorney-General. This prompted some legitimate legal mischief on Turnbull's part.

'If Armstrong was not telling the truth over Havers' role, then we should ensure Havers is properly humiliated over this ludicrous advice [not to suppress *Their Trade is Treachery*],' Turnbull thought at the end of the first day's cross-examination. 'If Havers is a man of some pride, he will insist that Armstrong set the record straight.'[9]

It had been a very good day for the Defence.

45. PLAINTIFF FOR THE DEFENCE

ON BARON GROUND

Turnbull and Greengrass went for a cathartic walk around prestigious Rose Bay on Sydney Harbour on the evening after the successful first day's cross-examination of Armstrong. Greengrass tried to dissuade Turnbull from drawing such a long shot over the conspiracy theory involving Rothschild, the government and Pincher.[1]

Their media friends thought it too far-fetched, Greengrass informed him. When they returned home, Turnbull asked his wife Lucy to join them in thrashing out the theory. They discussed Jonathan Aitken's letter to Thatcher which asked her to clean out MI5 because of the Hollis legacy. Turnbull thought she could suffer no damage by following through on Aitken's recommendation, and then making a full public statement, which would include an assurance that nothing like that would happen again. Greengrass refuted this by saying that Australians and Americans might behave that way, but not the British. They were dedicated to secrecy for its own sake.

They turned to the question of the Rothschild connection. Turnbull now had his own mini-obsession, suggesting that his Intelligence background would make him likely to carry out an authority-backed deniable operation. Greengrass said this theory was based on assumptions about Rothschild and suggested they needed an admission of some sort from him.

They agreed that Wright had to be cajoled or bullied into speaking about Rothschild, whom he was most reluctant to discuss. Lucy suggested they should stir the Labour Opposition to call for Rothschild's prosecution. This, she surmised, would force the

Government to respond by saying they were going to investigate him, which in turn would cause him to defend himself, hopefully on the record.[2]

MORE EXAMS

The next morning, 19 November, saw the plaintiff seeking leave to appeal against Powell's directive that it should provide documents about *Their Trade is Treachery*, *A Matter of Trust* and several other books which had previously published data included in *Spycatcher*. This was rejected, much to a fatigued Turnbull's relief and the cross-examination continued in the afternoon, with the gallery now over-flowing because of the media attention the trial had attracted.

Turnbull worked on the knowledge that the CIA, which collected by far the majority of the West's Intelligence, allowed much more in the way of authorized books than British Intelligence. But Armstrong insisted that the Americans – the CIA and the NSA – would think less of MI5 if books like *Spycatcher* were allowed to be published. The arguments to and fro in the court were based on logic. Armstrong's seemed to be missing.

He again appeared the fall guy. It was as if Thatcher were at the back of the court room whispering orders in her familiar tone of honeyed huskiness. We must show Ron and George that we, at least, do not have a sieve for a Service.

Turnbull was getting nowhere, so he switched to the topic of the *World in Action* programme of July 1984. The defence hammered the fact that the British 'authorities' did nothing to stop the programme even though they had prior knowledge of its contents, which included Wright divulging official secrets. Turnbull managed once more to highlight the inconsistency of the government's decisions.

That evening he decided it was time to pressure Wright into talking about the Rothschild connection. Greengrass, the 'good cop', was sent in to discuss it with Wright and his wife Lois for half an hour before Turnbull, acting the 'bad cop', appeared.

Wright clutched his whisky glass, a permanent companion during the ordeal of the trial, and claimed that he didn't want his long-time friend involved because he was old, ill and that it might kill him.

Turnbull got tough and said it was a choice between spilling everything about his greatly respected mate, or he would lose the case. Wright kept reaching for the bottle to replenish his glass and pleading against disclosure about Victor. Turnbull pushed back his falling lock aggressively and repeatedly told him it was a must.

After a great deal of debate, according to Turnbull, Wright fell silent and nursed his glass. He drained it and then raised it in a toast. His voice had a fateful tone of resignation.

'Oh well, poor dear Victor,' Wright said. 'Throw him to the wolves.'[3]

THE BIG CHILL

At midday on the third day, Thursday 20 November, Turnbull introduced Rothschild's name. Armstrong's responses turned dead cold, a fact not lost on the audience, which fell silent during the exchange. The defence lawyer opened by asking if Rothschild, over time, had 'considerable contact with the government and considerable confidence placed in him by the government?' Armstrong agreed he had.

ARMSTRONG: He certainly has been. He is now getting on in years and has not been very well and is rather more remote from things.

TURNBULL: Did Victor Rothschild discuss the publication of *Their Trade is Treachery* with you prior to publication?

ARMSTRONG: No.

TURNBULL: You are sure of that?

ARMSTRONG: I am sure of that.

TURNBULL: Have you received any reports from the Security Service concerning Victor Rothschild's role in the publication of *Their Trade is Treachery*.

ARMSTRONG: I would not wish to answer these questions in open court since any information I have on these matters is confidential.[4]

Turnbull knew that Greengrass's CIA connections had made sure that Armstrong would have had a report. The defence lawyer protested but Justice Powell led the court in a closed one-hour session.

As it turned out, Armstrong was no more forthcoming than he

had been in the open session. However, Rothschild's name had popped up. The more astute members of the British press were alerted and ready to probe for more detail. But none was forthcoming, yet. Still, it was not difficult to judge that Rothschild was very much out of favour with Armstrong and the Thatcher government.

In the afternoon of 20 November, Turnbull swung hard into Thatcher's statement to the House after the publication of *Their Trade is Treachery* on 26 March 1981. Referring to leads (which suggested but did not prove there was a mole inside MI5) she said:

'None of those leads identified Sir Roger Hollis or pointed specifically or solely in his direction. Each of them could also be taken as pointing to Philby or Blunt.'

Armstrong ended up agreeing that this part of the statement was incorrect. The dates were wrong to make Blunt responsible after he left MI5 in 1945, or Philby after he was ineffective within MI6 after 1951. Again all the consideration went to the argument that there had to be a mole inside MI5. It was not the place to use lateral thinking and consider if there just might have been a mole *outside* MI5.

That evening Turnbull asked Wright if he thought Thatcher knew she was telling a lie. No, he replied with a chuckle, she was just saying what MI5 told her to. He implied that the politicians were puppets when it came to matters of Intelligence.[5]

THE KILLER INSTINCT

That night Turnbull returned to his office with Greengrass and the *Observer*'s David Leigh, who rang a contact in the office of Opposition leader Neil Kinnock in order to arrange a chat between him and Turnbull. The defence lawyer argued that the Labour leader should humiliate Michael Havers in Parliament about his incompetence over not slapping an injunction on *Their Trade is Treachery*.[6]

Kinnock was ambivalent. He suggested that the person behind it all was Thatcher, not Havers. He pointed out that both Rothschild and Havers were ill. Like Wright, he worried that putting pressures on them might cause their deaths. Turnbull was so surprised at Kinnock's humanity that he made a callous, unfortunate joke about having to make sacrifices for the revolution. Why not start with

Havers and Rothschild?[7] Kinnock was not amused, but he saw a chance to needle Thatcher. He asked for copies of transcripts of Armstrong's evidence.

Turnbull's brashness was measured and, to a degree, calculated. He knew that GCHQ at Cheltenham would record his phone calls to London and that the government could have transcripts of his manipulative tactics outside the courtroom. Forcing issues was very much a part of his style, and he loved using the media and politicians to this end.

Later in the day (Thursday 20 November, British time – it was eleven hours behind Sydney) Kinnock asked in Parliament why Thatcher had not sought an injunction against *Their Trade is Treachery*. Thatcher was well prepared. She avoided answering by saying that it would be 'inappropriate' for her to respond while the Wright case was going on. Havers answered a similar query the same way, thus for the time being not giving Turnbull any more advantages in court.

Thatcher was furious about Kinnock's intervention. The next day, Friday, a press secretary from Number 10 started using unattributable lobby briefings to accuse Kinnock of breaking the accepted bipartisan approach to security matters. It was even claimed that he could not be trusted with security matters, and consequently that he was unfit to be Prime Minister.[8]

Thatcher had struck a blow, but it was only the beginning.

PINCHER SQUEEZES BACK

On the evening of Saturday, 22 November, Turnbull rang Pincher at his Berkshire home. This time, the lawyer's tone was tougher. Pincher would be accused in court of corrupting Wright by offering him money, which would imply bribery.[9] Not surprisingly, the call ended acrimoniously.

Pincher was incensed. He 'called in' a former journalist colleague, Michael Evans, now Whitehall correspondent for *The Times*. One of Whitehall's great leakees had become the leaker.[10] Pincher disclosed how Wright had received 'many thousands of pounds' worth of royalties for *Their Trade is Treachery*. The story was a page one article in *The Times* on Monday the 24th.

'Until now,' it noted, 'it was believed that Mr Wright's sole motive for helping Mr Pincher . . . was that of a crusader exposing alleged traitors inside MI5 in an attempt to clean up British Intelligence. However, he had another motive, which was money . . .'

Further down the piece, it mentioned in passing 'a secret trip' which Wright made to Britain in August 1980, 'which was paid for by a good friend of his, Lord Rothschild, himself a former MI5 officer . . . The meeting between Mr Pincher and Mr Wright had been arranged by Lord Rothschild . . . *The Times* understands that Lord Rothschild telephoned him [Pincher] and asked if he would like to meet someone [Wright] who wanted to expose MI5 traitors . . .'[11]

This way, Pincher got in first on his and Rothschild's behalf before Turnbull could do any damage using Rothschild's name in or out of court, as he had threatened. At worst, the article made the embattled peer look like a meddler in MI5 affairs, and at best, a potty patriot. It happened to suit the Thatcher/Havers/MI5 position. They were so unamused by his linking of Pincher and Wright that they were now happy to have him exposed as an out-of-touch interferer.

Furthermore, Pincher's leak meant Wright now had a tarnished image: that of a greedy old spy, rather than an heroic old patriot, which was excellent for the government's case. It also made it tougher for Kinnock, who disliked being manipulated, to defend him.

Turnbull was furious, perhaps partly at himself for pushing Pincher. The lawyer, over-worked and tense, judged that it was time to wheel Wright out before the media for the full ritual sacrifice of Rothschild. He announced a press conference for 5 p.m. after court on Tuesday the 25th.

It would be *sub judice* to answer questions or stray from a prepared text. Turnbull was nervous as Wright delivered his remarks with a few stumbles. Looking at once resplendent and slightly ridiculous in his Aussie hat, the old spy was having his day in and out of court and revelling in what he saw as a revenge of sorts. Yet he, too, was unnerved to the point where his inability to pronounce his 'r's' was intensified. He was delivering a partial exposé of a man he held in higher regard than any other human being.

Wright knew better than anyone how much it would damage the ailing baron, who was sitting in his office at the Bank, devouring every line of press on the Sydney case. Rothschild's deep sonorous tones would have been ringing in his head: *Et tu, Peter?*

Wright first mentioned that the leak to *The Times* was an attempt to 'discredit' him in advance of evidence to be given in court that week. Then he told the story of the Rothschild-paid trip to London, and how Rothschild had persuaded him to get a book written rather than take his document to Thatcher. Pincher was then contacted.

'I was terrified of getting into trouble [a statement later retracted],' Wright added. 'Lord Rothschild assured me it was going to be all right. He told me that he would arrange for his Swiss [style] banking facilities to pay me half the royalties from the book.

'He knew I was in financial difficulties and I was grateful for his assistance . . . I could not conceive of him embarking on such a project without knowing it had the sanction, albeit unofficial, of the authorities. I sensed I was being drawn into an authorized but deniable operation, which would enable the Hollis affair and other MI5 scandals to be placed in the public domain as the result of an apparently inspired leak.

'All I know about Lord Rothschild and the ease with which *Their Trade is Treachery* was published leads me to the inescapable conclusion that the powers that be approved of the book.'

It was stunning stuff, and had the desired effect of swaying the media behind Wright again. The long-shot about deniable operations and a government conspiracy suddenly shortened. First reaction from analysts everywhere was that it seemed more than plausible. It appeared to explain, not everything, but quite a lot.

Turnbull the Bold had won more than a round, based again on a wrong premise. Time, distance and tactics were against the Government saving the contest. By following up on Wright's obsessions about Hollis, the defence lawyer was now basking in the false reflections from the wilderness of mirrors so skilfully crafted over nearly half a century by Philby, Blunt, and Modin, and gilded to greatest effect by the finest glacier of them all: the Fifth Man.

But had Rothschild, the master, now blinded himself?

FLEET STREET FEVER

On the other side of the world, the media reaction to the Rothschild revelations helped Wright's case, and Turnbull kept the pressure on by releasing one of Pincher's letters to the *Observer*'s David Leigh, who passed it on to Labour MP Dale Campbell-Savours. On Tuesday 25 November, he called for Rothschild to be prosecuted.[12]

The next day *The Times* editorialized: 'The [Rothschild/Wright/Pincher link] remains curious. Lord Rothschild surely has the responsibility to give his own version when the case is concluded in Sydney.'

With an attitude similar to the front-page article three days earlier and Armstrong's icy tone in court, the editorial referred to the 'noble lord' as an 'incurable busybody.'[13]

He was now a certified meddler. *The Times*' leader had confirmed it. Rothschild must have been greatly relieved by such an epithet. Under less worrying circumstances, it may have even given him a good chuckle. He could live with it. He could even work that back quickly to great patriot. It was a long way from the sobriquet of the Fifth Man, which he dreaded above all others.

However, the apparition of that Soviet agent, who had effectively died in 1963 when Philby defected, speedily reappeared in Parliament the same morning. First the Attorney-General, Michael Havers, himself under some pressure, announced that he was considering allegations that Rothschild had breached the Act. Then in a Commons motion protected by parliamentary privilege, Labour MP Brian Sedgemore called on Thatcher 'to state whether the security services ever carried out an investigation into suspicions . . . that he [Rothschild] was a Soviet spy and the Fifth Man.'

The motion 'infuriated' Conservative MPs, according to *The Times*' front page report. They alleged abuse of the Commons order paper to make innuendos against people outside Parliament.

A furious debate followed in the Commons. Apart from the wilderness of mirrors, the third Lord Rothschild had also created the politics of confusion. Thatcher on the hard right was currently frosty to him and was now joined by left-wingers. But many members of her Conservative back-bench were defending Rothschild. Labour and Conservative peers were also more or less united in expressing quiet, indignant support.

Pincher still admired him as did Wright, despite his recent knifing of his former close confidant, and they were firmly on the right. Kinnock on the left had just gone into bat for Wright and Turnbull in the centre. David Leigh, on the left, was working feverishly for Wright. There seemed no end to the very odd political bedfellows conjured by events in the Sydney court.

Underlining the strange alignments, Rothschild, a former covert member of the Communist Party and now an overt Labour peer, was given the chance for an honourable answer by the Conservative *Daily Telegraph* on the morning of the 27th. It politely ignored references to the Fifth Man:

'However well intentioned his motives, Lord Rothschild owes a public explanation of his role in bringing together Mr Peter Wright and Chapman Pincher . . . Since Lord Rothschild in the past, so far as we are aware, has never acted without some public interest in mind, it seems legitimate to demand what public interest was at stake in contriving an airing for Wright's thesis that there were traitors in high places at MI5 . . .'[14]

Turnbull's tactic of inciting the press was having an effect in stirring Parliament. The phones ran hot at Rothschild's Cambridge and St James's Place residences. Iain Walker of the *Daily Mail* got through at the Bank but the besieged Baron told him he wouldn't be speaking until after the trial, and any appeal, which inferred there would be no comment for possibly months, or even years. Walker received a letter confirming their conversation.

Rothschild never intended to comment, because nothing he said would justify his action, unless he went into detail about his concern that he would be accused of being the Fifth Man, which he knew would be dangerous. As it was, he was already seeing the accusation in print again.

On 26 November, Michael Evans reported:

'Lord Rothschild . . . was once quite incorrectly rumoured to be the Fifth Man in the famous Cambridge spy ring . . .'[15]

This remark would have been intended to kill rumours rather than hint that Rothschild was the Fifth Man. Yet it seemed to have the same effect as the Auberon Waugh piece in the *Spectator* in

1980. Other instant profiles in the press and media inserted careful references to his links to Blunt, Burgess and alluded to the as yet unexposed Fifth Man. Rothschild had been defending himself against prying journalists for nearly twenty years and he was almost at the point where he had to do something drastic.

It began in 1968. When Phillip Knightley was writing about Philby, he had tried to contact Rothschild, who had responded by having his lawyers deliver a written warning to the journalist about linking his name to those of Soviet agents. The probes and innuendo peaked in 1980. Then, earlier in 1986, lawyers reading the manuscript of a Blunt biography were worried about a sentence concerning Rothschild's recommendation of Blunt to MI5 in 1940. The lawyers thought Rothschild might sue.

Such was the climate of legal prudence or caution created, that he had been able to rely on his own lawyers and the self-censorship of others to keep the innuendo in check. But the situation was now different. No legal action could stop Wright, Turnbull and the court revelations, which he feared would fuel renewed speculation about him being a Soviet agent. They were outside Rothschild's reach, a cause of stress with little he could do about them.

He had his last-ditch insurance in his back pocket – the list of his achievements for MI5, which proved he couldn't have been a Soviet agent. But it wasn't quite the right time to leak it to the press or do anything else with it. He just had to continue his routine of going to his office at the Bank, and wait for the outcome of the trial.

His silence, though, had ramifications which caused him to rethink his strategy. Fleet Street had caught the espionage bug. If it couldn't get explanations then it had to have pictures. Early on the morning of 27 November, after reading the papers, Rothschild left his St James's Place flat and hurried to his chauffeur-driven car, but could not avoid Ros Drinkwater, a staff photographer at *The Times*, who snapped him, head down and annoyed. The chauffeur drove down to the Mall as usual, but Rothschild noticed that Drinkwater was following them, riding on the pillion of a motor-cycle.

'Do a U-turn,' Rothschild ordered his driver. 'Get rid of them!'

The chauffeur obeyed in an illegal manoeuvre. Drinkwater kept on the car's tail. Rothschild was furious. He repeated his order to lose Drinkwater. The car ran through a red light on the Embankment as it sped on a roundabout route to the Bank's building in the City.

Once in the private road outside the Bank, Rothschild jumped out and hurried for the door, flanked by N. M. Rothschild employees. In the melee that ensued, Rothschild slipped and fell to the ground. Another photographer – the *Mail on Sunday*'s David O'Neill – rushed forward to snap him. O'Neill was manhandled and his Nikon camera was smashed. Drinkwater arrived to see O'Neill in the centre of the scuffle. Several employees then tried to stop her. She jumped clear and got into a position to photograph O'Neill. The employees tried to stop her but she got the shots and ran for it.

The Times carried the story the next morning with a witty, telling caption under the O'Neill photo which said 'Their Trade is Photography.'[16]

Rothschild was shaken. Now the Bank, too, was in an ugly spotlight. He would have to consider fighting back sooner.

46. THE GHOST OF THE FIFTH MAN

MANY FINGERS POINTING

Rothschild stayed home on Friday, reluctant to run the gauntlet of press photographers waiting outside his St James's Place flat and at the Bank. The phone had not stopped ringing since before 7 a.m. Tess was filtering calls, as she had done all week. She had been forthright in her responses and, in her own brisk way, charming. She referred to herself as Tess, and dispensed with her title. She was not aiming at the common touch. Rather, shehad a lingering, deep-seated belief that peerages were out-dated.[1]

Victor was not ready to speak about Peter Wright, she told yet another Fleet Street query. It was not possible. Not while the Sydney trial was in progress.

'But, um, Lady Rothschild, it's not *sub judice* for him to,' the journalist persisted.

He wouldn't comment, she repeated. He really could not.

Victor relieved his wife and answered a call. The journalist asked if that was Lord Rothschild.

'He's gone out,' he thundered and slammed the phone down.

This happened a few times and the atmosphere made them both agitated. When Tess answered the phone again, she had lost patience. For the first time she was more brusque than brisk. Why, she asked, was everyone being so awful to Victor? The persistent reporter asked her for a comment. She advised him to say that she had total confidence in her husband.[2]

By midday on 28 November, he could not even leave the flat to go to lunch. He was both anxious and angry. Never before, not even in the pressurized days after Blunt was revealed as the Fourth Man, had he been under siege. There was a lack of respect out there now, partly engendered he suspected, by the irreverent tone of *The Times*, which had dared to call him a busybody.

They could see the waiting press vultures through a window. Tess was urging him not to be precipitate, so was his sister Miriam. The family was rallying. But the situation was becoming intolerable. He felt he had to do something otherwise he could see the vicious rumour-mongering continuing unabated.

Over the weekend of 29 and 30 November he began to consider asking for clearance from the government. It was an act of desperation, but he felt he was at that stage. Again, others close to him suggested he wait until the matter 'died down'. The press had been after Armstrong and Havers last week, and him this week. It would be someone else next week. But, Rothschild countered, they were not suffering innuendo about being Soviet agents.[3]

A family member pointed to the last paragraph in the *Sunday Times* profile, which carried no by-line but would have been written by Simon Freeman and Barrie Penrose: '. . . this weekend as Rothschild broods grumpily about the intrusion into his privacy, it is hard not to feel just a little sorry for him – whatever the truth.'[4]

He was getting the sympathy vote. Rothschild thought this might evaporate if he did nothing. More profiles and other references in the Sunday press helped make up his mind. On Monday and Tuesday, 1 and 2 December, he discussed the matter with lawyers, a couple of family members and two close friends. They were divided on what his response should be, but could tell he was determined.

On Wednesday he wrote to the *Daily Telegraph*, which had been kindest to him. He knew they would print his letter on the front page:

3 December 1986

Dear Editor and Readers

Since at least 1980 up to the present time there have been innuendos in the press to the effect that I am 'the fifth man.' In other words a Soviet agent.

The Director General of MI5 should state publicly that it has unequivocal, repeat unequivocal, evidence that I am not, and never have been a Soviet agent. If the regulations prevent him from making a statement which, in the present climate I doubt, let him do so through his legal adviser or through any other recognizably authoritative source.

I am constrained by the Official Secrets Act, but I write this letter lest it be thought that silence be an indication of anything other than complete innocence. I shall not make any other public statement to the Press until further notice.

Yours truly
Rothschild.

The paper's editor, Max Hastings, visited Rothschild's office to collect the letter, which was an international scoop in itself. The paper published the letter on Thursday, 4 December. It kept its fair and gentle approach to his lordship in an editorial. The letter was 'a *cri de coeur*' which could end Rothschild's 'trial by rumour, gossip and innuendo'.[5]

Thursday was question time in Parliament and Thatcher was called on to make a statement. She declined, saying that the government was considering the matter. MPs from both sides of the House sympathetic to Rothschild asked for a response as soon as possible. The prime minister was annoyed that the letter had not been cleared with Number 10, which would have given her time to consult with MI5. But Rothschild knew she would have objected to it appearing until after the Sydney court case. He judged that the pressures on him were too great to wait that long.

STOLEN LIMELIGHT

The media was now dominated by the Rothschild affair and the *Spycatcher* trial slipped off the TV screens and front pages of papers in Britain and Australia. The case lost its excitement when Armstrong (who admitted to Turnbull in private that he was 'just a fall guy') left the witness box. Tying up the legal ends didn't have the same drama for the court, the gallery or the media.

In Sydney, Turnbull, who had waited with bated breath for a statement by Rothschild about his links to Wright and Pincher, was mystified by his letter to the *Daily Telegraph*, which seemed a strange 'outburst'. The defence lawyer had been so totally consumed in the exhausting trial that he could not keep abreast of events in London.

However, the defence, which had taken the high ground in the first two weeks so effectively, looked certain to win the judgement, which would not be pronounced by Justice Powell for months.

Also on 4 December, a key point in Rothschild's list or evidence was leaked to Michael Evans at *The Times*. The story was placed beautifully, from Rothschild's point of view, on page one of the paper's edition of 5 December – just below the story of Thatcher's silence on Rothschild's plea for clearance.

Evans' article concerned the apparent 'nailing' of Philby in 1962, when Rothschild cajoled Flora Solomon into telling MI5 about her doubts about Philby. This was supposed to be part of Rothschild's unequivocal evidence that he was not, and never had been, a Soviet agent. The article, which was copied around the world in all major Western papers, in a flash turned around almost everybody who read it. Rothschild's image as a possible Soviet agent and potential traitor was wiped clean and replaced with that of heroic patriot.

The evidence was a bold bluff and Rothschild certainly would not have been showing anyone the list's contents now, if someone dared to ask for it. Its compilation by Wright would have looked very odd, if not suspicious.

The former head of both MI5 and MI6, Sir Dick White, was asked if he knew about evidence Rothschild claimed MI5 had. White said he knew nothing about it. The evidence did not exist in MI5 files in the form into which it had been compiled by Rothschild and Wright.[6]

However, White loyally added: 'I haven't the slightest doubt that Lord Rothschild was not a Soviet spy.'

White would have been compelled to say this. He had been unwittingly spilling vital information to Rothschild when he was running him as an agent in Iran and China, and for the rest of the time he was outside the service. Like Wright, White had confided vital aspects of British Intelligence in the important years, 1945 to 1963, and until the end of the 1960s at least.

Again, like Wright, he was not ready to face the possibility that Rothschild had ever been a Soviet spy. It would have reflected too much on White's discretion. By telling Rothschild secrets when he was not employed by MI5, White knew that he, too, was in breach of the Act.

Friday also saw Thatcher responding with a statement issued from Number 10:

> I have now considered more fully Lord Rothschild's letter in the *Daily Telegraph* yesterday in which he referred to innuendos that he had been a Soviet agent. I consider it important to maintain the practice of successive governments on security matters. But I am willing to make an exception on the matter raised in Lord Rothschild's letter.
>
> I am advised that we have no evidence that he was ever a Soviet agent.

The chill, one-line clearance had many friends of Rothschild, journalists and politicians frowning. Why was she so lacking in magnanimity? Could she not have added at least something about his record of MI5 service during the Second World War.

Apparently the advice from MI5 had influenced her tone. It did not want any further disclosures about Rothschild or the matter in general, because he had been a suspect and also, probably, because of the immunity deals fiasco. Thatcher could later afford to be generous to Rothschild concerning his behaviour when she was Minister for Education under Heath. In her autobiography she praised him, which was magnanimous considering that he was viewed as a Heath man and she and the former prime minister were rivals. But when it came to Rothschild's Intelligence background, that was different.

When pressed the next day, 6 December, in an interview Thatcher insisted she had been misinterpreted over her statement on Rothschild, but was no more forthcoming.

'That is clearance,' she replied. 'Leave it at that.'

It was not a time for rejoicing.

AN AFTER-GLOW OF INNUENDO

An after-glow of comment occurred in the Sunday press, the day Britain traditionally relaxes and imbibes reflective essays on the nation's affairs in more papers than any other country. The Rothschild issue was kept flickering in Sydney the following day, Monday 8 December, when Wright finally limped to the witness box to read his long-awaited statement.

He repeated much of the detail now public about Rothschild and his relationship with him. The court went *in camera* at one point when Rothschild's MI5 activities were raised. They included mention of his involvement in the overthrow of Iranian prime minister, Mohammed Mossadeq, in 1953, and his relationship with the Russian Peter Kapitza.[6]

Aware of the furore in London, Wright inserted a line when back in the open court, which had been stored in his memory since 1980 when he compiled Rothschild's evidence:

'I am absolutely certain that neither [Victor or Tess] at any time spied for Russia.'[8]

Rothschild would have wished he hadn't bothered. He also could have done without other remarks such as 'Victor was always very secretive' and 'he loved intrigue and conspiracies and was always involved in secret deals and arrangements, especially with politicians . . .'

Yet at least Wright had vouched for his former close companion, and the story was buried inside the papers. Thanks to Rothschild's own initiative, the storm had blown over. After nearly seven years of combat, he had again won a huge battle with the media and Parliament. There was still the likely publication of *Spycatcher* to come, but this would once more place the emphasis on Hollis and away from Rothschild.

He was drained and dispirited by the tension of it all. Yet the war was not over. On 17 December, the Metropolitan police at the direction of the DPP (Department of Public Prosecutions) began inquiries into Wright's allegations against Rothschild and Pincher concerning the links between the three which led to the publication of *Their Trade is Treachery*.

47 . NO RESPITE

THE POLICE DILEMMA

The police had a tough, even impossible task in trying to bring a prosecution against Rothschild and Pincher. There were many hurdles, such as the near impossibility of putting Wright in a British witness box, which would have been essential seeing that he had been the accuser. The only written accusatory evidence was his in the Sydney trial affidavit.

The kernel of the accusation was that Rothschild and Pincher had conspired to draw him into a deniable operation in which he would divulge secrets and breach the Act. As a starting point, he was demonstrably incorrect and the two accused could have called upon everyone from the Prime Minister, Attorney-General, and head of MI5 downwards to be subpoenaed to support their case.

Secondly, there was no proof that Rothschild had given Pincher secrets in this case. Only Wright could be shown to have passed the journalist information. This left Rothschild outside the reach of the law. The fact that he had introduced Wright to Pincher was neither here nor there, if he had not himself passed on secrets.

This left the police with a quandary. *Their Trade is Treachery* had plenty of data which could possibly come under the heading 'secrets'. But which were they? Furthermore, were they accurate? If they were factual divulgences, why had the government not injuncted the book in the first place, when it had seen the manuscript before publication? (This was Turnbull's strong base argument, which he supported with the false themes about Hollis and Rothschild.)

The government could have defended itself by saying that Rothschild had created his own operation. Once they became aware of the book, they decided to let it be published, primarily because it was wrong in its main premise that Hollis was a Soviet spy. This big disclosure secret was not true, and therefore not a secret at all.

Thatcher, Havers and MI5's head, Sir Anthony Duff, could have argued further that they had not moved to injunct because it would have impeded freedom of speech, particularly as the speech, in this case, in the main was codswallop. They could have shown that Thatcher said the Hollis accusation was codswallop in Parliament days after the book had appeared, thus allowing the 'anyone may say anything' principle (Freedom of Speech) and have it rebuffed (more Freedom of Speech).

If this had been accepted, the DPP could then have said in court, yes but what about the other hundreds of little secrets, which were still published? This would have led to an interminable case as experts were called to say whether this line or that word was secret. It would still be going on in the year 2001 if they were to cover everything that had been written on the subject.

Then a grey, still huskily hectoring Baroness Thatcher would argue the point of principle that old spies could not be allowed to profit from their government service under most circumstances (except those the government approved). A quick, aged DPP would have replied that in the case of *Their Trade is Treachery*, 'Wright *did* profit from divulging secrets', which would have again led the court round in an unending, circular dance about what information was codswallop and what was factual and secret.

But this scenario, with the Prime Minister traipsing in and out of the witness box, and MI5's dirty linen – particularly the immunity deals for KGB agents like Blunt from 1964 to 1966 – being aired for the world to see and laugh at was never going to happen.

The police would not have been told this in a conspiracy to pervert the course of justice. The Government knew that the Metropolitan police were practical coppers loaded with common-sense and a desire to get on with more important, solvable cases. They were not expected to enter the wilderness of mirrors. Not when it led nowhere.

Besides, they had a plausible, acceptable way out. Wright, the essential witness, would never leave Tasmania, especially as he knew he would be arrested the moment he touched down in Britain. There was also the argument that such a case would cost ridiculous amounts of public money. Britain, Rothschild's middle rank power, could not afford it. It would have dawned early on Scotland Yard's chief superintendent, probably from their first meeting, that there were going to be enormous difficulties in putting Rothschild in the dock. He had been an MI5 officer and knew too many secrets.

If the combative Pincher had been in the dock he could defend himself by subpoenaing Rothschild, which would have brought on the same difficulties. Nevertheless, the police were professional and thorough. Their integrity was at stake too. If they could find something, anything that warranted charges which could conceivably bring a conviction they were duty-bound to expose it.

They first saw Rothschild, recently turned seventy-six, a week before Christmas, 1986. Armed with Wright's Sydney trial affidavit (the part read to the open court only) and prepared responses to its points, he had his lawyer present as the chief superintendent began his questioning, while an inspector took down responses, in longhand.

There were many long pauses for the inspector to catch up, and Rothschild probably wished he was still smoking. Earlier in the year, he had given up thirty years of chain-smoking his favourite Balkan Sobranie, which his doctor had told him were bad for his heart.

Rothschild was wary, as the questions strayed into part of the affidavit which Wright had read to the Sydney court *in camera*. First he was asked about Sir Shapoor Reporter, the one-time MI6 collaborator in Iran. Wright had implied that Rothschild was involved in the 1953 overthrow of Mossadeq. Rothschild denied it. That was bad enough but another question about Peter Kapitza, the Russian atomic physicist, shocked him, and made him realize what a loose cannon Wright had become.[1]

NO CASE FOR PROSECUTION

Rothschild explained how he had helped Wright investigate Kapitza and that was all. In the end the chief superintendent and his scribbling inspector saw him three times for a total of ten hours. The policeman asked how he met Pincher; why he bought Wright a first-class air-ticket (which Rothschild proved was an economy ticket); why he had paid for the Wrights' expenses; the circumstances of his linking Wright to Pincher; why there had been secret banking arrangements. They painstakingly took him through different points from Wright's affidavit, and from several angles.

The chief superintendent again disturbed Rothschild by asking questions for which he and his lawyer were not prepared concerning Wright's *in camera* statements. For instance, they asked if he had introduced Wright to former Labour Cabinet Minister, Roy Jenkins. Neither could recall any such meeting. It was a small point, but added to the number of apparently inaccurate and misleading remarks in the affidavit, the weight of contradictions began to sway the police. Even if they could get Wright to stand as a witness, his accusations were riddled with claimed and definite errors. His Sydney court statement was hardly a sound base for making a criminal prosecution.

Pincher was then interviewed, beginning on 18 February 1987. Like Rothschild he quickly found that they were not 'going through motions to pacify Parliament'. He later reported that the chief superintendent observed that he and Rothschild were exposed 'like being alone in the middle of a parade ground' and that nobody was coming to their rescue.[2]

The policeman probed further about Wright's *in camera* claim that Pincher was an MI5 agent, which the journalist would have found amusing if he had not been the subject of criminal investigation. He realised Wright's reference was connected to his 'few services done for MI5, none of them for payment'.

Pincher was also asked about a quote in one of his letters to Wright:

'Five is on its way to you through the V-Channel.'

If Pincher had passed over his own money then there may have been a case for mounting a bribery charge under the Act. But he had not. It had been paid by the publisher, Sidgwick & Jackson, via Overbridge, the offshore company Rothschild had set up to handle income for Wright.[3]

The bemused police were then compelled to knock on the publisher's door in Museum Street, London. They interviewed the equally bemused publisher, William Armstrong.

Armstrong knew Pincher well, and trusted his judgement on his sources. The publisher knew nothing about the Rothschild connection until the revelation in the Sydney trial. Yes, he had been given an address for royalties to be sent to Overbridge. No, he didn't ask about it. Why should he? The whole purpose of publishing a hot book on espionage was to trust the author and not query his sources. If they had to be revealed there would not be a book.

Armstrong did speak about the mysterious figure known as the arbiter – a distinguished middle man who would judge for the publisher (and in this case the government) the taste and prudence of proceeding with new book projects.

Again unbeknown to William Armstrong and Pincher, the arbiter took the manuscript of *Their Trade is Treachery* to MI6's Chief, Sir Arthur Franks, who didn't object to the book. The Arbiter then gave William Armstrong the thumbs up. He could publish.

This later gave rise to further speculation that *Their Trade is Treachery* had been a deniable operation. But it showed a misunderstanding of the quaint British business of secrecy, which is so much part of the culture. Thatcher, Havers, Sir Robert Armstrong and Co. did not authorize the book and would have preferred that it had never been published. Once the project was underway, the publisher, William Armstrong, had to cover his company from risk by finding out if there would be objections from British Intelligence to the book being published.

But the people shown the manuscript in Intelligence were themselves bound by secrecy and good, old-fashioned honour. Once handed the book by the Arbiter, British Intelligence had to decide whether it was damaging. If they could live with it being consumed by the public, Sidgwick & Jackson could go ahead with an unwritten indemnity. If MI6 was against it, the publisher would have backed off, knowing that the exercise would be futile. The government would have crushed it.[4]

This was a long way from a midnight meeting at Chequers with Mrs Thatcher sitting down with Havers, Armstrong and British Intelligence Chiefs to agree that Lord Rothschild should be called in to solve a problem of how to expose Hollis as a Soviet spy.

Learning all this and confused at a higher level, the Chief Superintendent and his loyal scribbling assistant, cold-footed it to see the Arbiter. The two policemen were meeting lots of nice Establishment types and having lots of hot tea and biscuits, while being drawn dangerously close to the wilderness of mirrors.

They entered it on 4 March, by taking files from Pincher's study, including two box-files marked 'Hollis'.[5] Less than two weeks later the DPP and the Attorney-General called a halt to police inquiries. They were apparently convinced that Wright's allegations were unfounded.

While waiting for a final verdict from the DPP's office, Pincher showed he was unconcerned by whatever it would be by continuing to publish information damaging to the morale of British Intelligence.

'In the middle of police inquiries,' he wrote in *The Spycatcher Affair*, 'on 19 April 1987, I [disclosed] that Sir Maurice Oldfield, the former chief of MI6, had been a secret homosexual and, as a result, had been driven to conceal his problem by falsifying his positive vetting statements over many years. From prime sources I knew how this had come to the notice of security authorities in 1979 and 1980, when Oldfield had retired from MI6 but was serving as Co-ordinator of Intelligence in Northern Ireland.'[6]

Pincher went on to deny that this had been leaked from MI5, and that he had been 'sitting on the information' for two years – since 1985.

Was Rothschild the source? It would have been consistent with his relationship with Pincher, which by 1985 had spanned two decades. A clue is given by Anthony Cavendish, a former MI6 officer who wrote *Inside Intelligence*, a book in defence of his old friend Oldfield whom the author claimed had been subject to 'a vicious smear campaign.'[7]

Oldfield told Cavendish that he had lied during vetting about his homosexuality. Believing this was about to be broken as a story on Fleet Street, he had told cabinet secretary Sir Robert Armstrong his story, and resigned.

'Maurice told me,' Cavendish wrote, 'that the only other person he had discussed it with was Victor Rothschild.'

THE DECISION

Decisions about Rothschild and Pincher were held back until after a general election. Unlike Pincher, Rothschild was extremely worried by the delay. He fretted that the police might have evidence with which to charge him, without the Wright accusations. He spoke to his local Cambridge MP, Robert Rhodes James, who let it be known that 'his distinguished constituent Lord Rothschild and his family were suffering intolerable distress because of the continuing uncertainty.'

The Attorney-General responded in a written parliamentary answer on 8 July:

> Allegations made against Lord Rothschild and also against Mr Chapman Pincher have been investigated by the police. The Director of Public Prosecutions has now decided that the investigation has not disclosed evidence justifying the bringing of proceedings against either Lord Rothschild or Mr Chapman Pincher. The Director has consulted me and I have agreed with this decision.

Rothschild had yet again fought off the spectre of the Fifth Man. But the struggle had caused great stress which had taken its toll on his health and his will.

48. THE END OF AN ERA

SPYCATCHER'S REVIEWERS

Wright's sensational stand against the British government brought generous applause from two great old spies a long way from the drama in the Sydney court room. James Angleton, dying of lung cancer, could not read enough about it, and asked contacts in Australia if they could send him the transcript. He was delighted that his old friend, one of the few individuals from British Intelligence whom he liked and trusted, was having his revenge and finally making a telling point about mole penetration, which Angleton had made a retirement cause for himself in the US.

Angleton also endorsed the attack on Hollis. The *Spycatcher* trial had become a *cause célèbre* among old spies everywhere.

The other prominent old spy enthusiastic in his support of what Wright, Heinemann and Turnbull were achieving was Kim Philby. He and Rothschild had led Angleton, Wright and the media into the wilderness so adroitly that enmity between MI5 and MI6 continued into the 1980s, assisted by the forced resignation of Maurice Oldfield and the confusion, involving the UK government, over whether Hollis was a Soviet spy. In the war between the KGB and the West, it was a major coup for the Russians.

This victory could not have been displayed more symbolically than on the back cover of Phillip Knightley's biography, *Philby*. It had a photograph of the cunning old Soviet spy, a mischievous glint in his eyes, holding a copy of *Spycatcher* as if it were his own achievement. In effect, it *was* his and Rothschild's. Philby was too clever to give the book any verbal endorsement in his final interview with Knightley. That would have given clues that the KGB regarded the Hollis story as disinformation. Instead, he was happy to hold up

Spycatcher as if to say, 'now here is a jolly good read . . . very, very interesting stuff.'

If he had been asked about Hollis, he would have given the standard reply that he did not know if he were a Soviet agent or not, thus creating speculation that he could have been. He may also have added, as Modin did in interviews with me, that Hollis 'may have been a member of the GRU'.[1]

Modin, like Philby, was just keeping Rothschild's self-interested operation running. Modin would have known if Hollis had been KGB or GRU. It was useful for Modin, Philby and the KGB to keep the doubt rolling for as long as possible. Doubt was a key technique in the espionage glazing business. It helped to keep British Intelligence in confusion.

But while the KGB was still winning some of the long-running espionage battles, communism, the ideology it was underpinning, was collapsing. With Gorbachev in power the Marxist, Leninist, Stalinist social experiment of seventy years was exposed as a monumental failure. Seven decades of construction was being wrecked quickly by Eastern Europe's millions, with little or no resistance. The Soviet Union, which had been held together by a combination of terror and corruption, was showing signs of cracking up into its component Republics.

DEMISE OF A COUSIN

On 13 March 1987 Justice Powell, after ten weeks' deliberation and an in-depth 286 page report, dismissed the British Government's case against Wright and Heinemann and ordered it to pay costs. Turnbull's logic had won against Thatcher's principle. The British Government appealed to the NSW Court of Appeal, just late enough to ensure the hearing was postponed as long as possible, thus extending the ban on legal publication once more. In effect, this move on top of the court case was ensuring that when *Spycatcher* did legally hit the shops it would already be a huge bestseller.

A month later, partly inspired by Wright's victory down under, Angleton, in his last recorded interview with the *New York Times*, spoke of the CIA's 'five leads of penetration', which had been left unresolved in the mid-1970s when he had been forced from his position of power.

'Moles', he said, 'were a way of life . . . [penetrations] should never be thought of as an aberration . . . anyone who gets flustered by it is in the wrong business.'[2]

It was a last justification for the nearly quarter century of paranoia and obsession since Philby's defection, which had humiliated the American. Angleton died on 11 May 1987, aged sixty-nine, and with him went a sizeable portion of the suspicious mentality which had clouded Western Intelligence.

'He may have been driven half-mad with it [penetration],' an old CIA colleague said, 'but look at it another way. His crazy obsession made it much tougher to penetrate our services. If he had not been paranoid, we might have been far more deeply compromised. Philby did us [the CIA and British Intelligence] a great service.'[3]

THATCHER FIGHTS ON

The NSW Court of Appeal adjourned on 31 July to consider its three-person decision. Soon afterwards the House of Lords did its sombre best to boost *Spycatcher* sales even further by a majority decision to uphold the book's ban. In a proclamation which had comedy writers reaching for their quills and computers, they went further and banned first, any extract in publications, and second, any reference to the allegations in *Spycatcher*, even if they were uttered in open court in Australia.

Now every formerly disinterested soul in the UK wanted to read the book, which was going to overtake *Lady Chatterley's Lover* as the most sought-after banned tome in British history.

People could buy the book in the US (Heinemann Australia had earlier made a rights deal with Viking Penguin) from 13 July 1987, where it was a big success, and Europe, but not in Australia or Britain. Wright himself had been made a non-person. He could not be quoted, even if his words had been spoken in an Australian court.[4]

Spycatcher was being smuggled into the UK and produced at risqué dinner parties, rather like a new exotic drug. Book shops could not sell it, but several – especially in the cluster of second-hand outlets around London's Charing Cross Road – were holding copies under the counter.

The Economist, in protest, had a blank page where a *Spycatcher* review would have been run. The less reverential *Daily Star* ran a picture of the Law Lords upside down under the headline: 'YOU FOOLS!'

Not all of them were. By a majority of one, Lords Templeman, Ackner and Brandon were in favour of the ban. Lords Bridge and Oliver found in favour of allowing the newspapers to publish information extracted from *Spycatcher*.

Lord Bridge saved the Lords from looking moribund with the critical observation:

'Freedom of speech is always the first casualty under a totalitarian regime. The present attempt to insulate the public in this country from information which is freely available elsewhere is a significant step down that very dangerous road. The maintenance of the ban, as more and more copies of the book, *Spycatcher*, enter this country and circulate, will seem more and more ludicrous.'

At least someone was in touch with reality.

The NSW Court of Appeal on 24 September 1987 came down 2 to 1 in favour of Heinemann and Wright, but Thatcher would not give in. The British Government asked for a continuation of the injunction so it could appeal to the High Court in Canberra. This was granted, and Heinemann had to fight the injunction again. Lucy Turnbull's father, Tom Hughes, appeared for Heinemann and Wright, and the injunction was finally lifted on 28 September.

The book had already sold 750,000 copies in the US and Europe and now it could officially go on the market. Sandy Grant, weary from the string of court actions, could now do what Heinemann had set out to do two years earlier: legally publish. Another 140,000 were printed for distribution in Australia (70,000), Ireland (20,000) and Chicago (50,000, all of which went to Holland to be pushed out in Europe).[6]

A book which most readers uninitiated into espionage would have found esoteric, and one which the buffs would have found old hat, became the century's most sought-after publishing commodity in quality non-fiction. It meant that the essence of the story – that

Roger Hollis was probably a major Soviet spy who never got caught – was now firmly in the mind of the world's reading public.

This misconception had been tossed about by no more than a few people for twenty years. Thanks to Rothschild's initial organization and help to Peter Wright, it was now known by millions. In KGB operational terms this would be seen as one of the most widely known disinformation exercises in its history, if it had planned it.

Rothschild could have done without the media overkill and the strains that went with it. But his efforts still had the desired effect in the long-run. All the emphasis now as the media publicized *Spycatcher* – widening the audience for the key concepts in the book by many more millions – was on Hollis. Very few reviewers, if any, mentioned Rothschild, who was portrayed as a bit player on the fringes of Intelligence. Wright could not have praised him more. And with the prospect of making millions of dollars, the old spy could not now get in touch with him to thank him. Too much enmity had built up between them since 1980, mainly because Wright had gone public.

Meanwhile, Thatcher was still not giving up. On 14 October 1987 the Australian High Court granted the British government leave to appeal against the earlier decision. She could now only win limited victories in banning *Spycatcher* elsewhere, such as in Hong Kong where the *South China Morning Post* was stopped from running extracts. Thatcher demonstrated her excessive desire to win by sending Armstrong to New Zealand in an effort to stop the *Dominion* newspaper publishing extracts. The peripatetic cabinet secretary had to sit in a Wellington witness box for more humiliation. The UK government lost again. His feelings this time were not recorded, but photographers kept their distance. However, just to show that fall guys don't run last, Thatcher gave him a life peerage. She hadn't forgotten his other more distinguished performances in an outstanding career as a civil servant.

Meanwhile sales of *Spycatcher* broke records. Australia had already racked up an incredible 715,000 copies and sales were running into millions worldwide.

Yet the battle was no longer about stopping publication. That had mostly been won by Heinemann and Wright. Thatcher was fighting on because if she won the final court decision in Australia, she could

recoup all the publisher's and Wright's profits on the book. The
irony of that would be the fact that the feisty PM would become a
de facto publisher herself, reaping huge benefits from telling spy
secrets in defiance of the Act. It would be a most devious taxation
ploy with Thatcher, Armstrong, Bailey, Havers and the British
Treasury having the last laugh.

PHILBY'S FINAL DEFECTION

Philby died on 11 May 1988, exactly a year after his former friend
Angleton. He told Phillip Knightley shortly before his death that
recent times had been 'the happiest in his life'. In early 1988 his
biographer had found him stammer-free and in good spirits.[6] He
had expected to live a few more years, but made his final defection
before the complete dissolution of the Soviet Union, which was
crumbling around him. If Philby felt depressed or defeated by the
failure of the ideology for which he had been prepared to fight and
deceive his own country, he did not show it. He wanted to leave the
proud impression that he had fought the good fight for the other
side, brutally at times, but no more so than his counterparts in the
West.

To him, betrayal, deception and, if necessary, murder were all
part of the struggle. It would have been interesting to ask him about
his attitude to the crash of communism.

Was Philby so much the dedicated, blind communist that he may
even have believed that the breakdown in the system was just an
historical hiccup? Did he believe the ideology would prevail in the
next century? Or might he have admitted he had backed the wrong
side after all?

Unfortunately, Knightley, who was returning to interview him at
the end of May, never got the chance to put questions like this to
him. Philby's legacy would be an army of agents and double agents
– Kim clones – penetrating institutions in the West well into the
twenty-first century.

His funeral took place on 13 May, his body lying in state in the
KGB's Dzerzhinsky Square HQ. The line of mourners filed past
his red-draped, carnation-filled, open coffin for two hours. Modin

headed the KGB contingent when the cortège moved to Kuntsevo military cemetery in the western suburbs of Moscow.

It was a telling moment for the Russian, and seemed a fitting time for him to retire from the KGB at the mandatory age of sixty-five. The most important of the defectors in the Ring of Five was gone. Only the Fifth Man remained.

In the turmoil of the new revolution in Russia, pensions for Soviet citizens were trapped by spiralling inflation and devalued to a point where they could not be relied on for survival. Modin and his family found life a struggle.[7]

He and other retired agents were allowed to tell their stories to the West for money to supplement their pensions, as long as they spoke about operations already blown and known to MI6 and the CIA. It was reverse Thatcherism with a Russian twist. Gorbachev acknowledged that the old Soviet system had failed its key KGB agents. He allowed them to earn more, whereas the British government blundered by not giving Wright a fair pension. Encouraged by what outsiders like Boyle and Pincher were making from writing books based on information supplied by insiders, he had set out to supplement his meagre income. Now his Russian counterpart had the same idea.

THE BIGGEST CASUALTY

The end of the costly battle came on 2 June 1988 when the Australian High Court gave its judgement. Surprisingly it tossed out all the old arguments and went for one suggested to Turnbull by his wife Lucy. The British government's case was dismissed on the grounds that it was an attempt to enforce the penal or public laws of Britain on Australia. It was a point of international law, which had not been explored in the initial court battle.

The judgement was that one country could not force its laws on citizens or entities of another. It was a point of legal principle, with which Thatcher, a lawyer and woman of principle, would no doubt concur. She had to, in any case, regardless of her real feelings. It was her biggest blow as prime minister. Grumbling in the Tory ranks started soon afterwards, and her support slipped to a position where it would only be a matter of time before the Conservative Party power brokers would dump their most successful post-war leader.

Rothschild's attempt to avoid being named as the Fifth Man had, indirectly, claimed its most substantial victim.

49. LAST VIGIL FOR
THE FIFTH MAN

THE BLACK DOG OF DISGRACE

The threat of revelation haunted Rothschild in his final years. English journalist Simon Freeman, who co-wrote the *Conspiracy of Silence*, about Blunt, started a book on Rothschild, but gave up, mainly because Establishment doors remained closed on the subject. A publisher with the same idea found the 'pressures' too much and also abandoned the project.[1,2]

According to close family members, Rothschild went into a 'deep, black depression' in the last two years. He had long given up his mathematics tutorials, which had successfully 'polished' his brain cells. In the past, when depressed and moody he would play the piano alone, but even that outlet had all but disappeared for him.[3]

Stress and his own perception that he had been partly exposed and therefore disgraced, compounded his poor health. Not too long before his death, his sister Miriam had been at a radio studio, when the subject of the Fifth Man was raised and discussed privately by participants in a programme. No one associated the spy with her brother.

Miriam had never lost faith in him. Loyal as ever, she phoned Victor to tell him that he was not suspected and therefore off the hook. But even his sister's attempt to cheer him failed.[4]

THE FIFTH MAN'S NOTICEABLE PASSING

The third Lord Rothschild died of a heart attack aged seventy-nine on 20 March 1990. He would have been pleased with the glowing obituaries that followed. Hardly any of the important ones dwelt on the Fifth Man connection. He was treated well and positioned with the great and the good, that special breed of the aristocracy who gave themselves to public life and made Britain tick, however erratically.

In mid-May 1990, a memorial service was held for Rothschild in the West London Synagogue, Upper Berkeley Street. Rabbi Hugo Gryn officiated. Addresses were delivered by Sir Leonard Hoffmann, Lord Swann, and MP William Waldegrave.

Before Rothschild's death, Modin teased Western journalists by saying that the Fifth Man was alive and happy, living out his retirement in England. After Rothschild died, Modin's tune changed slightly. He could not now admit the Fifth Man was dead, so he added the odd remark to me and others: 'The Fifth Man's funeral would not go unnoticed because of his work in England after his main espionage activity [for Russia] was over [in 1963].'[5] Certainly Rothschild's memorial service attracted attention. Thatcher turned up, as did former prime ministers Ted Heath and James Callaghan. Apart from the family there was a more than respectable number of the high and the mighty and the famous. Sir Dick White and Chapman Pincher, naturally, were among the faces paying their deepest respects to a man they all admitted they had known, but not deeply. He remained an enigma.[6]

A VERDICT FOR HISTORY

Rothschild suffered from and survived on his great birthright. His background, wealth, special intellect and drive gave him a sense of importance that allowed him to gravitate above the normal machinations of society and make judgements of influence for it. His forebears had done it. It was a matter of course for any member of the famous family with his talent, if he or she wished to take it.

The fact that the third Lord Rothschild decided that society should be changed by a new ideology was not surprising, given the political climate in which he, a Jew, and therefore an Establishment outsider in the 1930s, matured intellectually. Communism would not have been such an overwhelming, awe-inspiring concept for him as it had been for most of the other products of the Cambridge political cauldron of the 1930s. Yet he was impressed by many aspects of it.

As a born autocrat, he saw virtue in by-passing normal democratic institutions, and getting on with his way of governing, which was a little like Churchill's belief in his sense of destiny to rule, and a lot like the totalitarians who ran Russia from Lenin onwards.

Communism, neat and formulaic, appealed to his youthful, outstanding scientific mind, which thrived on logic and definable laws. To enforce the attraction, the Soviet communists were planning a modern society based on scientific development. By comparison, Britain seemed archaic, outmoded and a society based on privilege rather than equal opportunity.

On top of that, communism was diametrically opposed to fascism, and fascism was striving to eliminate all Jews, starting with rich, powerful, international and cultured Semites like the Rothschild family. For Victor at Cambridge in the 1930s there was a perfect, circular logic in him siding with the communists. It made even more sense when the Soviet Union took the brunt of Hitler's forces in the Second World War.

Along the way, Rothschild became committed to the cause. The end of the war and the defeat of fascism didn't stop his adherence. He was excited by the clandestine, and the heady prospect that the Ring of Five and others could succeed in changing Britain.

The Fifth Man involved himself in technically traitorous activity in helping the Soviet Union obtain many important weapons research secrets, including those concerning the bomb during and after the war. He was not alone in that. People of great conscience and achievement in that specialized and deadly science, such as America's J. Robert Oppenheimer, Nobel Laureate, Enrico Fermi, and Niels Bohr were happy to help the communists build the ultimate weapon.

The difference was that they were driven by guilt about the deadly consequences of their work, which could only be assuaged by a balance of power where both the world's great military nations were put on an equal footing. Rothschild believed in this too, yet was driven not by guilt but ideology. He was a man of fierce commitment, which he displayed similarly in striving to save his race. He started his support of the Jews in the 1930s, maintained it during the war and continued in aiding the creation and then defence of Israel.

From 1945 to 1963, the Fifth Man became enmeshed in the Cold War spying game on the Soviet side, and developed into a full-blown traitor in preventing MI5 from winning the subterranean Intelligence war, especially where new hi-tech methods were introduced, by passing the technology on to the Russians.

After 1963, things went horribly wrong for the well-intentioned Baron.

Just like communism after Krushchev, Rothschild became the autocrat who lost his way. The Soviet Union was not necessarily going to dominate the planet, as planned and predicted at Cambridge. Capitalism, for all its miserable faults, had survived, as had Churchill's 'best worst' system, Western-style democracy, which had been scorned by Rothschild. He knew at base it was a charade. From his perspective, the country was really run by the Establishment elite, of which he was a prominent member.

He did his best, which was considered brilliant, idiosyncratic and outstanding, to redeem himself and stand apart from his image as an espionage agent, first as a Shell science executive and then as head of the government Think Tank. But slowly, surely the truth crept up on him. His genius and guile allowed him to manipulate lesser mortals around him and to keep the facts at bay after the espionage watershed year of 1963, when Philby defected and Blunt was exposed.

But in the end he too was all but consumed by the spectre of

THE FIFTH MAN

NOTES, SOURCES, BACKGROUND

1: THE SALIENT SPIES

1) The Grove Tavern in Hammersmith Grove, London SW6, was Gorsky's favourite meeting place. Modin and another former KGB agent, Colonel 'B', described in interviews (July 1993) how it was reached and worked.

2) The Fifth Man only met Gorsky once or twice at the Grove Tavern according to Modin and ex-KGB Colonel 'B' (interviews, July 1990, February 1992, July and August 1993). According to several sources, including Modin, ex-KGB Colonel 'B', ex-KGB Colonel 'D', and others, the key KGB people at the Soviet Embassy from 1940 to 1956 knew Rothschild personally and met him both secretly and socially many times.

3) First Burgess, then Blunt and others informed Moscow (and Modin) of their feelings about Gorsky, who was considered too high-handed in dealing with them. (Interviews with Modin, July and August 1993.)

4) *Russia at War, 1941–1945*, Vladimir Karpov.

5) *The Germans at War*, Bin Shipeck.

6) *Codebreakers*, edited Hinsley and Stripp.

7) When Cairncross claimed he was the Fifth Man to get rid of journalists outside his home in the South of France, Modin contradicted him, and asked how he could possibly know. 'The identity of the Fifth Man is known only to me and a few (KGB) colleagues,' Modin commented (Moscow *New Times* magazine, June 1992). Modin also said that Cairncross spied for Russia after the war, which Cairncross denies. This has caused some enmity between the two men and Cairncross is confused about why Modin is apparently ranking him among the Ring of Five. It is clear from my interview with Modin that he is hiding the real identity of the Fifth Man and another spy. However, he confirmed that Cairncross had been one of his agents. As KGB Resident or a Control in London for a decade,

scores of British agents met him. At least a dozen key post-war British spies were under his command.

8) Information supplied by Modin, March 1992, confirmed in interviews July, August 1993.

9) *KGB*, Andrew and Gordievsky, Chapter 8.

10) Cairncross claimed to have had a car paid for by the KGB late in the war. Modin denied this. However, Cairncross may have bought a vehicle for himself.

11) Little is known of Krotov, but he was involved in creating the Moscow Centre files on several key double agents.

12) Krotov and the KGB Resident wanted the absent-minded Cairncross to stay on at Bletchley Park, according to Colonel 'B' (interview July 1993), especially after his useful work concerning the Battle of the Kursk. But it was not a major problem if he left. Rothschild, Blunt and Philby were sending enough data to keep the Centre and Stalin well-informed.

13) Modin (also see *KGB*, Andrew and Gordievsky).

14) Modin (interview July 1993).

2: SON OF A TROTSKYITE

1) *Stalin*, Isaac Deutscher.

2) The historical sources for this chapter come from various books, notes, etc., concerning the Russian Revolution and the Soviet Union between the wars. Outstanding references include:
The Life and Death of Trotsky, Robert Payne, *Lenin and the Bolsheviks*, Adam B. Ulam, *A History of the Russian Secret Service*, Richard Deacon, *The Russian Revolution*, Leon Trotsky.

3) See *Trotsky*, Robert Payne; *The Russian Revolution*, Trotsky.

4) ibid.

5) Modin was always known as an agent who understood the intellectual side of Marxism, according to former KGB Colonel 'F', a few years Modin's senior (interviewed July, August 1993). This set him apart from the KGB agents in the 1930s and 1940s and those who joined later than him in the 1950s and 1960s, who tended to be 'under-educated'. By the mid-1970s and 1980s, the agents were becoming better educated – tertiary trained. Modin himself taught them, as did Kim Philby and Donald Maclean briefly, on foreign affairs.

6) Modin's written files were known for their clarity and depth. These

qualities were also obvious when he delivered papers to KGB inductees and others in the 1980s.

7) Interview, Yuri Modin (July, August 1993).

8) This was a standard dismissal notice, according to ex-KGB Colonel 'F'. He knew much about the purges of Trotskyites in the late 1930s and listed the standard questions put to those accused.

3: SON OF A BANKER

1) Information from St Catherine's House, London.

2) *Meditations of a Broomstick*, Victor Rothschild.

3) Interview with Miriam Rothschild (December 1993).

4) ibid.

5) ibid.[2]

6) Interview with Miriam Rothschild (December 1993). Also see *Wisden Cricket Monthly*, January 1987.

7) ibid.[2]

8) Quote from contemporary at Harrow (discussion 1980).

9) ibid.[2]

10) ibid.[2]

4: CAMBRIDGE CAULDRON

1) *Climate of Treason*, Andrew Boyle.

2) Interviews, Miriam Rothschild and Tess Rothschild (December 1993).

3) Blunt had several close friends in the art world. Amongst them was Argentinian/French Anton Bros (interviewed March 1989), a successful Argentinian dealer in the 1930s. According to Bros, Blunt spoke a lot about the Rothschilds in the 1930s, especially when VR gave him money to buy paintings. Bros claimed VR financed 'several' smaller purchases for Blunt. Bros also said that Blunt told him he wanted to make the Apostles more 'arts oriented'. Its Marxist direction was already 'established by 1932'.

4) Quote from *Mask of Treachery*, John Costello, p. 143.

5) Sources include ex-KGB Colonel 'D' (interviewed July, August 1993).

6) ibid.

7) ibid.

8) Anton Bros (interview March 1989).

9) According to an intimate friend of Blunt, who did not wish to be named, Blunt told him how he attracted others, including Rothschild, into his circle and the Apostles (interview May 1984).

10) Interview with Modin and other sources (July, August 1993). Modin was very impressed with Burgess's knowledge of Marxist theory. The Russian said he was the best read on the subject of all Top Five spies. The Fifth Man thought the theory 'irrelevant' yet understood its basics. Philby took it seriously, but failed to learn much. Blunt did enough to tie it all in with his art interests. Maclean made an effort, but Modin never discussed Marxism with him. Cairncross had studied it and took it seriously.

11) *Meditations*, Victor Rothschild.

12) Miriam Rothschild (interviews December 1993).

13) ibid.

14) Interview with contemporary of VR's, Dr Dudley Andrews, Melbourne (August 1990).

15) Interview with ex-KGB Colonel 'E' who had been told this by Burgess (July, August 1993 and faxed responses April 1992).

16) Interview with Peter Wright (June 1988), who discussed the Apostles' activities in some detail, having investigated them when searching for Soviet agents in the 1960s.

17) Interview with a close Rothschild family member (December 1993).

18) Letter from Victor Rothschild to Keynes, Keynes Papers.

19) Interview, ex-KGB Colonel 'D' (August 1993), who was informed by Philby.

20) Interviews with ex-KGB Colonels 'D' and 'C' (July, August 1993). Both had private chats with Philby about his early days. Philby did not say he personally recruited VR for the Comintern. However, he mentioned that VR was on a list of ten he suggested to the Comintern should be approached for recruitment.

Colonel 'D' said Philby used VR as an example to counter the growing 'anti-Zionist' feeling amongst KGB ranks in the late 1970s and the 1980s. After several political incidents in the early 1980s, young KGB members became 'paranoid' that there were 'Zionist plots' behind them. Philby tried to calm down the mindless hysteria. Some younger KGB members only believed him when they were stationed in the West.

21) According to Miriam Rothschild, Rozsika thought VR too immature and adolescent at twenty-three to marry (interviews December 1993).

22) Interview with relative in London (June 1993). He did not wish to be named.

5: THE CONVERSION

1) Burgess told Colonel 'B' who assisted in his debriefing in Russia from 1951 to 1955 (interview July 1993).

2) Philby told his KGB pupils how he enthused potential recruits. Ingratiation and inspiration were used as part of his *modus operandi*.

3) Philby claimed to ex-Colonel 'D' (his former student) and others, that all his suggested British selections for recruitment were initially keen to be 'doing something'. However, several 'did not have the conviction' to follow through when approached by the Comintern (interview July 1993).

4) Philby told all potential agent recruits this, according to his former KGB students.

5) According to former KGB Colonels 'D' and 'E', Kapitza left several scientists agents 'in place' at the Cavendish, including Rothschild. They kept Soviet science informed on all British developments until well after the war.

6) Philby emphasised the need for finesse when hooking new recruits. The 'HARP' invitation to meet Maly and Deutsch was used 'a couple of times' according to ex-KGB Colonel 'F' (interviews July, August 1993).

7) Otto's recruiting techniques were given as examples to KGB students of Philby and others.

8) The KGB's recruiting techniques have been studied and well-tried since the 1920s. They are still used today. Several of the KGB interviewees, including Modin, were willing to talk about some methods of recruitment.

9) According to ex-Colonel 'D' and other KGB agents, the text or 'themes' for attracting different 'types' of recruits varied. For example, Jews had to be sold a different line than atheists, communists, socialists, journalists and members of different religious faiths.

10) Interview with Miriam Rothschild (December 1993).

11) This was a standard quote at the time, which was meant to inspire new recruits to enlist for the cause.

12) According to ex-Colonel 'D', this was expressed specifically to VR. Usually the Comintern encouraged new recruits by mentioning names which would influence them. However, this was restricted to those within

a 'cell'. Sometimes those within a cell were kept ignorant of fellow membership.

13) Interviews with Modin (July, August 1993).

14) Interview with ex-Colonel 'D' (July 1993). Confirmed in interview with Miriam Rothschild (December 1993). Rozsika was 'impressed' by financial advice given by Burgess.

15) Interview with ex-Colonel 'D' (July 1993). Confirmed by Rothschild family member. They claimed that Rozsika looked after VR's finances – investments etc. – until her death in 1940.

16) See several references including *Rothschild*, Derek Wilson.

17) See several references including *The Rothschilds*, Frederic Morton.

18) Ex-Colonels 'D' and 'E' explained the dilemma specifically created by VR. Modin explained in general terms the Centre's attitude to recruiting agents who did not meet exact Centre criteria, or who could not be 'controlled' for various reasons. If they had firm attitudes to contentious issues, which ran contrary to the Soviet Union or the Centre's policy, Controls and the Centre were uneasy about full recruitment.

19) Ex-KGB Colonels 'D' and 'E' could not or would not say if VR had been recruited as a leading agent later.

6: BLACKMAIL FOR LIFE

1) Interview with Modin (July 1993).

2) ibid.

3) 4) 5) ibid. Modin's recall was strong on these moments. They were amongst the most poignant of his life and changed its direction. They also saved his life. Had he not been recruited, he would have been at the Stalingrad Front. None of his fellow Kadets sent there returned alive.

However, Modin attempted to fudge certain matters. He did not want to seem like an informant. The ex-KGB officer, Colonel 'F', who knew of the circumstances of Modin's recruitment added helpful perspectives. He was of the opinion that Modin had been partly trapped into recruitment. However, another KGB man aware of the incident suggested Modin had informed on his fellow kadet in order to attract the KGB so they might recruit him.

7: THE POSITIONING

1) According to former KGB Colonel 'D', VR insisted on explaining the information he was supplying. At this stage, it was mainly data published in obscure journals and papers (interview July 1993).

2) Several KGB interviewees were aware of 'thousands' of items supplied by the scientists in Britain. The Centre did not have the expertise to understand the data and it was hardly ever filed. However, some agents' files, including those of Blunt, Burgess and Donald Maclean included such data. According to ex-KGB Colonels 'B', 'D' and 'F', Rothschild and several other Cambridge scientists passed scientific information to Kapitza.

3) Information supplied by Wright to the author (interview June 1988).

4) *The Times*, 26 September 1976.

5) See *The Rothschilds: A Family of Fortune*, V. Cowles. Other information came from family sources.

6) Interview with the author (December 1993).

7) Interview with family members (May, June, December 1993 – London and Paris).

8) Joan Bakewell's article 'Lord Rothschild', *Observer*, January 1978.

9) Malcolm Muggeridge quoted in 'Profile', *Observer*, 29 March 1987.

10) Nicolas Tomalin, *Sunday Times*, 1 November 1970.

11) *Rothschild – A Story of Wealth and Power*, Derek Wilson. Information also from family sources.

12) According to Rothschild family sources in France, Austria and Britain, Burgess was sent on 'business missions' for the family. It was a cover for certain assignments, some connected with refugees leaving Germany and Austria (interviews, May, June, December 1993).

13) The Protestant Pastor Martin Niemöller and Catholic Cardinal Innitzer both resisted Hitler's *Führerprinzip*, which included a programme of racial purification as well as plans to end the separation of church and State. *The Times*, 12 December 1938.

14) Interview with ex-KGB Colonel 'D', a student of Philby's (interview August 1993).

15) From *Deadly Illusions*, Costello and Tsarev.

16) Burgess's KGB file No. 83792, Vol. 1. Letter report of a meeting with Le Grand, 19 December 1938.

17) Philby to former KGB Colonel 'E', in lectures to students about the early illegals and tradecraft. (April 1992, July, August 1993).

18) Interviews with ex-KGB Colonels 'B', 'D' and 'F' (July, August 1993).

8 : THE PLACEMENTS

1) Interviews with ex-KGB Colonel 'F' and Modin (July, August 1993).

2) Details of the appointments involving Rothschild come from family and sources, including ex-senior personnel in British Intelligence, who did not wish to be named (interviews May, June, August, December 1993).

3) Interviews with Modin (July, August 1993).

4) ibid.

5) VR's report on the British Machine Tool Industry with a covering letter by Guy Liddell, dated 4 July 1940. US Embassy Archive. See also *Mask of Treachery*, Costello, Chapter 19.

6) Fellow students at Cambridge (interviews Melbourne, April 1993).

7) *Mask of Treachery*, John Costello, Chapter 15 (Straight to Costello).

8) *Mask of Treachery*, Costello, Chapter 15.

9) Interview with Tess Rothschild (December 1993).

10) Malcolm Muggeridge, *Chronicles of Wasted Time: The Infernal Grove*.

11) Interview with Miriam R. (December 1993).

12) According to several KGB sources, including ex-Colonel 'F', the Fifth Man – 'a scientist by training' – was at Porton Down for several months in 1940. Blunt initially acted as the middleman between Gorsky and the scientist (interviews June, August 1993).

13) For further data read *The Sacred Warrior* by Denis and Peggy Warner. This data was extracted from US Archives. It shows how prepared the allies were with Germ Warfare. On 2 February 1944, the US's General Porter said they would need eight months to construct a plant for the production of (biological) agents 'An operation force of 250 would be required . . . the plant would produce anthrax spores, botulinus toxin and other agents. It was estimated that the unit would produce one million anthrax spores, or 250,000 four-pound bombs filled with botulinus toxin . . .'

Under Stalin's directive during the Korean War, the communists started a propaganda war which claimed the Americans would drop germ bombs on China and North Korea. Meanwhile Soviet scientists were stockpiling the same weapons. The necessary data for such development had been passed to them since 1940, beginning with the Fifth Man.

14) Address on 23 October 1975 to the Imperial College.

15) According to two KGB sources, Colonel 'F' and Colonel 'C', the scientist – the Fifth Man – was asked to move to MI5 (interviews April, 1994; July, August 1993).

16) See J. Colville, *The Fringes of Power*, and *Rothschild*, Derek Wilson.

17) Ex-KGB Colonel 'B' remarked that British Intelligence was given help by the KGB concerning German fuses. Colonel 'F' claimed there were 'exchanges of data' between British Intelligence and the KGB concerning German sabotage bombs (interviews July, August 1993).

18) Information from a Rothschild family member. Confirmed by a retired Cartier executive (interview December 1993).

19) Rothschild to a family member. Relayed to the author (interview May 1993).

20) Information from two Rothschild family members (interviews May, December 1993).

21) *Meditations*. The recipient of the 'Field Telephone Conversation', according to Rothschild was 'Miss Cynthia Shaw, later Mrs Fulton'.

22) Conversation with Major Richard (Dick) Smith, detonation expert (May 1993).

9: AT THE PIVOT

1) *Meditations*.
2) ibid.

10: SILENCE OF THE LUBYANKA

1) Interview with Modin (July 1993).

2) Information from ex-KGB Colonel 'F' (July, December 1993).

3) Reported in *The Economist*, December 1993. Reprinted in the *Australian*, 3 January 1994.

4) Information from ex-KGB Colonel 'F' (July 1993; January 1994).

5) ibid.

6) Interview with Modin (July, August 1993).

7) Interview with ex-KGB Colonel 'F' (July, August 1993).

11: THE ATOMIC ALTERNATIVE

1) This comment was reported to a Weizmann family member by Dr Chaim (interview July 1992). The family member claims that at the time Weizmann was unaware of VR's secret work or intentions – apart from his activities with the Mossad precursor.

2) Interview with ex-KGB Colonel 'F' (July 1993). He referred to the Fifth Man. Former members of the British Mission, the Maud Committee, Cavendish Laboratories, Porton Down, Birmingham University physics labs and J. P. Thompson's team at Imperial College were all impressed by Rothschild's broad knowledge of research into weapons of war, including radar.

3) *Finest Hour*, Martin Gilbert, and other sources.

4) Ex-KGB Colonel 'F' and other sources spoke of the Fifth Man's briefing of Churchill on the Allied efforts to make an atomic bomb. Colonel 'F' made the point that, in effect, the Fifth Man was briefing two important laymen, Churchill and Stalin, simultaneously (interview July 1993).

5) *New Scientist*, 28 November 1992. Article 'In Good Conscience'.

6) Interview with Sir Mark Oliphant (January 1994).

7) Several ex-KGB officers spoke of the data which had been coming in to the Centre since 1940 about the efforts to make the atomic bomb via the U-235 route. Dr Klaus Fuchs supplied much of this, but the Fifth Man supplied some of it and the broader perspective on its possibilities.

8) Interview with ex-KGB Colonel 'F' who spoke about the 'British scientist'. With the author's prompting, he referred to the scientist as the Fifth Man (July 1993). Ex-Colonel 'B' said that the Fifth Man had a 'good overall understanding of nuclear weapons research' (interview August 1993). Modin suggested that the Fifth Man had a comprehension of advanced weapons research but would not be specific (interview July, August 1993).

9) Interview with Oliphant (January 1994).

10) Magnetrons were the base for radar and are used in micro-wave ovens today. Oliphant remarked that he would like 'a dollar' for every one made, since he had been its inventor (interview January 1994).

11) According to Colonels 'B' and 'F', late in 1942 or early in 1943 the KGB received specific information about the new radar technology from the Fifth Man via Blunt. It was accompanied by photos and drawings. Modin also divulged that the Fifth Man had given important radar data and admitted Blunt had provided some 'brilliantly artistic three-dimensional drawings'.

12) Although Beria's team of scientists received great amounts of data from a variety of spies in Britain and the US, ex-KGB Colonel 'F', Colonel 'B', and Colonel 'E' confirmed that the plutonium data, complete with hand-written diagrams came *first* from the Fifth Man. (Fuchs, for example, was working for Peierls and Frisch. Anything he passed on to the Russians would have involved the U-235 route to the atomic bomb.) It changed the direction of Russia's nuclear weapons programme at the time and was the major clue to the beginning of its reactor energy programme. Later, the Russians stopped copying the Anglo-American plutonium bomb and developed their own 'Fusion' bomb.

13) Interview with ex-KGB Colonel 'F' (July 1993).

12: MISSION: DESTROY AND COVER-UP

1) Lord Cadogan diary and notes, 15 April 1943, David Dilks (editor).

2) Interview with ex-KGB Colonel 'B' (May 1992). He claims this was the beginning of Maclean's major stress as a spy. He was frightened by the Poles, who he felt certain would murder him if they knew he himself was a KGB agent.

3) See references to Sikorski in Martin Gilbert's books on Churchill, *Finest Hour* and *Road to Victory*.

4) PM's personal telegram T.592/3, 'Most Secret and Personal', 26 April 1943; Churchill Papers, 20/110.

5) PM's personal telegram, T.606/3, no. 452 to Moscow, 'Personal and Most Secret', 28 April 1943; Churchill Papers, 20/111.

6) ibid.[2] Colonel 'B' did not use the word 'eliminate'. He preferred to say 'if Sikorski were not on the scene'. When pressed, he would not say Stalin wanted Sikorski assassinated, but the inference was there.

7) ibid.[2] and [6]

8) ibid.[5]

9) According to Colonel 'B', Maclean always reported Sikorski's move-

ments out of Britain, so that the KGB in other countries could monitor him and the contacts he made.

10) See *Road to Victory*, Martin Gilbert, p 426.

11) Interview with MI6 contact.

12) Interview with ex-KGB Colonel 'B' (May 1992).

13) ibid.

14) ibid.

15) Ex-KGB Colonel 'B' claimed to know the basic contents of the report, as described. His information was mostly confirmed by British MI6 contacts (interviews May 1992, September 1993).

13: ENTER THE MEXICAN WARRIOR

1) The Russian bomb tested in the 1950s was based on Fusion technology.

2) Winston Churchill, quoted in *Philby*, Phillip Knightley, Chapter 9.

3) Interviews with Modin (July, August 1993).

4) Interview with James Harris-Brown (October 1991).

5) William Hick's letter to Angleton's wife, Cicely, 23 May 1989. See also *Cold Warrior*, Tom Mangold, Chapter 2.

6) Interview with a former CIA agent, who worked 'closely' with Angleton in the 1950s and 1960s before being forced to retire because of ill-health. He would not admit it, but may have been a member of Angleton's SIG – Special Investigation Group (December 1993).

7) ibid.

14: 1944: THE TURNING

1) *The Fringes of Power*, John Colville. According to Australian wine expert, Mari Gillingham, the Rothschilds never produced a Chateau Yquem, but Colville's quote is intact.

2) ibid.

3) The directive was issued on 12 February 1944 – from the report by the Supreme Commander to the Combined Chiefs of Staff on the operations in Europe of the Allied Expeditionary Force – 6 June 1944 to 8 May 1945.

4) Modin, ex-KGB Colonels 'B' and 'F' all remarked in general about the success of the Ring in Paris (interviews July, August 1993).

5) Information from Andrew Boyle in *The Climate of Treason*, other writers who had interviewed Muggeridge about the topic, and other sources who were informed in private by him.

6) Interviews with Modin and other KGB officers (July, August 1993). From 1941, Stalin often knew about information headed for British PMs, *before* it reached them. This flow of data was at its peak from 1943 to 1945, including the Yalta Conference between the Superpowers. This prior knowledge continued on foreign affairs until 1951, thanks primarily to Burgess.

7) ibid.[5]

8) ibid.[5]

9) VR in *Random Variables*.

10) ibid.

11) *The Rothschilds*, Frederic Morton (the chapter on Hitler v. Rothschilds).

12) This quote comes from VR himself, when discussing Peter Wright's need to leave MI6 and the UK (*Spycatcher*, Peter Wright).

13) Interview with an officer who witnessed VR's technique, and interview with Tess Rothschild (December 1993).

14) Interview with a retired British officer involved in the same interrogation work (January 1994). Modin also informed the author that Blunt had passed details of the interrogation of German prisoners to the Centre. It could only have come from VR.

15) *One Woman's War*, Asja Mercer. Rothschild's part in this and other Pilsen interrogations was verified by several sources.

16) ibid.

17) ibid.

18) Interview with retired Israeli Intelligence chief (September 1993).

19) ibid.

15: THE REASSESSMENT

1) *New Scientist*, 24 October 1992, 'In the Beginning There was Uranium'.

2) Some of the basic science in these areas was obtained for the KGB by the Fifth Man, according to several KGB sources. Later, Klaus Fuchs at Los Alamos gathered detail on his own initiative or on orders from the Centre based on what they had already obtained from the Fifth Man and others.

3) Interview with ex-KGB Colonel 'F' (July, August 1993). Confirmed by an interview with ex Colonel 'E'.

4) *KGB*, Andrew and Gordievsky, Chapter 10. See reference to Peter Kapitza.

5) Interviews with Modin and ex-KGB Colonel 'B' (July, August 1993). See also *Mask of Treachery*, John Costello (Chapter on 'Most Secret Matters').

6) Interviews with Modin and ex-KGB Colonel 'B' (July, August 1993).

7) Modin, ex-Colonel 'F' and ex-Colonel 'B' all spoke of many 'social' contacts between VR and the Soviets in London. He was seen as a 'friend' of the Soviet Union. 'He was a very strong, a very good Socialist', Colonel 'F' noted.

8) Ex-Colonel 'B' and ex-Colonel 'F' spoke of VR's vigorous work on behalf of the Jewish movement.

9) 5) should be compared with remarks by ex-Colonel 'B' and ex-Colonel 'F' that the Fifth Man remained a vital contributor of bomb espionage data *after* the end of the Second World War.

10) Sources include *The Traitors* by Alan Moorehead, *British Scientists and the Manhattan Project* by Ferenc Morton Szasz, *The New Scientist*, 17 October 1992 (article 'Soviet Union "Copied" American atom bomb').

16: CHANGE OF FOCUS

1) VR made this kind of remark on several occasions in and out of Parliament in attempts to publicly disassociate himself from Zionism, which some members of his family espoused openly.

2) For more on Israel's origins see *Israel at the Cross Roads – Palestine from Balfour to Bevin*, by Christopher Sykes.

3) Speech in the House of Lords, 31 July 1946.

4) Ex-KGB Colonels 'B', 'C' 'F' all spoke of the Fifth Man's operations in Washington in the post-war period. He gave instructions to Maclean. According to ex-KGB Colonel 'F', the Fifth Man was not the only agent advising Maclean at the AEC.

5) Interview with Sir Mark Oliphant (January 1994). Oliphant said that the radioactive bomb was a contentious issue in the immediate post-war years.

6) ibid.

7) ibid.

8) Interview with an American at the meeting (November 1993).

9) ibid. See also *The Spycatcher Affair* by Chapman Pincher (Chapter called 'The Climate of Secret Suspicion').

10) *They Awakened the Genie*, Moscow News 1989, No 41.

11) *Burgess and Maclean* by John Fisher (Chapter on 'Homer Comes to Washington'). Confirmed by ex-KGB Colonel 'F'. See also *KGB* by Gordievsky and Andrew (Chapter on 'Cold War – The Stalinist Phase').

12) Interview with ex-KGB Colonel 'B'. Also see *KGB*, Gordievsky and Andrew.

13) ibid.[10]

17: MR MODIN GOES TO LONDON

1) Interviews with Modin (July, August 1993).

2) ibid.

3) ibid.

4) ibid.

5) ibid.

6) ibid.

7) ibid.

8) ibid.

9) ibid.

10) ibid.

11) In this case Modin mentioned Rothschild, as he did on several occasions in our interviews. He knew him well.

12) ibid.[2]

13) *The Times*, 7 August 1993.

14) Interview with an international businessman who worked undercover for MI6 in the 1950s and 1960s. He knew Blunt and showed the author correspondence between them.

15) From *Herald-Sun* (Melbourne), 7 February 1994.

16) First of three interviews with ex-KGB Colonel 'F' (July, August 1994).

18: MASTER OF THE BACK-CHANNEL

1) Interview with ex-KGB Colonel 'F', who at one point specialized in Middle Eastern Intelligence operations.

2) *Story of My Life*, Moshe Dayan.

3) Interview with close relative of Chaim Weizmann.

4) Interview with Colonel 'F', who referred to Rothschild openly here (July, August 1993).

5) *Flying Under Two Flags*, Gordon Levett, Chapter 20.

6) ibid.

19: A BOMB FOR THE FIVE

1) *The Traitors*, Alan Moorehead. See also *The Atom Bomb Spies*, H. Montgomery Hyde.

2) *My Silent War*, Kim Philby.

3) From interviews with Tom Mangold in *Cold Warrior*.

4) Interview Modin (July, August 1993).

5) ibid.

6) *Spycatcher*, Peter Wright.

7) Interview ex-KGB Colonel 'F' (July 1993).

8) ibid.[4]

9) ibid.[4]

10) *After Long Silence*, Michael Straight, p. 251.

11) Modin verified this (interview July, August 1993).

12) Straight had met Burgess at an Apostles dinner in 1949 and claimed in *After Long Silence* to have expressed hostility to Burgess's pro-Soviet and anti-American stance.

13) ibid.[9]

14) *Burgess and Maclean*, Anthony Purdy and Douglas Sutherland.

15) ibid.

16) Interviews with Alger Hiss (May 1979). Hiss outlined his controversial history to the author. He agreed that his career path was similar to Maclean's but denied he had ever been a Soviet agent. He had met Maclean.

17) ibid.[4]

18) ibid.[4]

20: END OF A NETWORK

1) Interviews Modin (July, August 1993).
2) Several other reports suggest Burgess was feigning a trip to the north of England. Modin says Scotland.
3) Interview with ex-KGB Colonel 'F'. He referred to Blunt and the Fifth Man.
4) ibid.[1]
5) ibid.[1]
6) *Philby*, Phillip Knightley.
7) *Spycatcher*, Peter Wright.
8) Interview with Modin (July, August 1993).
9) ibid.
10) ibid.
11) ibid.[7]
12) Interview with Peter Wright (June, 1988).

21: LEGACY OF A DICTATOR

1) Interview ex-KGB Colonel 'F'.
2) Interview, Modin (July, August 1993).
3) Interview Modin; ex-KGB Colonels 'D' and 'E'.
4) Interviews with ex-KGB Colonels 'D' and 'E' (July, August 1993). Both these men, 40 years and 41 years old respectively at the time of the interviews, were well-versed in all matters anti-Zionist. They had studied the recent KGB history under Philby, who had tried to disabuse the strongly anti-Jewish secret police organization of its beliefs about Zionism and its international influence. The author felt Philby had succeeded partly with one of them.
5) Interview ex-KGB Colonel 'F' (July, August 1993).
6) *Pravda*, 13 January 1953.
7) *Krushchev Remembers*, Talbott (editor/translator), Vol. 1.
8) Interview with ex-KGB Illegal 'G', who worked briefly in the Middle East (August, 1993). The author spoke with two 'Illegals' – those agents who hide their identity and operate outside Soviet Embassies. One of them specialized in operating by taking on the ID of a national. He did this on four occasions over twenty years.

9) Interview with a former senior MI5 officer (June 1988), who was briefed by Rothschild for White. Rothschild's activities in Iran were confirmed by an MI6 operative who had acted for MI6 in the Middle East (interview December 1993). Peter Wright also remembered Rothschild briefing MI5 in the 1960s and also in 1974 during the oil crisis when the UK Government sought special financial arrangements with the Shah (interview Peter Wright, June 1988).

10) ibid.

11) ibid.

12) ibid.

13) Interview with an ex-CIA operative, who specialized in Israel and the Middle East (New York, November 1993). The overthrow of Mossadeq was hailed as a great boost to CIA morale after its media mauling over the prediction of the Russian detonation of an atomic weapon, and several miscalculations and failures in the Korean War and Peace Talks. The Iranian coup was talked about 'endlessly'.

14) Interview with a former MI6 operative, who specialized in Middle Eastern and Far Eastern operations (December 1993).

15) ibid.

16) ibid.

17) ibid.[13]

18) ibid.[13]

19) ibid.[13]

20) Interview with Chuck T. Holloway (March 1991).

21) *The Shah*, Liang, p 137

22) *Countercoup*, Kermit Roosevelt.

23) ibid.[12]

24) Interview with ex-KGB Colonel 'F'.

22: THE VISITOR FROM NORWAY

1) Interview with Modin (July, August 1993). This was another vital meeting at the time and although Modin would not have been aware of its later historical interest, it was an electrified moment for him. He had never been that close to Philby and the Russian was in the UK under false pretences. Modin spoke extensively about this and other incidents with his agents in lectures to new recruits and others at the Andropov Institute in the 1980s in Moscow.

2) ibid.
3) ibid.
4) *My Silent War*, Kim Philby.

23: THE SEVERAL FACES OF VICTOR

1) Discussions with various people who knew VR.
2) Interview, Miriam R. (December 1993; January 1994).
3) *Observer*, article: 'The Autocrat who lost his Way', 29 March 1987.
4) Interview with close Rothschild family member (February 1994).
5) ibid.
6) Interviews with two former ARC staffers and two executives.
7) ibid.[3]
8) *British Scientists and the Manhattan Project*, Ferenc Morton Szasz, Chapter 7.
9) ibid.
10) *Random Variables*, VR.
11) Interview, Sir Mark Oliphant (February 1994).
12) Interview with source formerly linked with the Weizmann Institute. Supporting information acquired from former Israeli Intelligence sources.
13) ibid. Information divulged in the Mordechai Vanunu case supported these sources' claims about how Israel got the bomb technology. It had, by the mid-1980s, a stockpile of more than 100 nuclear weapons of various types.
14) *Spycatcher*, Peter Wright, and other sources.
15) ibid.
16) ibid.
17) ibid.

24: THE GOOD ACTING RESIDENT

1) Interview, Modin (July, August 1993), and other KGB sources.
2) *Foreign Devil*, Richard Hughes.
3) This reconstruction came mainly from Modin interviews (July, August 1993). It was supported by other accounts of Serov's behaviour at the Embassy and in London.
4) Interview with MI6 operative (September 1993).

5) Interview with former KGB Colonel 'F'.

6) ibid.[4]

7) Sources include *Their Trade is Treachery*, Chapman Pincher; *Spy-catcher*, Peter Wright.

8) Interviews with Modin (July, August 1993).

9) ibid.

10) Interview, Christopher Dobson (September 1993).

11) ibid.[8]

12) Interviews, Modin (July, August 1993).

13) *Spycatcher*, p 255.

14) Interview ex-KGB Colonel 'B' (July, August 1993). Also see *KGB*, Andrew and Gordievsky, Chapter 11 'The Cold War After Stalin'.

15) Sources for this included Modin and ex-KGB Colonel 'B'.

25: MOVES AND COUNTER-MOVES.

1) *Spycatcher*, Peter Wright, Chapter 7.

2) ibid.

3) Interview with former senior CIA officer (November 1993).

4) ibid.

5) *Spycatcher*, Chapter 8.

6) ibid.

7) *Sunday Times Magazine* article from June 1971, and *The Unsinkable Aircraft Carrier*, Duncan Campbell.

8) Interviews with three KGB sources (July, August 1993). They all spoke of a report but would not or could not comment on its authorship.

9) Ex-KGB Colonel 'F' claimed the Fifth Man was still operating as a Soviet agent in the late 1950s and early 1960s at least. But he would not comment on the authorship of the report.

10) These comments came from four former senior Shell executives in the UK and Australia, who preferred not to be named (interviews, January, February, March 1994).

11) Source, UK Department of Trade document, May 1978: British Soviet Joint Commission, London, 23–25 May 1975.

12) This article was called 'The National Guard' and was developed by Peter Laurie from his book, *Beneath the City Streets* (Penguin). It was difficult to acquire the article, which the author had copied at the Colindale Library, London.

26: MAKING FRIENDS

1) *Spycatcher*, Peter Wright. Chapter 9.
2) Three KGB sources, ex-KGB Colonel 'F', Colonel 'B', and ex-officer 'C' spoke of the effectiveness of the Fifth Man, particularly in supplying technical data into the 1960s. Blunt was used as the middle-man.
3) ibid.
4) *Spycatcher*, Peter Wright. Chapter 15.
5) *The Spycatcher Affair*, Chapman Pincher, Chapter 1, 'A Momentous Message' (Rothschild to Pincher).
6) ibid.
7) *Spycatcher*, Peter Wright, Chapter 9.
8) ibid.
9) ibid.
10) ibid.
11) According to KGB defector Golitsyn, reports on Peter Wright's technical developments – known as the Technics Documents – were in a safe at KGB HQ, Moscow. See *Spycatcher*, Peter Wright, Chapter 15.
12) According to several KGB sources, Blunt was the key conduit for information passed from the several British agents operating for the KGB. No one except the Fifth Man was in a position to pass so much data in such specialized fields.

27: ALIBI FOR A SPY

1) Interview with ex-Colonel KGB 'C' (July, August 1993).
2) Interview with former CIA operative '1' (November 1993).
3) *Spycatcher*, Peter Wright, Chapter 12.
4) Interview with former MI6 officer (September 1993). Supported in remarks in interview with Peter Wright (June 1988).
5) ibid.
6) *Philby*, Phillip Knightley, Chapter 15 'Confrontation in Beirut'.
7) Interview with Modin (July, August 1993).
8) ibid.
9) The sources for Modin's movements came from both the KGB and the CIA. The latter source claimed Modin travelled in disguise, but they were still aware of his movements.

10) Interview with ex-KGB Colonel 'D' (July, August 1993).

11) Interview with ex-KGB Colonel 'F' (July, August 1993).

12) Two sources for this information were a Mossad agent and an MI6 agent (interviewed June 1994).

13) *Philby*, Phillip Knightley, Chapter 15 'Confrontation in Beirut'.

14) *Spycatcher*, Peter Wright, Chapter 12.

15) ibid.

16) ibid.

17) Discussion with Phillip Knightley (June 1993). Knightley had specifically questioned Philby about the Rothschild/Solomon revelations.

18) ibid.

19) Discussion with Phillip Knightley (June 1993). Knightley said he wasn't sure what Philby was trying to say about Rothschild from their interview. He could not draw him any further on the subject.

20) ibid.[9]

28: A PREDATORY ENVIRONMENT

1) *Spycatcher*, Peter Wright, Chapter 14.

2) Interview with former MI5 officer (December 1993).

3) Interview with Peter Wright (June 1988). Wright changed his mind about VR after the *Spycatcher* trial in Sydney November–December 1986.

4) ibid.[1]

5) Interview with Modin (July, August 1993).

6) Interviews with ex-KGB Colonel 'E' (July, August 1993).

7) *Conspiracy of Silence*, Penrose and Freeman, Chapter 18.

8) There were various sources for this encounter. *Spycatcher*, *Conspiracy of Silence* and Modin – interview (July, August 1993).

9) ibid.[1]

10) ibid.[1]

11) Interview with Modin (July, August 1993).

12) *Random Variables*, VR, Chapter 'The File is Never Closed'.

13) *Spycatcher*, Peter Wright.

14) ibid.[11]

15) Interview with an ex-MI5 officer (January 1994).

16) *Conspiracy of Silence*, Penrose and Freeman, Chapter 'Maverick Conspirator'.

29: WILSON AND OTHER WITCHES

1) *Spycatcher*, Peter Wright, Chapter 14.

2) Interview, ex-KGB Colonel 'F' (July, August 1993).

3) Interview Peter Wright (June 1988).

4) Interview former business colleague of VR when VR was at N. M. Rothschild in the 1970s.

5) ibid.[3]

6) ibid.[3] A similar remark is made in *Spycatcher*, Chapter 14.

7) Nigel West, in his book, *Molehunt*, explored the possibility of Graham Mitchell being the MI5 mole. The book's appendices carried the complete White Paper with West's analysis of its errors.

8) *Spycatcher*, Peter Wright, Chapter 19.

9) *KGB*, Andrew and Gordievsky, Chapter 8 'The Great Patriotic War'.

10) Wright to a close friend (about March 1988). Relayed to the author (March 1994).

11) ibid.[8]

12) Interview with Shell executive (March 1994).

12a) *Spycatcher*, Peter Wright, Chapter 17.

12b) ibid.

13) Peter Wright first hinted at this extreme and unsubstantiated theory in a conversation with the author (June 1988). He expounded on it to a close friend.

14) Interview with Peter Wright (June 1988).

15) The letter is in the author's possession. The envelope is stamped 'Washington DC'.

30: WARS SILENT AND SHORT

1) Interview with Modin (July, August 1993).

2) *Kim Philby, The Spy I Loved*, Eleanor Philby, Chapter 8 'My First Russian Winter'.

3) ibid.[1]

4) Interview with ex-KGB Colonel 'F' (July, August, 1993).

5) Philby to Rufa, his Russian wife. Reported to the author by a KGB contact of hers.

6) *My Silent War*, Kim Philby.

7) Peter Wright to a close friend, reported to the author. Also confirmed in an interview with ex-CIA Officer '2', who was close to Angleton (1964–1969) and who had strong Mossad connections (December 1993).

8) Interview with ex-CIA Officer '2' (December 1993). He was aware of VR's Mossad involvement. The Officer indicated that he reported VR's 'activity' during this period, 1964–69 to Angleton.

9) Interview with Miriam Rothschild (December 1993).

10) *The Cousinhood*, Chaim Bermant, Chapter 28 'Final Generation?'

11) ibid.[8]

12) ibid.[8]

13) ibid.[8] Also interview ex-CIA Officer '2', who worked closely with Angleton.

31: BLUNTED

1) Peter Wright to a close friend after publication of *Spycatcher*.

2) Ibid. Wright reassessed his links with VR, and what had occurred between them during that period. After the *Spycatcher* trial he began to question VR's actions for the first time. By 1988, after the book was published, he was less deferential in his remarks about the man he formerly almost worshipped. By 1990, he was actively discussing with close friends and one other agent friend the possibility that VR was a Soviet agent. He would not let go of his obsession with Hollis in his analysis. Wright would compile lists of who knew what and when. He gave VR more ticks than Hollis, with each tick an indicator that he could have been a Soviet agent.

3) *Spycatcher*, Peter Wright, Chapter 17.

4) ibid.

5) Wright admitted that VR knew all about his inquiries, even those that were unauthorized. He believed that VR probably informed Hollis that he (Wright) was investigating him (Wright to author, June 1988).

6) ibid.[3]

7) Interview with former senior ASIO officer, who attended the conference (March 1994).

8) Wright to a close friend on several occasions and discussions in 1988 and 1989, in which they reassessed the possible spies within MI5.

9) ibid.[3]

10) ibid.[3]

32: NEW CHALLENGES, OLD ROLES

1) *The Cousinhood*, Chaim Bermant, Chapter 'Last Generation?'
2) *New Statesman*, 6 November 1970.
3) *Random Variables*, VR, Chapter 17, 'In and Out of the Think Tank'.
4) *Yes, Prime Minister* is a popular British TV sit-com about a PM and his relationships with manipulative civil servants.

33: THE CENTRE'S MIXED FORTUNES

1) Interviews with Modin, former KGB Colonel Michael Bagdonov and former KGB Colonel 'F' (July, August 1993).
2) ibid.
3) Interview with former KGB Colonel 'G'. See also *KGB*, Gordievsky and Andrew, Chapter 12 'The Brezhnev era' (July, August, 1993).
4) Interview with former KGB Colonel 'F' (July, August, 1993).
5) *Philby*, Phillip Knightley, Chapter 17.
6) *Independent*, 14 July 1993 p. 1.
7) Information given to the author by former KGB Colonel Michael Bagdonov, a close friend of Rufina Philby (July 1993). Bagdonov was trying to sell a book published about Philby, which he claimed he had co-written with Rufina. Bagdonov organized the London auction of Philby's possessions in July 1994.
8) ibid.
9) *Independent*, 14 July 1993.
10) ibid.[7]
11) The main sources for this material were three MI6 agents. For other references see *KGB*, Gordievsky and Andrew, Chapter 12 'The Brezhnev Era', and *Spycatcher*, Peter Wright, Chapter 23.
12) Wright gives credit to MI5's Harry Wharton and Tony Brookes. By 1971 Wright had still never actually caught a spy himself.
13) Interview with Peter Wright (June 1988).
14) Interview with Modin (July, August 1993).
15) ibid.

34: THE PM'S EYES AND EARS

1) *Spycatcher*, Peter Wright, Chapter 23.

2) ibid. Also see *The Wilson Plot*, David Leigh, Chapter 10.

3) *The Wilson Plot*, David Leigh, Chapter 10. This includes the actual report by Wright on Jack Jones, and David Leigh's analysis.

4) ibid.

5) *Spycatcher*, Peter Wright, Chapter 23.

6) ibid., Chapter 22.

7) ibid.

8) Sir Humphrey Appleby is the leading civil servant manipulator in the TV sit-com *Yes, Prime Minister*.

9) ibid.[7]

10) This information came from a confidential source not involved directly in British Intelligence.

11) *Spycatcher*, Peter Wright, Chapter 23.

35: GHOSTS AND WRITERS

1) *Inside Story*, Chapman Pincher, Chapter 36, 'Politicians and Zionism'.

2) *The Spycatcher Affair*, Chapman Pincher, Chapter 1 'A Moment's Occasion'.

3) Interview with former MI5 officer, employed by them at the time. He claims 'Wright instigated the anti-Wilson plot' (January 1994). This was verified by others who claimed Wright's book fudged the origin of the plot.

4) Interview with Wright (June 1988).

5) *Spycatcher*, Peter Wright, Chapter 23.

6) Interview with several KGB sources (July, August 1993). They referred only to the Fifth Man, but did not name him.

7) Wright referred to Blunt distrustfully on many occasions and said he could be 'vindictive'. Interviews with close confidant of Wright (November and December 1993). Also see *Spycatcher*.

8) ibid.[4]

9) Wright to a close confidant. Relayed to the author (November 1993).

36: IMPRESSIONS OF A KNEE-JERK BANKER

1) *The Wilson Plot*, David Leigh, Chapter 11.
2) ibid. Wright remarked about VR's reluctance at first to become involved.
3) *Inside Story*, Chapman Pincher, Chapter 11.
4) ibid.
5) *Spycatcher*, Peter Wright.
6) Wright to a close friend. Relayed to author, May 1993.
7) Interview with a close friend of Jacob Rothschild (September 1993).
8) Interview with Miriam Rothschild (December 1993).

37: AN EPOCH OF DISILLUSIONMENT

1) Interview with Modin (July, August 1993).
2) Stalin ruled a line through 20 million Soviet citizens killed in the Second World War, according to a Russian historian interviewed (August, 1993). The figure was said to be more like 40 million, but the numbers were unacceptable to the Soviet dictator. Most historians East and West agree that the figure was at least 20 million. Russians tend to use the figure of 40 million more in the 1990s, when they are freer to express themselves.
3) Rufa Philby said this in a lengthy conversation with Moscow's *Literaturnaya Gazeta* (July 1993).
4) *Philby*, Phillip Knightley, Chapter 18 'The Final Coup'.
5) Interview with ex-KGB Colonel 'E'.
6) ibid.
7) ibid.
8) ibid.
9) Written information supplied by former KGB agents (in possession of the author).
10) Description from various KGB interviews. See lay-out plan of KGB First Directorate in *KGB* by Gordievsky and Andrew.
11) Interviews with Modin and former KGB Colonel, Michael Bagdonov (July, August 1993).
12) ibid.

38: BEFORE THE STORM

1) Wright to a close confidant, who relayed the contents to the author. Also see *The Times*, 7 December 1986, front-page story by Maurice Chittenden.

2) *The Spycatcher Affair*, Chapman Pincher, Chapter 1 'A Momentous Message'.

3) ibid.[1]

4) Information on the Wrights in Cygnet in the 1970s came from various sources, including friends and people who visited them.

5) Article in *The Times*, 5 December 1986.

6) ibid.

7) ibid.

8) It is useful to read *Was There a Fifth Man?* by Wilfrid Basil Mann to understand how far off the mark Boyle was concerning the Fifth Man.

9) ibid.

10) *A Climate of Treason*, Anthony Boyle, Chapter 9 'Enter the Fifth Man'.

11) ibid.

12) *The Spycatcher Affair*, Chapman Pincher, Chapter 2 'The Hollis Affair'.

13) ibid.

14) ibid.

15) Information from friends of VR (interview, December 1993).

16) Copy of the letter shown to the author.

17) *Molehunt*, Nigel West, Chapter 6 'Other Connections'.

18) The source was interviewed by the author (December 1993).

19) *The Spycatcher Affair*, Chapman Pincher, Chapter 1 'A Momentous Message'.

39: VICTOR'S LIST

1) Interview with close Rothschild family friend (March 1994).

2) ibid.

3) ibid.

4) Interview with source close to Thatcher when she was PM (March 1994).

5) ibid.

5a) From the Wright affidavit in the Sydney *Spycatcher* trial, November, December 1986.

6) There were various sources for these quotes including: *A Spy's Revenge*, Richard V. Hall; *The Spycatcher Trial*, Malcolm Turnbull.

7) There is a minor dispute over the quote's reference to St James's Place or VR's Cambridge home. The author is satisfied with the integrity of the quote by Wright, who may have been mixed up over where the quote was uttered. This is understandable. He was reflecting on events six years earlier and he was at both places within hours of specific meetings with VR early in September. Efforts to make Wright's words in this case inaccurate or misleading are spurious.

8) Evidence in the *Spycatcher* trial, November 1986, Point 79, Wright's affidavit.

9) From Wright's unpublished papers.

10) *A Spy's Revenge*, Richard V. Hall.

11) *The Spycatcher Affair*, Chapman Pincher, Chapter 1 'A Momentous Message'.

12) ibid.

13) ibid., Chapter 3 'Encounter in Tasmania'.

14) ibid., Chapter 4 'Secret Intervention: Enter MI6'.

15) ibid.

16) The Pincher letters were submitted as evidence in HM Attorney-General v. Heinemann and Wright (the *Spycatcher* trial).

17) ibid.[14]

18) *KGB*, Gordievsky and Andrews, Chapter 11 'The Cold War After Stalin 1953–63'.

19) ibid.[8]

40: AND THEN THERE WERE TWO

1) Interview with Modin and ex-KGB Colonel 'E' (July, August 1993).

2) ibid.

3) ibid.

4) Modin interviews, July, August 1993. This anecdote had been told by an MI6 contact in a March 1986 interview when the author was researching *The Exile*. The MI6 contact hinted that Graham Greene had reported this to him. There is some conjecture over whether Greene

NOTES, SOURCES, BACKGROUND

continued on as an agent for MI6 on his travels after the Second World War. He would have been an invaluable source for MI6 because of his apparent left-wing leanings, which allowed him access to political leaders such as Cuba's Fidel Castro, and the Panama's General Omar Torrijos Herrara, about whom Greene wrote a flattering, most readable account in the book, *Getting to Know the General.*

5) *Britain Observed, A Russian's View*, V. V. Ovchinnikov.

6) ibid. Chapter 24 'The Watch With No Hands'.

7) Interview with Colonel 'E' and Colonel Bagdonov (July, August 1993).

8) ibid. Also see *KGB*, Andrew and Gordievsky, Chapter 14 'The Gorbachev Era, 1985–'.

9) ibid.[1]

10) *Conspiracy of Silence*, Penrose and Freeman, Chapter 23 'A Surfeit of Scandal'.

11) *Sunday Times*, 27 May 1984. Article by Simon Freeman.

12) Discussion with Simon Freeman, June 1993.

13) *The Times*, 19 July 1984.

41: A TRUE BRITISH MOLE

1) *KGB*, Andrew and Gordievsky, Introduction.

2) ibid.

3) Interview with former KGB Colonel 'E' (July, August 1993).

4) ibid.[1]

5) ibid.[3]

6) The US government released information on Ames after he was sentenced early in 1994 for his Soviet Intelligence work.

7) ibid.[3]

8) Interview with Bagdonov (July, August 1993).

42: THE DEVIL IN TASMANIA

1) Sources include people close to Wright (interviewed February 1993, March 1994). Also see *A Spy's Revenge*, Richard V. Hall.

2) ibid.

3) Wright expressed these views in private many times.

4) Publishing sources in the UK and Australia (interviewed February 1993, April 1994).

5) ibid.

6) Interview with Nick Hudson (March 1993, March 1994).

7) ibid.

8) ibid.

9) ibid.

10) ibid.

11) ibid.

12) ibid.

13) The author met Sandy Grant in 1986 and discussed with him aspects of the case on several occasions thereafter. Turnbull described him as 'calm' in *The Spycatcher Trial*, Chapter 1.

14) *The Spycatcher Trial*, Malcolm Turnbull, Chapter 1.

15) ibid. and several other sources close to Turnbull and Heinemann.

43: VICTOR THE VULNERABLE

1) Paul Greengrass to Malcolm Turnbull, *The Spycatcher Trial*, Chapter 7.

2) An MI5 officer to the author (April 1994).

3) From sources close to VR, relayed to the author (April 1994).

4) Several people who have spoken to Peter Wright, including the author, were impressed with his prodigious long-term memory.

5) *The Spycatcher Trial*, Malcolm Turnbull, Chapter 4.

6) ibid.

7) ibid.

8) ibid.

9) ibid.

10) ibid.

44: CAUGHT WITHOUT EQUITY

1) *The Spycatcher Trial*, Malcolm Turnbull, Chapter 5.

2) In the Westland Affair Thatcher was in conflict with aspiring leader

Michael Heseltine over a helicopter contract. Heseltine, the then Minister for Defence, wanted a European consortium to acquire the company, whereas Thatcher seemed to fancy an American company.

The Solicitor-General had written a letter of advice to the Minister for Trade and Industry, Leon Brittan, which criticized some of Heseltine's observations. This letter was leaked and apparently approved by someone at Number 10 Downing Street. It caused a scandal. Armstrong appeared before a parliamentary committee to explain, taking with him his version of events as gleaned from several press secretaries involved. He claimed there had been a 'misunderstanding' between officials at the Ministry of Trade and Industry and Number 10. Armstrong's version exonerated the PM and her press secretary.

3) See *A Spy's Revenge*, Richard V. Hall, and also *The Spycatcher Trial*, Malcolm Turnbull, Chapter 5.

4) From the transcript, HM Attorney-General v. Wright and Heinemann.

5) ibid.

6) ibid.

7) ibid.

8) *The Spycatcher Affair*, Chapman Pincher, Chapter 7, 'A Review by the Prime Minister'.

9) *The Spycatcher Trial*, Malcolm Turnbull, Chapter 5.

45: PLAINTIFF FOR THE DEFENCE

1) *The Spycatcher Trial*, Malcolm Turnbull, Chapter 6.

2) ibid.

3) ibid.

4) Transcript: HM Attorney-General v. Heinemann and Wright

5) *The Spycatcher Trial*, Malcolm Turnbull, Chapter 7.

6) ibid. Chapter 8.

7) ibid.

8) The sources for this were two MPs who were briefed by a press secretary at Number 10.

9) *The Spycatcher Affair*, Chapman Pincher, Chapter 16 'The Web of Deceit in Australia'.

10) ibid.

11) *The Times*, 24 November 1986, p. 1.

12) *The Spycatcher Trial*, Chapter 9, and *The Spycatcher Affair*, Chapter 16.

13) *The Times*, 26 November 1986.

14) *Daily Telegraph*, 27 November 1986.

15) *The Times*, 26 November 1986.

16) *Daily Telegraph*, 28 November 1986.

46: THE GHOST OF THE FIFTH MAN

1) Lady Rothschild usually refers to herself as Tess in phone conversations with journalists. The author had the same experience.

2) The quotes are a compilation from several journalists who tried and failed to interview VR during that hectic week.

3) Interviews with family members and friends of the Rothschilds (December 1993).

4) *Sunday Times*, 30 November 1986, 'Profile'.

5) *Daily Telegraph*, 4 December 1986.

6) *The Times*, 5 December 1986.

7) The sources were involved in the trial and present *in camera*. Interviewed January 1994.

8) From Wright's affidavit, trial HM Attorney-General v. Heinemann and Wright, 17 November 1986.

47: NO RESPITE

1) From Wright's affidavit, HM Attorney-General v. Heinemann and Wright, 17 November 1986. See also references in *The Spycatcher Trial*, Chapman Pincher, Chapter 21 'Enter the Police'.

2) *The Spycatcher Affair*, Chapman Pincher, Chapter 1 'Enter the Police'.

3) ibid.

4) Interview with and information supplied by William Armstrong, publisher, Sidgwick & Jackson (December 1993).

5) ibid.[2]

6) *The Spycatcher Affair*, Chapman Pincher, Chapter 21 'Enter the Police'.

7) *Inside Intelligence*, Anthony Cavendish, Chapter 18, p. 155.

NOTES, SOURCES, BACKGROUND

48: THE END OF AN ERA

1) Interview with Modin (July/August 1993).

2) *Cold Warrior*, Tom Mangold, Chapter 23 'Death of a Legend'.

3) Interview with a former CIA agent who worked with Angleton in the late 1960s.

4) Discussion with Sandy Grant, managing director, Heinemann Australia (October 1987).

5) ibid.[4]

6) *Philby*, Phillip Knightley, Chapter 18 'The Final Coup'.

7) ibid.[1]

49: LAST VIGIL FOR THE FIFTH MAN

1) Discussion with Simon Freeman, June 1993.

2) Discussion with the publisher concerned, June 1993. The author has a letter to this effect from the publisher.

3) Interview with Rothschild family members, December 1993.

4) Interview with Miriam Rothschild, December 1993.

5) Interviews, Modin (July, August 1993).

6) *The Times*, 15 May 1990.

BIBLIOGRAPHY

Andrew, Christopher, and Gordievsky, Oleg, *KGB*, Hodder & Stoughton, 1990.

Barron, John, *KGB Today*, Hodder & Stoughton, 1983.

Barry, Paul, *The Rise and Rise of Kerry Packer*, Bantam/ABC Books, 1993.

Bermant, Chaim, *The Cousinhood*, Macmillan, 1971.

Black, Ian, and Morris, Benny, *Israel's Secret Wars*, Hamish Hamilton, 1991.

Boyle, Andrew, *Climate of Treason*, Hutchinson, 1979.

Bullock, Alan, *Hitler and Stalin*, HarperCollins, 1991.

Cookridge, E. H., *Traitor Betrayed*, Pan Books, 1962.

   The Third Man, GPPS, 1968.

Costello, John, *Mask of Treachery*, William Morrow, 1988.

Costello, John, and Tsarev, Oleg, *Deadly Illusions*, Century.

Cowles, V., *The Rothschilds: A Family of Fortune*, Weidenfeld & Nicolson, 1979.

Deacon, Richard, *The Greatest Treason*, Century, 1989.

   A History of the Russian Secret Service, NEL, 1972.

Deutscher, Isaac, *Stalin*, Oxford University Press, 1949.

Eade, Charles, *Churchill By his Contemporaries*, Hutchinson, 1953.

Fisher, John, *Burgess and Maclean*, Hale, 1977.

Gilbert, Martin, *Exile and Return*, J. B. Lippincott, 1978.

   Road to Victory, Heinemann, 1986.

   Finest Hour, Heinemann, 1983.

His Majesty's Stationery Office, *Report by the Supreme Commander to the Combined Chiefs of Staff on the Operations in Europe of the Allied Expeditionary Force*, 1946.

Hall, Richard V., *A Spy's Revenge*, Penguin, 1987.

Hinsley F. H., and Stripp, Alan, *The Codebreakers*, Oxford University Press, 1993.

Hinsley, F. H., *British Intelligence in the Second World War*, Her Majesty's Stationery Office, 1981.

Hoare, Geoffrey, *The Missing Macleans*, Cassell, 1955.

Hyde, Montgomery H., *The Atom Bomb Spies*, Hamish Hamilton, 1980.

Jones, R. V., *Most Secret War*, Hamish Hamilton, 1978.

Karpov, Vladimir, *Russia at War, 1941–45*, Stanley Paul, 1987.

Knightley, Phillip, *Philby, KGB Masterspy*, Andre Deutsch, 1988.

Leigh, David, *The Wilson Plot*, Heinemann, 1988.

Lloyd, Selwyn, *Suez 1956*, Jonathan Cape, 1978.

Mangold, Tom, *Cold Warrior*, Simon & Schuster, 1991.

Manne, Robert, *The Petrov Affair*, Pergamon, 1987.

Morton, Frederic, *The Rothschilds*, Secker & Warburg, 1962.

Payne, Robert, *The Life and Death of Trotsky*, W. H. Allen, 1978.

Payne, Ronald, *Mossad*, Bantam Press, 1990.

Penrose, Barrie and Freeman, Simon, *Conspiracy of Silence*, Vintage, 1988.

Perry, Roland, *The Exile*, Heinemann, 1988.

Philby, Kim, *My Silent War*, Panther, 1968.

Pincher, Chapman, *Inside Story*, Sidgwick & Jackson, 1978.
   Web of Deception (The Spycatcher Affair), Sidgwick & Jackson, 1987.
   Traitors, Sidgwick & Jackson, 1987.
   Their Trade is Treachery, Sidgwick & Jackson, 1981.

Purdy, Anthony, and Sutherland, Douglas, *Burgess and Maclean*, Secker & Warburg, 1963.

Robotham, F. P., Titterton, E. W., *Uranium*, Abacus, 1979.

Rothschild, Lord Victor, *Meditations of a Broomstick*, Collins, 1977.
   Random Variables, Collins, 1984.

Shawcross, William, *The Shah's Last Ride*, Chatto & Windus, 1989.

Straight, Michael, *After Long Silence*, Collins, 1983.

Sykes, Christopher, *Cross-Roads to Israel*, Collins, 1965.

Szasz, Ferenc Morton, *British Scientists and the Manhattan Project*, Macmillan, 1992.

Trotsky, Leon, *The Russian Revolution*, Doubleday, 1959.

Turnbull, Malcolm, *The Spycatcher Trial*, Heinemann, 1988.

Ulam, Adam B., *Lenin and the Bolsheviks*, Collins, 1966.

West, Nigel, *Molehunt*, Weidenfeld & Nicolson, 1987.
   MI5, British Security Service Operations, Military Heritage Press, 1981.
   The Illegals, Hodder & Stoughton, 1993.

Wilson, Derek, *Rothschild*, Andre Deutsch, 1988.

Wright, Peter, *Spycatcher*, Heinemann, 1988.

INDEX

Lord Rothschild is referred to as VR